The Metropolis in Black & White

The Metropolis in Black & White

PLACE, POWER AND POLARIZATION

Edited by George C. Galster
and Edward W. Hill

CENTER
FOR URBAN
POLICY RESEARCH

Published by the Center for Urban Policy Research
New Brunswick, New Jersey 08903

Printed in the United States of America

Library of Congress Cataloging-in-Publication Data

The Metropolis in Black and White : place, power, and polarization /
edited by George C. Galster and Edward W. Hill.
        p.   cm.
    Includes bibliographical references.
    ISBN 0-88285-138-1
    ISBN 0-88285-139-X

    1. Inner cities—United States. 2. Metropolitan areas—United States.
3. Urban policy—United States. 4. United States—Race relations.
5. United States—Social conditions—1980– . I. Galster, George C.,
1948– . II. Hill, Edward W.
HN59.2.M48   1992
307.76'4'0973—dc20   91–45182
                                                          CIP
                                                          Rev.

Contents

Figures ix

Tables xi

Preface and Acknowledgments xv

I Overview

1 Place, Power, and Polarization: Introduction
GEORGE C. GALSTER AND EDWARD W. HILL 1

2 The Kerner Commission Twenty Years Later
NORMAN KRUMHOLZ 19

II Description and Analysis of the Issues

3 The Nature and Dimensions of the Underclass
EROL RICKETTS 39

4 What Happened to African-American Wages in the 1980s?
BENNETT HARRISON AND LUCY GORHAM 56

5   Changing Black Employment Patterns
         JOHN P. BLAIR AND RUDY H. FICHTENBAUM   72

6   The (Un)Housed City: Racial Patterns of Segregation,
         Housing Quality and Affordability
         PHILLIP L. CLAY   93

7   Race and Inner-City Education
         EDWARD W. HILL AND HEIDI MARIE ROCK   108

8   The Persistence of Differing Trends in African-American
         Mortality and Morbidity Rates
         AKWASI OSEI   128

9   Leadership and Race in the Administrative City: Building and
         Maintaining Direction for Justice in Complex Urban Networks
         LAWRENCE F. KELLER   143

10   Racial Politics and Black Power in the Cities
         GEORGIA A. PERSONS   166

III   Policy Prescriptions

11   A Cumulative Causation Model of the Underclass: Implications
         for Urban Economic Development Policy
         GEORGE C. GALSTER   190

12   The Underclass: Causes and Responses
         EROL RICKETTS   216

13   From Caste to Class to Caste: The Changing Nature of
         Race Relations in America
         CHARLES WASHINGTON   236

14 New Directions in Housing Policy for African-Americans
PHILLIP L. CLAY 258

15 The Case for Racial Integration
GEORGE C. GALSTER 270

16 Obstacles to Housing Integration Program Efforts
MITTIE OLION CHANDLER 286

17 Policy Prescriptions for Inner-City Public Schooling
HEIDI MARIE ROCK AND EDWARD W. HILL 306

18 Race and the American City: Living the American Dilemma
LAWRENCE F. KELLER 336

19 Beyond Black and White: Multicultural Understanding
and the Sharing of Power
TERRI LYNN CORNWELL AND SYLVESTER MURRAY 356

Suggested Further Readings 373

About the Authors 383

Figures

Chapter 1

FIGURE 1.1   The Relationships Between Place, Power and
Polarization   4

Chapter 2

FIGURE 2.1   Percent of Black Persons by Census Tracts in
Cuyahoga County, 1990   23

FIGURE 2.2   Central Neighborhood in the City of Cleveland by
Census Tracts, 1990   34

Chapter 4

FIGURE 4.1   Distribution of Employment by Full-Time Equivalent
Earnings   60

FIGURE 4.2   Distribution of Employment by Full-Time Equivalent
Earnings, by Race   63

FIGURE 4.3   Distribution of Employment by Full-Time Equivalent
Earnings, Men Aged 25–34   65

Chapter 8

FIGURE 8.1   Life Expectancy at Birth, According to Race and Sex:
United States, 1950–1983   130

FIGURE 8.2   Infant Mortality Rates by Race: United States, 1950–
1986   131

FIGURE 8.3   Average Annual Death Rates for Strokes, 1979–1981   133

FIGURE 8.4   A Model of Inter-Racial Health Disparities   138

Chapter 9
FIGURE 9.1   Spatial Illustration of Typical Units of American Local
               Government   152
FIGURE 9.2   Council-Mayor Form of Municipal Government   153
FIGURE 9.3   Commission Form of Municipal Government   155
FIGURE 9.4   Council-Manager Form of Municipal Government   156

Chapter 11
FIGURE 11.1   A Cumulative Causation Model of the Underclass
               Phenomenon   192

Chapter 13
FIGURE 13.1   Comparison of Caste and Class Dynamics   239

Chapter 15
FIGURE 15.1   The Vicious Circle of Prejudice and Inequality   273

Chapter 17
FIGURE 17.1   The Relationship Between the Four Standards and
               Nine Aspects in Public Schooling   309
FIGURE 17.2   The Relationship Between the Three Standards and
               Four Aspects in Public Elementary Schooling   315
FIGURE 17.3   The Relationship Between the Four Standards and
               Nine Aspects in Public Secondary Schooling   316

Chapter 19
FIGURE 19.1   Major Steps in Comprehensive Institutional Change   369

Tables

Chapter 1

TABLE 1.1   Percentage of Men with Zero Annual Earnings   8

Chapter 2

TABLE 2.1   Percentage of SMSA Populations Living Outside
Central City in 1970 and 1980, by Race   22

TABLE 2.2   Residential Dissimilarity of Blacks, Hispanics, and
Asians in 15 U.S. Metropolitan Areas, 1970–1980   24

TABLE 2.3   Black Delegates at National Political Conventions,
1940–1984   27

TABLE 2.4   Black Elected Officials, by Region, 1941–1985   27

TABLE 2.5   City of Cleveland Police Force   29

TABLE 2.6   Black Gains in City Employment, 1973–1980   30

Chapter 3

TABLE 3.1   Definitions of the Underclass   44

TABLE 3.2   Selected Estimates of Size of the Underclass   50

Chapter 4

TABLE 4.1   Distribution of Annualized (Full-Time Equivalent)
Wages and Salary Incomes Adjusted for Weeks and
Hours of Paid Employment, 1979 and 1987   62

Chapter 5

TABLE 5.1   Average Unemployment Rates by Race, 1948–1989   73

TABLE 5.2 Male Labor Force Participation and Unemployment
Rates, 1940–1990 76
TABLE 5.3 Youth Unemployment Adjusted for Differences in
Labor Force Participation Rates, 1990 78
TABLE 5.4 Sectoral Earnings and Growth Profile 79
TABLE 5.5 Occupational Structure of Three Sectors 81
TABLE 5.6 Sectoral Occupation Employment Ratios in Two
Service Sectors, 1988 83

Chapter 6
TABLE 6.1 Selected Housing and Economic Statistics for Blacks
and Whites in Urban Areas 94
TABLE 6.2 Social Class of Black Families, 1969–1986 97

Chapter 7
TABLE 7.1 Selected Characteristics of the 25 Most Populous
Cities, Fall 1986 110
TABLE 7.2 Public School Districts in Large Central Cities 111
TABLE 7.3 Percent Distribution of Persons Age 5 to 17 Years
Enrolled in School by Residence, October 1988 112
TABLE 7.4 Residence of School-Going Children Ages 5–17 by
Race and Ethnicity in 1986 113
TABLE 7.5 Percent Distribution of Central-City Residents Enrolled
in School by Age and Race 114
TABLE 7.6 Percent of Students at or Above Selected Reading
Proficiency Levels by Race and Age for Selected Years 118
TABLE 7.7 National Assessment of Educational Progress for Age
and Select Characteristics of Participants by Subject 120
TABLE 7.8 Educational Attainment, March 1987, Percent
Distribution by Highest Level Attained by Race, Sex
and Major Occupational Group 122

Chapter 8
TABLE 8.1 Cancer Mortality Rates by Primary Site and Race 135
TABLE 8.2 Death Rates by Selected Cause, Race and Sex 136

Chapter 10
TABLE 10.1 Black Mayors of Cities with Populations over 50,000,
1990 175

Chapter 14
TABLE 14.1 New Budget Authority for Assisted Housing, FY
1977–1988 263

Chapter 16

TABLE 16.1	Racial Attitudes Survey	288
TABLE 16.2	Key Elements and Objectives of Integration Programs	293
TABLE 16.3	OHFA Integration Assistance Loan Guidelines, 1985	294
TABLE 16.4	Revised Integration Assistance Guidelines, December 1988	295

Chapter 17

TABLE 17.1	Four Standards and Nine Aspects of Public Schooling	308
TABLE 17.2	Comparison of the Nine Aspects of Public Education with Two Theories of School Failure and Two Programs of School Reform	321

Chapter 19

TABLE 19.1	Number of Minorities in Municipal Administration	359

Preface and Acknowledgments

Airplane travel is often filled with unique and revelatory experiences. Such was the case during the spring of 1989 when we shared a flight from Cleveland to Baltimore, where a conference of urbanists was being held. As our view of the city gradually faded during our ascent through the clouds, it struck us that the general public and policy makers alike had long been examining urban racial issues in a similar fashion: at a distance through a fog. The stark inter-racial contrasts in the character of urban place, personal and group power, and socioeconomic polarization have been obscured by a decade of official indifference and misinformation. We wanted to open up those discussions once again—at least with our students.

Our goal has been to present for a broad audience a clear "down-to-earth" vision of the complex reality of race and the city, the multiple, interrelated causes of this reality, and alternative programmatic means of altering this reality. We began formulating this vision by listening. During seminars held at The College of Wooster and at Cleveland State University in the fall of 1989, we heard the voices of students, faculty, policy makers, and practitioners—people of different sexes, races, residences, and socioeconomic backgrounds—as they articulated their perceptions of urban racial issues. These perceptions—and, in some cases, what we believed to be misperceptions—were the grist for discussion papers authored by various Cleveland State and Wooster faculty.

After examining these papers, we were impressed with the discordant visions centered on common concerns, concerns that were to become the focus of this book: place, power and polarization. After receiving favorable feedback from our students and colleagues on the quality of these papers as vehicles for undergraduate instruction, we were convinced that the core of a book was in hand. Other leading scholars agreed to contribute their efforts to expand on this core. All papers represented original, previously unpublished work. Each was extensively critiqued by both editors and subjected to at least two rounds of revisions, so as to ensure their clarity and coherence.

The result is a book that we believe is accessible, scholarly, and balanced. Throughout, material is presented in a non-technical manner that does not presume prior knowledge of social scientific language. Nevertheless, the material is scholarly, not journalistic, in its attention to theory, analysis, and use of current evidence. Balance is achieved in several dimensions. The seventeen authors include economists, political scientists, sociologists, planners, and public administrators; five are women and seven are African-Americans. The papers provide a wide variety of analytic perspectives, public policy proposals, and ideological presuppositions; disagreements between authors are often explicit.

We have been fortunate to enjoy lavish support of our efforts to bring urban racial issues to the attention of a wide audience. Wooster's President Henry Copeland and Dean Yvonne Williams provided encouragement and resources for the "Race and the City" seminars. The Maxine Goodman Levin College of Urban Affairs and the Urban University Program of the Ohio General Assembly and the Board of Regents provided support for the seminars and general assistance in the production of this volume. Charlotte Wahl of Wooster assisted in the preparation of several chapters, and Ellen Baumgardner at Cleveland State copy edited the manuscript.

Special thanks are due to the scholars who contributed their papers to *The Metropolis in Black and White,* and thereby provided substance to our vision. Their prompt and professional responsiveness to our demanding requests for revisions, their personal encouragement, and, of course, their creative, insightful thoughts made this book a reality. We are deeply indebted to these individuals.

We have worked with the authors in this book to be consistent in the use of the terms African-American and black. African-American is primarily used to denote ethnicity. It can be compared with white, Hispanic, and Asian as an ethnic group. Black is used to conform with the Bureau of the Census' racial definitions, which would compare to the terms white and Asian. The root of the difference in the use of the terms lies with the Hispanic population. Hispanics are a multi-racial ethnic group containing black, white, and native peoples.

The Cleveland metropolitan area is frequently cited in this book. This is perhaps understandable since it is the home of several of the contributing authors. More than this, however, we believe that it is appropriate to cite Cleveland often in order to illustrate our points for several reasons. First, in many ways the area is typical of older, declining, industrial-based urban complexes. The central city has declined absolutely in population for many decades while the suburban fringe has grown. Now the city of Cleveland has approximately equal numbers of African-American and white residents (and its second African-American mayor), whereas the overall metropolitan area is comprised of three-fourths white residents. The city and suburbs are highly segregated, although some suburban municipalities are predominantly black and others are struggling to maintain a fragile racial diversity. Second, the area evinces several atypical, even extreme phenomena that hint at what urban race relations may become in most metropolitan areas. As Norman Krumholz shows in Chapter 2, Cleveland's Central neighborhood epitomizes the welter of social ills associated with concentrated poverty, public housing, and offical neglect. George C. Galster and Mittie Olion Chandler (Chapters 15 and 16, respectively) debate the merits of the unique, nationally recognized program for integration maintenance operating in Cleveland's eastern suburbs. Therefore, we are unapologetic about the prevalence of Cleveland in the following pages.

A final acknowledgment serves to amplify the dedications of this book. Raymond R. Day, Emeritus Associate Professor Sociology and Social Welfare, was the first faculty member hired into The College of Wooster's nascent Urban Studies Program in 1968. Beside his teaching responsibilities, Ray designed and directed the College's Urban Semester Program. Through his unflagging efforts over the years, hundreds of naive Wooster students have been enlightened by their internships in Birmingham, Portland, San Diego, and St. Louis. Across the campus, he proselytized the importance of Urban Studies as a valid area of academic inquiry and experiential learning. After retiring in 1983, Ray continued to support our efforts in a variety of ways. Perhaps nothing speaks more eloquently, however, than his endowment of an annual prize awarded to the senior urban studies major whose academic achievements and personal qualities make her or him most likely to assume a future leadership role in the field. It is not hyperbole to suggest, therefore, that the Urban Studies Program at The College of Wooster has been built upon the seminal efforts of Raymond Day. After a decade-long battle with cancer, Ray died on September 30, 1991.

David C. Sweet, Dean of the Maxine Goodman Levin College of Urban Affairs, has provided intellectual leadership and built a college where teaching and research based on service are highly valued. In 1978, David arrived at a small college with an undergraduate degree program and four faculty members. Today the college has graduated over four hundred students, has nineteen full-time faculty and five degree programs. The role the college plays in Cleveland is more impressive than its growth. David has created an exciting environment where inquiry and diversity are at its core. He has quietly supported students, whether they are at Cleveland's Law and Public Service Magnet High School or enrolled in the college's doctoral program. David Sweet has led in the creation of a singular institution.

George C. Galster
Professor of Economics
Chairperson, Urban Studies Program
The College of Wooster
Wooster, Ohio 44691

Edward W. Hill
Associate Professor
Maxine Goodman Levin College
    of Urban Affairs
Cleveland State University
Cleveland, Ohio 44115

PART I

Overview

1 Place, Power, and Polarization: Introduction

GEORGE C. GALSTER and EDWARD W. HILL

The *Metropolis in Black and White* is a stark title highlighting a stark fact: America's metropolitan areas appear to be more polarized along racial lines than at any time since the mid-1960s. The title also reflects one of the strengths of this book—its focus on the differences between those of African and European heritage in urban America and on the magnitude, origins, and consequences of those differences.

America's urban areas have become multi-cultural, typically containing large Hispanic and Asian populations in addition to African-Americans and whites, with substantial cultural diversity within each of these ethnic groups. Despite this fact, this book focuses on the two dominant racial groups because it is believed that black-white racial differences will outlast ethnic differences in metropolitan America and that *the* race issue in most urban areas is perceived as a black-white one; one that has been impervious to significant change over generations.

Statistically, the book's theme of place, power, and polarization is most powerful when blacks and whites are contrasted. African-Americans, on average, are the poorest, most segregated, most disadvantaged urban racial (or ethnic) group, precisely because they are most deeply entangled in the web of interrelationships connecting place, power, and polarization. Since these interrelationships form a comprehensive, interlocking set of social structures that oppress African-Americans, they can be judged to be racist at their core.

Race, not merely class, continues to play a pivotal role in shaping the life-chances of urban African-Americans. It is not, however, solely a question of straightforward acts of discrimination by individuals and institutions. Rather,

1

institutionalized racism involves less-obvious connections between flows of resources and power over metropolitan space, resulting in African- and European-Americans having different starting points in their quest for individual and group economic success. Achieving individuals can succeed in the United States, no matter their race, of this there is no question. African-Americans, however, must work much harder for their individual successes.

This is not to suggest that all African-Americans are deprived, depressed or powerless. Indeed the socioeconomic advancement of unprecedented numbers of African-Americans is noteworthy and heartening. Yet, such advancement belies the continuing difficulty of its achievement. The racist structure of U.S. metropolitan areas creates obstacles that, although not insurmountable to all, prove to be so for many. In the U.S., societal claims of equal opportunity ring hollow because African-Americans face comprehensive barriers that render their success less likely than comparable European-Americans. African-Americans will succeed in smaller proportions than whites due to overt discrimination, poorer educational backgrounds, lack of access to information about work opportunities, and low amounts of financial and political capital.

Perhaps the most visible symptom of metropolitan America's racist structure is a group that suffers from multiple disadvantages. These individuals and families are persistently poor, and have been referred to by some academicians and a larger group of newspaper reporters and popular commentators as the "underclass." While the persistently poor are not exclusively people of color, African-Americans are disproportionately represented in this group. One of the greatest dangers of the underclass debate (How large is the group? What are its causes? Where do they reside? Are there any cures?) is that the title underclass may be taken as a code word for black in popular discourse. There are three important points to remember: (1) not all African-Americans are poor--in fact, 32 percent are poor; (2) not all poor are African-Americans--29 percent of the poor are black; and (3) it is the combined effects of residential location, race, and class that trigger concern about inner-city residents who are both African-American and persistently poor.

Since the social and economic dislocations, and the consequences associated with being both African-American and persistently poor are so extreme for this group, a good deal of effort is spent in this book attempting to define, analyze, and ameliorate the conditions members of the underclass face in their lives (see Chs. 3, 11, 12, and Ch. 13). The condition of African-Americans who are persistently poor is an extreme expression of racial inequality, and it provides a crystallized picture of polarization between African- and European-Americans in the metropolis.

Indeed numerous topics covered in this book are primarily of relevance to middle-class African-Americans: earnings and occupational differentials (Chs. 4 and 5), housing affordability and integration (Chs. 6, 14, 15, and 16), and political power (Chs. 9, 10, and 18). Still others have applicability to all segments of the African-American community: the legacy of benign neglect (Ch. 2), health (Ch. 8), public education (Chs. 7, and 17) and intergroup relations within organizations (Ch. 19).

This chapter begins by defining the conceptual framework for comprehending the metropolis in black and white, a holistic framework that serves to organize the rest of the book. After explaining this framework, its power is shown by using it in an analysis of contemporary trends in the economic performance of African-Americans. (It was decided this book would focus primarily on the topic of race in the metropolis relying on social scientific methods and statistical data in the investigation and this decision is reflected throughout this volume.) The next section reviews previous attempts to formulate comprehensive models of urban race relations and establishes an intellectual context for this work. The organizational rationale for the book is then provided and key points of the upcoming chapters are highlighted. Finally, this chapter concludes by proposing some questions about the future of race relations in the metropolis.

CONCEPTUAL FRAMEWORK

The model of urban race relations presented in this book is based on three interrelated concepts: place, power, and polarization. These interrelationships are portrayed in Figure 1.1.

Place is meant to convey the location and isolation of the African-American community. The inner-city poor live in places that are spatially segregated (Ch. 2), harbor a myriad of housing (Ch. 6) and health problems (Ch. 8), possess an inferior education system (Ch. 7), and are embedded within a fragmented system of metropolitan governance (Ch. 9). Middle-class African-Americans who live in segregated suburbs do not face the same intensity of problems as do the inner-city poor, but they do confront segregation and receive different levels of public services when compared to whites with similar incomes.

There are two dimensions to power. The first begins with personal empowerment and moves to collective power. The second dimension encompasses institutionalized sources of power, economic and political. African-Americans may be holding more visible elective offices (Ch. 10), but whether this represents broader-based economic and political resources for fundamental change in the lives of the inner-city African-American poor is debatable (Chs. 2 and 13).

Polarization is seen in growing economic and social disparities, such as the diminishing portion of the population that earns middle-class wages. These disparities are evident both within the African-American community (Chs. 3 and 4), and between it and the white community (Ch. 5).

FIGURE 1.1

The Relationships Between Place, Power and Polarization

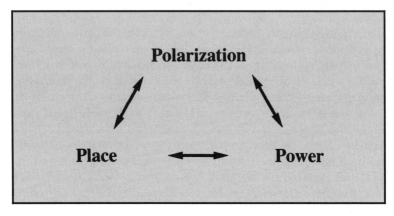

Place, power, and polarization are interrelated by a series of mutually causal connections (shown as double arrows in Figure 1.1). In other words, these three concepts can be viewed in the context of an interlocking nexus of social, spatial, and economic relationships. The causal connections between place, power, and polarization are multiple and complex. An attempt is made to sketch the most important ones in this chapter. The chapter also demonstrates how the model offers an explanation for the major empirical conundrum related to race in the city: rising black wages in the face of declining black labor force participation rates.

Place influences polarization in two ways. First, the residences of the minority poor and the sites of unskilled and semi-skilled jobs are in different locations within metropolitan areas. Increasing numbers of low skilled jobs are situated in suburban factories and shopping malls. The minority urban poor tend to be concentrated in inner-city ghettos; in contrast, poor whites are more evenly dispersed throughout the metropolis. Douglas Massey and Mitchell Eggers (1990) show that from 1970 to 1980 there was a *decrease* in residential segregation between different white income groups in 41 of 60 metropolitan areas studied. The same was true in 52 areas for Hispanics and 59 for Asians. Conversely, there was an *increase* in residential segregation between different black income groups in 51 of the areas. Because information about most jobs is obtained through word-of-mouth, the inner-city poor are, therefore, less likely to apply for suburban jobs than suburban residents. Because the inner-city poor are disproportionately African-American this has distinct racial implications.

Even if the inner-city poor were to apply, these jobs often do not pay high enough wages to compensate for the cost of the commute—assuming that the poor own serviceable automobiles. In short, semi-skilled jobs and those who would best fill these jobs are located in two different parts of the metropolitan area. The African-American poor are less likely to benefit from the growth in low-skilled jobs than are suburban whites (Kasarda 1990; Ch. 11; Ch. 12).

There is also an indirect, more lasting effect of place on racial differences in labor market performance. Both the social composition of the classroom and the amount of money spent on public education depend on the municipality in which the school is located. Moreover, both factors have been shown to influence the quality of education. Research indicates that the social composition of the classroom has a more profound effect than expenditures on education (Darling-Hammond et al. 1985; Hanushek 1986). Racial segregation in housing, therefore, will affect the quality of schooling children of color will receive due to the socioeconomic makeup of the classroom. Schooling will, in turn, affect the performance of the child in the job market two decades later. Place, then, is an important contributor to racial polarization.

But polarization affects place as well. The economic deprivation of the African-American population contributes to their disadvantages in housing (Ch. 6) and health care (Ch. 8). Inasmuch as upper- and middle-income households of all races tend to move away from areas of rampant poverty, polarization contributes to the out-migration of the central city's tax base. Weakened fiscal capacity, of course, contributes to the inferiority of education and other services delivered to the inner-city African-American community. Finally, poverty precludes many from escaping from the ghetto simply because they cannot afford to reside in the less-segregated areas that have a better quality of life.

Similarly place and power affect one another also. Housing segregation may provide enough density of minority voters so that African-Americans can be regularly elected to local political offices (Ch. 10). It is questionable, however, whether a place characterized by poorly educated and alienated citizens who hold few economic resources can ever be considered as having power.

This is a point that is debated in the following chapter because office-holding power does have its rewards. Such power permits the institution of public policies that hold the potential for changing various aspects of life in the inner-city. More directly, such power results in greater access to well-paying public employment both by the city itself and independent public bodies, such as school boards, transit agencies and public works authorities. How this power might be wielded, what policy options may be pursued, and the likely effects of those policies on place, is discussed in Part III of this book.

Finally, consider the interrelationship between polarization and power. At the personal level, the poverty that epitomizes economic and social polarization causes a growing sense of powerlessness on the part of people of color, especially those who did not become part of the middle class before the onset of the 1979 recession. Washington (Ch. 13) implies that mobility ladders are blocked for many African-Americans, removing their connection to the world of work. Drugs and the culture of the street are winning over those who suffer from anomie. He posits that the development of a distinct class structure within the African-American community has been arrested and that a caste structure is emerging.

A person's future orientation and ability to shape that future fundamentally depends on his or her own sense of power. People who feel that they have no future, and no power to affect their future, are more vulnerable to the web of social pathologies associated with poverty (Clark 1965). A person who suffers from anomie will have little reason to invest money, time or energy in his/her future. Of course, this merely serves to reinforce deprivation (Ch. 3). In other words, personal powerlessness spawns subsequent polarization.

An example may help clarify this point. If young people feel that their job prospects are bleak, they will have little incentive to stay in school, thereby not investing in their future earning potential. In fact, this may be highly rational behavior if, due to economic restructuring, discrimination, and segregation, their prospects are dim. It is also a self-fulfilling prophecy because they will not have the skills to secure a good job that might become available to them. This means that the young person will have little chance to use the world of work as a way of moving into the working or middle classes and racial polarization based on earnings will continue.

Increasing poverty and alienation reduces the likelihood of the deprived segments of the African-American community exercising any substantial electoral clout. Growing polarization within the African-American community may well mean that the more affluent and powerful members of that community will grow less sympathetic toward the concerns of the less well-off members, and will tailor public policies accordingly. In effect, the existence of an African-American class structure can fracture the political agenda pursued by African-American political and economic leaders because different classes can have different interests once overarching concerns, such as ending legal segregation, are achieved. This phenomenon is no different from what has occurred with other ethnic groups throughout American history. Moreover, the possibility of this occurring brings forth a controversy about the extent to which the spoils of elected office have benefitted all segments of the African-American community (Chs. 2, 10, and 18). Finally, such intra-community polarization may influence how power is wielded by white policy makers at all governmental levels. Visible African-American "success stories" may convince white policy makers that race is no longer an issue (O'Neill 1990), whereupon their policy initiatives will have different consequences for polarization in the city.

While the three parts of the model are interrelated, there is a causal chain which several of the chapter authors look to as a way of finding solutions to the racial divide that exists in the modern American metropolis. Residential segregation (place) and economic deprivation (one aspect of power) have built on the history of legal segregation and discrimination to reinforce social and economic polarization. Polarization then feeds back to reinforce differences in place and power. This means that the way to bridge the current racial divide is to vigorously attack housing segregation and to promote access to good jobs for people of color. The catch, however, is that promoting access to good jobs in a stagnant, or declining, economy is politically trying because redistribution is more difficult when the pie is not growing. The majority will feel extremely threatened.

A PERSPECTIVE ON THE ECONOMIC PERFORMANCE OF AFRICAN-AMERICANS

Now that the model has been explained, consider how it can be used to reconcile two apparently contradictory pieces of information about the labor market experience of African-Americans. James P. Smith and Finis R. Welch (1989) report that the average earnings of black male workers increased until 1979, when the black-to-white earnings ratio began to decline (the decline in this ratio throughout the 1980s is a finding that has been replicated in numerous studies). Yet, Gerald Jaynes (1990) calculates that the employment and labor force participation rates of young black males have decreased at the same time. If earnings are increasing, it is reasonable to expect that more, rather than fewer, workers will enter the labor market, especially during an unusually long period of prosperity such as that which the United States experienced from 1982 to 1990.

The numbers tell the tale. The percentage of employed black males with 12 years of education fell from 90 percent in 1969, to 77 percent in 1979, and to 69 percent in 1984. Black males with only some high school education fared worse: 86 percent were employed in 1969, 62 percent in 1979 and in 1984. The fall in employment rates was matched by declines in labor force participation rates (Jaynes 1990).

In 1984, 28 percent of black men from age 20 to 24 and 16 percent from age 25 to 54 earned no income at all! (Table 1.1) While the percentage of men of both races reporting no annual earnings increased from 1969 to 1984, the gap between blacks and whites grew at an alarming pace. For example, there was an

TABLE 1.1

Percentage of Men with Zero Annual Earnings

Year		Ages 20–24	Ages 25–54	Ages 55–64
1969	Black	16	8	22
	White	8	4	1
	Difference	8	4	21
1979	Black	23	16	35
	White	7	5	22
	Difference	16	11	13
1984	Black	28	16	42
	White	9	5	26
	Difference	19	11	16

Source: Jaynes and Williams, 1989, p. 311.

8 percentage point black-white difference in 1969 between young male workers, age 20 to 24. This grew to 16 points in 1979 and to 19 points by 1984 (remember that 1984 was a year when the economy expanded). The growth in the portion of the young male black population with no earnings explains why the black-to-white ratio of average weekly earnings of *employed* males can go up (from 65 percent in 1969 to 72 percent in 1979 and then falling to 67 percent in 1984) and, at the same time, the annual per capita earnings ratio of *all* black and white males has remained essentially flat (it was 57 percent in 1969 and 1979 and 56 percent in 1984). The increase in non-employment is not factored into the average weekly earnings data, while the non-employed are part of the latter figures.

These data imply that the increase in average earnings for working black males has been offset by an increase in black male non-employment and that there has been an increase in earnings inequality within the African-American population. This is confirmed by Harrison and Gorham in Chapter 4. The significance of these trends is seen by resulting changes in poverty rates.

In 1989, 12.8 percent of all Americans were part of families with incomes below the nation's official poverty threshold; by contrast, slightly more than 30 percent of black families were considered to be poor (*New York Times* 1990). This is a vast improvement from 1959 when 55.1 percent of the black population lived below the official poverty line, but it is not a major advance over the poverty rate in 1979 when 31 percent of the black population was classified as being poor (Sawhill 1988).

Blair and Fichtenbaum (Ch. 5) investigate several competing reasons to explain the divergence in the earnings and employment performance of blacks. They pay special attention to the role that racial discrimination can play and the form it can take in explaining differences in these numbers. Blair and Fichtenbaum note that the restructuring of the economy affected African-Americans in disproportionate numbers but that factor alone cannot explain the occupational differences between whites and blacks. They conclude that "a comprehensive solution to employment problems experienced by African-Americans must include . . . the use of affirmative action and strengthening enforcement of civil rights legislation" and that "civil rights enforcement must be supported by an economy and society that generates opportunities for advancement."

Gerald Jaynes (1990) and William J. Wilson (1987) provide a compelling explanation for the divergence in the earnings and employment data. Jaynes emphasizes that the reported data on earnings are a statistical artifact biased by the relative increase in non-employment among African-Americans. The reason given for this truncation is the increase in the number of low-skilled potential workers accepting government transfer payments and non-wage income instead of opting to fill low-skill, low-wage jobs. In essence, this is a supply-side view of the labor market where low-skilled jobs do not offer high enough wages to attract potential workers into the labor market. This has a lopsided impact on the African-American community because the community is disproportionately low skilled.

The complementary demand-side variant of this hypothesis is offered by Wilson (1987). Wilson holds that demand for low-skilled workers, especially minority workers, is lacking in inner-cities (pp.100–104,180–81); and that "when the factor of joblessness is combined with high black-male mortality and incarceration rates, the proportion of black men in stable economic situations is even lower than that conveyed in the current unemployment and labor-force figures" (p.83). Jaynes summarizes Wilson's thesis:

> A slowing of economic growth and the shift from heavy manufacturing to service jobs, with a concurrent decline in real wages, should be expected to produce a period of great economic and social distress. Among those workers who are displaced or become educationally or spatially misplaced, the rise in unemployment and the increased competition for moderate- to high-pay jobs may lead to a rise in the number of discouraged workers, who discontinue active job search for long periods of time. The rise in government transfer programs probably aided their decisions, but there is little theoretical or empirical evidence for believing that transfers were the major factors. . . . (1990, p.22)

The Jaynes-Wilson explanation is correct as far as it goes. The conceptual framework for this book suggests that the tripartite themes of place, power, and polarization provide yet a deeper, more comprehensive view because they delve into what Jaynes and Wilson take as given.

For instance, they take the disproportionate number of low-skilled African-American workers as given. This book emphasizes how this situation results from the mutual interactions between place, power and polarization. Perceived personal powerlessness prevents some from procuring adequate skills and training, what labor economists call human capital. Others try but find their attempts thwarted by poor health care and inadequate educational preparation, resulting from a substandard educational system that exists within their place of residence. The reason for these inferior public services can be traced to the locational decisions of firms and the immediate interests of the local power structure—a power structure shaped by polarization within the African-American community, as well as between that community and the majoritarian society.

Jaynes and Wilson take the spatial mismatch between the location of low-skilled jobs and the residences of low-skilled African-Americans as given. In contrast, this book probes into why most African-Americans remain residentially segregated in central cities and illuminates the effects of power and polarization. First, the paucity of African-American purchasing power in the housing market, and the power of whites to exclude through zoning and discriminatory barriers, rule out the possibility of people of color suburbanizing in large numbers. In addition, firms have located where they have due to the spatial features of the modern metropolis: inferior public services in central cities, weak household purchasing power of inner-city residents, and the high cost of redeveloping inner-city land for productive purposes when compared to suburban "greenfield" development.[1] Third, public transit systems are designed to transport suburban households from their homes to the central business district. They are not designed to move central households to suburban worksites. This is another reflection of power imbalances.

INTELLECTUAL CONTEXT FOR THE MODEL

Traditionally, racial integration and poverty have been considered as separate problems. Poverty is seen by many economists and policy makers as an outcome of a labor market process that is divorced from space. Worker characteristics are taken as given instead of being dependent on where the prospective workers grow up and now live. Traditionally, racial discrimination is viewed as a powerful intervening variable on the demand side of this market (Ch. 5), and is also hypothesized to have an effect on the skills obtained by individuals on the supply side of the labor market. Discrimination is not viewed by labor economists outside of the context of the labor market.

Racial discrimination in the housing market has also been viewed as a distinct problem separate from other forms of discrimination. Some sociologists focus on economic disparities as a cause of segregation; others see economic disparities as an outcome of segregation. Certain political scientists concentrate on how the exercise of power affects various groups within the city. Others examine the economic and social foundations of power with scant attention paid to its spatial dimensions.

Fortunately, there are five notable exceptions to the above generalizations, and they are cited below as an intellectual framework for this current effort. In his 1944 classic, *The American Dilemma*, Gunnar Myrdal provided the seminal notion of cumulative causation. Whites' prejudices and their power to discriminate against people of color result in segregation and inter-racial economic disparities which, in turn, reinforce the original prejudices. This process plays itself out over time in a fortifying, cumulative manner. Decades later, in the wake of riots in numerous cities, the Report of the National Advisory Commission on Civil Disorders (1968) replayed Myrdal's theme.

In his 1987 book, *The Truly Disadvantaged*, William J. Wilson argued that the combination of the historical burden of racism, the decline of manufacturing in the inner-city, and the out-migration of middle-class African-Americans from the inner-city resulted in an isolated, permanently deprived underclass. Wilson reminds us of the social and psychological dimensions of polarization—both within the African-American community and between it and the white community—and how those dimensions become intensified in the context of segregated communities. Communities that differ in their residents' sense of personal efficacy are communities that differ in their collective political power.

Douglas Massey and Mitchell Eggers (1990) carefully examined the causes of spatial concentration of poverty among different racial groups. They found that concentrated urban poverty in 1980 was principally confined to blacks who lived outside of the West and to Hispanics who resided in the Northeast. They also concluded that the spatial concentration of poverty is directly rooted in residential segregation. Their research indicates that changes in the structure of employment caused more minorities to slip from the middle class into poverty. The fact that these same people were segregated in minority neighborhoods *and* suffered disproportionately in the labor market resulted in increased concentrations of poverty in inner-city minority neighborhoods.

George Galster and W. Mark Kenney (1988) attempted to statistically quantify the linkages in a model similar to Myrdal's. In a 1980 sample of 40 metropolitan areas, they found strong evidence that discrimination in labor and housing markets, prejudice, residential segregation, and inter-racial income disparities were linked in a mutually supportive fashion. The industrial structure of the local economy also had a clear impact on the nexus of social problems that resulted in inter-racial income disparities. The perspectives provided by these five works reappear throughout the chapters of this book.

ORGANIZATION OF THIS BOOK

There are numerous ways to organize a book of readings, and the scheme chosen for this one resulted from a great deal of thought and discussion. The text is subdivided into three sections. The first section (Chs. 1 and 2) provides an overview of key issues, an integrative conceptual framework, and a historical perspective. The second section (Chs. 3–10) describes the current state of place, power, and polarization in U.S. metropolitan areas and analyzes their causes and interconnections. Chapters 3, 4 and 5 primarily deal with polarization; Chapters 6, 7, and 8 with place; and Chapters 9 and 10 with power. The final section (Chs. 11–19) focuses on policy proposals relating to race and the metropolis. Chapter 11 draws on the prior chapters to provide a model for understanding spatial, human, and labor market causes of polarization and shows how the model can be used to help evaluate a wide range of urban public policies. This chapter establishes a context for the more focused policy discussions for economic development of the underclass (Chs. 12 and 13), housing and residential integration (Chs. 14, 15 and 16), public education (Ch. 17), governmental structural reforms (Ch. 18), and institutional changes for enhancing cross-cultural communication as a prelude to expanding employment prospects for people of color (Ch. 19). A major contribution of this book is its perspective. This perspective is reflected by both the positive chapters in the first two sections of the book and amplified in the more normative chapters in the third section.

Separating the descriptive and analytical chapters (Sections I and II) from the prescriptive chapters (Section III) is purposeful. The central goal is to emphasize that the problems of race and the metropolis can be more fully understood from the perspective of a unified conceptual framework embodying place, power, and polarization. The origins of a particular problem—and, thus, the appropriate policy prescriptions—cannot be viewed in isolation from other interrelated phenomena because of their reinforcing interconnections. The text, therefore, is *not* organized around "topics," wherein each particular facet of the overall metropolitan racial situation is discussed in isolation and then followed by a particular policy recommendation for that topic. It is hoped that the organization of this book serves to encourage a more encompassing approach to both causal analysis and comprehensive policy prescription.

With this organizational strategy in mind, an introduction to the specific chapters follows. In his historical overview of the issues (Ch. 2), Krumholz agrees with the fundamental insight of the National Advisory Commission and argues that the connection between spatial isolation and polarization is even more applicable now than it was 20 years ago. The troubling reality which Krumholz emphasizes is that the position of many African-Americans has worsened since the mid-1970s, despite the passage of civil rights legislation, significant electoral gains by African-American politicians, and major improvements in the racial attitudes of whites.

Ricketts discusses polarization in Chapter 3 when he traces the origin of the term underclass, its various definitions, and how the size of this group has increased. His estimates indicate that approximately 2.5 million people live in underclass areas and that one-half million are in the underclass. Ricketts provides an intellectual framework for understanding the connection between the world of work and the world of the nearly permanent urban poor. In Chapter 4, Harrison and Gorham statistically demonstrate how a decline in the proportion of African-American families who are members of the middle class and a phenomenal rise in the proportion who hold low-paying jobs has accompanied the restructuring of the American economy alluded to by Wilson and Jaynes. Blair and Fichtenbaum (Ch. 5) link this relative decline in African-Americans' status to the types of jobs and occupations held by blacks and whites. Their analysis of why this has occurred, coupled with their presentation of the various theoretical explanations offered by the academic community, ties together the impact of race on place and polarization.

Several chapters in the second section of the book extend the analyses of Massey and Eggers and Galster and Kenney by examining in detail various outcomes of the interaction between place, power, and polarization. Clay (Ch. 6) describes differences in housing quality, affordability, and homeownership among blacks and whites and documents trends that will affect the racial dimension of housing in the coming decade. Osei (Ch. 8) presents evidence on persistent differences in mortality and morbidity rates between blacks and whites and argues for an explanation of these differences based on both class and race. Hill and Rock (Ch. 7) show how inner-city educational problems are based on race and class isolation and how the quality of inner-city education has not kept pace with the demands of the workplace. In concert, spatial inequities in housing, health, and education serve to racially polarize the economic, social, and political spheres of the metropolis.

The theme of place and political power is amplified in Chapters 9 and 10. Keller (Ch. 9) argues that race is a moral issue that confounds the current structure of urban government. Urban government is characterized formally by a crazy quilt of overlapping jurisdictions fragmented across the metropolitan area and informally by local politicians (of all races) practicing "transactional politics" aimed at short-run parochial gains. These two characterizations, according to Keller, preclude governance: the effective coordination of a diverse set of organizations, and the activities surrounding them, to obtain desirable policy outcomes. Thus, a spatially fragmented metropolis creates a structure of power that precludes an effective political response to economic and racial polarization. The structure of government in the metropolis reinforces racial polarization and transactional politics feeds on polarization. This inhibits true political leadership that can tackle the moral issue of race and engage in what Keller calls "transformational politics."

Persons (Ch. 10) provides a detailed analysis of the electoral success of African-Americans in municipal elections, placing it within the context of the history of ethnic urban politics. She pays particular attention to the emergence of African-American mayoralties as "both the embodiment of a continued dispersion of political power in cities, and as the latest catalyst for ethno-racial conflict." Persons notes that such political empowerment has produced mixed benefits, and that whatever gains have been made are threatened by, among other things, changing racial patterns in both central cities and suburbs.

What policies may be helpful in overcoming this nexus of problems? The analyses provided in the second section of the book indicate that a comprehensive solution must account for numerous interlocking problems: structural economic change, racial residential isolation, discrimination in housing and jobs, inadequate levels of learning, and political conflict and jurisdictional fragmentation. The chapters in the book's third section provide alternative strategies with which to respond to this daunting complexity that is the metropolis in black and white.

Galster (Ch. 11) attempts to synthesize the learning from the second section in a neo-Myrdalian model and discusses its implications for alternative types of urban economic development policy. This chapter reinforces the mutual causation that lies behind the conceptual model. It serves as a transitional chapter, as the authors move from positive analysis in the second section to normative prescription in the third.

Policies responding to economic polarization are presented first. Ricketts (Ch. 12) examines four alternative explanations of the growth in the minority urban underclass and the policy implications of each of these hypothesized causes. Washington (Ch. 13) shows how the interplay of state and federal racial policies has affected the life-chances of both underclass and middle-class African-Americans. He ironically notes that, whereas historically the federal government (and the federal court system) has led the fight against racism, during the last decade it has led the efforts to reverse economic and political gains of minorities. Washington states that this reversal threatens to return the nation to a caste system of race relations, one that is supported by an established power structure and that supports spatial and economic polarization.

The residential life of inner-city African-Americans—in particular the location and quality of their homes and schools—is the focus of the next four chapters. Clay (Ch. 14) presents policies that will increase housing opportunities for African-Americans yet may well perpetuate their spatial isolation. In contrast, Galster (Ch. 15) makes a case for making residential integration a central part of urban public policy and reviews ongoing efforts to create stable integration. Chandler (Ch. 16) responds to Galster by citing practical and political difficulties in integration maintenance efforts as seen from the perspective of the African-American community. She argues for more choice in integrative policies.

Rock and Hill (Ch. 17) present a model of four aspects of education for which public school systems are held accountable. They then discuss two prominent theoretical reasons given for the failure of inner-city public schools to fulfill these aims and two approaches that have made a difference in inner-city schools: Edmond's (1979) observations on the effective schools movement and Commer's (1987) on the New Haven Schools Project. Hill and Rock conclude by offering a radical strategy for promoting educational reform that can incorporate the best from these two approaches.

Keller (Ch. 18) and Cornwell and Murray (Ch. 19) conclude the book. Keller provides structural remedies to the problem of governance in a multicultural metropolis. He argues that without a better congruence between place and power, America will be unable to engage in transformational politics that transcends narrow interests. Cornwell and Murray discuss the necessity of multicultural understanding in the coming decades and provide strategies for opening cross-cultural communications in the workplace. Cornwell and Murray's recommendations are placed within the context of public sector employment (reflecting Murray's experience as city manager in Cincinnati) but their recommendations apply equally well to workplaces in the private sector. They emphasize that progress will be gradual and that, while housing integration is one way to attack the problems of place and polarization, opening up the workplace to people of color directly attacks the connection between power and polarization.

WHAT ABOUT THE FUTURE?

The problem of equal opportunity for people of color in the United States is actually a nexus of problems built on a solid foundation of racism. Place—where people live, work, and socialize—cannot be ignored as a major component of this foundation. Powerlessness—personal and collective, economic and political—combines with spatial isolation to polarize American society. It is clear that progress from a polarized society toward an inclusive, multicultural society will not occur unless spatial isolation of people of color—especially African-Americans—ends.

The question remains: what will cause this racist foundation of place, power, and polarization to crumble? Will it crumble due to the good wishes and intentions of white America? It will take more than this.

The legacy of years of segregation and discrimination, coupled with institutionalized racist practices, means that a powerful shock to the economy is required to overcome African-Americans' accumulated disadvantages of residence and skills. That shock is easy to foresee and it is one which current policy is ignoring: the coming labor shortage. If the American economy is to grow it will need to incorporate people of color and women into the workforce as never before. The labor force in the year 2000 will become slightly older, more female, less white and it will grow at a slower rate (Hill and Rock 1990). The problem is that America is not preparing for the coming labor shortage. Those who have been marginalized will not have the skills required to take advantage of the shortage. The resulting harm to the nation could be so dramatic as to necessitate a major policy response. This response will not be based on a sense of social justice or equity; it will become a question of national economic security.

There are three possible responses. The first is the one hoped for—deeper investment in the poor, accompanied by legal action to increase the mobility of the excluded. Once the prospect of mobility is realistically offered and demonstrated, self-help efforts on the part of achieving individuals will be rewarded. Increased immigration is the second possible response. Labor will be imported from other nations to relieve the shortages and lessen economic pressure to invest in the native-born poor. The third possible response is the continued exporting of employment. It is feared that a combination of the second and third responses will take place.

This book offers a variety of strategies that might be considered to ensure the first response. Chapters 11, 12 and 13 offer conceptual underpinnings for urban economic and human development programs. The remaining chapters of the third section of the book offer specific proposals in the areas of housing (Chs. 14, 15 and 16), public education (Ch. 17), metropolitan government (Ch. 18) and inter-racial relations within employment settings (Ch. 19). No attempt has been made to force a consensus among the policy discussants; these chapters sometimes reflect sharp differences in emphasis. Some are more optimistic than others. Nevertheless, they are viewed as representative of the sort of hard-hitting policy discussions that have been largely absent from the current political scene and that must occur if a serious effort at healing the black-white divide is to succeed in America's metropolitan-based society.

This collection is primarily intended to be used as a textbook in undergraduate classes. It is the hope of all those who have contributed that this work will stimulate thoughtful debate on the future of U.S. cities and metropolitan areas, the future of inter-racial relations, and of our own roles in a multicultural society. Please engage in that debate because the problems of racial tensions and of poverty are persistent and tragic facts of American life. They have lasted far too long to be called crises. They cry for solutions.

NOTES

1. Land is available for redevelopment in central cities but it often requires huge amounts of funds to offset three types of costs. The first type consists of legal costs associated with assembling a site out of what is usually a group of smaller parcels. The second is the costs associated with razing existing buildings and disposing of the material. The third type is the often exorbitant expenses involved with cleaning up environmental hazards at former industrial sites. Quite often the extent of environmental damage is not known until excavation has begun and the new owner, and often the lender, are obligated to press on with the clean up no matter the cost. This is a huge risk and is deterring the reuse of older industrial sites.

REFERENCES

Aaron, H. 1990. Symposium on the economic status of african-americans. *Journal of Economic Perspectives* 4(1):3–8.

Clark, K. 1965. *The dark ghetto*. New York: Harper and Row.

Comer, J. 1987. New Haven's school-community connection. *Educational Leadership* 44(6):13–16.

Darling-Hammond, L., et al. 1985. *Tuition tax deductions and parent school choice*. Santa Monica, CA: RAND (R-3294-NIE).

Edmonds, R. 1979. Effective schools for the urban poor. *Educational Leadership* 37:15–27.

Galster G. and M. Kenney. 1988. Race, residence, discrimination, and economic opportunity. *Urban Affairs Quarterly* 24(3):87–117.

Hanushek, E. 1986. The economics of schooling: production and efficiency in public schools. *Journal of Economic Literature* 24(3):1141–77.

Hill, E. and H. Rock. 1990. Education as an economic development resource. *Government and Policy (Environment and Planning C)* 8(1):53–68.

Jaynes, G. 1990. The labor market status of black americans: 1939–1985. *Journal of Economic Perspectives* 4(1):9–24.

Jaynes, G. and R. Williams, eds. 1989. *A common destiny: blacks and american society*. Washington, DC: National Academy Press.

Kasarda, J. 1990. City jobs and residents on a collision course: the urban underclass dilemma. *Economic Development Quarterly* 4(4):313–19.

Massey, D. and M. Eggers 1990. The ecology of inequality: minorities and the concentration of poverty, 1970–1980. *American Journal of Sociology* 95:1153–88.

Myrdal, G. 1944. *The american dilemma: the negro problem and modern democracy*. New York: Harper and Row.

National Advisory Commission on Civil Disorders. 1968. *Report of the national advisory commission on civil disorders*. New York: Bantam Books.

New York Times. 1990. U.S. reports poverty is down but inequality is up. September 27: A10.

O'Neill, J. 1990. The role of human capital in earnings differences between black and white men. *Journal of Economic Perspectives* 4(1):25–45.

Sawhill, I. 1988. Poverty in the U.S.: Why is it so persistent? *Journal of Economic Literature* 26(3):1073–1119.

Smith, J. and F. Welch. 1989. Black economic progress after Myrdal. *Journal of Economic Literature* 27(2):519–64.

Wilson, W. 1987. *The truly disadvantaged*. Chicago: The University of Chicago Press.

2   The Kerner Commission Twenty Years Later

NORMAN KRUMHOLZ

The National Advisory Commission on Civil Disorders (named the Kerner Commission after its chairperson) was appointed in 1967 to investigate the causes of the racial disturbances that swept many American cities. In its report issued one year later, the commission described a city-suburb polarization that was rooted in racial and economic differences. America, it warned, was becoming a racially divided and unequal nation. The commission deliberated on various strategies that might avert this destructive polarization.

In its final report, the Kerner Commission considered three possible strategy options. The first strategy involved doing nothing more about the problem than was being done at the time. The commission rejected this approach, not because the federal Great Society programs of the time—model cities, antipoverty programs, Medicare and Medicaid, educational enrichment, etc.—were not working, but because the commission believed that this approach would likely perpetuate two racially separate and unequal societies. The second strategy considered was one of "ghetto enrichment" through major increases in federal programs and funding, but with no basic change in racial segregation. This approach, often called "gilding the ghetto," was also rejected because the commission believed that equal opportunity was impossible as long as the races were segregated. The final strategy, which was unanimously recommended, emphasized both ghetto enrichment and racial integration.

For a period during the 1960s and early 1970s, national events were moving in a direction that seemed supportive of the Kerner Commission's recommendations and likely to improve the prospects for racial integration. These events included legislative changes, changes in social attitudes, and positive changes in the economy. In 1964, the Civil Rights Act banned discrimination in all public accommodations, outlawed discrimination in employment of all types, and forbade discrimination in any program involving the use of federal funds. The Voting Rights Act of 1965 attacked the disenfranchisement of African-Americans and brought floods of new voters into the electoral process. The Civil Rights Act of 1968 banned discrimination in the rental or sale of housing. One by one, these laws destroyed the legal basis for racial segregation (Farley 1984).

Over the same period of time, racial attitudes among whites also improved. Many polls taken during the 1960s showed that there was substantial resistance to racial integration. By 1972, however, 85 percent of all whites interviewed in a study agreed that it would make no difference to them "if a black with just as much income and education moved onto their block" (Pettigrew 1973).

Economic opportunities also increased for African-Americans during the 1970s, partially as a result of anti-discrimination legislation, partially as a result of more tolerant racial attitudes, and, perhaps most crucially, as a result of the unprecedented high and sustained rate of national economic growth from 1940 to 1970. By the 1980s, more blacks with more resources than ever before were becoming respected members of the middle class and increasingly choosing to locate in the suburbs (Freeman 1976; Wilson 1978). Despite these gains, however, the economic status of blacks relative to whites has stagnated since the mid-1970s because of the slowdown in the U.S. economy.

Notwithstanding the passage of the fair housing and civil rights laws and substantial economic progress in many regions, African-Americans located in older industrial cities with large minority neighborhoods, such as Cleveland, Ohio, still continue to be subjected to high degrees of residential segregation. And by indices such as unemployment, income, and poverty, the gap between blacks and whites remains almost as wide in 1990 as it was in the 1960s when racial riots brought national guardsmen into the streets of Cleveland and other American cities. In the 1980s, national policy shifted away from the social domestic programs, a course generally maintained in the 1970s. Instead of the Kerner Commission's unanimously recommended policy of racial integration and ghetto enrichment, America has tacitly adopted a policy calling for standing still or retreating, a policy that involves substantial cutbacks in the federal resources that were available in 1968. In effect, U.S. national policy has accepted continued racial segregation, as well as high levels of poverty.

This chapter presents an overview of racial progress and lack of progress in three important areas: housing desegregation, political participation and power, and economic status. It concludes that despite evidence of progress since 1968 in certain areas, the American dilemma has not been resolved. While the gulf between black and white America has narrowed in some respects, it is far from closed. Finally, the chapter concludes with brief recommendations for what must be done to remedy the situation.

HOUSING DESEGREGATION

In its report, the Kerner Commission noted that "discrimination and segregation have long permeated much of American life...." (National Advisory Commission on Civil Disorders 1968). Recognizing the different experiences of African-Americans in comparison to other immigrant groups, the Commission stated:

> Thousands of Negro families have attained incomes, living standards and cultural levels matching or surpassing those of whites who have "upgraded" themselves from distinctly ethnic neighbors. Yet most Negro families have remained within predominantly Negro neighborhoods, primarily because they have been effectively excluded from white residential areas...by intimidation or violence.... Often, real estate agents simply refuse to show homes to Negro buyers.

And the Commission continued, "Many middle-class Negro families, therefore, cease looking for homes beyond all-Negro areas or nearby 'changing' neighborhoods. For them, ... the psychological efforts and costs" of change are too high (National Advisory Commission on Civil Disorders 1968, p. 244).

Residential segregation of blacks is far greater than that of any other racial or ethnic group. It was not an unplanned spontaneous process, nor has the segregation disappeared or been weakened much since the Kerner Report. The legal and social changes that affected the status of African-Americans from 1960 to 1980 have had limited effects on residential segregation (Kain 1985).

African-Americans are still not free to live where they wish, regardless of their economic status; discrimination concentrates most African-Americans into separate residential areas. Especially for poor blacks this is a disaster, forcing them into areas where a high percentage of economically poor and undereducated families live, and where educational and employment opportunities are greatly limited. Residential segregation continues to represent a fundamental cleavage between blacks and whites in American society. It does not seem likely to change soon.

Racial segregation is often enforced through harassment and violence. When the Cuyahoga Metropolitan Housing Authority [CMHA] in Cleveland, Ohio, leased homes in white neighborhoods to black tenants, the homes were often attacked (*Cleveland Plain Dealer* 1989). In one such incident in 1987, a firebombing killed an elderly black tenant. In suburban areas of Washington, D.C., newly-arrived black families were often greeted by burning crosses (Valente 1983). In 1984, over 30 attacks were reported on the homes of blacks living in integrated areas of Chicago (Blackstone 1985). Resistance to the arrival of minority families is a longstanding part of life in most American cities.

Massey and Denton have provided a recent description of the extent of racial segregation in American cities and how it has changed between 1970 and 1980 (Massey and Denton 1987). They confirm that racial segregation continues to prevent many blacks from coming into contact with whites.

TABLE 2.1

Percentage of SMSA Populations Living Outside Central City in 1970 and 1980, by Race

SMSA	1970			1980		
	% Negro	% White	Ratio W/N	% Black	% Nonblack	Ratio NB/B
Atlanta	26.6	85.0	3.19	43.3	90.7	2.10
Baltimore	14.2	69.3	4.86	22.6	78.0	3.46
Boston	19.9	76.8	3.86	22.6	79.2	3.50
Chicago	10.4	60.5	5.81	16.2	68.1	4.21
Cincinnati	17.9	73.4	4.10	24.9	79.2	3.19
Cleveland	13.5	73.3	5.44	27.3	79.2	2.90
Columbus	8.2	51.6	6.31	7.3	54.1	7.43
Dallas-Fort Worth	12.6	53.6	4.25	15.7	63.4	4.03
Denver-Boulder	5.2	55.1	10.61	22.3	67.1	3.00
Detroit	13.2	76.8	5.83	14.8	87.2	5.90
Ft. Lauderdale	68.6	59.1	0.86	67.3	73.8	1.10
Houston	18.8	43.0	2.29	16.7	51.5	3.08
Indianapolis	2.2	38.1	17.37	2.9	45.7	15.53
Kansas City	3.4	67.8	20.02	29.2	71.8	2.46
Los Angeles-Long Beach	31.5	57.8	1.83	42.2	57.4	1.36
Miami	59.8	76.0	1.27	68.9	80.7	1.17
Milwaukee	1.4	52.8	38.96	2.5	60.7	24.49
Minneapolis-St. Paul	6.8	63.1	9.27	16.6	71.0	4.27
New York	6.9	23.9	3.47	8.1	26.4	3.27
Philadelphia	22.6	67.4	2.99	27.8	72.6	2.62
Portland, Ore.	7.4	63.6	8.65	16.9	72.0	4.25
Riverside-San Bernardino	54.5	73.5	1.35	58.8	76.6	1.30
Sacramento	28.1	70.0	2.49	39.9	74.9	1.88
St. Louis	32.9	81.9	2.49	49.4	87.3	1.77
San Antonio	16.3	27.1	1.66	20.7	27.2	1.31
San Diego	14.6	50.3	3.44	25.6	54.6	2.13
San Francisco-Oakland	33.1	69.2	2.09	37.2	73.0	1.96
San Jose	39.4	57.1	1.45	33.3	51.5	1.55
Seattle-Everett	8.1	60.5	7.49	18.5	67.7	3.65
Tampa-St. Petersburg	23.5	58.2	2.48	28.0	71.7	2.56
Washington, D.C.	25.0	90.0	3.60	47.5	91.4	1.92
All SMSAs						
Weighted mean	18.1	59.8	3.30	25.8	65.4	2.54
Unweighted mean	20.9	62.1	6.12	28.2	67.9	3.98

Source: Kain, Black Suburbanization in the Eighties, 1985.

The Massey and Denton study focuses on two measures of residential segregation: evenness and exposure. Evenness refers to the differential distribution of blacks and whites among census tracts in an urban area; exposure describes the degree of potential contact within tracts.

Using data from the 1980 census, the researchers found major patterns of racial housing segregation in most cities and metropolitan areas, and extreme patterns of segregation, which they called "hypersegregation" in ten metropolitan areas (Massey and Denton 1989). Those ten cities contain 29 percent of the nation's black urban population. The Cleveland area, for example, remains one of the most segregated housing markets in the United States with most blacks living on the east side of the Cuyahoga River and most whites living on the west side. In 1970, 92 percent of all blacks in the region lived within the central city and east of the Cuyahoga River. Since World War I, Cleveland's housing market has been characterized by restrictive covenants, blockbusting, steering, and intimidation designed to keep black homeseekers confined to a homogeneous

FIGURE 2.1

Percent of Black Persons,
by Census Tracts in Cuyahoga County, 1990

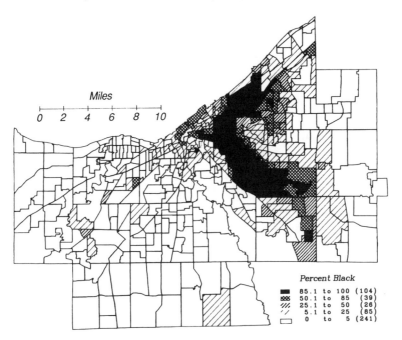

Percent Black

■ 85.1 to 100 (104)
▧ 50.1 to 85 (39)
▨ 25.1 to 50 (26)
▨ 5.1 to 25 (65)
☐ 0 to 5 (241)

Source: 1990 Census of Population and Housing, PL94-171 Data (preliminary count).
Prepared by: The Northern Ohio Data & Information Service (NODIS), The Urban Center, Maxine Goodman Levin College of Urban Affairs, Cleveland State University.

ghetto and its fringes. Through the years, numerous lawsuits have been brought against local politicians and real estate companies for such practices up to the present day.

The Massey and Denton study (1987) rated 60 of the nation's largest cities on a scale of 0 to 100, with 0 being totally integrated and 100 being totally segregated. Cleveland scored 87.5 on the segregation scale, which means that 87.5 percent of all blacks would have to move to achieve integration. This rating is only a slight improvement over 1970 when the city's rating was 90.8. Cleveland is one of 15 cities with large black concentrations whose average segregation rate improved only slightly during the 1970 to 1980 decade.

The bleak findings in the Massey study with respect to Cleveland are underscored in a 1986 report by the Cuyahoga Plan, a local nonprofit agency set up in 1974 to track, document, and encourage racial integration in housing in the Cleveland area (Obermanns 1986). The report analyzed racial percentages in 1968 and 1986 for 35 Cleveland neighborhoods and 54 suburbs in Cuyahoga County. The Cuyahoga Plan's report found that 20 years after Title VIII of the Civil Rights Act of 1968 was signed into law, the same number of city neighborhoods—22—were racially isolated (a community is considered racially

TABLE 2.2

Residential Dissimilarity of Blacks, Hispanics, and Asians in
Fifteen U.S. Metropolitan Areas, 1970–1980

| Metropolitan Area | Dissimilarity Between Anglos and | | | | | | | | |
| | BLACKS | | | HISPANICS | | | ASIANS | | |
	1970	1980	Change	1970	1980	Change	1970	1980	Change
Chicago	.919	.878	−.041	.584	.635	.051	.558	.439	−.120
New York	.810	.820	.010	.649	.656	.007	.561	.481	−.080
Atlanta	.821	.785	−.036	.359	.329	−.031	.458	.291	−.167
Cleveland	.980	.875	−.033	.523	.554	.031	.450	.358	−.093
Baltimore	.819	.747	−.072	.442	.381	−.061	.473	.389	−.084
Birmingham	.278	.408	.031	.285	.221	−.065	.379	.261	−.118
Cincinnati	.768	.723	−.045	.378	.303	−.075	.433	.330	−.103
Detroit	.884	.867	−.017	.479	.451	−.029	.461	.375	−.086
Gary–Hammond	.914	.906	−.008	.591	.562	−.028	.420	.350	−.070
Indianapolis	.817	.762	−.055	.383	.332	−.051	.402	.360	−.042
Jersey City	.752	.765	.013	.548	.488	−.060	.465	.450	−.015
Nassau–Suffolk	.744	.755	.011	.291	.362	.070	.422	.345	−.077
Newark	.814	.816	.002	.604	.656	.052	.502	.344	−.158
Paterson–Clifton	.779	.815	.037	.610	.722	.112	.466	.404	−.061
Philadelphia	.795	.788	−.007	.540	.629	.089	.491	.437	−.053

Source: D.S. Massey and N. Denton. 1987. Trends in the residential segregation of blacks, Hispanics, and Asians: 1970–1980. *American Sociological Review* 52 (December): 815.

isolated when 90 percent or more of its population is of one race). There was, however, some movement: some neighborhoods that were racially diverse in 1968 had become almost entirely black by 1986; other neighborhoods, mostly on Cleveland's predominantly white west side, went from virtually all white to racially mixed.

The report also pointed out that racial integration in the suburbs had improved, mostly in the eastern suburbs. This improvement took place as the result of a substantial suburbanization of Cleveland's black population between the 1960s and the 1990s. In 1960, only 4,492 (between 1 and 2 percent) Cleveland-area blacks lived in the suburbs; 250,818 lived in the city. From 1960 to 1970, however, the black population in the suburbs increased by 453 percent. The huge suburban increase reflected the fact that there were almost no suburban blacks in 1960. A good part of the increase, however, was limited to one community, East Cleveland, where the black percentage rose in one decade from 2 to 51. By 1980, 27 percent of the black population in Cuyahoga County had suburbanized, and by 1990, 33 percent of the black population was living in Cleveland's suburbs (U.S. Bureau of Census 1980, 1990).

In 1968, 4 of the 54 suburbs were considered racially diverse compared with 11 in 1986; but much of the black population that had suburbanized in the 1960s was concentrated in the inner-ring suburbs of East Cleveland and Warrensville Heights, and those cities were virtually re-segregated. Most blacks in both central city and suburban areas continue to live in highly segregated, racially-isolated neighborhoods. Whereas black families in Bedford Heights, Cleveland Heights, Shaker Heights, Warrensville Heights and similar suburbs have substantially better occupations, higher incomes, and higher rates of home ownership than do central-city blacks, East Cleveland may be seen as an extension of Cleveland's Glenville ghetto (in 1987 East Cleveland's poverty rate was two percentage points higher than Cleveland's). Of the 21 large western suburbs, none had a non-white population of more than 6 percent in 1986, and 12 western suburbs were virtually all white.

As noted earlier, residential integration in Cleveland has been made more difficult by periodic acts of terror, including shootings, firebombings and acts of vandalism. Fueled by such acts, the patterns of racial segregation in Cleveland have stubbornly resisted all fair housing laws.

POLITICAL PARTICIPATION AND POWER

Unlike other citizens whose rights of basic citizenship—voting, equal treatment before the law, the right to hold public office—have been taken for granted, African-Americans have had to struggle frequently for those rights through litigation and protest. The political participation of African-Americans, therefore, has been an intensely social and collective process.

National Participation

At the national level, African-Americans predominantly voted Republican until the Great Depression. The Republican party was seen as the party of Lincoln, more inclined to favor concerns of African-Americans than the Democratic party since the Democratic party was heavily influenced by its conservative southern wing. A shift toward the Democrats was begun in the 1930s by Franklin D. Roosevelt's New Deal policies. As a response to fundamental needs of African-Americans, this process underscored an expanded and more generous role for the federal government in job creation and social welfare. A significant fraction of black political loyalty, however, held firm with the Republican party during the 1950s. While the Democrats sent out confused and ambiguous signals on civil rights during that decade, Earl Warren, a former Republican governor of California who was appointed Chief Justice of the Supreme Court by a Republican president (Eisenhower), decided the key school desegregation decision of 1954 in *Brown* v. *Topeka Board of Education*.

The wholesale shift of blacks to the Democratic party began in earnest in 1964 when Lyndon B. Johnson, a Democratic president, signed into law the Civil Rights Act of that year, while the Republican presidential candidate of that year (Senator Barry Goldwater) voted against it. President Johnson also began the medical and social programs of the Great Society and followed the landmark 1964 Civil Rights Act with the Voting Rights Act of 1965 and the Civil Rights Act of 1968. Civil rights issues reinforced economic interests and generated powerful black political partisanship.

Since 1964, African-Americans have been virtually unanimous in their support for national candidates affiliated with the Democratic party, and voter participation rates, which before 1964 lagged far behind white rates, have begun to approach white voter participation rates. The participation of African-Americans in Democratic party conventions has also sharply increased over participation in Republican national conventions. Since the Kerner Report was written, African-American delegates to the Democratic national political convention have gone up from 209 to 697 (see Table 2.3).

Local Participation

The number of elected black officials in the entire nation before World War II stood at only 33. Up to 1965, it grew slowly, but since then, with the passage of the Voting Rights Act of 1965, it has grown dramatically. Growth in the number of elected black officials is especially noteworthy in the South, where black candidates were rare before 1965. Since that year, African-Americans have been elected to every major public office except president and vice president.

TABLE 2.3

Black Delegates at National Political Conventions, 1940–1984

	Democratic Conventions			Republican Conventions		
	Black		Total	Black		Total
Year	Delegates	Percent	Delegates	Delegates	Percent	Delegates
1940	7	0.6	1,094	32	3.2	1,000
1944	11	0.9	1,176	18	1.7	1,057
1948	17	1.3	1,234	41	3.7	1,094
1952	33	2.6	1,230	29	2.4	1,206
1956	24	1.7	1,372	36	2.7	1,323
1960	46	3.0	1,521	22	1.6	1,331
1964	65	2.8	2,316	14	1.0	1,308
1968	209	6.7	3,084	26	1.9	1,333
1972	452	14.6	3,103	56	4.2	1,348
1976	323	10.6	3,048	76	3.4	2,259
1980	481	14.4	3,331	55	2.7	1,993
1984	697	17.7	3,933	69	3.1	2,235

Source: Data from the Joint Center for Political Studies in Jaynes and Williams, 1989.

TABLE 2.4

Black Elected Officials, by Region, 1941–1985[a]

Year	Northeast	North Central	South	West	Total
1941	10	20	2	1	33
1947	21	35	6	4	66
1951	29	31	16	6	82
1965	63	104	87	26	280
1970	238	296	703	132	1,369
1975	503	869	1,913	218	3,503
1980	570	1,041	2,981	298	4,890
1985	694	1,150	3,801	371	6,016

Note: [a] Regions are those of the Bureau of the Census.

Source: Jaynes and Williams, *A Common Destiny: Blacks and American Society,* 1989.

In 1988, the national total of elected black officials was 6,829; the first African-American governor of any state was elected in Virginia in 1989; an African-American is the majority whip of the U.S. Congress; and in 1990, African-Americans control the office of mayor in many of America's largest cities, including Baltimore, Los Angeles New York and Philadelphia (see Ch. 10). While the increase in number of public officials is noteworthy, blacks, comprising 11 percent of the U.S. population, have elected only 1.5 percent of all U.S. public officials. The largest increase in elected officials has occurred at the local levels of government, with city and school board members predominating.

To a large extent, political success at the local level is determined by the racial composition of the local electorate. The higher the percentage of voting-age blacks in the population, the higher the probability of electing a black candidate. In an ironic way, widespread racial discrimination and segregation in housing has provided a solid base for black political success. Once in office, a black mayor is expected to increase the black share of the municipal workforce, raise the level of positions to which blacks are appointed, and place a high priority on municipal contracting with minority firms. Cleveland provides an example of how this process works.

One facet of racial segregation in Cleveland and elsewhere is the rise of black politicians, backed largely by black voters, to local political dominance. The concentration of the black population in Cleveland—which in 1990, was about one-half of the total population—has produced substantial political power. Carl B. Stokes, the first black mayor in a U.S. city with a population over 500,000, was elected to two-year terms in 1967 and again in 1969 with more than 90 percent of Cleveland's black vote. His brother, Louis Stokes, was elected to the U.S. Congress in 1969, where he continues to serve. George L. Forbes, former City Council President (1973–89) and clearly the most powerful political figure in Cleveland, enjoyed the solid support of the black community, as did 10 of the 21 members of the Cleveland City Council. Black Cleveland voters have also helped elect a number of black judges, state representatives and senators, and a county commissioner.

Benefits of Power

To a certain extent, this political muscle has been translated into jobs and other benefits for the African-American community much in the same way earlier ethnic groups, such as the Irish, took advantage of the benefits of office. This has been true in city government and in other public agencies where the city exercises political influence. In 1987, for example, the City of Cleveland employed 8,195 people; 3,584 (43 percent) were black. This included substantial numbers at the highest director and commissioner levels, which 20 years

TABLE 2.5
City of Cleveland Police Force

	All Ranks		Sergeants		Lieutenants		Captains		Above Captain	
	Total	Black	Total	Black	Total	Black	Total	Black	Total	Black
1968	2,216	165	155	6	78	0	26	0	17	0
1988	1,743	403	201	28	81	7	25	6	15	5

Source: City of Cleveland, 1988.

ago were off limits to blacks. It also included a rising number of employees at all levels in the traditional white police and fire departments (see Table 2.5).

The appointments of African-Americans in city hall represent more than jobs. It is generally believed that African-American representation in the delivery of city services improves those services in black neighborhoods. Similarly, when African-American representation on the police force goes up, African-American citizens are subject to less harassment.

African-American representation is also rising where city politics can influence other public agencies outside city hall. In 1988, the Greater Cleveland Regional Transit Authority (RTA) employed 2,733 people; 1,283 (47 percent) were black (Abram 1988). Since bus drivers at RTA with two years experience earn $13.50 an hour plus a 30 percent benefit package, this represents a substantial income stream. In 1988, the Cuyahoga Metropolitan Housing Authority [CHMA] employed 549 people; 403 (73 percent) were black. The Cleveland Board of Education, with a 1987 budget of $440 million, employed 10,205 people in 1988; 5,281 (52 percent) were black. In all of these institutions, the number of jobs held by blacks was substantially higher than the level 20 years ago when none of these agencies even had an affirmative action plan. African-American political power has also expanded the number of jobs held by blacks in the private sector, in part by affirmative action pressures on all contractors doing business with the city and on all firms taking advantage of public economic development subsidies.

In addition to seeking the increase of employment opportunities in the public sector, African-American political leaders in Cleveland have also expanded the participation of minority-owned firms in public and private contracting and purchasing. RTA, for example, sets a goal of 17.4 percent for the amount of minority contracting *(Cleveland Plain Dealer* 1989). This reflects both the 10 percent federal "set-aside" requirements relating to federal grants and the local political initiatives to influence the spending of local revenues. For its own part, the city of Cleveland sets aside a minimum of one-third of city works contracts

TABLE 2.6

Black Gains in City Employment, 1973–1980

City	Percent Black Population, 1980	Percent Blacks Hired	
		1973	1980
Los Angeles (1973)[a]	17	22	24
Totals			
Administrators		1.3	6.7
Professionals		5	8.8
Newark (1970)	58.2	—	49.6
Totals			
Administrators		—	19.5
Professionals		—	51.6
Atlanta (1973)	66.5	41.5	60.7
Totals			
Administrators		13.5	35.0
Professionals		19	47.2
Detroit (1973)	63	45.1	55.2
Totals			
Administrators		12.1	41.2
Professionals		22.8	39.2
Gary (1967)	70.3	—	77.3
Totals			
Administrators		—	72.3
Professionals		—	70.8

Note: [a] Date in parentheses is date of the first election of a black mayor.

Source: Personnel departments of each city. Washington, D.C. data were not made available.

for minority entrepreneurs. In 1988, more than $86 million in contracts were awarded by the city to minority- and female-controlled enterprises (Cleveland Department of Personnel 1987).

African-American gains in Cleveland are similar to those in five other black-mayor cities. In each of these cities, it is clear that affirmative action efforts have resulted in substantial increases in public sector employment (Eisinger 1984).

Although in some quarters it is argued that African-American control of central cities is a "hollow prize" and that power, authority, funding, and patronage all lie outside the central city (Friesma 1969), African-American politicians in Cleveland and elsewhere have convincingly refuted the idea and have demonstrated their mastery of the political process, providing tangible economic benefits to some of their supporters. Taking political control of city hall, then, is a prize of substantial value to the African-American citizens of a city, and a prize worth fighting for.

Public sector patronage does not, however, offer a strategy for full employment. Public sector jobs in Cleveland would support no more than 8 to 10 percent of the total black population of Cuyahoga County. Still, these jobs should help create a sizable, economically-secure, middle-class group in the African-American community, a group with steady work, good pay, and excellent fringe benefits. Their gains may be expected to build a substantial level of economic security and leadership for succeeding generations.

ECONOMIC STATUS

Writing in 1944, the famous Swedish sociologist Gunnar Myrdal summarized the economic position of America's black population:

> Except for a small minority enjoying upper or middle class status, the masses of American Negroes . . . are destitute. They own little property . . . , their incomes are not only low but irregular. They thus live from day to day and have scant security for the future. (Myrdal 1944)

Myrdal's assessment was riveting and accurate. At the time of his observations most Americans were poor. Forty-eight percent of all white families and 87 percent of all black families lived below the federal poverty line. The overwhelming majority of blacks lived in the South and worked in agriculture. One-third of southern blacks were sharecroppers or tenant farmers with little hope of surmounting their condition. Per capita black incomes were 39 percent of white incomes.

Even as Myrdal wrote, however, blacks were moving north. Pulled by the promise of jobs in the war economy, and pushed by the mechanization of agriculture and the repressive conditions of the South, blacks streamed to the cities of the North. The net emigration eventually totalled 3.5 million blacks, or more than 25 percent of the entire black population. The rapid and sustained economic growth during World War II and the next 25 years was essential to black gains in economic status. By 1964, only 36 percent of black families and 9 percent of white families were living below the poverty line, and black income was about one-half of white income. The urban industrial north was far from the promised land, however, and in the 1960s, frustrated by their continuing stature as second-class citizens, blacks rioted in city after city.

The employment status of blacks in the industrial world echoed Myrdal's comments on the agricultural status of blacks 25 years earlier. The Kerner Commission in 1968 spelled out the situation:

Negro workers are concentrated in the lowest-skilled and lowest-paying occupations. These jobs often involve substandard wages, great instability . . . extremely low status . . . little or no chance for meaningful advancement. (National Advisory Commission on Civil Disorders 1968)

Now two decades later, black-white economic differences continue to be substantial and economic gains of blacks during World War II through the end of the 1970s have stagnated. For example, in 1985, 31 percent of all black families and 11 percent of all white families lived below the poverty line, an increase over the respective 1974 poverty rates of 29.3 percent and 7.3 percent. Also black family real income in 1984 was only 57 percent of white income, the same relative position as in 1971. This lack of economic progress since the early 1970s reflects the stagflation of the 1970s, the national shift away from industrial production toward a service economy, and the unstable employment patterns for many blacks, particularly those workers who have the least education. In the last 25 years, this dynamic has helped produce a sharp economic split within the African-American community.

Some people within the African-American community, those better equipped through education and training to take advantage of the new civil rights and affirmative action legislation, have advanced dramatically since the 1960s. Many others, however, have been left far behind. As the rate of poverty reduction began to decline in the early 1970s, approximately one-third of all black families remained in poverty throughout the 1980s. This divergence had much to do with the educational attainments of young black men. In the 1980s, black men aged 25–34 with some college earned 80 to 85 percent as much as white men in the same age bracket; but young black men who had not finished high school could not compete in the stagnant economy and many dropped out of the labor force altogether.

Polarization of black family incomes has also taken place. In 1970, 15.7 percent of black families earned more than $35,000; by 1986, over 21 percent earned this amount. During the same years, the percentage of black families earning less than $10,000 also increased from 26.8 to 30.2 percent. Since 1960, the income polarization has been accompanied by the growth of female-headed black families, with whom the incidence of poverty is highest. It is no exaggeration to state that, generally, the polarization of black-family incomes is between the two-parent middle-class family and the female-headed lower-class family. Predictably, the growth in the number of female-headed households has meant that more black children would experience the effects of poverty. In 1969, a year after the Kerner Report, 58 percent of all poor black children were in female-headed families; in 1984, 75 percent of all poor black children were in such families. How those youths will affect labor markets, education policy, and social welfare requirements are major issues for the future, and poses a challenge to the nation's ability to solve the technical, economic, and social problems of the twenty-first century.

The geographic location of these persistently poor black families is more and more likely to be in central cities and in neighborhoods where a high proportion of residents is also poor. In 1986, at least two out of five poor blacks lived in census tracts where one-fifth or more of the population lived in poverty. As a direct result, poor blacks are likely to see, interact, go to school, and go to religious services with mainly other disadvantaged black people. They are, as a result of their increasing isolation, facing more and more obstacles to full participation in American life. A closer look at a specific impoverished black Cleveland neighborhood may help illustrate this point.

The Persistently Poor and the Central Neighborhood

Since the 1960s, expanding housing and economic opportunities have been drawing thousands of African-Americans out of Cleveland's older ghettos. Left behind are disorganized families and unskilled, alienated individuals who have become increasingly concentrated as the better-equipped people move out. Their very concentration exacerbates the most negative features of their lives (Wilson 1985; Orfield 1985). This group is relatively small, but it is extraordinarily destructive to its own members and the people and property around them. It has hardly been touched by the policies of the last 20 years, although some observers have argued that the existence of this group is the distorted result of past policies that have encouraged better educated, more mobile African-Americans to leave the ghetto and, thus, deny the remaining families their leadership (Wilson 1987). The actions of some members of this residual group are frequently marked by violence, reflecting their deep anger and frustration. Results of the violence are widespread fear, property destruction, and physical injury.

The behavior of this persistently poor group is a response to a long history of racial discrimination, inadequate education, and thwarted opportunity. Their plight has been aggravated by the flight of industrial jobs and the shift of the local and national economy from manufacturing to service industries. For example, in the 1970s, Cleveland lost 34,580 manufacturing jobs, while the area suburbs gained 23,800 jobs (Zeller 1988). Since the Kerner Report, African-American political power and training/employment programs have had only a minimal impact on this group. Instead of traditional work, their culture is dominated by welfare programs, petty crime, and street hustles. The extent of the economic and social distress of Cleveland's persistently poor population can be seen in the Central neighborhood, the city's first and oldest ghetto (see Figure 2.2). The growth, decline, and present tragic isolation of Cleveland's Central neighborhood go back into the history of the city.

FIGURE 2.2

Central Neighborhood in the City of Cleveland by Census Tracts, 1990

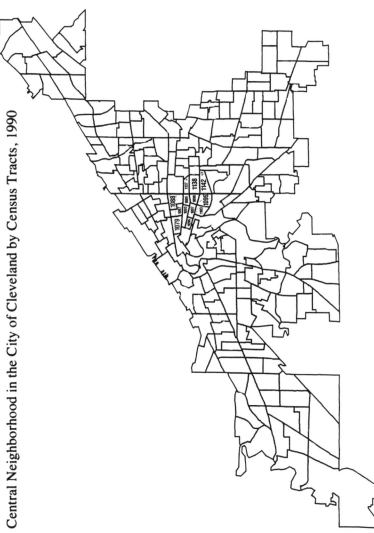

Source: 1990 Tiger/Line Prototype File, Bureau of the Census. *Prepared by:* The Northern Ohio Data & Information Service (NODIS), The Urban Center, Maxine Goodman Levin College of Urban Affairs, Cleveland State University.

Cleveland's black population is almost as old as the city itself, with the first black settlers arriving in 1809, thirteen years after the city was founded. Throughout most of the nineteenth century, Cleveland had a small black population that enjoyed a higher social and economic status than most other black communities in the North. Black and white housing was interspersed, segregation in accommodations was infrequent, and inter-racial violence was rare.

As the size of the black population grew, however, conditions deteriorated. By the turn of the century, African-Americans were increasingly segregated and concentrated in the Central neighborhood (defined as the area on Cleveland's east side, bounded by E. 22nd Street, E. 71st Street, Quincy Avenue and Woodbury Run). They were often excluded from restaurants, theaters, and public accommodations. More crucial, blacks were not hired to work in the city's burgeoning manufacturing industries, where prejudice by employers was matched by that of trade unions. At the height of Cleveland's industrial expansion in the 1920s, only 10 percent of all black employees worked in the skilled trades.

Still, drawn by the hope of a better life, black migration from the South continued. By 1920, there were 72,000 blacks in Cleveland, almost all of whom lived in the Central neighborhood. Discrimination in housing, employment, and public accommodations increased and the steady growth of the ghetto began to create segregated schools. The Depression devastated both white and black races, but blacks suffered much higher rates of unemployment and at earlier stages. Housing and economic conditions in the Central ghetto continued to deteriorate in the 1930s and 1940s as overcrowding increased.

By 1950, 62,408 people lived in Central in what was generally the worst housing in the region. As the public housing program of the New Deal took hold beginning in the late 1930s, the Central neighborhood was targeted for many of the projects. The projects that were built were racially segregated and contributed to overcrowding since they demolished more low-income housing than was constructed. Ernest J. Bohn, Director of CMHA from its founding (1933 to 1968), essentially permitted Cleveland City Council to exercise control over public housing site locations. The City Council was anxious to build the housing in order to enjoy the patronage benefits of contracting and construction, but the council did not want to bring blacks to white neighborhoods. As a result, most of Cleveland's public housing was built where it was politically simple and feasible, namely in already black neighborhoods. The urban renewal of the 1950s followed a similar pattern. The St. Vincent's project, for example, bulldozed thousands of low-rent homes, displacing the mostly black occupants and replacing the housing with institutional developments.

Today, Central is the location of 5,186 units of subsidized housing distributed in 6 major housing projects: Longwood Homes (820 units), Olde Cedar (608 units), Cedar Extension (410 units), Carver Park (1,144 units), Outhwaite

Homes (1,020 units) and King-Kennedy (1,184 units). It is the most dense concentration of public housing in the state of Ohio. It is also the city's most troubled residential neighborhood by nearly every measure of deterioration, poverty, unemployment, crime, and social dislocation (U.S. Department of Housing and Urban Development 1989). Central is also the most isolated neighborhood in Cleveland, a factor that reduces the ability of its residents to overcome their poverty and distress (Coulton, et al. 1990).

Central's 1980 statistics outline the extent of the problem:

- Median family income was $4,280.
- Unemployment rates were by far the highest in the city.
- Seventy percent of households were one-parent, female-headed households, as opposed to a 29 percent city-wide rate.
- Birth rate was the highest in the city.
- Sixty-two percent of adults, 25 years of age or older, had not finished high school.
- Median age was 24.6 years, 31 percent of the population was 14 years of age or younger, making Central the "youngest" city neighborhood.
- Between 1960 and 1970, 49 percent of the population left Central, the highest rate of loss in the city and more than three times the city-wide loss of 14 percent. Between 1960 and 1980, nearly 30,000 residents left this area of less than one mile in radius. Most out-migrants moved to better black neighborhoods like Hough and Glenville.
- Median sales price of homes during 1980–1983 was about $4,000.
- Violent crime, as measured by the rate per thousand of homicide, rape, and assault, was the highest in the city and was typically three to four times higher than the city-wide rate. Homicide was the leading cause of death among black young men aged 25–35.
- Only 4.3 percent of housing units were owner-occupied, contrasted with 44 percent city-wide.
- Because of high crime rates, poor maintenance, and widespread vandalization of property, over 20 percent of CMHA's apartments were vacant.

Development of policies that can deal in a practical way with the poverty, isolation, and despair of Cleveland's Central neighborhood and similar black neighborhoods across urban America is the country's most difficult challenge of the 1990s. That challenge can be met by aggressive local and national policies and programs.

CONCLUSION

Locally, where African-Americans make up a substantial portion of the electorate, their best bet is to take political control of city hall and the jobs, contracts, and other benefits offered. Other ethnic groups have done so in their time, why not African-Americans? Local leaders must also do everything they can to improve the quality of public education in the city; to develop an agenda to press the regional, state, and federal government for more resources; and to provide support for local programs such as tenant management of public housing projects, community-based nonprofit housing corporations, and flexible public transit systems that will connect the isolated neighborhoods of the persistently poor with suburban job opportunities.

At the national level, proponents of racial equality must push for a national jobs and income program, as well as vigorous enforcement of open housing and affirmative action laws. Efforts to eliminate racial segregation should emphasize measures to reduce and, ultimately, eliminate discrimination in mortgage lending and real estate practices. Moreover, such efforts deserve strong staffs, budgets and support from top policy makers.

It is clear, however, that such efforts will take place in a chilly climate. Since the Kerner Commission, the national record suggests an indifference, if not deep opposition, to such programs. Yet, pressure for racial integration and equality must be maintained. There is no other way to go and remain consistent with the promises of American society. This is a racially heterogeneous society committed to creating a racially integrated society. The goal is for all those who pay allegiance to the same political symbols and participate as citizens in the same national life to consider themselves Americans. A dedication to the integration of the races is part of this goal. If people of optimism and good will continue on this course with energy, imagination, and, above all, persistence, America may in the next 20 years be able to realize more of the recommendations of the Kerner Commission.

REFERENCES

Abram, G.A. 1988. Letter from Abram, Director of EEO, RTA, to author, November 3.

Blackstone, K. 1985. Racial violence and harrassment escalate in Chicago area. *Chicago Reporter* 14(January): 1, 6–7.

City of Cleveland. Department of Personnel. 1987. *EEO Report, December 31*. Cleveland, Ohio.

Cleveland Plain Dealer. 1989. RTA board waffles on minority goals. February 15: A16.

———. 1989. A red flag on racism. January 20: A8.

Coulton, C.J., et al. 1990. *An analysis of poverty and related conditions in Cleveland area neighborhoods*. Cleveland, OH: Center for Urban Poverty, Mandel School of Applied Social Science, Case Western Reserve University.

Eisinger, P. 1984. Black mayors and the politics of racial economic advancement. In *Readings in urban politics*, H. Hahn and C. Levine, eds. New York: Longman.

Farley, R. 1984. *Blacks and whites: narrowing the gap?* Cambridge, MA: Harvard University Press.

Freeman, R.B. 1976. *Black elite: the new market for highly educated black americans*. New York: McGraw-Hill.

Friesema, H.P. 1969. Black control of central cities: the hollow prize. *Journal of the American Institue of Planning* (Fall): 75-79.

Jaynes, G.D. and R.M. Williams, 1989. *A common destiny: blacks and american society*. Washington, DC: National Reading Press.

Kain, J.F. 1985. Black suburbanization in the eighties: a new beginning or a false hope? In *American domestic priorities*, J.M. Quigley and D.L. Rubinfeld, eds. Berkeley, CA: University of California Press.

Massey, D. and N. Denton. 1987. Trends in the residential segregation of blacks, hispanics and asians, 1970-1980. *American Sociological Review* 52: 802-25.

———. 1989. Hypersegregation in U.S. metropolitan areas. *Demography* 26(3)(August): 373-91.

Myrdal, G. 1944. *American dilemma: the negro problem and modern democracy*. New York: Harper and Row.

National Advisory Commission on Civil Disorders. 1968. *Report of the national advisory commission on civil disorders*. New York: Bantam Books.

Obermanns, R. 1986. *Housing desegregation in Cleveland and Cuyahoga county since 1968*. Cleveland, OH: The Cuyahoga Plan.

Orfield, G. 1985. Ghettoization and its alternatives. In *The new urban reality*, P.E. Peterson, ed. Washington, DC: The Brookings Institution.

Pettigrew, T. 1973. Attitudes on race and housing: a social psychological view. In *Segregation in residential areas*, A.H. Hawley and V.P. Rock, eds. Washington, DC: National Academy of Sciences.

U.S. Bureau of Census. 1984. *American housing survey, 1984, Cleveland*. Washington, DC: U.S. Government Printing Office.

U.S. Department of Housing and Urban Development 1989. *The viability of public housing in Cleveland's central area*. Cleveland, OH: Cleveland Regional Office.

Urban League. 1987. *State of black children*. Cleveland, OH: Cleveland Urban League.

Valente, J. 1983. Crossburning vandalism reported in Maryland suburbs. *Washington Post*, 30 August, C2.

Wilson, J. Q. 1975. *Thinking about crime*. New York: Basic Books.

Wilson, W. J. 1978. *The declining significance of race*. Chicago, IL: University of Chicago Press.

———. 1985. The urban underclass in advanced industrial society. In *The new urban reality*, P.E. Peterson, ed. Washington, DC: The Brookings Institution.

———. 1987. *The truly disadvantaged: essays on inner city woes and public policy*. Chicago, IL: University of Chicago Press.

Zeller, G. 1988. *Poverty indicators*, Vol. 6. Cleveland, OH: Council for Economic Opportunities.

PART II

Description and Analysis of the Issues

3 The Nature and Dimensions of the Underclass

EROL RICKETTS

In 1962 Gunnar Myrdal provided the first systematic discussion of the emergence of an underclass in the United States in his book, *The Challenge to Affluence*. Myrdal argued that the word "under-class" [sic] does not seem to be used in English, and that its absence from common usage is understandable because most Americans consider American society classless. The word seems to have been virtually invented by Myrdal, because there is no evidence of significant, prior scholarly usage, and in Swedish it is an obscure term which translates literally to lower class (Gans 1990a).[1]

Myrdal used the term underclass to refer to an emergent group of permanently unemployed, unemployable, and underemployed. Ironically, Myrdal viewed the creation of the underclass as a consequence of economic development. He argued that over the last few generations a process had been underway that, while it opened more opportunities to more people, it also closed opportunities to some. Moreover, he argued that the process, "threatens to split off a true 'under-class' that is not really an integrated part of the nation but a useless and miserable substratum" (Myrdal 1962, p. 35).

Myrdal's concept of the underclass is remarkably close to recent renditions (cf. Glasgow 1980; Auletta 1982; Clark and Nathan 1982; Kasarda 1983; Wilson 1985; Ricketts and Sawhill 1988; Van Haitsma 1989; Ricketts 1989). However, more has happened since 1962 than simply a uniting of the two elements of Myrdal's hyphenated word, under-class. Like Myrdal, other 1960s liberal observers such as Oscar Lewis (1966) and Michael Harrington (1962) emphasized that the marginalization and isolation of the poor had its origin in economic organization or economic change. Indeed, in the 1960s liberal analysts used the term underclass to draw attention to the most pressing conditions of poverty (e.g., Gans 1968; Rainwater 1969).

However, the specific discussion of the underclass was obscured by the controversial debate on the culture of poverty which occurred simultaneously. From what can be discerned from the literature, discussions of the underclass and the culture of poverty were separate conversations in the 1960s, although both conversations evidenced a view of poverty as hardened and difficult to change.

When the discussion of the underclass reemerged in the early 1980s it became steeped in controversy because a number of observers, primarily journalists, argued that the underclass was caused by the culture of poverty (see, for example, Lehman 1986). As Wilson (1985) argues, liberal analysts had abandoned the study of hard-core poverty problems during the 1970s and in the vacuum journalists and conservative scholars rejuvenated the concept of the culture of poverty as a cause of the underclass.

What was more noteworthy than the resulting controversy was that the reemergence of the discussion of the underclass evinced that the perception of poverty had changed. In the early 1960s, poverty was thought of as a condition that was fairly intractable because it was either seen as a consequence of the culture of poverty or as a consequence of the economical structure. By the mid-1960s, poverty began to be viewed as tractable and susceptible to a war on poverty, but by the early 1980s poverty was again seen as virtually intractable.

This chapter examines the circumstances that contributed to the reemergence of a policy focus on the underclass. It also reviews definitions of the underclass and discusses the dimensions of the underclass.

The reader should be aware of how the terms underclass and poverty are used in this chapter. The underclass is regarded as a special kind of poverty— multi-faceted poverty to be exact (poverty being conditions below the accepted minimum standards of living in any society). For example, the Council of Ministers of the European Community defines the poor as "persons, families and groups of persons whose resources (material, cultural and social) are so limited as to exclude them from the minimum acceptable way of life in Member States in which they live" (Room 1990). In this chapter low income or income poverty (what the lay person regards as poverty) is viewed as only one aspect of poverty. The underclass, as defined in this chapter, is a non-racial category, in which membership is determined by specific criteria, although it is recognized that in the United States blacks and other minorities are significantly overrepresented in the underclass.

ORIGIN OF THE UNDERCLASS: THE PERCEPTION OF POVERTY, 1960–1990

To understand the current national debate on the underclass, it is important to examine how the perception of poverty changed over the last three decades.

In the early 1960s, discussions of the culture of poverty emphasized that poverty was well entrenched and enduring across generations (see Harrington 1962; Lewis 1966; Clark 1965). Although Lewis had argued that the culture of poverty was both an adaptation and a reaction by the poor to their marginal position in a class stratified, highly individuated, capitalistic society, he argued that once the culture of poverty was brought into existence, it tended to perpetuate itself from generation to generation because of its effect on children who absorb the basic values of the culture. Consequently, he argued that the elimination of income poverty may not eliminate the culture of poverty.

Harrington's less systematic version of the culture of poverty emphasized the vicious cycle of low parental education leading to bad jobs, leading to low education for children, although it carried a similar message as Lewis's: the conditions of the culture of poverty were hard to escape. Harrington argued that the poor were victims of circumstances of birth from which they were unlikely to escape, even if they were virtuous.

This perception of poverty changed over the course of the War on Poverty and poverty came to be seen as a condition of not having sufficient income. Subsequently, the United States's social policy increasingly focused on addressing poverty through income and in-kind transfer programs. Another contributing factor was the controversy that developed in response to the publication of the Moynihan Report which in turn discouraged the study of the cultural and familial aspects of poverty. The report, *The Negro Family: The Case for National Action* (1965), which is commonly known by the name of its principal author, generated bitter debate because, on the basis of 1950 and 1960 data, it characterized the black family as "crumbling" and as "a tangle of pathology." The report came at a time of increasing black intellectual and political asendancy, and blacks served notice that unflattering discussions of black family life were off-limits. As poverty came to be seen as an economic phenomenon, scholars gradually abandoned the culture of poverty thesis.

The culture of poverty thesis was also undermined by subsequent research which suggested that the culture of poverty thesis overstated the extent of intergenerational poverty (see, for example, Levy 1977; Rainwater 1981; Duncan, et al. 1984; Corcoran, et al. 1985). This research showed that there was tremendous movement in and out of poverty and relatively few of the poor were consistently poor over several years.

However, by the mid-1970s, enthusiasm for the War on Poverty programs waned, as there was a perception based on early follow-up research that the programs had had little effect. During the course of the War on Poverty, although income poverty was reduced, there was simultaneous growth in dependence on government in the incidence of many social pathologies. Midway through the 1980s, levels of social dislocation and poverty were not much lower than the pre-War on Poverty levels. Although the economy had grown, the rate of pre-transfer poverty had increased; teenage pregnancy and out-of-wedlock births had grown at an alarming rate and crime and the rate of welfare dependency had also increased. What emerged was a sense that the War on Poverty programs had failed. Indeed, programs such as Aid to Families with Dependent Children (AFDC) were being increasingly accused of fostering some of the social ills they were intended to cure (see Murray 1984).

Most of the discussion about the effects of government policy became focused on the status of blacks, who were a principal target of War on Poverty programs. In the main, the evidence showed that a portion of the black population had achieved considerable social mobility during the 1960s and 1970s, but it also showed that another portion of the black population was being left behind—increasingly trapped in poverty with little hope of escaping. Scholars such as Wilson (1982; 1984) argued that affirmative action programs contributed to bifurcated social stratification within the black community and the increasing isolation of poor blacks, because the more highly educated blacks were more able to use affirmative action programs for self-advancement and migrated out of traditional black neighborhoods leaving a residual disadvantaged group behind.

At the same time, research showed poverty was more entrenched than previously thought. Research by Bane and Ellwood (1986) suggested that, because of methodological problems, earlier research (e.g., Levy 1977; Rainwater 1981; Duncan, et al. 1984) underestimated the extent of continuous spells of poverty.

In estimating the persistence of poverty, earlier research looked at the proportion of the poor who were consistently poor for say three or four years of the time period the data were available—typically eight to ten years. The research underestimated poverty spells because it did not account for the entire spell for those already in poverty prior to the start of the series and the entire spell for those continuing in poverty after the last years of the series.

To overcome this methodological problem, Bane and Ellwood (1986), using the same University of Michigan's Panel Study of Income Dynamics [PSID] data as some earlier studies of persistent poverty (e.g., Levy 1977; Coe 1978; Hill 1981; Rainwater 1981; Duncan, et al. 1984), calculated and used entry and exit probabilities to estimate the duration of spells. This research showed that there was considerable entry into and exit from poverty, but it also showed the duration of poverty spells was considerably longer than previously estimated. Among the findings, the study showed that over 50 percent of those who would be identified as poor in cross-sectional surveys were in a spell of poverty that would last ten or more years, and the average poor black child was in a poverty spell lasting almost two decades.

It was partly because of a sense that government social programs had failed, despite considerable anti-poverty spending, and partly because research such as that by Bane and Ellwood showed that poverty was more entrenched than previously thought, that renewed focus was given to the culture of poverty as a cause of social pathologies associated with the underclass.

DEFINITIONS OF THE UNDERCLASS

Although the low-income population and the underclass are often confused, scholars have defined the underclass fairly independent of income poverty. This section reviews some of the most pointed recent conceptual definitions of the underclass. Table 3.1 lists the explicit elements of various authors' definitions.

In one of the first scholarly treatises on the underclass (which has gone largely unnoticed), Glasgow (1980) argued that the underclass is comprised of (1) many of the long-term working poor who had parents who were also poor, (2) those who prefer to remain unemployed rather than accept jobs providing minimal financial rewards, and (3) those who seek but cannot find meaningful employment and end up accepting low-level jobs for short durations. While Glasgow noted that members of the underclass are not exclusively blacks or other ethnic minorities nor are they exclusively city dwellers, he noted that a disproportionately large number of the underclass are black men between 14 and 27 years of age who inhabit the decaying cores of nearly every major city. Further he argued that members of the underclass are not necessarily culturally deprived, lacking in aspirations, or in motivation to achieve. They are foremost able-bodied and physically healthy black men who are left, by lack of opportunity, to seek other options for economic survival, including private entrepreneurial schemes, working the welfare system, hustling, quasi-legitimate schemes, and outright deviant activity as alternatives to work.

Auletta (1982) groups the underclass into four categories: (1) passive poor or long-term welfare recipients; (2) hostile urban street criminals who are often school dropouts and drug addicts; (3) hustlers who earn their livelihood in the underground economy and rarely commit violent crimes, but like street criminals may not be poor; and (4) street people—traumatized drunks, drifters, homeless shopping-bag ladies and released mental patients.

Clark and Nathan (1982) stipulated that the underclass includes people who lack education, experience in the labor market, options for social mobility, stable family relationships, as well as income—especially earned income. Clark and Nathan also stressed the geographical dimension of the underclass. They argued that the underclass is concentrated in the large cities, especially the Northeast and North Central cities. They also noted the concentration of underclass status among racial minorities—particularly blacks and Hispanics.

Wilson (1985) described the underclass as a heterogeneous grouping of families and individuals who exist outside the mainstream American occupational system. He included in this group individuals who lack training and skills and either experience long-term unemployment or are not a part of the labor force, individuals who engage in street crime and other forms of aberrant behavior, and families who experience long-term spells of poverty and/or welfare dependency. Wilson argued that although the underclass is heterogeneous and has distinct subgroups, the different subgroups live and interact in the same

TABLE 3.1

Definitions of the Underclass

Authors	Not in Labor Force	Unemployed/ Under-employed	Black	Hispanic	Welfare Dependent	Criminal	Deviant in Behavior	Unskilled	Drug Addict/ Seller	High School Dropout	Long-term Poor	Working Poor
D. Glasgow 1980	X	X	X				X				X	X
K. Auletta 1982	X				X	X			X	X		
K. Clark and R. Nathan 1982	X		X	X				X		X		
B. Wilson 1985	X	X			X	X	X	X			X	
S. McLanahan 1986	X	X					X					

TABLE 3.1 (continued)

Definitions of the Underclass

Authors	Not in Labor Force	Unemployed/ Under-employed	Black	Hispanic	Welfare Dependent	Criminal	Deviant in Behavior	Unskilled	Drug Addict/ Seller	High School Dropout	Long-term Poor	Work-ing Poor
E. Ricketts and I. Sawhill 1988	X					X	X			X		
M. Van Haistma 1989	X											
C. Jencks 1989	X					X	X	X				
E. Ricketts 1989	X				X							
C. Murray 1990	X				X	X						

TABLE 3.1 (continued)
Definitions of the Underclass

	Hustler	Able-bodied	Unmarried/Teen Parent	Definitions of the Underclass						
				Central City Resident	North-east Resident	Home-less	Nonpoor	In Unstable Family	Social Cultural Isolation	Socially Costly Behavior
D. Glasgow 1980	X	X								
K. Auletta 1982	X						X			
K. Clark and R. Nathan 1982				X	X	X		X		
B. Wilson 1985									X	
S. McLanahan 1986									X	

TABLE 3.1 (continued)

Definitions of the Underclass

	Hustler	Able-bodied	Unmarried/Teen Parent	Central City Resident	North-east Resident	Home-less	Nonpoor	In Unstable Family	Social/Cultural Isolation	Socially Costly Behavior
E. Ricketts and I. Sawhill 1988		X	X							X
M. Van Haistma 1989									X	
C. Jencks 1989			X							
E. Ricketts 1989		X								
C. Murray 1990			X							

depressed communities and have become increasingly isolated socially from mainstream patterns and norms of behavior.

McLanahan, et al. (1986) pointed out that the common dimension of various groups considered to be in the underclass is weak attachment to the legitimate labor force and, to a lesser extent, cultural isolation and persistent weak labor force attachment and persistent cultural isolation. They argued that having low income and being in the underclass should not be equated, although there is a good deal of overlap between the two conditions. McLanahan, et al., argued that what distinguishes the underclass from the poor is the persistence of nonemployment and persistence of isolation from mainstream values and behavior.

Ricketts and Sawhill (1988) defined the underclass as consisting of able-bodied individuals whose behaviors depart from mainstream norms such as attending school, delaying parenting until at least age 18, working at a regular job, and obeying the law, and whose behaviors are costly to society.

Van Haitsma (1989) has defined the underclass as those persons who are weakly connected to the formal labor force and whose social context tends to maintain or further weaken their attachment.

Jencks (1989) disaggregated the underclass into an economic underclass, a moral underclass, and an educational underclass. The economic underclass includes all working-age men and women who cannot get or keep a steady job. The moral underclass are those individuals who treat the ideals of obeying the law, getting married before parenting, and going to work daily as impractical or irrelevant. And the educational underclass consists of those individuals who lack the information and skills they need to pass as members of the working class. He further breaks the moral underclass into a criminal underclass and a reproductive underclass. Jencks justifies the use of his three major categories as being consistent with the societal sense of classes such as the middle class which is defined in terms of occupations, commitment to norms of behavior, and cultural and social skills.

Ricketts (1989) defined the underclass as able-bodied, working-age individuals who do not sell their labor in the mainstream or regulated economy and who have no legitimate means of support other than the welfare system. This does not include women with small children, students, or the disabled. Spousal support, support provided by friends and relatives, and inheritance which are derived from accumulated wealth from earnings in the mainstream economy, are considered legitimate means of support.

Murray (1990) defines the underclass as a subset of the poor "who chronically live off mainstream society (directly through welfare or indirectly through crime) without participating in it. They characteristically take jobs sporadically if at all, do not share the social burdens of the neighborhoods in which they live, shirk the responsibilities of fatherhood and are indifferent (or often simply incompetent) mothers."

Although many observers have stressed the absence of agreement about whom to include in the underclass, as Table 3.1 shows, there is a high degree of consistency between the above definitions. They all stress detachment from work in the mainstream economy and various behaviors that are at variance with mainstream American norms as defining principles of the underclass.

DIMENSIONS OF THE UNDERCLASS

Since analysts started measuring the underclass in the late 1970s, there has been a transition from using long-term income poverty to using geographically concentrated income poverty, and more recently, to using multi-faceted poverty to measure the size or extent of the underclass (cf. Levy 1977; Gottschalk and Danziger 1986; Ricketts and Sawhill 1988). As Table 3.2 shows, estimates of the size of the underclass have also been a function of the various working definitions. Overwhelmingly, researchers have relied on data on the low-income population to estimate the size of the underclass and some of the variance in the estimates results from the different ways in which income poverty has been measured.

Levy's study of the size of the underclass (see Levy 1977) is an example of the genre of studies of persistent poverty based on the PSID low-income data (e.g., Coe 1978; Hill 1981; Rainwater 1981; Duncan, et al. 1984). Most of these studies make no pretense to be estimating anything but long-term income poverty, but because of temporal and methodological differences between the studies, the range of the estimates is vast. Ruggles and Marton (1986) note that if all the estimates are standardized to the 1978 population, the estimates would range from about 3 million to 20 million potential members of the underclass (12 to 80 percent of the poor) or from roughly 1 to 7 percent of the total U.S. 1978 population.

Based on PSID data for 1967 to 1973, Levy estimated that the underclass, whom he described as the permanent poor, were roughly 50 percent (10.6 million) of the average annual poverty population of 19.6 million for those years. Levy defined the permanently poor as those who were poor for 5 of the 7 years under observation. His analysis showed that there was considerable movement in and out of poverty and little evidence poverty status was transmitted intergenerationally, which he took as evidence discrediting the culture of poverty view. However, he cautioned that what appeared to be upward mobility out of poverty was better thought of as people returning to their permanent income— conceived as mean lifetime income around which annual income fluctuated.

Using a similar approach, Ruggles and Marton (1986) estimate that about 24 percent of the poverty population or 8 million people are in the underclass, based on their estimate that persistently poor persons were half of the 33 million

TABLE 3.2

Selected Estimates of Size of the Underclass

Definition	Date	Number (in millions)	Percent of U.S. Poverty	Percent of U.S. Population
a. Persistently poor who are neither elderly nor disabled.	1985	8.0	23.5	3.5
b. Poor living in poverty areas—defined as census tracts with poverty rates above 40 percent in the 100 largest SMSAs.	1979	1.8	7.1	.8
c. Poor at least 5 years between 1967 and 1973.	1967	10.6	50.0	5.3
d. Upper bound: All persons living in poverty areas— defined as census tracts with poverty rates above 20 percent in the 100 largest SMSAs.	1984	3.7	11.0	1.6
Lower bound: Long-term AFDC recipients living in poverty areas.	1984	< 1.0	2.9	.4
e. Black and Hispanic poor living in poverty areas— defined as census tracts with poverty rates above 20 percent in the 100 largest SMSAs.	1979	4.1	15.1	1.8
f. Upper bound: All persons living in underclass areas— defined as census tracts with high incidence of multiple social ills.	1979	2.5	—	1.0
Lower bound: Able-bodied, working-aged people with no regular attachment to the labor force living in underclass areas.		.5	—	< 1.0

Notes: a. Ruggles and Marton, 1986.
b. Sawhill, 1987.
c. Levy, 1977.
d. Gottschalk and Danziger, 1986.
e. Nathan, 1986.
f. Ricketts and Sawhill, 1988.
Panels a through e are reprinted from Ricketts and Sawhill, 1986 (reprinted by permission of The Urban Institute).

people in poverty in 1985 and able-bodied, non-elderly persons were half of the persistently poor.

Gottschalk and Danziger (1986), recognizing the inherent problems of measuring the underclass with published data, in the absence of a standard definition, provide a number of alternate estimates of its size. They argue that it is hopeless to try to measure the size of a culturally defined underclass with existing surveys. The best that can be done is to measure the underclass in terms of observable characteristics, whatever their causes. One method is to measure the underclass in demographic terms such as long-term AFDC recipients. For example, assuming all long-term AFDC recipients (those who stay on the program longer than the six years that it takes to raise a child to school age) and absent fathers connected to long-term AFDC recipients are in the underclass, Gottschalk and Danziger estimate 18 to 24 percent (or 6 to 8 million) of the 33.7 million poor population would be in the underclass.

Nathan (1987), defining the underclass as black and Hispanic populations in urban poverty areas in the 100 largest SMSAs, estimates that 6 to 15 percent of the U.S. poverty population was in the underclass in 1980 depending on how restrictive the definition of poverty areas is. If a poverty area is taken to mean a census tract with 20 percent of the population in poverty, then 15 percent of the poverty population would be in the underclass. If the poverty area is defined more restrictively, as a census tract with 40 percent or more of the population in poverty, then the underclass would be 6 percent of the poor.

In contrast to studies that have used individual and geographic income poverty data to estimate the size of the underclass, Ricketts and Sawhill (1988), based on their working definition of underclass areas as census tracts with a high incidence of multiple social ills and the underclass as those individuals residing in these areas who engage in socially dysfunctional behavior, estimate that roughly 1 percent of the population or 2.5 million persons live in underclass areas. If the underclass is thought of as only able-bodied, working-aged people with no regular attachment to the labor force living in underclass areas, there is roughly a half million people in the underclass. These estimates of the underclass are the most widely accepted and cited (see, for example, The Budget of the United States Government, Fiscal Year 1991, pp. 141–42).

Is the underclass growing? Although only a few studies have tackled the problem of determining whether or not the underclass is growing and the extent of that growth, there is some consensus that the underclass is growing. One national study (Ricketts and Mincy 1990) indicates that the underclass in 1980 was roughly three times what it was in 1970.

A study by Jencks that disaggregates the underclass into economic, criminal, reproductive, and educational underclasses concludes the economic underclass is probably growing; the criminal underclass seems to be shrinking, especially among blacks; the reproductive underclass is shrinking when measured by teenage motherhood but growing when measured by unwed motherhood; and the educational underclass seems to be roughly constant among whites and shrinking among blacks.

A study by Coulton, et al. (1990) indicates that the underclass has grown rapidly in Cleveland, based on a study of the growth of poverty areas with a poverty rate of 40 percent or more. Between 1970 and 1980, the proportion of Cleveland's population living in these areas grew from 21 to 27 percent, but between 1980 and 1988 it grew from 27 to 48 percent.

In sum, it is clear that studies of the underclass have yielded conflicting estimates because of definitional, methodological, and temporal differences between the studies. Estimates of the size of the underclass range from less than 1 million to 11 million or from 3 to 50 percent of the poverty population in respective years. In general, studies based on the persistence of income poverty have yielded estimates of the size of the underclass that are higher than those based on geographical concentration of the income poor. Given the wide range of the estimates, the fundamental question in deciding which numbers are reasonable is whether or not they are appropriate measures of the underclass as most observers have defined it.

CONCLUSION

In a brilliant essay entitled "Center and Periphery," sociologist Edward Shils (1970) argues that one can think of society as having a center and a periphery. Historically, the center of society has been the domain of the elites and the periphery the domain of the disenfranchised. Shils argues that the recent history of western civilization has been characterized by increasing expansion of the center to include groups in the periphery through such events as the extension of the voting franchise and the civil rights revolution. Taking Shils's argument as a historical truism, what is different now is that the United States is faced with a counter-tendency whereby an increasing number of Americans are disenfranchised, primarily by economic change, from participating in mainstream society. This is exemplified by the paradox of half of the minority community making significant progress into the American mainstream while the other half is being increasingly excluded. But this process is not limited to minority Americans; it is also the fate of many whites, and without appropriate policy attention, it may become the fate of even more Americans.

The presence of an underclass in American society is really not new. One can think of the many immigrant groups—the Irish, the Italians, the Eastern European Jews—who came in at the bottom of the society and worked their way up out of underclass conditions to positions of eminence. In the pyramidical metaphor of the American occupational structure, a group's economic and social standing is viewed as a consequence of the group's tenure in the society. Groups come in at the bottom of an expanding occupational structure and work their way up through the inter-generational transmission of parental occupational status into education of children and, hence, the occupational status of children. What makes the current situation of the underclass different from that of previous groups is that economic change itself, instead of providing opportunities for inclusion, seems to be disconnecting thousands of Americans from the mainstream socioeconomic structure.

In addition, the underclass problem may be more universal and, hence, more likely to be linked to the international economic structure than previously thought. The American debate on the underclass has been cast in very narrow terms, but judging on the basis of indicators of the emergence of the underclass—the growth in idleness, out of wedlock births, teen parenting, and so on—the underclass problem may be worldwide. A recent article by Charles Murray (1989; see also Murray 1990) suggests that judging by the criteria used for being in the U.S. underclass, the underclass in Britain is growing significantly. For example, the illegitimacy ratio rose from 10.6 percent in 1979 to 25.6 in 1988 in Britain, outstripping the U.S. rate of 24.5 percent in 1987. Murray argues that this cannot be attributed to the minority population of Britain, because the British illegitimacy rate would only fall from 25 to 24 percent if the black population were excluded. Another example is Sweden where, based on 1985 data, 1 in 3 children are born out of wedlock, compared to 1 in 7 in the United States. This sense of the problem suggests that the underclass is a more universal and difficult problem than previously assumed.

To conclude, it seems fair to say that although underclasses in American society are not new, the current underclass poses more profound problems because it seems to be primarily an epiphenomenon of changes in the economic structure. Second, the underclass is made up of able-bodied, working-age individuals who are detached from the labor force and, hence, engage in socially costly behaviors to secure income. Finally, the problem is fairly recent and seems to be growing rapidly.

NOTES

1. Gans notes that Myrdal's usage of "under-class" drew on an old Swedish term "underklass" which together with "overklass" was used in the nineteenth century and brought into literary use by August Strindberg around 1900.

REFERENCES

Auletta, K. 1982. *The underclass*. New York: Random House.
Bane, M. and D. Ellwood. 1986. Slipping into and out of poverty: the dynamics of spells. *The Journal of Human Resources* 21:2-23.

Clark, K.B. 1965. *Dark ghetto: dilemmas of social science*. New York: Harper and Row.

Clark, K.B. and R.P. Nathan. 1982. The urban underclass. In *Critical issues for national policy: a reconnaissance and agenda for further study*, 33–53. Washington, DC: National Research Council, Committee on National Urban Policy.

Coe, R. 1978. Dependency and poverty in the short and long run. In *Five thousand american families: patterns of economic progress*, G.J. Duncan and J.N. Morgan, eds., 273–396. Ann Arbor, MI: Institute for Social Research.

Corcoran, M., G.J. Duncan, G. Gurin and P. Gurin. 1985. Myth and reality: the causes and persistence of poverty. *Journal of Policy Analysis and Management* 4:516–36.

Coulton, C.J., J. Chow and S. Pandey. 1990. An analysis of poverty and related conditions in Cleveland area neighborhoods. *Technical report*. Cleveland, OH: Center for Urban Poverty and Social Change.

Duncan, G.J., R.B. Coe and M.S. Hill. 1984. The dynamics of poverty. In *Years of poverty and plenty*, G. Duncan, ed., 33–70. Ann Arbor, MI: Institute for Social Research.

Gans, H. 1968. Culture and class in the study of poverty: an approach to anti-poverty research. In *On understanding poverty: perspectives from the social sciences*, D.P. Moynihan, ed. New York: Basic Books.

———. 1990a. Personal communication with author.

Glasgow, D.G. 1980. *The black underclass: poverty, unemployment, and entrapment of ghetto youth*. San Francisco, CA: Jossey-Bass.

Gottschalk, P. and S. Danziger. 1986. Poverty and the underclass. Testimony before the Select Committee on Hunger, 99th Cong., 2d Sess.

Harrington, M. 1962. *The other America: poverty in the United States*. New York: Macmillan.

Hill, M.S. 1981. Some dynamic aspects of poverty. In *Five thousand american families: patterns of economic progress*, M.S. Hill, D.H. Hill and J.N. Morgan, eds., 93–120. Ann Arbor, MI: Institute for Social Research.

Jencks, C. 1989. What is the underclass—and is it growing? *Focus* 12(1):14–26.

Kasarda, J.D. 1983. Caught in the web of change. *Society* 21:41–47.

Lehman, N. 1986. The origins of the underclass? *The Atlantic* (June): 31–55 and (July): 54–68.

Levy, F.S. 1977. How big is the american underclass? Working Paper 009-1. Washington, DC: The Urban Institute.

Lewis, O. 1966. The culture of poverty. *Scientific American* 215:19–25.

McLanahan, S., I. Garfinkel, and D. Watson. 1986. Family structure, poverty and the underclass. Paper prepared for Workshop on Contemporary Urban conditions sponsored by the Committee on National Urban Policy of the National Research Council. Washington, D.C., July 16–17.

Moynihan report, The negro family: the case for national action. Washington, DC: U.S. Department of Labor, Office of Policy Planning and Research, 1965.

Murray, C. 1984. *Losing ground: american social policy 1950–1980*. New York: Basic.

———. 1989. Underclass: the alienated poor are devastating America's cities: is the same happening here? *The London Sunday Times Magazine*, November 26.

———. 1990. The british underclass. *The Public Interest* 99:4–28.

Myrdal, G. 1962. *The challenge to affluence*. New York: Pantheon Books.

Nathan, R. 1986. Will the underclass always be with us? *Society* (March-April): 57–62.

Rainwater, L. 1969. The american underclass: looking back and looking up. *Transaction* 6(4):9.

_____. 1981. *Persistent and transitory poverty: a new look.* Working Paper No. 70, Joint Center for Urban Studies of the Massachusetts Institute of Technology and Harvard University.

Ricketts, E.R. 1989. Making sense of the national debate on the underclass. Unpublished.

Ricketts, E.R. and R. Mincy. 1990. Growth of the underclass: 1970–1980. *The Journal of Human Resources* 25(1): 137–45.

Ricketts, E.R. and I. Sawhill. 1988. Defining and measuring the underclass. *Journal of Policy Analysis and Management* 7(2): 316–25.

Room, G. 1990. Final report of the programme evaluation team for the commission of the european communities. Bath, England: University of Bath.

Ruggles, P. and W.P. Marton. 1986. Measuring the size and characteristics of the underclass: how much do we know? Unpublished paper. Washington, DC: The Urban Institute.

Sawhill, I. 1987. Anti-poverty strategies for the 1980s. In *Work and welfare: the case for new directions in national policy,* Center for National Policy, Alternatives for the 1980s, No. 22. Washington, DC: Center for National Policy.

Shils, E. 1970. Center and periphery. *Selected essays by Edward Shils.* Chicago, IL: University of Chicago.

Van Haitsma, M. 1989. A contextual definition of the underclass. *Focus* 12(1): 27–31.

Wilson, W.J. 1982. Race-oriented programs and the black underclass. In *Race, poverty and the urban underclass,* C. Cottingham, ed., 113–32. Boston, MA: Lexington Books.

_____. 1984. Race-specific policies and the truly disadvantaged. *Yale Law and Policy Review* 2: 272–90.

_____. 1985. Cycles of deprivation and the underclass debate. *Social Science Review* 59:541–59.

4 What Happened to African-American Wages in the 1980s?

BENNETT HARRISON and LUCY GORHAM

The debate about class polarization *within* the African-American community in the United States dominates many contemporary discussions of the political economy of race. Leading the inquiry, University of Chicago sociologist William J. Wilson (1987) writes of a growing black middle class, which is leaving a large black, mostly urban "underclass" behind, both in terms of social and geographic mobility. As relatively more affluent blacks suburbanize, and otherwise move into higher status situations, successful role models are systematically removed from the inner city scene. This fracture in the community hypothetically contributes to the Myrdalian cumulative causation of urban black poverty feeding on itself.[1] Theorists and concerned citizens alike fear that only some quite dramatic combination of social interventions around human capital formation and drug control, on the one hand, and a new commitment to self-help within the African-American community on the other, can offer the hope of eventual upward mobility for the poorest urban (or, for that matter, rural) blacks.

In this chapter, drawing on material from a larger project conducted for the Rural Economic Policy Program of the Aspen Institute and the Ford Foundation,[2] Current Population Survey [CPS] microdata is used to validate the perception that the black (as well as the white) population indeed underwent family income polarization in the 1980s. The extent to which this may be traced (at least in part) to a similar polarization in the distribution of individual earnings is also examined in this chapter.

The principal finding is that practically all the growth in the number of high-income black families since 1979 *must* be the result of packaging different forms of income (such as wages and rents) or from wages of more than one family member. The reason for this inference is that the relative density of the upper tail of the distribution of individual black earners has actually *diminished* since 1979, the last business-cycle peak year prior to 1990.[3] That is, the incidence of well-paid black workers, both men and women, has *fallen* during the 1980s (the same is true for white men, but there has been considerable growth in the number and incidence of high-wage white women over this period).

In the political-economic climate of the past decade, characterized by extensive privatization (Donahue 1989), by the slowdown in growth of permanent government employment and a decline in the number and percent of black recruits into the U.S. military,[4] and by the continuing private sector shift from manufacturing to services, black families may no longer be able to rely on the wages of one family member to propel them into the middle class—if indeed many ever could. In the absence of a truly major national policy effort to promote affirmative action in hiring and promotion, comparable worth, higher hourly wage rates for part-time workers, and extensive job training tied to well-paid stable employment opportunities, most black families, even more than white families, need two or more earners to attain a middle-class standard of living. Black women who are single parents will find it particularly difficult to support families. In that context, whatever one may think about the "underclass" thesis in its entirety, this research strongly validates the concern of Wilson and others about the critical importance of creating social and economic conditions in the inner-city that facilitate the reproduction of two-parent (or at least two or more earner) African-American families.

POLARIZATION OF FAMILY INCOMES SINCE 1979

It is clear from a recent Census Bureau report on poverty that the black population is experiencing polarization in family income. In 1979—the last business-cycle peak before the recessions of 1980 and 1982—34.7 percent of all black families had annual incomes under $12,500 (in 1987 dollars), while 7.9 percent had incomes of $50,000 or more. By 1987, the low-income share had risen to 37.1 percent, the high-income share to 9.5 percent, and the middle had fallen from 57.4 percent to 53.4 percent of the population of black families (U.S. Bureau of the Census 1988, Table 3).

This trend toward income polarization appears in the data on white families, too, although (as many researchers have recently noted) with whites the growth at the top of the distribution has exceeded the growth at the bottom (Danziger, et al. 1989). In 1979, 12.4 percent of white families received less than $12,500 in inflation-adjusted income from all sources, while 20.8 percent received $50,000 or more. By 1987, the low-income share among white families had risen slightly, to 13.5 percent, while the high-income share increased to 24.4 percent.

Clearly, the distributions of both black and white family income are undergoing polarization. The question remains: are the sources of this potentially social disruptive trend different for blacks and whites? Black families are less likely to have two wage earners than white families. Between 1979 and 1987, the proportion of white families with two or more wage-earners rose from 57 percent to 59 percent. But for black families, the change was in the opposite direction, from 50 percent in 1979 down to 46 percent in 1987.[5]

Moreover, it is generally thought that blacks possess fewer or less valuable income-bearing assets (businesses, rental properties, stocks and bonds, etc.) than whites. Inter-racial wealth comparisons are notoriously difficult to make, but using one particular indicator (liquid assets), the Federal Reserve System has provided useful information. In 1983, when the FED last surveyed consumer finances, only 66 percent of "nonwhites and Hispanics" had any assets at all, compared with 93 percent of whites. In that year, median total financial assets held by whites amounted to approximately $4,500; for nonwhites and Hispanics the comparable figure was only $1,000.[6]

Dramatic as they are, these differences do not rule out the possibility that part of the emergence of a class of black *families* with high incomes—Wilson's growing black middle class—is the result of significant growth in wages and salaries of *individual* black workers with "good jobs at good wages." After all, median years of black schooling have increased over time, and some equal employment opportunity and affirmative action hiring and promotion practices have become institutionalized in both the public and private sectors. Moreover, just as residence in the inner-city may, according to Wilson's thesis, cut poor blacks off from the social networks through which access to information about (and referrals to) good jobs are transmitted, the suburbanization of thousands of black households over the past twenty years plausibly *increases* employment access for members of these more mobile households.[7]

In this chapter, a highly disaggregated analysis of the March 1980 and March 1988 CPS computer tapes is conducted in order to explore the extent to which individual black workers with at least some wage income gained increased access during the 1980s to high-paying jobs. The short answer: by most indicators, they have not.

CHANGES IN THE DISTRIBUTION OF INDIVIDUAL EARNINGS FOR ALL WORKERS: 1979–1987

This chapter defines "low earners" as individuals whose annual wage and salary incomes (WSI) leave them below the official poverty line for a family of four persons, adjusted for inflation by the now-standard CPI-X1 deflator of the

U.S. Census Bureau. "High earners" are arbitrarily (but not unreasonably) defined as those earning at least three times the poverty line. In 1987, these normative standards amounted to a bit under $12,000/annually and about $35,000/ annually, respectively.

People's work experience varies enormously over the course of the year. Some people work year round and fulltime, often for the same employer. Others work regularly—by which is usually meant year round—but on part-time schedules. Still others (e.g., farm workers and people employed in other highly seasonal activities such as tourism, construction, and the fashion industry) may well work fulltime (or even overtime) when they *do* work, but for considerably fewer than 50–52 weeks a year. Finally, especially the youngest and the oldest among the population will often be employed "casually"—that is, both part-time *and* for only part of the year. How can this heterogeneity of work experience be incorporated into an analysis of wages that gives an indicator to meaningfully compare across demographic groups?

The procedure selected is straightforward. Each individual's annual WSI is recorded from the CPS tapes. This is divided by the number of weeks in which the respondent worked for wages "last year;"[8] and then again by the number of hours the respondent "usually" worked when (s)he did work. The resulting figure is multiplied by (52 weeks × 40 hours) to arrive at a work experience adjusted estimate of "annualized," or "fulltime equivalent," WSI. Such an indicator enables seasonal, occasional and part-time workers to be systematically incorporated into a comprehensive count of how many people receive "low," "middle," and "high" annual earnings.[9]

Figure 4.1 illustrates the relevant percentage shares of each group and how they have changed over time. Over this period, low-wage employment—the number of people working below the poverty line—grew by almost 40 percent, while high-wage employment rose by only about 2 percent.[10] Nearly 11 million net additional poverty-level jobs were filled in the United States over the course of this (incomplete) business cycle, but only 261,000 "new" high wage jobs were filled.[11] As Figure 4.1 shows, the proportion of the workforce earning poverty-level wages rose from 25.7 percent to 31.5 percent over this period, while the proportion earning three or more times poverty actually *fell*, from 14.2 percent to 12.7 percent.

Some scholars have suggested that this proliferation of low-wage employment in the 1980s is mainly a consequence of the entry of the post-World War II "baby-boom" generation into the labor market of the late 1970s (Lawrence 1984). If so, and if it is assumed that young workers are generally weak substitutes in production for older ones (either because of lack of accumulated specific human capital or because of the presence of seniority-wage payment principles operating in the workplace), then the "crowding" effect of the baby-boomers should not be expected to depress the wages of middle-aged, more experienced employees. Yet, even workers between the ages of 35 and 54

FIGURE 4.1

Distribution of Employment by Full-Time Equivalent Earnings

ALL WORKERS — 1979

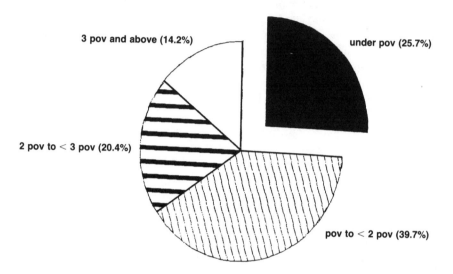

3 pov and above (14.2%)

under pov (25.7%)

2 pov to < 3 pov (20.4%)

pov to < 2 pov (39.7%)

ALL WORKERS — 1987

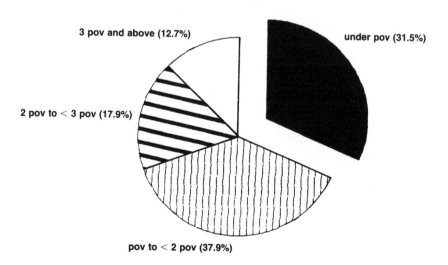

3 pov and above (12.7%)

under pov (31.5%)

2 pov to < 3 pov (17.9%)

pov to < 2 pov (37.9%)

(an interval that most labor economists consider to include the peak earning years) underwent rising poverty-level employment during the 1980s. This group experienced a 52 percent increase in the number of its members earning wages below the poverty line, compared with a 14.2 percent increase for those being paid three or more times poverty wages. During the 1980s, the low end of the earnings distribution became "thicker," and the high end "thinner," for *every* age group. This is a finding that strongly challenges the baby boom hypothesis—as has now been fairly generally acknowledged by other researchers (cf. Burtless 1989).

RACIAL DIFFERENCES IN THE TRAJECTORY OF EARNINGS INEQUALITY IN THE 1980s

The results presented so far form a backdrop against which to evaluate the original question. As demonstrated earlier there has indeed been a measurable increase in the number and proportion of African-American families with what are commonly considered to be "middle-class" incomes. The question now is: to what extent have individual black workers gained increased access to high-wage (and, for that matter, to middle-level) employment since 1979?

Table 4.1 and Figure 4.2 display a comparison of the black and white earnings distributions for the period under study. The comparison is stark indeed. The table shows that between 1979 and 1987, whites experienced nearly a 31 percent increase in the number working under the poverty line, while for blacks, the increase was 44 percent. Whites, as a whole, suffered a decline in the number of high-wage workers over this period of under 1 percent, while among blacks there were actually 7 percent fewer high-wage workers in 1987 than in 1979. Put another way, by 1987 there were two-and-a-half times as many whites earning high wages as blacks, and blacks were 33 percent more likely to be working below the poverty line than whites. As shown elsewhere (Gorham and Harrison 1990; Harrison and Bluestone 1988, 1990), these trends—especially at the low end of the distributive spectrum—constitute a reversal of the pattern of the period 1963–1979, during which the proportion of jobs paying low wages was falling for all racial and demographic groups.

As the slices in Figure 4.2 make clear, this increase in wage inequality in the 1980s has fallen with special force on the African-American community. The incidence of poverty-level employment among whites has risen from 24.3 percent of all white full-time equivalent workers to 29.3 percent. Among blacks, the comparable proportion working under the poverty line rose from 33.9 percent to 40.6 percent. For both races, the proportions earning three or more times the poverty line have fallen since 1979.

TABLE 4.1

Distribution of Annualized (Full-Time Equivalent) Wages and Salary Incomes Adjusted for Weeks and Hours of Paid Employment, 1979 and 1987[a] by Race (in thousands)

	Median Annualized (Full-Time Equivalent) Earnings ($1987)	Less Than the Poverty Line		Poverty to Less Than Two Times POV[b]		Two Times Poverty to Less Than Three Times POV[b]		Three Times Poverty and Above		Total
		Number	Percent of Total	Number	Percent of Total	Number	Percent of Total	Number	Percent of Total	
Blacks										
1979	$13,816	3,533	33.9%	4,286	41.2%	1,843	17.7%	750	7.2%	10,413
1987	$13,520	5,081	40.6%	4,941	39.5%	1,791	14.3%	695	5.6%	12,509
Changes, 1979–87										
Number	($296)	1,548		655		(52)		(55)		2,096
Percent	-2.1%	43.8%		15.3%		-2.8%		-7.3%		20.1%
Percent Points			6.7%		-1.7%		-3.4%		-1.6%	
Whites										
1979	$16,886	21,043	24.3%	33,936	39.2%	18,192	21.0%	13,341	15.4%	86,513
1987	$17,168	27,649	29.3%	35,502	37.7%	17,850	18.9%	13,237	14.0%	94,239
Changes, 1979–87										
Number	$282	6,606		1,566		(342)		(104)		7,726
Percent	1.7%	31.4%		4.6%		-1.9%		-0.8%		8.9%
Percent Points			5.0%		-1.5%		-2.1%		-1.4%	

Notes: [a] "Annualized" or full-time equivalent earnings = actual annual wage and salary income divided by actual weeks worked times usual hours per week, the result multiplied by (52 × 40).
[b] "POV" refers to the U.S. Census poverty budget for a family of four persons, adjusted for inflation by the CPI-X1.
Errors in totals due to rounding.

Source: Authors' estimates from March 1980 and March 1988 Current Population Survey.

FIGURE 4.2

Distribution of Employment by Full-Time Equivalent Earnings, by Race

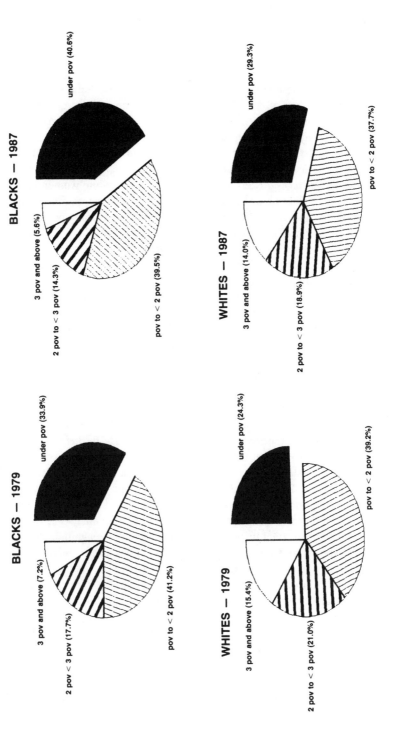

In order to search for the existence of at least *some* subset of the black population that has done well in the political-economic conditions of the 1980s, age, race, and gender were cross-tabulated. The detailed statistics are presented elsewhere (Harrison and Gorham 1990), but are briefly commented on here. Black women in their prime working years (ages 35–54) underwent greater progress than any other group in the black community, experiencing a 33 percent increase in the incidence of high-wage employment. But to put this into perspective, there was also a 37 percent increase in poverty-level employment among the same age-race-gender group. By comparison, white women in the same age bracket experienced an 88 percent increase in jobs paying three or more times the poverty line, and a 38 percent increase in those earning poverty-level wages. Finally, the relatively high percentage increase in well-paying jobs for middle-age black women is a classic example of growth from a low absolute base; in 1987, this group receiving higher wages still constituted less than 5 percent of all black women aged 35 to 54.

But the truly staggering "news" is the situation in the 1980s of black men in their late twenties and early thirties. What has happened is startling. The recent history of this particular age group is depicted graphically in Figure 4.3.

The low wages of the youngest group (ages 16–24) are no surprise. Both pathological and generally benign processes (such as the continuing sorting out of job and lifestyle opportunities and choices) are well-known to explain the late "settling down" of this age group (Osterman 1982). The statistics on white youths are not much different.

But consider what has happened in the past decade to black men aged 25–34. They have experienced a *161 percent increase in their numbers who work under the poverty line*! Or, as Figure 4.3 shows, the share of all such persons earning below the poverty line nearly doubled in only 8 years from 18.4 percent to 34 percent. The share of black men in this age bracket who were successful enough to earn above three times the poverty line halved over the same period, from 10.8 percent of all such workers to 5.8 percent. And, of course, these statistics systematically understate the problem's magnitude by not counting those who have dropped out of the active labor force altogether and earn no (reported) wages. To discover such deprivation a full quarter century after the launching of the War on Poverty, in general, and the various programs targeted to black and other minority youth, in particular, is deeply disheartening.

RACIAL DIFFERENCES IN THE SCHOOLING-EARNINGS NEXUS

This chapter was intended to seek evidence of growth since 1979 in the number and proportion of blacks earning more than $35,000 a year, adjusted for inflation. Such growth could account for the increasing proportion of high-

FIGURE 4.3

Distribution of Employment by Full-Time Equivalent Earnings, Men Aged
25–34

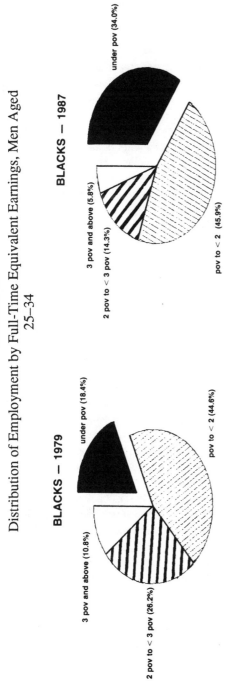

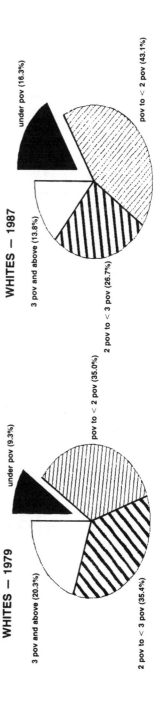

income black families during the last decade. Instead, it found that the number and proportion of well-paid black workers has actually *fallen* since 1979—even as the incidence of blacks working below the poverty line exploded. How can these devastating developments be explained? The most obvious place to turn first, for at least part of an explanation, is to see what has happened to returns to high school and college graduation for blacks and whites.

Certainly going no farther than a high school diploma has not helped blacks since 1979. Over the course of the decade, blacks without any college education at all experienced a 34 percent increase in the number working below the poverty line (compared with a 24 percent increase among whites with the same amount of education). Given what is known all too well about the deteriorating quality of so many secondary schools to which black youngsters had access in the 1980s, perhaps this finding is not surprising (although there now seems to be a national consensus that the quality of primary and especially secondary education has fallen among whites, as well). Moreover, as the demand for blue-collar factory labor has diminished with deindustrialization, and given the comparatively low rate of unionization outside of manufacturing, it can be argued that unionization is no longer an effective substitute for college education as an instrument of upward mobility, especially for blacks and others workers of color (Blackburn, Bloom, and Freeman 1989; Bluestone 1989).

But then consider the comparative data on those who have completed 4 or more years of college. In 1987, 17.1 percent of whites with this much schooling still worked under the poverty line. Among blacks, the comparable proportion was 20 percent. Presumably these are mainly young people, still in university or just starting to work. But then look at the high end of the wage spectrum. Only a bit over 1 in 8 African-American college graduates were earning as much as $35,000 a year in 1987. White college graduates were twice as likely to be paid this much as were blacks with equivalent years of schooling (26.1 percent versus 13.1 percent).

Suppose just blacks in 1987 are compared to blacks back in 1979. Over this period, the absolute number of black men with a 4-year college education who received annualized earnings of at least $35,000 did increase, by 467,000 (Gorham and Harrison 1990). But the number of well-educated African-American men receiving *low* wages grew even more, so that the fraction of all black male college graduates who had high wages actually *fell*—from 23.4 percent in 1979 to 19.5 percent in 1987.

For black women college graduates, the findings are even more discouraging. Between 1979 and 1987, despite a new addition to the American labor force of 407,000 black women with at least 4 years of college, the number earning $35,000 a year or more *declined* by 10,000, with the share of such women who received high earnings also dropping, from 12.4 percent of all black women college graduates to 7.6 percent.

CONCLUSIONS AND THOUGHTS ABOUT FUTURE RESEARCH

For all workers between at least 1963 (the earliest year for which CPS microdata are available) and the late 1970s, the incidence of employment at poverty wages fell steadily, while the share of workers earning high wages rose. This was also true for nonwhite workers.[12] Since the 1970s, these trends have sharply reversed for most demographic groups—what Harrison and Bluestone (1988, 1990) called the "great U-turn." As seen, in the course of the reversal away from greater equality, blacks have suffered especially severe setbacks.

The increase in wage polarization among workers of all races since the late 1970s occurred in both urban and rural areas (Gorham and Harrison 1990). They have been most extreme in the traditional "Blackbelt" states of Alabama, Kentucky, Mississippi, and Tennessee, although the U-turn happened to some extent in every region of the country except New England. If growing impoverishment despite working for a living is a sign of unequal distribution of *power*—the ability to enforce claims on economic resources—then all of this statistical evidence confirms the continuing importance of *place, power*, and *polarization* in American economic life.

In trying to arrive at an explanation for these reversals, further research might well investigate the racial impacts of the pronounced slowdown in growth of federal government employment, in general, and of hiring and promotions associated with the administration of social welfare programs, in particular.[13] Moreover, given that unionization has, since the 1960s, been especially advantageous to blacks, especially in the service sector (Freeman and Medoff 1984), the growing resistance of employers to trade unions and the generally anti-labor tone of recent opinions by the U.S. Supreme Court (Clark 1989; Freeman and Medoff 1984) could be partly responsible for the truncation of the black-wage distribution. Ongoing research by Barry Bluestone, Mary Stevenson, and Chris Tilly in Boston and by John Kasarda in Chapel Hill is pursuing the hypothesis (central to Wilson's own explanation for the growth of a black underclass) that the continuing structural shifts in the economy away from blue-collar manufacturing have disproportionately reduced employers' demands for the labor power of black workers, especially (but, as just seen, not exclusively) those with weak educational backgrounds. The relaxation of enforcement of equal protection laws and the sharply reduced funding of government-sponsored job training programs in the 1980s are also likely candidates for inclusion in the causal modeling that deserves the highest priority from the research community, in light of the descriptive findings presented here.

In any case, whatever the particular determinants of the racial differences in earnings distributions that have been measured, a strong conclusion about the debate over the growth of a black middle class in the 1980s already seems possible. Given the extraordinary tenacity with which the American economic system continues to crowd black *workers* into the lowest-paying jobs (or to devalue jobs entered by black men and women), as recently as 1987 it seems likely that the key to upward social mobility for black *families* does—as Wilson and others argue—turn mainly on the presence of multiple wage earners in the household.

The obstacles to multiple wage-earning in the urban African-American family are especially formidable. Disproportionately high rates of incarceration, recidivism and suicide among black men reduce the marriage pool (Wilson 1987). Disincentives still remain in the public assistance system that deter black men from allowing themselves to be "discovered" living with their welfare-recipient mates (Darity 1986; Ellwood 1988). Where women are the sole bread-winners, the society is still unprepared to insist that they be paid anything resembling the old "family wage" once earned by white male factory workers—even when those women have college degrees (Harrison and Gorham 1990). And the deteriorating quality of U.S. inner-city schools especially reduces the chances that, when multiple wage-earning families *are* formed, both adults will have the skills (or at least the credentials) to get a decent job.

Inadequate employment opportunities at good wages, unacceptably low rates of skill formation due to a grossly uneven educational system, race and sex discrimination are hardly new problems in American life. For a time, it appeared that their combined contribution to polarization among workers and between the races was finally being eroded. Sadly, the 1980s can only be looked back on as a sobering reminder that the scourge of inequality is still very much with us.

NOTES

1.   For an early attempt to apply Myrdalian cumulative causation or positive feed-back models to the study of inequality and labor market segmentation, see Vietorisz and Harrison (1973).

2.   The Structure of Employment and Earnings in Nonmetropolitan and Metropolitan Labor Markets: Trends, Causes and Policy Implications, Ford Foundation, Grant No. 880-0411.

3.   There has been a 47 percent growth in the number of high-wage white women over this period, but a 3 percent decline in the absolute number of high-wage African-American women. For an analysis of racial differences in the labor market outcomes of women that poses a sobering challenge to the feminist movement, see Malveaux (1985).

4.   Between the 1970s and the 1980s, the growth rate of government employment at all levels fell by a factor of four (at the level of the federal government, most of what growth did occur was in the military) (Council of Economic Advisers 1989, p. 357). Moreover, since 1985, the typical probationary period prior to achieving permanent status in the federal civil service was increased from one to up to four years. The Federal Office of Personnel Management ordered all government agencies to substitute tem-

porary for permanent employees "whenever possible," noting that "temporary employees are not eligible for federal health benefits, may be dismissed 'at will,' and have no appeal rights or other protection against adverse personnel actions" (Pear 1985). Historically, permanent civil service employment has been a major source of upward mobility for blacks (Harrison and Osterman 1974). On the decline in military recruiting of blacks see U.S. Congressional Budget Office (1989).

5. U.S. Bureau of the Census, 1988, Table 1 for 1987 data; U.S. Bureau of the Census, 1981, Table 20 for 1979 data.

6. "Survey of Consumer Finances," Table 10. The FED does not specifically identify black financial activity in its surveys. A more recent FED survey did not become available for study in time for inclusion in this report.

7. According to former Census Bureau Director Vincent Barabba, between 1970 and 1979 there was "an increase of 39 percent in the number of black suburbanities. This growth rate far overshadows the black growth rate in any other geographic area, and suburban blacks now represent 20 percent of all blacks instead of the 16 percent that we noted in 1970" (Barabba 1979).

8. For further details on data and methodology, see Gorham and Harrison (1990). It is well understood by survey researchers that people who report zero annual earnings often hold occasional jobs, but at low wages. It follows that, by excluding records reporting zero wage income during the year prior to the interview, the share of low-wage employment for any group each year is certainly *understated*.

9. This measure masks the problem of low earnings of those who are involuntarily employed less than year round and fulltime. This chapter is certainly not denying the usefulness of research that distinguishes fully employed from partially employed workers (cf. Ehrenberg, et al. 1988). For purposes of this study, it seemed useful to construct a composite indicator that aggregates people with different work experience.

10. This chapter focuses attention on the lower and upper tails of the various wage distributions estimated. The reader is welcomed to make use of the additional statistics presented in the tables in Harrison and Gorham (1990) to study the interior wage brackets.

11. Of course, these increments do not consist exclusively of literally "new" jobs. Existing jobs may have been downgraded or upgraded, as well. The net changes (or increments) incorporate all such gross flows.

12. The CPS does not permit a breakout of blacks from the superset "nonwhites" during the 1960s. In the March 1980 CPS, blacks constitute 84 percent of all nonwhites who had some wages in 1979.

13. For persuasive evidence that these sectors played a major role in advancing the economic position of blacks during the 1960s and early 1970s, see Brown and Erie (1981), Darity (1986), and Harrison and Osterman (1974).

REFERENCES

Barabba, V.P. 1979. How demographic changes will shape the '80s. Address before the annual meeting of the American Council of Life Insurance (December).

Blackburn, M., D. Bloom and R. Freeman. 1989. Why has the economic position of less-skilled male workers deteriorated in the United States? In *A future of lousy jobs?*, G. Burtless, ed. Washington, DC: The Brookings Institution.

Bluestone, B. 1989. Commentary on Blackburn, Bloom and Freeman. In *A future of lousy jobs?*, G. Burtless, ed. Washington, DC: The Brookings Institution.

Brown, M. and S. Erie. 1981. Blacks and the legacy of the great society. *Public Policy* (Summer).

Burtless, G. 1989. Earnings inequality over the business cycle. In *A future of lousy jobs?*, G. Burtless, ed. Washington, DC: The Brookings Institution.

Clark, G.L. 1989. *Unions and communities under siege.* Cambridge, MA: Cambridge University Press.

Council of Economic Advisers. 1989. *Economic report of the president.* Washington, DC: U.S. Government Printing Office (January).

Danziger, S., P. Gottschalk and E. Smolensky. 1989. How the rich have fared: 1979–1987. American Economic Association *Papers and Proceedings* 79 (May).

Darity, W.A., Jr. 1986. The managerial class and industrial policy. *Industrial Relations* (Spring).

Darity, W.A., Jr. and S.L. Myers, Jr. 1980. Changes in black-white inequality, 1968–78: a decade of progress? *Review of Black Political Economy* (Summer).

Donahue, J. 1989. *Privatization.* New York: Basic Books.

Ehrenberg, R., P. Rosenberg and J. Li. 1988. Part-time employment in the United States. In *Employment, unemployment and hours of work*, R. Hart, ed. London: Allen and Unwin.

Ellwood, D. 1988. *Poor support.* New York: Basic Books.

Freeman, R. and J. Medoff. 1984. *What do unions do?* New York: Basic Books.

Gorham, L. and B. Harrison. 1990. Working below the poverty line. Rural Economic Policy Program of the Aspen Institute, Washington, DC (Fall).

Harrison, B. and B. Bluestone. 1988. *The great u-turn: corporate restructuring and the polarizing of America.* New York: Basic Books.

———. 1990. Wage polarization in the U.S. and the 'flexibility' debate. *Cambridge Journal of Economics* (September).

Harrison, B. and P. Osterman. 1974. Public employment and urban poverty. *Urban Affairs Quarterly* (March).

Heckman, J. 1989. The impact of government on the economic status of black Americans. In *The question of discrimination: racial inequality in the U.S. labor market*, S. Shulman and W. A. Darity, Jr, eds. Middletown, CT: Wesleyan University Press.

Lawrence, R.Z. 1984. Sectoral shifts and the size of the middle class. *Brookings Review* (Fall).

Levy, F. 1988. Incomes, families, and living standards. In *America's living standards*, R. Litan, R. Z. Lawrence and C. L. Schultz, eds. Washington, DC: The Brookings Institution.

Malveaux, J. 1985. The economic interests of black and white women: are they similar? *Review of Black Political Economy* 14(1)(Summer): 5–28.

Osterman, P. 1982. *Getting started: the youth labor market.* Cambridge, MA: MIT Press.

Pear, R. 1985. Temporary hiring by U.S. is pushed under new policy. *New York Times,* January 2:1.

Survey of consumer finances 1983. 1984. *Federal Reserve Bulletin* 70(9)(September).

U.S. Bureau of the Census. 1981. Money income of households in the United States: 1979. *Current population reports,* Ser. P-60, No. 126. Washington, DC: U.S. Government Printing Office (June).

U.S. Bureau of the Census. 1988. Money income and poverty status in the United States: 1987 (advance data from the March 1988 current population survey). *Current population reports,* Ser. P-60, No. 161. Washington, DC: U.S. Government Printing Office (September).

U.S. Congressional Budget Office. 1989. Social representation in the U.S. military. Washington, DC (October).

Vietorisz, T. and B. Harrison. 1973. Labor market segmentation: positive feedback and divergent development. *American Economic Association Proceedings* (May).

Wilson, W. 1987. *The truly disadvantaged.* Chicago: University of Chicago Press.

5   Changing Black Employment Patterns

JOHN P. BLAIR and RUDY H. FICHTENBAUM

Economists have a nearly schizophrenic view of work. On the one hand, work is viewed as a cost necessary to earning a living. On the other hand, work is essential to human development. Work is one of the ways we define ourselves, achieve self-esteem, the respect of others and contribute to society. Thus, when African-Americans are deprived of work opportunities, they suffer both from lack of income and socio-psychological problems associated with unemployment.

This chapter examines African-American employment patterns and racial employment differences. The first section describes various aspects of black employment, including the high levels of unemployment and ominous trends in these patterns. The second section evaluates the principal theoretical explanations for black-white employment differentials.

PATTERNS OF EMPLOYMENT AND UNEMPLOYMENT

Discrimination in access to employment is one of the most severe hardships afflicting African-Americans. The old rule of "last hired, first fired," continues and there remain important occupations from which African-Americans are almost totally barred. The burden of unemployment is especially heavy on African-American youth.

Super Unemployment

Official statistics show that for more than a quarter of a century the unemployment rate among blacks has been generally more than twice that among whites and the gap is widening (see Table 5.1). In 1990, the black unemployment rate was near 10.4 percent, compared to the national average of about 5.3 percent. Even if other economic factors are ignored and the focus is on unemployment alone, it is clear that the African-American population lives in a condition of permanent depression.

Official unemployment rates, however, understate the extent of the black-white employment gap because neither discouraged workers, nor part-time workers, are considered to be unemployed. These types of hidden unemployment greatly increase the true unemployment rate compared to the official statistics, especially for African-Americans.

Discouraged Workers

Discouraged workers would like to have a job but they have given up looking for work because they do not believe jobs are available. Since they are not actively looking for work, they are not considered unemployed—they are simply not counted in the labor force. In 1989, 81 percent of the white male civilian

TABLE 5.1

Average Unemployment Rates by Race, 1948–1989

Years	White	Black[a] and Other Minorities	Black[a] and Other Minorities % of White
1948–1953	3.8	6.5	172
1954–1963	4.8	10.2	213
1964–1973	4.1	8.3	202
1973–1985	6.6	14.8	224
1986–1989	5.1	12.8	247

Note: [a] For 1974–1989 refers to African-American only; before that period they are for all non-whites.

Source: BLS *Handbook of Labor Statistics*, 1973 T. 61, *Survey of Current Business*, May 1974, *Economic Report of the President 1984*, T. B-33, and *Employment and Earnings*, January 1986–1990, T. 4.

non-institutionalized population age 16 and over were part of the labor force, but only 72.6 percent of black male civilian non-institutionalized population 16 and over were in the labor force. Hill (1988) showed that states with slack labor markets have higher dependency rates than tight labor-market states. The dependency rate is a measure of the portion of the population dependent upon the earnings of others.[1] Hill's finding strongly supports the notion that when it is difficult to get a job, many workers become discouraged and drop out of the labor market. The low participation rate of African-Americans screens massive numbers of discouraged workers.

One indication that the discouraged worker effect is greater among black workers than among white workers can be found by comparing labor force participation rates in good times and bad. Workers are more likely to believe they can find work in prosperous periods and, therefore, actively start looking for a job. Between 1983 and 1987, the economy experienced slow but steady employment growth. As jobs became available, the labor force participation rate of white workers increased by 1.5 percent, whereas the black labor force participation rate increased by nearly twice that amount, 2.8 percent. This suggests that a greater portion of black than white workers would be willing to work if jobs were available.

Further evidence that the discouraged worker effect is greater for blacks than whites can be found in information collected by the Department of Labor on the reasons why people are not in the labor force. In 1990, 7.5 percent of whites who were not in the labor force, wanted a job. In contrast, 17.8 percent of black workers not in the labor force wanted jobs. These numbers indicate that a disproportionate number of blacks are excluded from the official unemployment count and that, while the true magnitude of unemployment is greatly understated for all workers, it is especially understated for black workers.

The low black labor force participation rate has been used by some commentators, such as Viscusi (1986) and Holzer (1986) to support a claim that black-white differences in employment are due to a lower desire to work on the part of African-Americans. However, a Department of Labor study (1986) of work attitudes dispels such myths stating:

> The figures also show that a larger proportion of blacks than of whites are job-oriented: Those employed plus those seeking work (unemployed) plus those wanting a job but not actually seeking one constituted 66 percent of the black population and 62 percent of the white population . . . the figures help dispose of the myth that blacks are less interested in jobs than whites. (Department of Labor, p. 2.)

Leonard Goodwin (1972), in a Brookings Institution study, found no difference between whites and blacks in "work orientation." However, a larger proportion of blacks, especially poor blacks, do not think they can obtain jobs. Blacks, as well as whites, poor as well as rich, have a low opinion of "quasi-illegal" activities and prefer honest work by an overwhelming majority.

Underemployment

Workers who can only find part-time jobs might be considered partly employed or underemployed. Yet official unemployment statistics count such workers as fully employed. In recent years the magnitude of this involuntary part-time employment has increased because employers have been hiring more and more part-time workers. Part-time workers generally receive few, if any, fringe benefits, earn lower pay, are less likely to participate in a union, and seldom receive time and a half for overtime because they are not covered by the Fair Labor Standards Act.

In 1990, 10.7 percent of black men in the labor force and 17.8 percent of black women in the labor force worked part-time. In contrast, 10 percent of white men and 25.1 percent of white women worked parttime. What is most revealing is that among those black men working parttime, 51 percent wanted full-time jobs but could not find them and among black women working part-time, 36 percent wanted full-time jobs but could not find them. In contrast, 36 percent of white men working parttime wanted full-time jobs and only 19.6 percent of white women working parttime wanted full-time jobs.

Measuring Hidden Unemployment

A better measure of the true magnitude of unemployment can be obtained by counting as unemployed:

- Half of those involuntarily working parttime for "economic reasons."
- All of those "wanting a job now," except those not actively seeking work because of school attendance, ill health or disability, home responsibilities, or because they think they cannot find work.

With these adjustments, the unemployment rate in 1990 for white males increases from 4.4 percent to 8.8 percent. For white females, the unemployment rate increases from 4.7 percent to 12.6 percent. For black males, the unemployment rate increases from 11.5 percent to 22.1 percent, and for black females the unemployment rate increases from 11.0 percent to 26.6 percent. These figures give a more accurate indication of actual unemployment differences between African-Americans and whites.

The Increasing Severity of African-American Unemployment

According to Table 5.1, the average rate of black unemployment during the past decade has been higher than at any time since the Great Depression and, relative to whites, it is at record high levels. Due to treatment of discouraged and underemployed workers in the unemployment statistics, the actual trends have been considerably worse than indicated in Table 5.1.

The labor force participation gap has also widened. In 1940, the percentage of black males in the labor force was slightly higher than that of white males— 83.7 percent against 82.5 percent (see Table 5.2). This is as expected, as relatively fewer African-American youth could afford to continue their education, and relatively few older African-Americans could afford to retire. Thus, in 1940, 46.1 percent of young minority males aged 16 and 17 were reported as in the labor force, as against 27.4 percent of whites aged 16 and 17; and 49.0 percent of minorities aged 65 and over were reported as in the labor force, contrasted with 41.2 percent of whites in that age group.

By 1950, the post-war competition for jobs increased (it became more difficult to get a job) and the labor force participation rate of blacks fell to 2.3 percentage points lower than that of whites; in 1960, it was 5.2 percentage points lower; in 1970, 7.6 percentage points lower; and in 1980, 9.4 percentage points lower. In 1990, after 8 years of job growth it remains 6.6 percentage points lower!

TABLE 5.2

Male Labor Force Participation and
Unemployment Rates, 1940–1990

Year	Labor Force Participation Rates			Unemployment Rates		
	White	Black	White-Black Difference	White	Black	Black-White Ratio
1940	82.5	83.7	1.2	14.6	18.0	1.23
1950	81.8	79.5	−2.3	4.6	7.8	1.70
1960	80.9	75.7	−5.2	4.6	8.7	1.89
1970	77.4	69.8	−7.6	3.6	6.3	1.75
1980	76.1	66.7	−9.4	5.9	12.3	2.08
1990	78.1	71.5	−6.6	4.4	11.5	2.61

Source: U.S. PC80-1-Cl 1940–1989, 4 *Employment and Earnings,* July 1990, Table A4.

Over the 50-year interval, there was a decline of 4.4 percentage points in the white male participation rate, and a 12.2 percentage point decline in the reported black male participation rate. Masses of blacks have, in fact, been relegated to the semi-permanent reserve army of the unemployed. They are able to get jobs only under conditions of extreme labor shortage. Otherwise, they are simply not counted as workers or as students or as any other socially meaningful category of persons.

Future Polarization: African-American Youth Unemployment

The catastrophic employment situation of African-American youth has been well publicized. Ten years ago, more African-American youth got into college, or at least into 2-year community colleges, than do currently. Since the late 1970s, the proportion of African-American students in college has been declining. The great majority of African-American youth today cannot attend college and many who start college drop out because of economic pressures or because they are ill-prepared by segregated school systems (see Ch. 7 for a detailed discussion). The problem is exacerbated because jobs being created in central cities where many black youth live and look for work have increasingly stiff educational requirements (Kasarda 1989).

Among black youth ages 16–19, the official unemployment rate in 1990 was 38.8 percent and for black youth ages 20–24 it was 17.6 percent. Overall, black youth were 2.5 times more likely to be unemployed than white youth. Although black youth unemployment decreases as education increases, a significant gap in unemployment rates remains. For instance, black high school graduates had an unemployment rate of 19.6 percent compared to a 7.2 percent unemployment rate for similarly educated white youths in 1990. Clearly education, although extremely important, cannot be the sole solution to the problem of black youth unemployment.

After adjusting for differences in labor force participation rates to account for the high portion of discouraged workers among black youth, young black women are 3.75 times more likely to be unemployed when compared with young white women, and black youth with 1 to 3 years of college education are almost 4 times more likely to be unemployed after adjusting for differences in labor force participation rates. (See Table 5.3.)

Structural Change

The U.S. economy has undergone major economic changes associated with a shift from goods-producing to service-providing activities. These structural

TABLE 5.3

Youth Unemployment Adjusted for Differences in
Labor Force Participation Rates, 1990[a]

	Black	White	Ratio Black to White
Total 16–24	38.7	9.7	399
16–19 years	53.8	14.2	379
20–24 years	29.9	7.3	410
Men	36.7	9.4	390
Women	40.5	9.9	409
Less than 4 years of high school	56.7	16.7	340
4 years of high school	31.3	7.2	435
1–3 years of college	23.3	7.2	324
4 years of college or more	5.5	6.2	89

Note: [a] Unemployment rates for black youth calculated assuming that labor force
participation rates for black youth are equal to labor force participation rates
for white youth.

Source: Employment and Earnings, July 1990, Table A7.

changes are anticipated to continue into the next century. The reasons and reper-
cussions of the restructuring are too numerous and complex to describe here.
Nevertheless, structural changes within the U.S. economy have adversely
affected the economic opportunities of African-Americans.

Table 5.4 provides a foundation for understanding the nature of the industrial changes that continue to reshape the U.S. economy. It compares employment changes between 1978 and 1988, years approximating business-cycle
peaks.[2] Three industrial sectors stand out as particularly important to African-
American progress—manufacturing, services, and professional services. In each
of these three sectors, black employment as a percentage of total employment
was equal to or greater than the percentage of blacks in the workplace. In 1988,
blacks accounted for 9.4 percent of the total workforce. Furthermore, column 2
indicates that all three sectors employed a large percentage of the total black
workforce. Together, manufacturing, services, and professional services,
accounted for nearly half of all black employment. A comparison of columns 1
and 3 indicates that the percentage of black employment in each of these sectors
has remained stable in spite of the decline in manufacturing and the rapid
growth of the two service sectors.

TABLE 5.4

Sectoral Earnings and Growth Profile

	1978 % Black Employment in Industry	1978 % of Total Black Employment	1988 % Black Employment in Industry	1978–88 Total Employment Growth	Annual Average Projected Growth Rate 1988	1888 Average Weekly Earnings
Construction	7.1	3.9	6.8	25.8	1.2	251
Manufacturing	9.8	19.1	10.2	-.8	-.1	218
Transportation	11.0	6.1	14.3	30.8	.6	252
Wholesale trade	5.7	1.8	5.7	26.6	1.7	197
Retail trade	6.4	9.0	8.3	22.0	1.7	96
Finance, insurance, and real estate	7.6	3.7	8.0	46.5	1.3	107
Services	11.9	28.8	11.8	38.9	2.5	143
Professional services	11.2	18.6	11.9	29.4	2.8	175
Public administration	13.4	6.1	14.4	8.2	1.9	NA[a]

Note: [a] NA = not available.

Source: Employment and Earnings, 1979 and 1989.

The manufacturing sector has traditionally provided the greatest prospects for black progress (Rose 1979). Annual earnings are substantially above the national average, jobs in the manufacturing sector usually include fringe benefits (medical insurance is especially important) and individuals can often qualify for such jobs without post-secondary education. For many Americans, manufacturing jobs were an important step on the intergenerational mobility ladder, providing sufficient income to help children move into higher paying white-collar, professional jobs. Unfortunately, the promise of manufacturing has been diminished because of the prospects for slow growth through the year 2000. (Change in manufacturing employment was positive during the recovery phase of the current business cycle but over the entire cycle it was slightly negative.) As indicated by column 5 of Table 5.4, the Bureau of Labor Statistics anticipates the current annual average decline in manufacturing employment of 0.1 percent to continue. The decline in employment demand in this sector is likely to depress wages as well.

Services and professional services are sectors with significant growth potential. In fact, they are anticipated to be the fastest-growing job categories. Consequently, African-American economic progress is to some extent dependent on the ability of African-American workers to substitute jobs in the service industries for jobs that would have existed if manufacturing growth had kept pace with the economy.

Service industries contain jobs in a highly varied mix of occupations. On the one hand, they include some of the highest-paying professional and executive jobs. On the other hand, a large portion of service sector jobs are in low-paying occupations. Workers in the low-paying occupations are often only able to obtain part-time positions that lack medical insurance, other fringe benefits, and contractual job security.

During the 1980s, the gap between rich and poor widened and families in the middle have been squeezed (Harrison and Bluestone 1988; Ch. 4, this volume). This shift in the earnings distribution has undoubtedly made it more difficult for African-Americans who aspire to the middle class. Table 5.5 shows how the shift from manufacturing to service sectors contributed to this phenomenon. The occupational makeup of manufacturing, professional services, and other services sectors are shown (the occupations are ranked according to their median income). Table 5.5 indicates that manufacturing provided more jobs in the middle-earnings occupations. In contrast, the two service industries are structured with a high portion of jobs at the two extremes and fewer in the middle-earnings categories. The bimodal nature of compensation in the service sectors would be even more pronounced if the numerous benefits received by those in the higher-paying occupations were compared to the (lack of) benefits in the lower-earning categories.

TABLE 5.5

Occupational Structure of Three Sectors

	1988 Median Earnings	*Occupation as a Percent of Total Industry Employment*		
		Manufacturing	*Professional Service*	*Other Service*
Executives, administrators and managers	28,635	12.0	10.6	11.9
Professional specialities	26,876	8.2	41.3	28.7
Technical and related support	22,425	3.3	6.4	4.9
Precision production, craft and repair	20,696	19.0	1.6	4.6
Transportation and material moving	18,234	4.0	1.2	1.3
Machine operatives, assembly and inspectors	14,695	31.1	0.9	2.0
Administrative support (incl. clerical)	13,780	11.2	18.3	19.8
Sales	13,727	3.5	0.6	2.1
Handlers, equipment cleaners and laborers	8,252	5.6	0.4	1.0
Service (except household)	7,297	1.6	18.0	19.5
Household services	2,201	—	—	4.0
Percent in:				
Top three occupations		23.5	58.3	45.5
Middle six occupations		68.8	33.2	29.8
Bottom three occupations		7.2	18.4	24.5

Source: Calculated from data in *Employment and Earnings*, 1989.

The bottom portion of Table 5.5 highlights the bimodal nature of compensation in the two service sectors and contrasts it with the manufacturing sector. About 69 percent of manufacturing jobs are in the middle-paying occupations, compared with 33 percent for professional services and 30 percent for other services. Only about 7 percent of manufacturing jobs are in the three lowest-paying occupations.

In light of the bifurcated nature of the two service sectors, the effect of restructuring on African-American progress through the job market is likely to depend upon the occupations of the African-American population. Blacks who would have traditionally been employed in manufacturing are unlikely to find comparable occupations in the service industries. They are more likely to hold lower-paying occupations with fewer skill requirements. It is very difficult for someone already in the workforce to move to a higher-skilled occupation without additional education. As work requirements become more credentialized, shifts to higher-skilled occupations will become even more difficult.

Table 5.6 shows the percentage of total white employment divided by the percentage of total black employment for each occupational-industry category. A ratio of one indicates that the number of whites in a particular category divided by the total white work force equals the comparable ratio for blacks.[3] The lower (higher) the number, the more overrepresented (underrepresented) blacks are based upon their (already underrepresented) share of the labor force.

Table 5.6 indicates that blacks tend to be concentrated in the lowest-paying occupations in the two service sectors and are underrepresented in the higher-paying occupations. This generalization is true for all sectoral categories, including manufacturing (not shown). However, as indicated in Table 5.5, the majority of the jobs in manufacturing are in occupations in the middle of the occupational spectrum. Therefore, as restructuring has resulted in jobs shifting from manufacturing to service industries, job opportunities for African-Americans have shifted from middle-earning occupations to lower-earning occupations. If present trends continue, continued growth can be anticipated in lower-paying occupations.[4]

Economic restructuring and associated shifts in the types of jobs available raise the question of the rate at which African-Americans are employed in better-paying occupations. Since 1970, there has been a slight improvement in the share of blacks in "better" jobs, although this trend has slowed considerably during the 1980s. This is particularly the case in the middle- and blue-collar occupations which have been severely affected by plant closings and layoffs.[5]

There were some gains for black workers in the area of white-collar employment. Black women gained more than black men. Undoubtedly, the increased access of African-Americans to white-collar jobs, and especially the increased employment of African-American women in these jobs, represents a real improvement compared to the kinds of employment previously available to

TABLE 5.6

Sectoral Occupation Employment Ratios in
Two Service Sectors, 1988

| | | White-Black Employment Ratio | |
Occupation	*Median Earnings*	*Professional Service*	*Other Service*
1. Executives, administrators and managers	28,635	1.45	1.99
2. Professional specialists	26,876	1.45	2.09
3. Technical and related support	22,425	0.81	1.25
4. Precision production craft and repair	20,696	0.77	1.40
5. Transportation and material moving	18,234	0.51	0.55
6. Machine operatives assembly and inspectors	14,695	0.59	0.60
7. Administrative support (incl. clerical)	13,780	0.94	1.57
8. Sales	16,884	1.05	5.13
9. Handlers, equipment cleaners and laborers	8,252	0.69	0.49
10. Service (except household)	7,297	0.30	0.56
11. Household services	2,201	—	0.31

Source: Calculated from data in *Employment and Earnings*, 1989.

African-Americans. *But it was not all gain.* It was part of a process in which white-collar employment increased very rapidly and the technical and economic boundary between white- and blue-collar employment became less distinct. In many cases, occupational gains occurred as earnings were reduced in previously high- or medium-paying white-collar occupations.

THEORIES OF EMPLOYMENT DIFFERENTIALS

Many blacks are not fully involved in the labor market either because they are confined to lower-paying segments of the occupational structure or because they lack jobs altogether. This section examines the extent that each of several theories can contribute to understanding the reasons for low attachment by African-Americans to the world of work, or, conversely, the reason why employers do not fully utilize this source of potential labor.

Productivity

Conventional microeconomic theory leads to the conclusion that employment and compensation are based on the value of the extra output each worker produces. For example, assume: (1) all other inputs were held constant (that is no additional machinery or materials need be purchased); (2) a worker produces five extra units per hour; and (3) the extra output could be sold for $10 a piece. The firm would be willing and able to hire the worker for $50 per hour or (preferably from the firm's perspective) less. On the other hand, if the worker could produce only one extra unit per hour, then the value of the employee to the firm would be only $10 per hour. Consequently, the worker would not be hired if the wage demanded was over $10 per hour.

This productivity explanation has been used by some economists to explain black-white employment differentials. If blacks are less productive than whites, it follows that firms will hire whites rather than blacks and/or pay white workers more than blacks.

The productivity explanation is weakened because it is difficult or impossible to measure productivity differentials among individuals for most jobs. Furthermore, there is absolutely no evidence that black workers as a group are less productive. Recognizing that individual productivity cannot be measured, economists frequently assume that discrimination does not contribute to employment differences and thereby attribute the differences in employment opportunities to productivity. By ignoring racism and accepting a competitive model of the labor market, it is easily deduced that African-Americans must be less productive if they earn lower wages and suffer higher unemployment. This is an example of reaching a conclusion by reasoning from what is likely a flawed set of assumptions.

African-American educational gains (see Ch. 7) undermine the productivity theory but do not refute it. One would expect educational gains to be associated with improved job performance. One possible explanation for the failure of increases in African-American educational attainment to be reflected in changes in black employment opportunities is that educational attainment is measured by years of schooling—not what is actually learned. The low quality of central-city education may result in individuals passing courses in school but not enhancing their education.

Pathological Behaviors

A second explanation for the black-white employment differential is that a disproportionate number of African-Americans have behavioral traits that prevent them from attaining, or succeeding at, jobs. The behavioral traits explanation is similar to the productivity explanation in that both attribute employment differentials to differences in the quality of labor between African-Americans and whites. In other words, both theories point to deficiencies in the supply of black labor.[6]

But which comes first, poor work attitudes or poor job prospects and the need for welfare (Gottschalk 1990)? Social psychologists have attributed dysfunctional job behavior to the marginalization of the poor, which causes or reinforces feelings of low self-esteem and cause social deviance. Economists who have studied the dual labor market have reported that traits of dependability and punctuality are not valued in some lower paying, irregular jobs (Doeringer and Piore 1971). Consequently, individuals trapped in such jobs may lack incentives to develop more productive behaviors.

Theories that explain black-white employment differentials using behavioral differences are consistent with Wilson's (1987) idea that race is of declining significance in black-white economic status. According to this perspective, African-Americans are relegated to unemployment or low-paying jobs because they are part of the underclass, not because they are black *per se*.[7]

Hout's (1984) analysis of the increased importance of family background compared to race in determining success of African-Americans supports Wilson's hypotheses. Hout's findings suggest that race may be less important than in the past, but it is still important.

It is somewhat ironic that Wilson, while arguing that race is of declining significance in explaining African-American poverty, also argues that the African-American poor are fundamentally different from poor whites. The reason for the differences, he suggests, is that poor whites do not suffer from social isolation and, therefore, live in communities where the social fabric is intact. Why his theory of poverty applies primarily to African-Americans, requires explanation. (See Ch. 3.)

Is there any evidence that supports Wilson's hypothesis? Using census data, Danziger and Gottschalk (1987) showed that the share of income among the lowest 40 percent of blacks declined significantly between 1939 and 1979 because of the increasing percentage of blacks earning no income, up from 14.5 percent in 1939 to 21 percent in 1979. (Among whites, the portion of the population earning no income declined during the same period.) Danziger and Gottschalk view these findings as evidence that there is a black underclass, cut off from the American mainstream. While the increase in inequality among black families in general and the increase in the number of black males with no earnings are particularly alarming, the authors recognize that it does not substantiate the claim that the black underclass has distinctly different values.

Although dysfunctional attitudes on the part of some African-Americans undoubtedly exist, evidence that there are substantial differences between the attitudes of African-Americans and whites is weak. Few, if any, studies show attitudinal or value differences between African-Americans and whites (Goodwin 1972).

William Ryan (1976) labeled the behavioral explanations of poverty "blaming the victim." He believed African-Americans are really victims of the economic system. Individuals who have succeeded often prefer to blame victims rather than blame the economic system or bad luck. By implication, successful individuals can claim credit for their own status and success.

Institutional Barriers to Unemployment

Institutional barriers to attaining and maintaining jobs are a frequently discussed cause of employment differentials. Individuals with productive skills are often hampered from obtaining jobs or from advancing to better-paying jobs by institutional barriers. Examples of institutional barriers include lack of knowledge regarding specific employment opportunities, geographic immobility, and wage rigidities.

Lack of Job Knowledge

One explanation for the lack of employment opportunities for African-Americans is that they do not have access to information about job openings, in part because of residential segregation and informal recruitment methods such as unsolicited walk-in applications, referrals from current employees and use of employment agencies (Rosenfeld 1975).

Braddock and McPartland (1987) examined African-American job-search patterns. They reasonably assumed that if an African-American graduated from a segregated high school, they lived in a predominantly black area and had fewer white contacts than did blacks graduating from integrated schools. Consequently, blacks who lived in segregated environments would tend to use segregated networks to obtain job leads. The authors found that use of segregated networks led to poorer-paying, more segregated jobs. Desegregated networks lead to better-paying, less segregated work. In other words, segregation in schooling and housing affects the quality of job information available to blacks. The problem of information is compounded because many of the fastest job growth areas are in the largely white suburban areas of major metropolitan areas.

Geographic Immobility

Many African-Americans live in areas of the country that have undergone substantial economic restructuring, particularly the larger Northern urban areas. Consequently, the manufacturing jobs they aspired to and were qualified for have been growing very slowly—if at all. In an ideal labor market, individuals could easily move to places with better job prospects. However, some individuals are bound to areas of low opportunities and, therefore, will be unable to take advantage of opportunities elsewhere.

While a theoretical link between residence and lack of employment opportunities seems strong, the empirical evidence is weak. Ellwood (1986) found that black employment rates were not significantly influenced by residential location or by commuting distances.

Wage Rigidities

Wage rigidities combine with the previously discussed productivity argument to suggest another explanation for black-white employment differences. If wages are set above the equilibrium level, more individuals will be seeking jobs than there are jobs available. By definition unemployment will result.

The scope for setting wages above the equilibrium level goes far beyond minimum wage laws. Wages are generally sticky downward in the American economy. Collective bargaining agreements and custom also tend to keep wages above the equilibrium.

When wages are rigid and a surplus of job candidates exists, someone must decide who among the qualified candidates will get the jobs. Criteria could include excessive educational requirements, use of informal friendship and "old-boy" networks and outright (though often subtle) discrimination. Each of the above techniques for rationing jobs is likely to work in favor of whites over blacks.

A strength of the wage rigidity hypothesis is that it often appears that blacks are disproportionately excluded from jobs where wages appear to be well above market levels and job qualifications are vague, management and supervisory jobs are examples. However, by itself, the wage rigidity theory fails to explain why blacks should be disproportionately disadvantaged (the additional assumption of discrimination is needed to do that), nor does it explain why wages are persistently above equilibrium levels in some sectors and not in others.

Overt Discrimination

The most simple and direct explanation of black-white employment differentials is discrimination. However, discrimination is a difficult behavior pattern to document because it can be subtle. Recently, courts have made it more difficult to prove legally that discrimination exists by limiting the admissibility of statistical data indicating discrimination. However, economists have demonstrated the existence of overt discrimination in many studies. These studies cannot pinpoint individual acts of discrimination with a clear victim and an identified beneficiary (which is what the courts appear to be demanding), they identify institutional patterns of discrimination. These studies document institutional racism.

Braddock and McPartland (1987) collected data on hiring practices among firms and selected worker characteristics, such as race, sex, educational attainment, and academic test scores. They found that employer's ratings of a candidate's ability to perform various jobs were influenced by race after controlling for the applicant's non-racial characteristics. They found that white workers are more likely to be found in good jobs even after accounting for individual non-racial differences. Their findings provide consistent evidence of discrimination for jobs requiring a high school education. The findings are important, since most jobs fall in this category. However, less evidence of discrimination was found among jobs requiring a college degree. These results may have implications for the class-race issue if it is assumed that college-educated African-Americans have fewer low-classed behavioral characteristics.

African-Americans are also discriminated against as candidates for internal promotion. The search for internal candidates takes three primary forms: (1) encouraging specific employees to apply, (2) directly offering the job to an employee without a search, and (3) posting or circulating a written vacancy notice. Braddock and McPartland (1987) found that the more open the process (such as circulation of a written notice), the greater the likelihood that African-Americans will be promoted.

Shulman (1987) provided data that attributed the narrowing wage gap and the widening employment gap to discrimination. He suggested that it is easier to discriminate against African-Americans in hiring than in compensation because hiring is a subjective judgment, where it is difficult to prove discrimination, particularly in a specific instance. Consequently, he concluded that "[e]mployers may thus choose to satisfy the wage provision of Title VII of the Civil Rights Act while shirking the employment provisions." He pointed out that the ratio of employment to wage complaints filed with the Equal Employment Opportunity Commission [EEOC] increased from 6.81 in 1978 to 9.21 in 1982. While recognizing that not all complaints are valid, the increase in the types of complaints suggests that the way African-Americans are being discriminated against is changing.

Further evidence that discrimination is a major employment barrier is provided by Heckman and Payner (1989). They showed that federal anti-discrimination policies contributed to the improvement of black job performance in manufacturing in South Carolina in the mid-1960s. Even accounting for other possible explanations for the success of African-American workers in manufacturing, federal anti-discrimination policy appears to have promoted the job prospects for African-Americans. There was evidence of greater African-American employment in counties that sold more goods to the federal government and thus were more sensitive to EEOC regulations. Since anti-discrimination policy improved the job picture for blacks, it may be inferred that discrimination was an impediment.

Smith and Welch (1989) showed that minority representation expanded more rapidly among firms that were required to report to the EEOC on hiring practices than firms not required to report. Minority employment expanded particularly fast in managerial and professional occupations. Their findings can be attributed to the lesser ability of reporting firms to discriminate. However, critics of affirmative action programs could argue that the Smith and Welch findings reflect the fact that reporting firms hired unqualified African-Americans ("unqualified" is almost impossible to define rigorously for most jobs) simply to please the EEOC.

Finally, Boston (1988) has shown that African-American workers are disproportionately overrepresented in secondary labor markets, that is in jobs with low wages and benefits, poor working conditions and high turnover. Conversely, they are underrepresented in primary labor markets that have high pay and benefits, chances for career advancement, well-defined work rules and low turnover. Moreover, when he examined mobility patterns between sectors, Boston found that 60.9 percent of whites who were in the secondary labor market and changed jobs remained in the secondary labor market. However, for blacks he found that 76.2 percent of those who were in the secondary sector and changed jobs remained in that sector.

CONCLUSION

Today the African-American community is facing an economic crisis of grave proportions. While a few African-Americans have joined the ranks of the middle class the vast majority of African-Americans live either below the poverty line or just above the poverty line. Evidence presented in the first part of this chapter indicated that African-Americans suffer disproportionately from unemployment and are more likely to end up in low-paying jobs.

During the 1970s and the early 1980s, many economists and policy makers argued that the basic solution to the economic crisis facing the African-American community was to create more jobs. Their philosophy can best be expressed in the saying that "a rising tide lifts all boats." However, after eight years of expansion in the 1980s—the longest peace-time expansion in U.S. history—the relative economic position of most African-Americans has actually deteriorated. Labor force participation among African-American males has declined relative to whites, unemployment relative to whites has increased, and the black to white earnings ratio for male workers has deteriorated annually since 1979 (Smith and Welch 1989). For those lucky enough to have a job at all, the odds are that most work in low-paying jobs with few benefits and no prospect for career advancement.

Education is currently center stage as a solution to the African-American employment problem. While education can increase worker productivity and hence job prospects, it is doubtful that improvements in education alone will solve the economic crisis in the African-American community. It is true that many of the new high-paying jobs being created require more education. At the same time, economic restructuring is resulting in the creation of low-wage, unskilled jobs in occupations where African-Americans are well represented. Given the nature of hiring practices, it is likely that most African-Americans will continue to end up in low-paying jobs in the absence of strong, deliberate policies to avoid such outcomes. Anti-discrimination laws must be strictly enforced.

Anti-discrimination and affirmative action programs have worked, as evidenced by the progress made during the mid-1960s and early 1970s when government was more active in regulating and enforcing civil rights laws. However, even during periods of active enforcement, institutional barriers and overt discrimination were reduced but not eliminated. During recent periods of lax enforcement, problems of employment discrimination have worsened.

A comprehensive solution to employment problems experienced by African-Americans must include a series of measures designed to wipe out the effects of discrimination through the use of affirmative action and strengthening enforcement of civil rights legislation. Given the current disadvantaged state of African-Americans in the labor market, civil rights enforcement must be supported by an economy and society that generates opportunities for advancement.

NOTES

1.   The labor force (LF) is composed of all people who are either unemployed (U) but actively seeking work, and those who are employed (E). Therefore: $LF = U + E$. The unemployment rate (UR) is the portion of the LF who are unemployed and actively seeking work: $UR = (1 - E/LF) \times 100$. The dependency rate (DR) measures the portion of the population (P) that is dependent upon the earnings of others: $DR = (1 - E/P) \times 100$. The labor force participation rate $(LFPR)$ is the portion of the population that is part of the labor force: $LFPR = (LF/P) \times 100$ or $(E + U/P) \times 100$.

2.   The economy has continued to grow since 1988 and growth has been very slow. Thus, 1988 was not technically a cycle peak. The peak most likely occurred in late June or July 1990.

3.   For instance, the 1.25 for technical and related support occupations in the other service industry indicates that there are 1.25 times as many whites in that category as would be expected if whites and blacks were evenly distributed among all occupational groups.

4.   Sales occupations appear to be an exception to the tendency for blacks to be overrepresented in lower-paying occupations. A possible explanation for this variation may be that sales is itself an occupation with a bimodal earnings distribution. At the top are the 55 percent of sales workers who work fulltime and earned annual incomes of $22,209 in 1988. At the bottom are the part-time workers, who have average annual earnings of only $3,093.

5.   The middle- and better blue-collar occupations include the Department of Labor's groups of precision production, craft and repair; machine operators, assemblers and inspectors; and transportation and material moving occupations.

6.   Another type of behavior that affects African-Americans but is not directly related to job performance may be cultural traits such as mannerisms, diction, dress, and so forth, that are negatively perceived by employers. In some cases, such behaviors may not bother an employer directly but the employer may fear the behavior will be viewed poorly by customers or co-workers. Behaviors of this type are included in the discussion of arbitrary discrimination.

7.   The historical burden of racism, however, is seen as an important reason for a disproportionate number of African-Americans being part of the underclass. In addition, Wilson emphasizes the disappearance of manufacturing employment opportunities in Northern cities as another reason for the growth in the urban underclass.

REFERENCES

Bielby, W.T. 1987. Modern prejudice and institutional barriers to equal employment opportunity for minorities. *Journal of Social Issues* 43(1): 79–84.
Boston, T.D. 1988. *Race, class and conservatism*. Boston, MA: Boston University, Hyman).
Braddock, J.H. II and J.M. McPartland. 1987. How minorities continue to be excluded from equal employment opportunities: research on labor market and institutional barriers. *Journal of Social Issues* 43(1): 5–39.
Danziger, S. and P. Gottschalk. 1987. Earnings inequality, the spatial concentration of poverty, and the underclass. *American Economic Review* 77(2): 211–15.
Doeringer, P. and M. Piore. 1971. *Internal labor markets & manpower analysis*. Lexington: D.C. Heath
Ellwood, D.T. 1986. The spatial mismatch hypothesis: are there teenage jobs missing in the ghetto? In *The black youth employment crisis*, R.B. Freeman and H.J. Holzer, eds., 147–85. Chicago: University of Chicago Press.
Franklin, J. and J. P. Blair. 1983. The role of mobility in national urban policy. *Journal of the American Planning Association* 49(3): 307–15.
Goodwin, L. 1972. *Do the poor want to work*. Washington, DC: The Brookings Institution.

Gottschalk, P. 1990. AFDC participation across generations. *American Economic Review* 80(2): 367–71.

Harrison, B. and B. Bluestone. 1988. *The great u-turn*. New York: Basic Books.

Heckman, J.J. and B.S. Payner. 1989. Determining the impact of federal anti-discrimination policy on the economic status of blacks: a study of South Carolina. *American Economic Review* 79(1): 138–72.

Hill, E.W. 1988. Differences in the dependency rate among states in 1985. *Economic Development Quarterly* 2(3): 217–35.

Holzer, H. 1986. Black youth nonemployment: duration and job search. In *The black youth employment crisis*, R. Freeman and H. Holzer, eds., 23–70. Chicago: The University of Chicago Press.

Hout, M. 1984. Occupational mobility of black men: 1962 to 1973. *American Sociological Review* 49(June): 308–22.

Kasarda, J.D. 1989. Urban industrial transition and the underclass. *Annals of the American Academy of Political and Social Sciences* 501: 26–47.

Rose, H.M. 1979. The diminishing urban promise: economic retrenchment, social policy, and race. In *Fiscal retrenchment and urban policy*, J. Blair and D. Nachmias, eds., 159–83. Beverly Hills: Sage Publications.

Rosenfeld, C. 1975. Jobseeking methods used by american workers. *Monthly Labor Review* 98(8): 39–42.

Ryan, W. 1976. *Blaming the victim*. New York: Vintage Books.

Shulman, S. 1987. Discrimination, human capital, and black-white unemployment: evidence from cities. *The Journal of Human Resources* 22(3): 362–76.

Smith, J.P. and F.R. Welch. 1989. Black economic progress after Myrdal. *Journal of Economic Literature* 28(June): 519–64.

U.S. Department of Labor. Bureau of Labor Statistics. 1986. *Unemployment of black workers*. Washington, DC: U.S. Department of Labor.

U.S. Department of Labor. 1990. *News Release*, 90–344 (July 6).

Viscusi, K. 1986. Market incentives for criminal behavior. In *The black youth employment crisis*, R. Freeman and H. Holzer, eds., 301–46. Chicago: The University of Chicago Press.

Wilson, W.J. 1987. *The declining significance of race*. Chicago: University of Chicago Press.

———. 1988. The ghetto underclass and the social transformation of the inner city. *The Black Scholar* (May/June): 15.

6 The (Un)Housed City: Racial Patterns of Segregation, Housing Quality and Affordability

PHILLIP L. CLAY

The fortieth anniversary of the Housing Act of 1949 passed recently with hardly any acknowledgement. That historic legislation committed the nation to a policy that every American family should have "... a decent home ... in a suitable environment." In 1990, the nation is far from this goal, although some progress has been made. In 1990, as in 1949, African-Americans lag behind their white counterparts to the extent that the goal has been achieved.

Housing is a major component in the bundle of goods that define social and economic well-being for American families. It is an indicator of the social status of families and individuals. It is the largest investment most people make and comprises the majority of most families' net worth. It is also the largest part of most households' budgets, generally around 20 percent, but often a third or more for families of limited means.

The lack of available affordable housing and its poor quality forces families into a serious crisis or places them at great inconvenience and risk. The great expense of housing amounts to a burden that can override other important aspects of well-being for poor families, such as proper nutrition or medical care. Even decent, affordable housing in a deteriorated, crime-ridden environment is not sufficient; families living in such a community may well be victims of a disinvested and hostile environment where services, including education, are often of poor quality. While the family may not have a housing problem, it is deprived of the services and amenities commonly associated with housing.

Despite the many problems that remain, all population groups have made substantial progress in housing over the last 40 years. Though the ill-housed are well below the one-third of the population that President Roosevelt saw during

PHILLIP L. CLAY

the Depression, America still has a long way to go: more than 10 million households (out a total of more than 100 million) are still are inadequately housed or,
to an increasing extent, not housed at all. Black households have continued to be
especially deprived and, even though their housing conditions (as illustrated in
Table 6.1) have improved over the last 40 years and some in recent years, the
gap between blacks and whites continues (Schwartz, et al. 1988; U.S. Bureau of
the Census. Housing and Urban Development 1988).

The steady progress blacks experienced relative to whites over this longer
period has, however, been short-circuited in the last decade. For example, during the 1980s, for the first time, the rate of homeownership for the entire population, and especially for blacks, has declined as poverty and economic mar-
ginality for the population have increased (Joint Center for Housing Studies
1990). While housing affordability is not a problem limited to African-

TABLE 6.1
Selected Housing and Economic Statistics for Blacks and Whites in Urban Areas

	Blacks	*Whites*
Percent poor:		
1959	55	18
1969	32	10
1979	31	9
1988	32	10
Median income of renter (1989) in $000s	$13,100	$22,600
Percent of renter households in poverty (1989)	39	19
Median net worth of renter families (1988)	$735	$7729
Ratio of black-to-white income:		
1970	.61	
1980	.58	
1988	.57	
Percent with inadequate units 1975/1983	28/22	8/7
Percent households with any housing problem (1975/83)	52/51	8/7
Percent with housing cost burden greater than 25% 1975/83	16/24	13/19
Percent of homeless adults (1989)	41	46
Percent homeownership (1989)	45	70
Percent qualifying for home purchase in 1986 (based on 20% downpayment	1.5	16.9

Sources: Joint Center, 1990 and Committee on Ways and Means, 1990.

Americans, the pattern of segregation and ongoing discrimination makes access to housing an additional problem African-Americans face on top of other difficulties caused by poverty, which African-Americans face to a greater extent than whites. Unlike whites, blacks are not able to maneuver the market or move freely among sectors of the market to maximize housing satisfaction. This dual burden of race and poverty leads to more serious housing problems for blacks.

The purpose of this chapter is to look at the housing problems of blacks and analyze their origins.[1] This assessment starts with well-known statistics on racial inequality in housing and views the sources of these inequalities from several different perspectives. The chapter makes traditional analyses where measures of housing progress and deprivation are noted. It also takes a more indirect view and emphasizes the changes in policy and in the environment surrounding the housing market that affect opportunities for housing progress. This approach enables assessment of both the shifting nature of the problems blacks face and the changing effectiveness of various approaches to deal with the problems. Some of these issues are continued in Chapter 14.

ORIGINS OF HOUSING PROBLEMS AFRICAN-AMERICANS FACE

The problems African-Americans face in obtaining shelter do not arise solely from changes in the market; broader social, economic, and political trends are important as well. Table 6.1 provides some statistics that compare blacks and whites on a variety of socioeconomic and housing indicators. When these numbers and trends are considered, it should come as no surprise that there are problems, and that on some dimensions they are becoming worse.

For example, more than half of black households (three-quarters of very low-income households) experience substandard, crowded housing, or pay more than 30 percent of their income to obtain housing. An estimated 1 to 3 million persons are homeless, with the most rapid growth in the number of homeless being families (as opposed to single adults). African-Americans form the largest ethnic/racial group in this expanding homeless population (Committee on Ways and Means 1990). The surprise is that the problems are not more pervasive.[2] What explains the continuing problems African-Americans have with housing?

Increasing Poverty

After a 20-year decline in the national poverty rate (from a rate of 20 percent in the 1960s), the nation experienced a major increase in the incidence of poverty among all households—from just under 12 percent in 1970 to as much as 15 percent in the early 1980s and 13 percent in 1989. More than 30 percent of blacks were in poverty in 1989, representing a very slight increase over 1980. In major cities, such as Cleveland, Detroit, and Newark, the incidence of poverty is even higher—as much as 40 percent of African-American households. This higher incidence of poverty among blacks compared to whites has remained steady in recent years steady despite the recent 7 years of general economic expansion.

The difference between how black and white families operate in the market is wide and extends well beyond economic features to demographic features. African-American families, for example, are younger, larger, and more often the victims of small shifts in the economy (i.e., faster unemployment in recessions and slower rebound in recoveries). They have fewer family resources or wealth to leverage and rely on when problems arise. They are less likely to have more than one wage earner in the household or a worker whose income is rising in real terms. They are twice as likely to have a household head who is unemployed (see also Ch. 4).

There has been a large increase in the percentage of children who live in poor households, especially among blacks. In 1986, 15 percent of white children and 43 percent of black children lived in poor families (U.S. Bureau of the Census 1988). This is direct evidence for the concentration of poor black children in low-income neighborhoods and for the concentration of black poverty in African-American families (as opposed to individuals, for example). These households have limited resources to devote to housing. Any sacrifice for housing cuts into other needs children have.

Emergence of Underclass Neighborhoods

The African-American community has experienced a major class shift in the last decade. Table 6.2 shows that the middle class has expanded steadily, while the non-poor working class has declined as a share of the black population. The poor, whether working or not, have expanded steadily; this expansion is most significant for the resulting concentrations.

During the 1980s, America experienced a significant increase in areas of black poverty concentration. While the increase in black poverty has followed the general pattern, the percent of poor in inner-city areas has increased, and the number of such concentrations increased sufficiently to prompt use of the term "underclass" to describe this persistently poor population concentrated in urban ghettoes. Various authors have captured the nature of this population and the areas in which they live (Wilson 1987; Bane and Jajorsky 1986; Gephart 1989).

All of the difficulties of producing and maintaining housing in cities are compounded in these areas, which are not only abandoned by whites, merchants, and investors, but by non-poor blacks as well. The burden of supporting

TABLE 6.2

Social Class of Black Families, 1969–1986

	1969	*1983*	*1986*
Upper class	3	4	9
Middle class	25	25	27
Working class (non-poor)	44	35	34
Working class (poor)	14	14	—
Non-working poor ("underclass")	14	23	30

Source: Based on calculations of U.S. Census data in, Andrew Billingsley, "Understanding African-American Family Diversity," in *The State of Black America 1990* (New York: The National Urban League, 1990), 97.

a housing submarket falls on people who lack sufficient resources to be effective consumers.

The Accelerating Cost of Housing

Over the last 15-year period when real incomes for most Americans were declining, housing prices, rents, interest rates and other aspects of housing costs (i.e., land, labor, etc.) leapt forward and have remained at historically high levels, as measured by the Consumer Price Index [CPI]. The CPI measure shows that the increase for housing exceeded the rise overall prices. In some places (such as the Northeast and California) and in some years (1986–1989), the housing cost increases were much more dramatic, with several consecutive years of double-digit increases (Case, et al. 1989). The new development here is that housing is now more costly relative to income for a broad range of households, not just for blacks and the poor.

This broadening of the housing constituency puts housing on state and local governmental agendas, in some cases for the first time. The broadening of constituency originated first to assist families who were not the target of the federal housing policy. These included mainly first-time homebuyers. The state and local agendas were stretched as federal resources shrank and communities found themselves with demands from the low-income needy. Blacks, as a significant element of that group, looked to states for relief that had historically been federal.[3] Less than a dozen of the 50 states made more than a token response (Terner and Cook 1990.) What some states (and cities) did took very much the character of helping non-poor, non-central city families deal with affordability.

Neighborhood Disinvestment

African-Americans are concentrated in major cities such as Chicago, Los Angeles, New York, and Washington, where there has been an escalation in the cost of housing, including prices and rents in existing housing in traditional inner-city, low-income areas. Sometimes prices move in connection with middle-class upgrading (gentrification), which leads to displacement or rising prices that overburden incumbent residents.

African-Americans are also concentrated in Midwest and Southern central cities, where housing prices were moderate to depressed throughout the 1980s. Previously in these cities, there was less incentive for housing investment amid the disinvestment in the economic sector. Housing was often abandoned. With more moderate costs, housing conditions and quality continue to be problems in these cities (Clay 1989). New housing proliferates in the suburbs. The fact that prices and rents in the city are low means there is little investment basis for the expansion of housing opportunities. Low income can only support low rents while costs and interest rates rise. Blacks, who could have, moved to formerly all-white areas. As a result, formerly all-black areas (including working-class areas) have become severe pockets of poverty.

Critical to the needs of African-Americans in both expanding and depressed settings is the preservation of existing housing resources on which they rely but which are at risk of loss (Clay 1987). The loss to the subsidized occurs when contracts and use restrictions expire. Without the protection of contracts, the vast majority (up to 80 percent) of federally subsidized housing would be lost to low-income use over the next decade.[4] Further, erosion of the private stock is also likely to occur as quality declines and there is not the rent potential to justify private, unassisted rehabilitation.

Segregation and Discrimination

Having affordable housing is important, but it is also important that African-Americans have access to that housing and that current patterns of segregation be disrupted. Residential isolation is associated with other types of isolation, such as isolation from quality schools and responsive public services.

No comprehensive assessment has been made of the exact status of housing desegregation since 1980. The 1980 census is the last date for which comprehensive data are available. The 1990 census will allow America to test how much progress it has made with respect to segregation. Until these data are available, only speculative estimates can be made.

Any progress in residential desegregation made during the 1980s will prove to have been limited and selective (Clay 1979).[5] The 1990 census will show some additional shifts of blacks from rural areas to metropolitan areas and, to a modest degree, from central cities to the suburbs. This latter trend often occurs, however, in a manner that does little for desegregation and simply extends central-city patterns of segregation into adjacent suburbs or leapfrogs to traditional low-income suburban areas (Lake 1981). The census, therefore, will probably reveal continued high levels of segregation and perhaps even an increasing level in some cities (Wilkerson 1989). The census may also reflect the rise of new and more densely populated areas of black poverty.

While we have to wait to see what the census reveals about the patterns of segregation and the extent to which the pattern might have changed, a number of studies have documented the powerful and persistent presence of discrimination in urban and suburban housing markets. A review of 71 housing audits reveals that racial discrimination continues to be a serious national problem. African-Americans attempting to buy homes face, on average, a 20 percent chance of encountering discrimination. Apartment-seekers face, on average, a 50 percent chance (Galster 1990a). There is also considerable evidence to suggest that racial steering occurs (Galster 1990b).[6] While there is debate over how best to do the analysis in this area and what the statistical data means (Clark 1989), the conclusion that there is a fair housing problem is widely shared.

Absence of National Policy

Given this evidence of housing problems, since 1980 the United States has not had a national policy or set of programs to address problems described in the sections above. The last decade is the only time in post-war history when this has been true. America now produces fewer than 30,000 new public houses or federally-subsidized units each year compared to an average of more than 150,000 units per year during the late 1970s. These subsidized units served not only to fill the critical gaps of low-income housing supply,[7] but also represented a major resource for minority households.[8]

If anything, the 1980s *de facto* policy has been one of retrenchment. For example, in public and assisted housing where a disproportionate number of the beneficiaries are African-American, programs have been cut more than 80 percent since 1980 (Schwartz, et al. 1988; Palmer and Sawhill 1982; Levitan 1985). While funding for vouchers/certificates increased significantly during the 1980s, these programs neither expanded desegregated opportunities (Struyk 1990) nor increased the supply of private affordable rental units.[9]

Studies also show that efforts to use public policy over the last 20 years have not met with notable success in achieving desegregation. Certificates and vouchers that were supposed to allow central-city black families to move to suburban housing have not produced the desired result. Affordable housing programs produced dwellings mainly in black areas because white areas resisted efforts to site housing in their areas. State and local programs have not targeted the poor. The result of special efforts to desegregate public housing or to disperse blacks in suburban communities over the decade have been modest at best (Struyk 1990).

KEY HOUSING TRENDS FOR THE 1990s

A number of developments in housing and real estate have significant meaning for housing opportunity and status for African-Americans. The past has not been productive for open access or equal opportunity. There have been problems with the nature of the market and structure of the housing system. Moreover, the future seems to include some of the same problems as well as new challenges. The new (and some old) features that define this environment are described below.

1. Increasingly, decisions about housing and real estate development in major cities will be made in the context of developing national or even global real estate and capital markets. While not every aspect of the development process will be driven by these extra-local forces, many, such as capital supply and interest rates, will be so driven (Lachman 1988). As a result, the extent and nature of residential development will be influenced by these international concerns, not necessarily by community needs and resources or U.S. policies, unless America returns to a policy of sheltering housing from shifts in the economy.[10]

    For African-American communities that suffered from disinvestment when decisions were local, the prospects for sensitive attention in a new, non-localized era are not encouraging without conscientious policy initiatives to make it so.

2. Trends in development finance described above also have meaning for housing producers and developers. In many areas, private investment in rental housing and in low- and moderate-cost housing for sale, is declining. Private investors increasingly are interested in commercial development or high-quality residential development. Tax disincentives and interests rates as well as alternative investments depress private investment interest in housing that would be of moderate cost. For black communities, this preference further reduces the prospect for private subsidized development. There is increasing reliance by government on nonprofit community-based development when there are public incentives, since fewer profits make firms less interested

(National Congress for Community Economic Development [NCCED] 1988; Clay 1990).

3. New housing will be in less demand in the 1990s for a variety of reasons. There is the imminent reduction in demand pressure caused by the end of the baby-boom generation entering adulthood (Masnick 1989). Upgrading existing housing will become more significant as households adapt housing units to family change and as turnover and rehabilitation combine to meet 20 percent or more of the new demand.

A particular casualty of this de-emphasis of new construction will be housing production targeted toward first-time homebuyers who will find it increasingly difficult to afford a new home and will turn instead to existing housing that might otherwise have filtered down.[11] In the past, new construction and the chain of opportunities it set off have been critical in opening new areas and bringing people into ownership who did not have the opportunity previously.

African-Americans did not benefit from this process in the 1950s, 1960s, and 1970s. The housing—old and new—often was available only in segregated areas and in the context of such exploitation as "steering" or "redlining." With more fair housing enforcement, matters might be different in the 1990s.

In the present environment, the nation will have to rely on African-Americans to penetrate existing communities and to deal with the existing pattern, culture of segregation, attitudes of exclusion, and practices of discrimination that are in place.

In addition, as the rental housing crisis (defined as a shortage of affordable rental units) continues in some markets and the best units are converted to condominiums, the rental sector may also experience change (i.e., tighter markets, higher rents, and little net addition to the rental stock).[12] Tenants will have a harder time finding quality units they can afford. Landlords can be more selective in choosing tenants (a development that sometimes provides a "cover" for discrimination). Families will have narrower choices and the high rents will result in a declining ability on the part of families to save in order to make the transition to homeownership.

Some exceptions to this general proposition may be in the South and parts of the West (except California) where prices are more moderate and where population growth still supports a broad spectrum of supply response. Since African-Americans are a significant part of the southern market, guiding this development and assuring equal housing opportunity will be especially important there. Given that the South continues to grow, the potential for substantial desegregation may be higher in the suburban South than in the metropolitan areas of the Northeast and the Midwest.

4.   As federal deregulation continues, local regulations in the development area become increasingly more important in influencing the cost of and access to housing. Because of local tax pressures, however, regulations will be increasingly used to support local fiscal and growth goals (Clay and Frieden 1984).[13] Local government actions, such as minimum lot zoning, environmental restrictions, and high development fees designed to limit growth or pass on to the developer (and buyers) the cost of infrastructure, all have the effect of raising the cost of housing and/or reducing the number of units produced (Frieden 1979). Either way, local regulation may become a barrier to developing affordable housing and economic (and, therefore, racial) dispersal. While some courts have prohibited such regulatory restrictions, these precedents have not been applied nationally.[14]

5.   As America enters a second decade of declining incidence of homeownership, especially among young people, African-Americans and low- and moderate-income households, there will be increasing political pressure to bring ownership within reach of low- and moderate-income families. Whether this pressure will percolate to the national level remains to be seen. Congress continues to wrestle with the deficit and the after effects of the Department of Housing and Urban Development and savings and loan scandals. As of this writing, both houses of Congress have passed (different) bills to address some of these issues to provide modest resources for poor and for first-time buyers.[15] While the small program will not change the overall dimensions of the need, after a decade of inattention to housing the legislation, if enacted, would be the proverbial "camel's nose under the tent."

6.   Large central cities have an uncertain future (Clay 1989). Some will continue to be areas of economic gain or stability (not decline), especially in the downtown. Economic development supports both economic opportunity for families and creation of a fiscal product to support state and local housing initiatives. The possibility for such a trend will not be spread evenly across urban America. If past history is indicative, it will be strongest in about a dozen industrial states and in the large metropolitan areas. In the near future (through the mid-1990s), the projections are for less development. Regional recessions (if not a national one), overbuilt markets, and corporate restructuring all point to a decline in all types of construction (Cahners Economics 1990).

Rapidly expanding foreign investment and periods of hyper-development (i.e., "economic booms") in central cities may return in the latter 1990s. These activities present both an opportunity and a risk. The opportunity arises from the momentum generated by investment, which can spur development of neighborhoods as well as residential opportunity in the downtown. On the other hand, there is the risk that downtown and industrial development will drain resources that might otherwise have been used for neighborhood development or divert resources that might have been used for that purpose. This especially will be the case in cities that are not willing to make links between the two development thrusts.

African-Americans in these cities have often found themselves displaced as white, middle-class households rediscovered and bid up prices and rents in the neighborhoods that blacks had used to improve their housing. While the extent of the urban renaissance (sometimes referred to as gentrification) was not overwhelming except in a few cities, it did occur to some degree in all of the cities whose downtown areas were revitalized. It is also true that such cities were in a better position than most to initiate their own programs for housing development, using their own funds or funds that came from programs such as linkage.

Blacks have not found the same opportunities that the revived cities gave to the middle class generally and to investors, developers, and others specifically, who used their resources to take advantage of the speculation frenzy. In the last decade, poverty rates may have stabilized, but they did not fall significantly despite seven years of economic expansion.

Taken together what do these trends mean for African-Americans? It is hard to imagine that the 1990s will duplicate the sustained level of economic expansion experienced in the 1980s. With a slower pace of economic expansion comes limitations in policy flexibility and more cautious private initiatives. The slower pace makes the future uncertain and offers the possibility that the period will see the further expansion of income inequality, which stands parallel to, and partly defines, racial inequality. While under different political agendas, this might not be fatal for public initiatives; under the present regime—federal and local—public efforts to help African-Americans or cities, in general, will be harder to enact.

While efforts to help all needy people may de-racialize public policy, there is no reason to believe that there is a broad constituency for helping the poor. Pressure to help the middle class may be more politically attractive but the benefits to African-Americans are likely to be, on the whole, small since the black middle class is smaller proportionately than the white middle class and because helping the middle class can be harmful to the poor. Such efforts can also reinforce class (and, therefore, racial) privilege.

CONCLUSION

This chapter underscores the problems blacks face in finding and affording decent housing. It also notes the special obstacles created by discrimination. More important, the chapter suggests that demographic, institutional, and other trends make the problem more complicated and embedded (in the economy, the class structure, regional differences, etc.) than is often recognized. Despite what is widely believed to be more racial openness than a generation ago, the racial problems of housing do not seem to be waning. The policy issues are explored in Chapter 14; however, it ought to be clear from this discussion that policy will have to be incorporated in the housing market, in the political economy of cities, and in creative fair housing initiatives that address the multiple and subtle ways in which African-Americans are sheltered differently than whites.

NOTES

1. The author gratefully acknowledges the research assistance of Angela Goode for her help in preparing this chapter.

2. While there is no census of the homeless, all the studies suggest that blacks are disproportionately represented and that blacks are especially prominent among homeless families who are the fastest-growing segment of the population. There are an estimated 800,000 people who have signed up for housing in the 25 cities surveyed 2 years ago by the National Conference of Mayors. These and others who have basic housing needs and no long-term source of relief are the "pre-homeless" (National Alliance to End Homelessness 1988).

3. State and local programs in the dozen states where significant and sustained initiatives have been made were targeted to working-class and middle-class households. Except in California, Massachusetts, and New York, the only benefit to low-income households was a leverage of federal funds, not the state's own funds.

4. There are four million units of housing developed under various programs that over the next decade face the expiration of use restrictions that protect the poor or face the end of subsidy contracts that cover part of the operating cost. Public housing is also at risk as some communities move to demolish it and others are allowing the units to be severely undermaintained (Clay 1987).

5. Based on anecdotal information, it is expected, for example, that there will be an opening of selected suburban communities near major cities and a reduction in isolation in selected middle-class areas in cities. Some closing of the North-South gaps are also suggested by the anecdotal information. This progress is balanced against more numerous concentrations of very poor all-black areas, the rise of low-income black

suburbs, and the black suburbanization as black reconcentration in some communities (Clay 1979).

6. Steering is the process by which real estate agents show prospects houses or apartments in neightborhoods of their race. Whites are shown areas with no or very few blacks and blacks are shown areas where blacks are already settled. The consequence of this practice is that homeseekers have fewer choices and that segregated patterns are reinforced (Galster 1990b).

7. The importance of this housing and the risks it faces have been documented (see National Low Income Housing Preservation Commission 1988). The extent to which blacks benefit varies based on the city; but in cities with large proportions of blacks, they depend heavily on this housing.

8. The issue of over concentration of public and subsidized housing in the minority community has been a major issue since the Supreme Court ruling in the *Gautreaux* case (1972) that public and assisted housing ought not to reinforce segregation. In 1974, the Department of Housing and Urban Development attempted with limited success, through site selection criteria, to spread assisted housing around. (For a discussion of this issue, see Calamore 1979.)

9. One of the assumptions of a voucher or certificate approach is that if poor people have success to additional resources that, when combined with their private income, are sufficient to cover the market rents, then housing producers and suppliers will create and maintain units for the poor. This is in contrast to the production approach where the government subsidizes the creation of units so that the poor can afford them as in the case of public housing.

10. Prior to 1979 with the advent of deregulation, housing was protected by a number of special provisions that kept interest rates low, provided for smaller down payments, and offered a counter-cyclical stimulus to the economy. Housing investment enjoyed preferential investment features and Congress voted a steady stream of subsidies.

11. America has created a system where this is likely. The reduction in rate of ownership in recent years is not a cyclical feature but appears to be built into the system. For example, deregulation allows lenders to feel less obligated to assist marginal families in becoming owners and because home prices in relation to incomes have changed dramatically. Blacks who have always lagged and several features discussed in this chapter exaggerate this tendency now—fewer intact families have the two incomes often needed, rising prices and competition (which forces up the price of previously existing affordable housing), and the higher level of savings required to enter the market.

12. One might think this pattern leads to more supply but the incentives when fully considered and weighed are quite the opposite.

13. Many communities that cannot or will not raise taxes will exact fees and impose restrictions that raise the cost of housing. Sometimes there is an environmental or a growth management justification (Frieden 1979).

14. For example, see *Burlington NAACP* v. *The Township of Mount Laurel* (Laurel II), 92 N.J. 456, A.2d 350 (1983). This case and others define an affirmative obligation on the part of suburbs to provide a range of housing options at cost within the range of the prospective residents.

15. Elements of one or both of the bills include funds for a small production pro-

gram that is leveraged by state and local funds, funds to support community-based housing developers, a program to help the poor buy their public housing units, a low-interest mortgage program, and resources and regulations to support preservation of subsidized units at risk of loss.

REFERENCES

Bane, M.J. and P. Jajorsky. 1986. Urban poverty areas: basic questions concerning prevalence, growth and dynamics. Working Paper of The JFK School of Harvard University, Cambridge, MA.
Cahners Economics. 1990. *Top U.S. construction markets for 1991.* Newton, MA: Cahners Publishing Company.
Calamore, J.O. 1979. Fair housing vs. Fair housing: the conflict between providing low-income housing in impacted areas and providing increased housing opportunities through spatial deconcentration. *Housing Law Bulletin* 9 (6) (November/December): 1–12.
Case, K. 1989. The distributional effects of housing price booms: winners and losers in Boston 1980–88. *New England Economic Review* (May/June): 3–12.
Clark, W.A.V. 1989. Residential segregation in american cities: common ground and differences in interpretation. *Population Research and Policy Review* 7:193–97.
Clay, P. 1979. The process of black suburbanization. *Urban Affairs Quarterly* (Fall): 11–14.
_____. 1987. *At-risk of loss: the endangered future of low income rental resources.* Washington, DC: Neighborhood Reinvestment Corporation.
_____. 1989. Choosing urban futures: the transformation of american cities. *Stanford Law and Policy Review* 1 (Fall): 28–43.
_____. 1990. *Mainstreaming the community builders: the challenge of expanding the capacity of nonprofit housing development organizations.* Cambridge, MA: MIT Department of Urban Studies and Planning.
Clay, P. and B. Frieden. 1984. Housing regulation and the housing consumer. *Society* (Winter).
Committee on Ways and Means. U.S. House of Representatives. 1990. *The 1990 green book: background material and data on programs within the jurisdiction of the committee on ways and means,* Appendix G. Washington, DC: U. S. Congress.
Ellwood, D. 1988. *Poor support: poverty in the american family.* New York: Basic Books.
Frieden, B. 1979. *The environmental hustle.* Cambridge MA: MIT Press.
Galster, G. 1990a. Racial discrimination in housing markets during the 1980s: a review of the audit evidence. *Journal of Planning Education and Research* 9: 165–76.
_____. 1990b. Racial steering in urban housing markets: a review of the audit evidence. *The Review of Black Political Economy* 18: 105–29.
Gephart, M. 1989. Neighborhood and communities in concentrated poverty. *Items* 43(December): 84–92.

Iredia, I. 1986. Attaining the housing goal? Unpublished paper, 19. Division of Housing and Demographic Analysis, Department of Housing and Urban Development, Washington, DC.

Joint Center for Housing Studies. 1990 *The state of the nation's housing 1990.* Cambridge, MA: Harvard University.

Lachman, L. 1988. *Decade to decade: U.S. real estate adapts to revolution in finance and demographic evolution.* New York: Schroeder Real Estate Associates.

Lake, R. 1981. *The new suburbanites: race and housing in the suburbs.* New Brunswick, NJ: Center for Urban Policy Research.

Levitan, S. 1985. *Programs in aid of the poor.* Baltimore, MD: Johns Hopkins University Press.

Masnick, G. 1989. U.S. household trends: the 1980s and beyond. Working Paper W89-1. Cambridge, MA: Joint Center for Housing Studies, Harvard University.

National Alliance to End Homelessness. 1988. *Housing and homelessness: a report of the national alliance.* Washington, DC.

National Congress for Community Economic Development (NCCED). 1988. *Against all odds: the achievements of community-based development organizations.* Washington, DC: NCCED.

National Low Income Housing Preservation Commission (NLIHPC). 1988. *Preventing the disappearance of low income housing.* Washington, DC: NLIHPC.

Palmer, J. and I. Sawhill, eds. 1982. *The Reagan experiment.* Washington, DC: The Urban Institute.

Schwartz, D., et al. 1988. *A new housing policy for America.* Philadelphia: Temple University.

Struyk, R. 1990. Race and housing: affordability and location. A paper presented at the Conference on New Perspectives on Racial Issues: Middle-Sized Metropolitan Areas. Madison, WI: University of Wisconsin.

Terner, I.D. and T. Cook. 1990. New directions for federal housing policy: the role of the states. In *Building foundations*, D. DiPasquale and I. Keyes, eds., 113–36. Philadelphia: University of Pennsylvania.

U.S. Bureau of the Census. Housing and Urban Development. 1988. *Statistical abstract of the United States.* Washington, DC: Department of Commerce, Bureau of the Census.

Wilkerson, I. 1989. Study finds segregation in cities worse than scientist imagined. *New York Times*, August 5: 6.

Wilson, W. 1987. *The truly disadvantaged.* Chicago: University of Chicago Press.

7 Race and Inner-City Education

EDWARD W. HILL and HEIDI MARIE ROCK

The United States faces a continuing educational crisis in its inner-city schools: racial isolation continues, children attending these same districts become poorer every year—increasing income and class isolation—academic achievement is unacceptably low, and drop-out rates are stubbornly and unconscionably high. Yet, there has been substantial improvement in the educational performance of minority students, when compared to majority students during the 1970s and 1980s. The problem educators face is that a substantial gap in academic performance remains and that the demands of employers are outpacing the gains of the average minority student.

Restructured advanced economies are demanding better trained labor for all but the most rudimentary positions and children who have been enrolled in inner-city school systems are, too often, not succeeding in this modern world of work (Hill and Rock 1990). The problems of inner-city education will affect the performance of the nation's economy as America looks to today's children to become tomorrow's workers.

The educational problems of America's inner-cities are not solely problems of local service delivery—problems that can be solved by better teaching techniques or technology. They are not isolated in one school district. The same set of problems occurs in city after city; they are national problems that need to be addressed in part by national policies. They also represent failures of policy not of technique. This chapter demonstrates the dimensions of the educational prob-

The authors wish to thank George Galster, Lawrence Keller, and Norman Krumholz for their comments on the chapter. The authors acknowledge partial support received from the Urban University Program of the Ohio General Assembly and Ohio's Board of Regents.

lems in America's inner-cities and the differences in the educational perfor-mance of blacks and whites. The roots of the policy failures are discussed in Chapter 17 and a solution is proposed in that chapter.

THE DILEMMA

The true measure of the success or failure of schools is not evaluated through standardized test scores; it lies in the success or failure of its attenders in the labor market. Smith and Welch (1989, p. 560) observe that

> [t]oday, the average new black worker is a high school graduate and trails his white competitor by less than a year of education . . . Dramatic improvements in the quality of black education increased the ability of blacks to translate their schooling into more dollars in the job market . . . This central role of education raises our deepest concerns about future prospects . . . The historical improvement in the quality of black school-ing resulted largely from Southern black migration to the better schools of the North and from the overall rise in quality of Southern schools. Because these trends have run their course, further improvements in black schooling depends critically on what takes place in urban black schools of the North.

They show that in 1980, for the first time in history, black inner-city male residents received lower weekly earnings than black males who lived elsewhere. They also found that from 1980 to 1985 the ratio of earnings of young black males to young white males deteriorated, a finding that has been replicated by O'Neill (1990). Smith and Welch conclude by stating that it would be "disturb-ing" if the deterioration were caused by the quality of black schooling because that would affect African-American labor market entrants over the next two decades. Their observations raise two questions:

1. Are the problems of inner-city education built on a foundation of racial and class isolation?
2. Is the quality of inner-city education deteriorating?

RACIAL AND CLASS PROFILE OF INNER-CITY PUBLIC SCHOOL STUDENTS

In 1986 the public school districts of the 25 most populous cities in the nation were responsible for the education of 5 million children (Cook 1988) (see Table 7.1). They represent 10 percent of all of the children in the nation. Public

TABLE 7.1

Selected Characteristics of the 25 Most Populous Cities, Fall 1986

Rank Order	City	Census Population Estimate	School Districts Serving the City	Number of Schools	Student Membership
1	New York, NY	7,262,700	1	978	938,606
2	Los Angeles, CA	3,259,340	2	620	601,764[a]
3	Chicago, IL	3,009,530	1	594	431,298
4	Houston, TX	1,728,910	7	385	325,257[a]
5	Philadelphia, PA	1,642,900	1	255	190,119
6	Detroit, MI	1,086,220	1	281	185,499
7	San Diego, CA	1,015,190	3	188	148,642[a]
8	Dallas, TX	1,003,520	3	207	140,569[a]
9	San Antonio, TX	914,350	14	293	207,260[a]
10	Phoenix, AZ	894,070	16	184	127,055[a]
11	Baltimore, MD	752,800	1	179	111,243
12	San Francisco, CA	749,000	1	112	64,786
13	Indianapolis, IN	719,820	1	89	57,310
14	San Jose, CA	712,080	17	202	142,815[a]
15	Memphis, TN	652,640	1	160	113,101
16	Washington, DC	626,000	1	182	85,612
17	Jacksonville, FL	609,860	1	145	102,966
18	Milwaukee, WI	605,090	1	145	90,657
19	Boston, MA	573,600	1	[b]	[b]
20	Columbus, OH	566,030	1	133	66,158
21	New Orleans, LA	554,500	1	139	84,204
22	Cleveland, OH	535,830	1	130	73,263
23	Denver, CO	505,000	1	113	60,315
24	El Paso, TX	491,800	3	128	119,430[a]
25	Seattle, WA	486,200	1	103	43,574

Notes: [a] Student membership is an aggregation of the membership over all of the school districts that serve the city. School districts do not necessarily have boundaries coterminous with a city's boundaries and often include geography beyond the city's limits. Therefore, the reported student membership may be more than the actual number of students who reside within the city.

[b] Data are not available from the state education agency.

Source: Cook, 1988, p. 5.

school districts in large central cities—central cities of Metropolitan Statistical Areas [MSAs] with populations of 400,000 or more, or with population densities of more than 6,000 per square mile—educated 11.6 percent of America's youth (see Table 7.2). Mid-sized cities (central cities of MSAs with either low population densities or with populations under 400,000) educated another 14.7 percent of America's children. In 1987, 26.3 percent of all children attended public school districts in large- or mid-sized cities (Johnson 1989). If one-third of these children were to drop out (given today's experience this is a reasonable estimate), nearly 9 percent of *all* youth, or 4.5 million potential workers, would be removed from the labor supply. These numbers alone are sufficient to compel the public to focus its attention on the performance of urban school districts.

A family's race and income largely determine their residence, which in turn exerts a strong influence over where a child attends school. Over half of school-age children of color reside in large- and mid-sized central cities while one-quarter of white children do so (Table 7.3). About one-fifth of all black youth live in non-metropolitan places; the white fraction is one-quarter. The major difference in the residential pattern of black and white youth is in the suburbs of central cities. Half of white school-age youth live in the suburbs of central cities, compared to between 22 and 25 percent of black youth.[1]

TABLE 7.2

Public School Districts in Large Central Cities

Atlanta, GA	Baltimore, MD	Berkeley, CA
Boston, MA	Bridgeport, CT	Buffalo, NY
Chicago, IL	Cleveland, OH	Columbus, OH
Dallas, TX	Denver, CO	Detroit, MI
El Paso, TX	Elizabeth, NJ	Fort Lauderdale, FL
Fort Worth, TX	Hartford, CT	Hialeah, FL
Houston, TX	Indianapolis, IN	Jacksonville, FL
Jersey City, NJ	Kansas City, MO	Long Beach, CA
Los Angeles, CA	Memphis, TN	Miami, FL
Milwaukee, WI	Minneapolis, MN	Nashville, TN
New Haven, CT	New Orleans, LA	New York City, NY
Newark, NJ	Oakland, CA	Oklahoma City, OK
Paterson, NJ	Philadelphia, PA	Phoenix, AZ
Pittsburgh, PA	Providence, RI	Rochester, NY
St. Louis, MO	San Antonio, TX	San Diego, CA
San Francisco, CA	San Jose, CA	Santa Ana, CA
Seattle, WA	Syracuse, NY	Washington, DC
Yonkers, NY		

Source: Johnson, 1989.

TABLE 7.3

Percent Distribution of
Persons Age 5 to 17 Years Enrolled in School by Residence,
October 1988

	Race (in percent)		
Northeast	White	Black	Other
Central city	25.6	72.3	49.4
Suburban	55.8	25.9	49.1
Non-metropolitan	18.6	1.8	1.6
Midwest	White	Black	Other
Central city	16.8	79.4	32.3
Suburban	43.8	18.1	38.3
Non-metropolitan	39.5	2.5	29.4
South	White	Black	Other
Central city	20.5	40.9	29.6
Suburban	43.4	21.5	45.6
Non-metropolitan	36.1	37.6	24.8
West	White	Black	Other
Central city	28.8	52.7	45.0
Suburban	50.4	43.8	39.8
Non-metropolitan	20.8	3.4	15.2

Source: Authors' calculations from the Current Population Survey, October 1990.

The locational pattern differs a bit among the four major regions of the nation: Northeast, Midwest, South and West.[2] African-American children are more concentrated in central cities in the Northeast and Midwest and are not well represented in the rural portions of these regions. There is, however, a substantial African-American presence in the non-metropolitan portion of the South. The West is characterized by a relatively large suburban presence of people of color; 43.8 percent of black school-going children and 39.8 percent of children classified as being neither white nor black (this group is composed of people of Asian heritage, native Americans, and a portion of the Hispanic population).[3]

Even though only 25 percent of all white children live in central cities, they represent nearly two-thirds of the school-going children living in these places (Table 7.4).[4] The highest concentration of white school-going children living in

TABLE 7.4

Residence of School-Going Children Ages 5–17
by Race and Ethnicity in 1986
(percentage distribution)

	White	*Black*	*Hispanic Origin*
Metropolitan	74.5	78.9	90.3
Central City	23.6	55.5	47.7
Suburb	50.9	23.4	40.1
Non-metropolitan	25.5	21.2	12.3

Note: People of Hispanic origin may be classified as being white, black or other.

Source: Enrollment Status of Persons 3 to 34 Years Old by Residence, Age, Race, Hispanic Origin: October 1986, Table 2, U.S. Bureau of the Census, Current Population Report, School Enrollment — Social and Economic Characteristics of Students, October 1986 (No. 249).

central cities is in the West, followed by the Northeast. Central-city school districts educate a much larger proportion of the population of students in the Southwest than elsewhere in the nation and a larger share of white children live in the central cities of metropolitan areas in the West than in the other regions.[5] This is most likely due to the large geographic size of western cities, especially in the Southwest. Typically, these cities are more actively engaged in annexation than eastern and mid-western cities which results in the central cities in the West containing a larger portion of their metropolitan areas' population.

The portion of the central-city school-going population which is white tends to be higher for children under 10, and ages 16 and 17. Apparently white families tend to move out of central cities when their children are old enough to attend junior high school and high school, thereby lowering their proportion in the population. Their proportion (not their numbers) then increase at ages 16 and 17; which is consistent with data presented in Table 7.5 which shows that African-American children have higher dropout rates than do white children.

Metropolitan areas are clearly segregated by race and income. Whites live in disproportionate numbers in suburbs and people of color in core cities. How do these residential patterns affect school integration? It is difficult to answer this question conclusively because the federal government does not maintain data on the racial composition of small suburban districts—even though when summed together they often account for the majority of students within a metropolitan area. Fortunately, Orfield and his collaborators have provided some insights on this question (Orfield, et al. 1987, 1988, and 1989).

TABLE 7.5

Percent Distribution of Central City Residents
Enrolled in School by Age and Race

Age	White	Black	Other
Northeast			
5–17	64.0	31.6	4.4
5–6	62.8	33.8	3.4
7–9	65.8	30.8	3.3
10–13	63.0	32.0	5.1
14–15	60.5	33.4	6.1
16–17	67.7	27.7	4.6
Midwest			
5–17	53.7	43.7	2.6
5–6	55.7	39.7	4.6
7–9	52.0	46.4	1.6
10–13	54.9	42.2	2.9
14–15	48.5	49.1	2.4
16–17	57.6	40.6	1.8
South			
5–17	59.5	38.1	2.4
5–6	58.8	38.4	2.8
7–9	55.0	41.4	3.6
10–13	62.0	36.2	1.8
14–15	62.2	36.0	1.8
16–17	59.4	38.3	2.3
West			
5–17	71.9	12.3	15.8
5–6	70.1	14.0	15.9
7–9	73.3	10.5	16.2
10–13	72.3	13.2	14.5
14–15	73.3	8.0	18.7
16–17	69.2	16.7	14.1

Source: Authors' calculations from the Current Population Survey, October 1990.

Orfield, et al. (1987) noted that the existence of many small, predominately white, suburban districts is the reason segregation within metropolitan areas is so high and that substantial integration has been achieved only in those areas with metropolitan area-wide desegregation plans. Their research indicates that there has been "no significant changes in the patterns established for both black and Hispanic desegregation by the early 1970s . . . Those states and localities with the highest level of integration tended to have very broad desegregation orders." (1987, pp. 35–36).

There has been progress since 1968. In that year 76.6 percent of black children attended schools that were at least 50 percent black, 83.9 percent of these children attended schools that were more than 90 percent black (this means that 64.3 percent of all black students attended schools where more than 90 percent of the students were black). In the 1984–1985 school year, 63.5 percent of black children attended 50 percent black schools and 33.2 percent attended 90 percent black schools (Orfield, et al. 1988). The small gains made in desegregating African-Americans since 1968 is contrasted with the increased segregation of Hispanic children. Orfield concludes that the progress made by African-Americans was at the behest of the courts.

There are two general types of metropolitan area-wide desegregation plans (Orfield, et al. 1989). The first are area-wide bussing plans based on the merger of city and suburban school districts, such as in Wilmington, Delaware, and Louisville, Kentucky. The second are desegregation plans where suburban districts are opened to voluntary enrollment by inner-city minorities. This is the key feature to the Hartford, Minneapolis, and St. Louis desegregation plans. Orfield stresses (1988) that declining white enrollments in central city and suburban districts will lessen the opportunities for integration and that desegregation does not occur by accident or by the processes of the marketplace. Desegregation only takes place through explicit, and often sweeping, efforts of the courts.

The spatial isolation of families with low incomes in central cities is a relatively recent concern. Families with choice—black, white, Hispanic and Asian—are migrating to the suburbs. Nearly 40 percent of those who moved from owner-occupied housing in Milwaukee to its suburbs in 1986 stated that concern over schools was their primary or secondary reason for moving (Bednarek 1987). Demographers in St. Louis found that the majority of persons who left the city from 1975 to 1980 were parents. They also found that ". . . overall out-migration rates for whites, 1970–80, were lower than they had been from the period 1960–70; the reverse was true for blacks. Out-migration occurred in every age group, except 55–64-year old non-white males . . . ." The city lost 74,000 black residents during the decade, while bordering St. Louis County gained 57,000 (Billingsley, et al. 1984).

The 1970s was a decade where black families gained access to the suburbs. This does not mean that suburban America is desegregated. It means that substantial numbers of black families have an expanded, but still restricted, range of residential choices (Hodgkinson 1985; Kain 1987).

The Community Advisory Committee (1985) to the St. Louis Public Schools concluded that the city has become less a place for families and is increasingly becoming a community made up of small households of all ages without children, black female head-of-households with children, a disproportionate number of whom are below the poverty level; an increasing percentage of young, highly-educated professionals, and an increasing concentration of elderly households . . . . (p. 7)

In 1987 the Council of Great City Schools, which represents 45 of the largest urban school districts, reported that 33 percent of all black youth, 27 percent of Hispanic youth and 20 percent of Asian youth were enrolled in their members' districts.[6] Of the pupils in these districts, 80 percent are eligible for subsidized lunches and 33 percent come from families receiving public assistance. These districts confront enormous dropout problems and are the focal point of the group that Wilson (1987) calls the truly disadvantaged, and Ricketts and Sawhill (1988) would call the children of the underclass. Orfield and his colleagues stated the problem best in their 1987 report:

Whatever may be the roots of the "urban underclass" it is certainly true that its children go to schools that are almost totally segregated by race and class and have no viable connection to any paths of mobility in education or employment. It may well be that the children being socialized and educated in these underclass schools are even more comprehensively isolated from mainstream middle-class society than were the black children of the South whose problems led to the long battle over segregated education in Dixie. (p. 37)

America's system of public schooling is segregated by race and by class; and that segregation is structural—it is based on the way in which America governs and funds public education. In effect the polarization of students is attributable to the children's place of residence. Does this polarization adversely affect academic achievement (what is learned) and attainment (the highest grade level attended or degree received)? America emphasizes achievement of basic skills because it is the foundation of education and has become a requirement for even modest success in the world of work. The child who reads well can do almost anything; the child who cannot is lost. If you are 14 and cannot read there is little future for you in ordinary American life.

EDUCATIONAL ACHIEVEMENT AND ATTAINMENT

There are marked differences in educational achievement of whites and blacks and smaller differences in attainment. The National Academy of Science's 1989 report, *A Common Destiny: Blacks and American Society*, noted three trends in the educational achievement of African-Americans and three in the enrollment and attainment status of African-Americans (Jaynes and Williams 1989). First, school achievement scores of blacks have increased at a faster rate than those of whites. Second, despite black gains, substantial gaps in achievement remain. The academy's third finding on achievement is both preliminary and disturbing: "among the youngest age group and birth cohort, there is evidence of a possible decline in black performance relative to whites" (pp. 348 and 352–54).

The academy's three findings on achievement presage those on attainment. First, blacks and whites no longer receive vastly different amounts of schooling, measured in terms of years attended. The overall gap, measured in terms of the median years, declined from 4 years in 1940 to less than one-half year in 1980 for young men. Second, important gaps still remain, especially in terms of rates of high school completion and college attendance. Third, the report notes a drop in college attendance by blacks from 1977 through 1982 not matched by a drop in white attendance. The following section builds on the academy's findings.

Achievement

The National Assessment of Educational Progress's [NAEP] Reading Report Card classifies students by age along a continuum of achievement ranging from "rudimentary" to "advanced". The classification "intermediate" (the level at which a person can search for specific information, interrelate ideas and make generalizations) is interpreted as being roughly equivalent to the expected achievement of a middle school, or junior high school, student (Table 7.6).

About 60 percent of all 13-year old children have been classified as being intermediate readers in each of the four years listed in Table 7.6. The rate for white children has increased steadily over time, from 63.8 percent in the 1970–71 school year to 66.9 percent in 1983–84. The rate for black children is substantially lower, though there has been marked progress. In 1970–71 only 20 percent of all black 13-year old children were intermediate readers. In the 1983–84 test 35.3 percent of black 13-year olds were classified as being intermediate.

Those who are classified as being either "adept" (able to find, understand, summarize and explain relatively complicated literary and informational material) or "advanced" readers (able to understand the links between ideas even when those links are not explicitly stated and to make appropriate generalizations even when the text lacks clear introductions or explanations) are considered to be "proficient" readers. Proficiency is a reasonable expectation of those who are about to end their secondary school careers. All advanced readers in Table 7.6 are part of the adept category, as each category in the table includes all children reading at, or above, the specified level.

TABLE 7.6

Percent of Students at or Above Selected Reading Proficiency Levels
by Race and Age for Selected Years

Race	Age	Year	Rudimen-tary 1	Basic 2	Intermed-iate 3	Adept 4	Advanced 5
All	13	1970–71	99.7	92.3	57.0	9.3	0.0
		1974–75	99.6	92.8	57.5	9.7	0.0
		1979–80	99.8	94.3	59.3	10.9	0.0
		1983–84	99.8	94.5	60.3	11.3	0.0
	17	1970–71	100.0	96.6	80.0	37.2	4.9
		1974–75	100.0	97.5	82.0	36.1	3.5
		1979–80	100.0	97.9	82.8	34.8	3.1
		1983–84	100.0	98.6	83.6	39.2	4.9
White	13	1970–71	99.9	96.0	63.8	10.9	0.0
		1974–75	100.0	96.2	64.3	11.5	0.0
		1979–80	99.9	96.7	66.0	13.1	0.0
		1983–84	99.9	96.5	66.9	13.6	0.0
	17	1970–71	100.0	98.4	85.4	41.4	5.5
		1974–75	100.0	99.1	87.5	40.6	4.0
		1979–80	100.0	99.3	88.9	39.9	3.6
		1983–84	100.0	99.2	88.9	45.1	5.8
Black	13	1970–71	98.3	72.2	20.4	0.4	0.0
		1974–75	98.0	75.3	23.9	1.5	0.0
		1979–80	99.4	84.1	29.6	1.4	0.0
		1983–84	99.4	87.1	35.3	2.3	0.0
	17	1970–71	100.0	83.6	41.1	6.9	0.2
		1974–75	100.0	86.0	45.0	7.1	0.0
		1979–80	100.0	88.8	45.8	6.1	0.0
		1983–84	100.0	96.5	65.8	15.5	0.8

Notes: 1. Able to follow brief written directions and select phrases to describe pictures;
2. Able to understand combined ideas and make references based on short uncomplicated passages about sequentially related information;
3. Able to search for specific information, interrelate ideas, and make generalizations about literature, science, and social studies materials;
4. Able to find, understand, summarize, and explain relatively complicated literary and informational material;
5. Able to understand the links between ideas even when those links are not explicitly stated and to make appropriate generalizations even when the texts lack clear introductions or explanations.

Source: Percent of Students at or Above Selected Reading Proficiency Levels by Race and Age: 1970–71 to 1983–84, Table 74, *Digest of Educational Statistics*, p.88. U.S. Department of Education, Center for Educational Statistics, 1987.

The proportion of all 17-year olds who were proficient readers declined from the 1970–71 school year (37.2 percent) to the 1979–80 year (34.8 percent). There was a rebound in the 1983–84 academic year to 39.2 percent. This pattern of decline followed by rebound held for all racial groups, but there were major differences in the percentage of students achieving proficient levels of reading comprehension by race. The white rate of achievement was above the national average. In 1970–71 41.4 percent of white 17-year old students were classified as adept or advanced readers; the corresponding figures were 39.9 percent in 1979–80 and 45.1 percent in 1983–84. The respective rates of achievement for black students were 6.9, 6.1 and 15.5 percent.

Even though scores for black students are increasing and the gap between white and black achievement is shrinking, the black rate remains substantially below the white rate. Regardless of the level of achievement and age group the pattern of narrowing, but still large, disparities in reading achievement scores between white and black students is consistent across all reading levels on the NAEP. For example, at the basic level the scores of white 13-year olds increased from 96.0 percent in 1970–71 to 96.5 percent in 1983–84. For the same period black student scores increased from 72.2 percent to 87.1 percent. The portion of white 17-year olds testing at the intermediate levels of achievement increased from 85.4 percent to 88.9 percent, while the black rate increased from 41.1 percent to 65.8 percent.

Spatial and racial differences in achievement, which overlap to a degree, are easily documented. The NAEP measures achievement for a multi-staged sampling of children at three different ages (Table 7.7). The results are reported, in part, by region, sex, race, ethnicity and type of community. The level of achievement of minority youth consistently falls below that of white youth in all academic areas measured. The largest differences, however, are in the crucial fields of reading, science and mathematics. Differences for black and white children increase with the age of the student. Because the reported scores for 13-year olds include most potential dropouts who will leave school by the time they are 17, the widening gap in scores with age is even more distressing. It means that black children with the deepest attachment to school are being left further and further behind their white counterparts.

The reading scores of all black 13-year old students in the 1979–80 NAEP was 14.3 percent below the national average and the score of all black 17-year olds was 16.6 percent below average in the 1979–80 academic year. The gaps in the mathematics and science test scores were nearly as large. Black 13-year olds were 12.3 percent below average in mathematics in the 1981 school year and 17-year old black students were 15.2 percent below average.

Differences in educational achievement affect the level of educational attainment due to the fact that students who do not achieve either do not receive psychic rewards from school attendance or tend to be uncommitted to learning.

TABLE 7.7

National Assessment of Educational Progress for Age and Select
Characteristics of Participants by Subject
(percent difference from national portion correct)

Subject	Reading	Music	Art	Citizenship	Social Studies	Science	Mathematics
Test Year	1979–80	1978–79	1978–79	1975–76	1975–76	1976–77	1981–82
Age 9 (Nation % Correct)	58.2	57.3	41.2	62.1	63.3	50.7	56.4
Race							
White	3.4	1.7	0.8	2.0	2.2	2.5	2.4
Black	-13.8	-8.2	-3.4	-7.4	-8.6	-12.9	-11.2
Hispanic	-13.3	-6.3	-3.3	-8.4	-8.5	-8.5	-8.7
Size and Type of Community							
Medium City	-0.4	-0.7	-0.7	0.2	0.3	-1.0	0.1
Main Big City	-3.4	-1.0	-0.4	-1.8	-2.0	-4.7	-2.2
Urban Fringe	3.2	2.0	0.5	2.5	2.6	4.3	3.0
Disadvantaged Urban[a]	-14.7	-7.4	-1.2	-8.9	-9.8	-11.7	-10.9
Advantaged Urban[b]	9.8	6.1	3.2	3.9	4.4	7.6	9.9
Age 13 (Nation % Correct)	74.0	52.3	47.0	63.2	62.9	49.1	60.5
Race							
White	3.3	1.3	0.7	1.4	1.6	2.9	2.6
Black	-14.3	-6.0	-3.5	-7.6	-8.2	-11.7	-12.3
Hispanic	-11.4	-5.9	-0.8	-7.6	-7.9	-10.3	-8.6

TABLE 7.7 (continued)
National Assessment of Educational Progress for Age and Select Characteristics of Participants by Subject
(percent difference from national portion correct)

Size and Type of Community							
Medium City	-0.4	-0.8	-0.2	-0.8	-0.8	0.6	2.5
Main Big City	-3.7	-0.9	-0.1	-1.0	-1.5	-2.2	-3.1
Urban Fringe	2.0	1.3	-0.6	2.9	3.0	1.9	3.9
Disadvantaged Urban[a]	-9.8	-5.6	-1.9	-5.5	-6.1	-11.1	-11.2
Advantaged Urban[b]	8.5	3.3	1.7	6.6	6.6	6.3	10.2
Age 17 (Nation % Correct)	79.1	50.0	50.6	67.4	67.6	53.5	60.2
Race							
White	2.9	1.2	0.8	1.6	1.6	2.6	2.9
Black	-16.6	-6.6	-4.6	-8.6	-9.4	-15.7	-15.2
Hispanic	-8.0	-6.2	-3.4	-8.2	-8.3	-10.8	-10.8
Size and Type of Community							
Medium City	0.7	0.2	0.6	-0.2	-0.2	1.7	1.8
Main Big City	-3.3	-0.6	0.2	-1.2	-1.2	-5.8	-2.8
Urban Fringe	1.1	0.1	1.4	0.8	0.8	2.8	2.1
Disadvantaged Urban[a]	-10.4	-4.9	-2.3	-5.8	-6.1	-12.3	-12.5
Advantaged Urban[b]	5.9	3.2	3.6	4.2	4.2	4.4	9.5

Note: [a] Students attend schools in or around cities with a population greater than 200,000 where a high proportion of the residents are on welfare or not regularly employed.
[b] Students attend schools in or around cities with a population greater than 200,000 where a high proportion of the residents are in professional or managerial positions.

Source: Digest of Educational Statistics, 1987, Tables 77, 78, 78, 79.

Attainment

Based on racial differences in achievement pronounced differences in educational attainment can be expected as well. The educational attainment of young adults, ages 25 to 29, is examined in Table 7.8 because they are old enough to have completed their educational careers and their attainment most closely resembles the expected distribution of attainment of those who are currently enrolled in schools.

The portion of the young black adult population who terminate their education without attaining a high school degree is much higher than the white rate. The dropout rate for black females, 17.9 percent, is higher than the rate for

TABLE 7.8

Educational Attainment, March 1987
Percent Distribution by Highest Level Attained
by Race, Sex, and Major Occupational Group

	High School		Post Secondary	
	Dropout	Graduate	1–3 Years	4 or More Years
All Persons Age 25 to 29[a]	14.0	42.4	21.6	22.0
White Male	14.4	41.9	20.4	23.3
Female	13.0	42.8	21.2	22.8
Black Male	15.2	51.9	21.3	11.6
Female	17.9	43.6	27.4	11.1
Employed Persons Age 25–64[b]	14.0	39.9	19.9	26.2
Exec., Admin., Manager	4.6	25.7	23.1	46.6
Professional	0.8	8.6	14.2	76.4
Technicians and Related	2.9	29.6	34.3	33.2
Marketing and Sales	7.9	41.0	24.1	27.0
Admin. Support and Clerical	5.3	54.2	27.9	12.6
Precision Prod. Craft Repair	22.0	53.5	18.2	6.3
Machine Setters and Operators	33.3	51.5	11.3	3.9
Transport & Material Moving	31.7	50.4	14.1	3.8
Helpers and Laborers	33.2	50.8	11.7	4.3
Farming, Forestry and Fishing	34.4	44.1	13.2	8.3
Other Service Workers	24.9	49.0	18.5	7.6

Notes: [a] Years of School Completed by Persons 15 Years Old and Over, Table 2; [b] Years of School Completed by Persons 25 to 64 Years Old, Table 6.

Source: Educational Attainment in the United States: March 1987 and 1986. U.S. Bureau of the Census, Current Population Report, Series P-20, No. 428.

black males, 15.2 percent. The dropout rates for both white females (13.0 percent) and white males (14.4 percent) are significantly lower than the corresponding black rates.

The National Academy of Sciences' report noted an inconsistency in the black dropout rate reported in the Current Population Survey, which Table 7.8 is based on, and city-specific reports on dropouts (Jaynes and Williams 1989, p. 338). The reported rate in many large city school systems is near 50 percent, yet, the rate reported in Table 7.8 for black men ages 24 to 29 is 15.2 percent. It is reasonable to suspect that this population is underrepresented in the Current Population Survey due to the fact that the survey is based on place of residence and is conducted by telephone. The survey does not directly include populations that are in the military, incarcerated, or homeless—all of whom are over-represented in the population of young black males. The Current Population Survey will also include those who have earned a high school equivalency certificate after dropping out.

The modal level of educational attainment for all young adults is a high school diploma. The difference is that 51.9 percent of the black male population terminate their education at this level, as do 43.6 percent of young adult black females, while only 41.9 percent of white males and 42.8 percent of white females end their formal education at this level.[7]

A major difference between the black and white populations is in the proportion attending post-secondary institutions for 4, or more, years. There is about an 11 percentage point racial difference in this rate, which exists for both males and females. The data indicate that young adult black men are also less likely than young adult black women to attend post-secondary educational institutions.

The gap in the proportion of black and white women attending post-secondary educational institutions for 4 or more years is largely accounted for by black females who have some post-secondary education, 27.4 percent compared to 21.2 percent. The gap between the two male groups is accounted for by black males who never attend a post-secondary school, 67.1 percent versus 56.3 percent.

Levels of educational attainment in both racial groups do not speak well for the future. Kasarda's (1989) work indicates that some post-secondary education is a requirement for success in urban labor markets—67.1 percent of young adult black males, 61.5 percent of young adult black women, 56.3 percent of young adult white men, and 55.8 percent of young adult white women have not reached this level of attainment.

Is the problem of inadequate levels of educational attainment in the United States strictly a problem of race? It unquestionably is linked to race and class but other data indicate that it is also a spatial problem. It is a problem of cities: due in part to the way in which children and schools are matched; due in part to the way in which public education is funded; due in part to the social pathologies children of the urban poor must contend with on the way to school, in school and possibly at home; and due in part to the lack of incentives society provides to stimulate good teaching and encourage effective parental involvement in the education of their children.

The dropout rate in New York City is 40 percent—New York is not alone in this regard. Chicago, Cleveland, Detroit, and Milwaukee all report dropout rates between 40 and 50 percent. Unfortunately city-specific data are not available on educational achievement to match these figures on attainment. If data on achievement were available, it would probably demonstrate that the problem is worse than indicated by reported dropout rates. It is also conceivable that these dropout rates are typical of large urban public school districts throughout the United States. If so, there is reason to be concerned about the futures of these children, the future of the cities in which they live, and the future of the nation.

CONCLUSION

The two questions asked at the start of this chapter have been partially answered. The problems of inner-city education are built on a foundation of racial *and* class isolation. This is especially true outside of the West region. The second question—is the quality of inner-city education deteriorating—is harder to answer. Data on educational achievement and attainment indicate that gains have been made by inner-city students. However, two caveats are required: (1) the gains are not keeping pace with changes in the economy and; (2) the data do not capture the effects of recent gang- and drug-related problems that some districts are experiencing.

The achievement of central-city students is considerably below that of their suburban and non-metropolitan counterparts. This gap is the result of a combination of three major forces. First, there has been a collapse in the socioeconomic environment of many inner-city neighborhoods. Secondly, inner-city public schools have become the social safety net of last resort. The failure of parents, churches, communities and government to deal with the effects of poverty, hunger, chemical abuse, and the devastated aspirations of many parents and their children forces schools to address the problems in some fashion. Contending with these non-pedagogical problems, however, impairs the ability of teachers to teach and students to learn. Finally, there is widespread institutional failure on the part of inner-city school districts which has caused them not to respond to competitive challenges imposed by suburban and private systems. These topics will be addressed in greater detail in Chapter 17, along with a proposal to radically restructure the public educational system. The importance of finding new ways of delivering education to inner-city students is critical not only to the students but to the cities in which they live.

NOTES

1.   The percentage varies with age.

2.   The Northeast region is comprised of the New England and Middle Atlantic Census Divisions; the Midwest region is made up of the East and West North Central Census Divisions; the South region is equal to the East and West South Central Census Divisions; and the West region combines the Mountain and Pacific Divisions.

3.   The residential pattern of children of Hispanic origin differs from that of both blacks and whites. The Hispanic population is predominantly urbanized, 90.3 percent versus 74.5 percent for whites and 78.9 percent for blacks. The major difference between the residential pattern of black and Hispanic school-age children is in the proportion living in central cities; the black rate is 55.5 percent and the Hispanic rate is 47.7 percent. Of Hispanic children, 40.1 percent live in suburban places—greater than the black proportion (23.4 percent) but less than the white (50.9 percent). Only 12.3 percent of Hispanic youth live in non-metropolitan places, which is far lower than both the white and black rates, 25.5 percent and 21.2 percent respectively. These figures are influenced by the large share of the Hispanic population who live in the more integrated West and the large proportion of the black population who live in segregated Northeastern and Midwestern metropolitan areas. All data are from "Enrollment Status of Persons 3 to 34 years old by Residence, Age, Race, Hispanic Origin: October 1986," Table 2 of the U.S. Bureau of the Census, *Current Population Report* (No. 249), *School Enrollment: Social and Economic Characteristics of Students: October 1986*.

4.   Table 7.4 must be interpreted with caution. The data are for school-going children who live in central cities of metropolitan areas in the four regions of the country. They do not indicate which children attend public or private schools or the actual location of those schools. Regional differences in the data presented in Table 7.4 will be understated if there are regional differences in the proportion of central city students who either attend private school or attend a public suburban school system.

5.   Thirty-two percent of all students in the United States attend districts with more than 20,000 pupils. Forty-one percent of Arizona's public school population is enrolled in districts with more than 20,000 pupils and 22 percent attend districts with at least 39,000 pupils; 58 percent of California's public school population attend systems with more than 20,000 pupils and 23 percent attend systems with more than 39,000 pupils; 29 percent of New Mexico's students attend Albuquerque's system, which has 72,000 students; 43 percent of Texas' public school students attend districts with more than 39,000; 60 percent of Utah's public school population attend systems with more than 20,000 pupils and 45 percent attend systems with more than 39,000 pupils. *Digest of Educational Statistics: 1988*, U.S. Department of Education (CS 88–600), Tables 35 and 71.

6. Most of the chapter discusses differences between black and white youth because comparable secondary data on educational attainment and achievement for children of Hispanic and Asian descent are not yet available.

7. Note that there is less than a 1 percentage point difference between black and white females. The black rate is 43.6 percent and the white rate is 42.8 percent.

REFERENCES

Bednarek, D. 1987. City finds people flee schools, crime. *Milwaukee Journal* 19 (November):18.

Billingsley, G., K. Zeff and D. Beisel. 1984. *Population analysis.* St. Louis, MO: St. Louis Public Schools.

Community Advisory Committee. 1985. *Phase I summary: the long-range plan.* St. Louis, MO: St. Louis Public Schools.

Cook, R. 1988. *Characteristics of the 25 most populous cities' school systems and the 25 largest public elementary and secondary school districts: Fall 1986.* Washington, DC: U.S. Department of Education, National Center for Educational Statistics (CS 88–041).

Council of the Great City Schools. 1987. *Challenges to urban education: results in the making.* Washington, DC.

Hill, E. and H. Rock. 1990. Education as an economic development resource. *Environment and Planning C: Government and Policy* 8:53–68.

Hodgkinson, H. 1985 *All one system: demographics of education.* Washington, DC: The Institute for Educational Leadership.

Jaynes, G. and R. Williams, eds. 1989. The schooling of black americans. *A common destiny: blacks and american society.* Washington, DC: National Academy Press.

Johnson, F. 1989. *Assigning type of locale codes to the 1987–88 ccd public school universe.* Washington, DC: U.S. Department of Education, National Center for Educational Statistics, CS 89–194.

Kain, J. 1987. Housing market discrimination and black suburbanization in the 1980s. In *Divided Neighborhoods*, G. Tobin, ed. Newbury Park, CA.: Sage.

Kasarda, J. 1989. Urban industrial transition and the underclass. *Annals of the American Academy of Political and Social Science* 501:26–47.

O'Neill, J. 1990. The role of human capital in earnings differences between black and white men. *Journal of Economic Perspectives* 4(4):25–45.

Orfield, G. and F. Monfort. 1989. *Status of school desegregation 1968–1986.* Alexandria, VA: National School Boards Association.

Orfield, G. and F. Monfort. 1988. *Racial change and desegregation in large school districts: trends through the 1986–1987 school year.* Alexandria, VA: National School Boards Association.

Orfield, G., F. Monfort and R. George. 1987. *School segregation in the 1980s: trends in the United States and metropolitan areas.* Washington, DC: Joint Center for Political Studies.

Ricketts, E. and I. Sawhill. 1988. Defining and measuring the underclass. *Journal of Policy Analysis and Management* 2(Winter): 316–25.

Smith, J. and F. Welch. 1989. Black economic progress after Myrdal. *Journal of Economic Literature* 2:519–64.

Wilson, W. 1987. *The truly disadvantaged*. Chicago: The University of Chicago Press.

8 The Persistence of Differing Trends in African-American Mortality and Morbidity Rates

AKWASI OSEI

In 1984, the Secretary of Health and Human Services in the Reagan administration, Margaret Heckler, sent Congress a report on the health of America. Two conclusions stood out in this report. First, America generally was in good health with people living longer and healthier lives. Second, "there was a continuing disparity in the burden of death and illness experienced by blacks . . . as compared with our nation's population as a whole" (U.S. Department of Health and Human Services 1985, p. ix). This was a candid admission of a persistent problem regarding health care in the United States: the low health status of blacks compared with whites.

Looking at the health picture of the United States reveals the subordinate position of African-Americans—both in terms of their disproportionate representation among poorer Americans and the general climate of neglect and inadequacy that characterizes their health status. This takes place in the context of prejudiced perceptions by other Americans leading to an inferior position and a certain powerlessness among African-Americans, whether position or power is defined politically, socially, or economically.[1]

There is a continuing polarization of African-Americans and other Americans, a chasm that impacts all aspects of life. This chapter demonstrates this polarization by focusing on key issues of health and health policy as they relate to African-Americans. Do they lag behind the rest of the nation in terms of access to health care and the type of health care they receive? Why are African-Americans disproportionately represented among sufferers of some of the nation's most debilitating health problems: cancer, acquired immune deficiency syndrome (AIDS), hypertension, cirrhosis, homicide, drug abuse, and heart

128

disease? Why is there a steady stream of reports that announce crises in African-American health conditions?[2] This chapter attempts to look for answers by examining the health status of African-Americans, assessing the role race has in this status, and offering some general policy recommendations on how the status may be upgraded.

The continuing disparity between the health of African-Americans and other Americans mirrors larger social and political problems. Indeed, studies have been carried out that establish the case that low health status is not only explained by biological factors, but is also heavily influenced by political, social, and economic factors (Miller 1989; Greenberg 1989; Pinkney 1987). Factors such as class and race affect the incidence of diseases and illness, as this chapter will demonstrate. Given the influence of the political and social climate, this chapter presents the argument that as long as African-Americans suffer social, economic, and political inequalities, their health status will continue to lag behind that of other Americans.

THE HEALTH STATUS OF AFRICAN AMERICANS

Probably the most accurate indicators of the generally low level of health among African-Americans is the mortality and average life expectancy rates. A simple but painful fact stands out when examining these statistics: mortality rates of blacks are, and have always been, substantially higher than those of whites (Ewbank 1989; NCHS Report 1988; Manton, et al. 1989). Despite a rise in the life expectancy rates among the general population, there exists a dramatic difference between the number of years blacks and whites are expected to live. This persistent differential was partly the reason why the Secretary's Task Force on Black and Minority Health was commissioned by Margaret Heckler in 1984 (Figure 8.1).

According to the report (U.S. Dept. of Health and Human Services 1985), life expectancy for females at birth is longer (78 years) than for males; black females (74 years) are expected to live shorter lives than white females, but longer than white males (72 years) and black males (65 years). Probably the most telling aspect of these figures is that *the 64.9 years that black males were expected to live in 1982 is lower than the 66 years of white males in 1950!* In other words, life expectancy for black males is now at a level achieved by white males over 30 years ago. Projecting this trend into the future—keeping in mind that the gap between blacks and whites has been somewhat consistent—one would not expect any convergence in the near future, especially if disparities persist in income, health, and social status.

Convergence in the near future appears unreasonable given the death rates of blacks and whites. Black males and females have death rates of 1,085 and 612

FIGURE 8.1

Life Expectancy at Birth, According to Race and Sex:
United States, 1950–1983

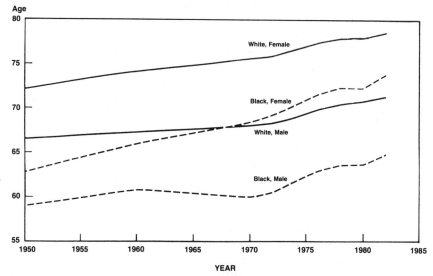

Source: National Center for Health Statistics, 1985.

per year per 100,000, respectively; the comparable figures for white males and females are 736 and 405, respectively. Comparing black death rates to whites, the report relied on a new indicator to further illustrate the rate differentials. This is called "excess deaths": the "difference between the number of deaths actually observed . . . among blacks and the number of deaths that would have occurred in that group if it experienced the same death rates as the white population" (U.S. Dept. of Health and Human Services 1985 p. 63). By this measure, as a result of the disparity in the death rate of blacks and whites, blacks endured about 59,000 excess deaths each year:

> Between 1979 and 1981, an average of 227,000 blacks died each year. Of these, 139,000 were under the age of 70 years. About 59,000 of these deaths among blacks under 70 would not have occurred had blacks experienced the same death rates as whites. These excess deaths represent 42.3 percent of all blacks who died before age 70. (U.S. Dept. of Health and Human Services 1985, p. 70)

The disparity in the death rates is even more dramatic when one controls for age. Between ages 24–63, there is a rise in black excess deaths; after 64, it declines. This means that blacks, especially males, are at high risk during their most productive and active years. But disparities in death rates appear at younger ages as well. The rate of black infant mortality has been roughly twice that of whites for an extended period of time (Figure 8.2).

FIGURE 8.2

Infant Mortality Rates by Race: United States, 1950–1986

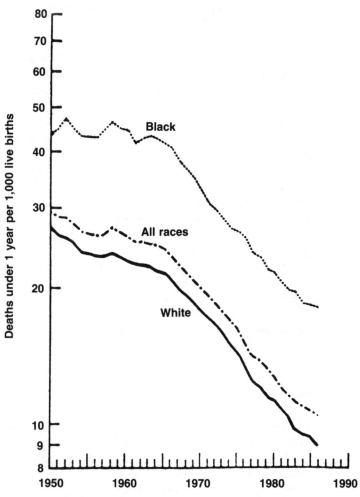

Source: National Center for Health Statistics, 1985.

Even though there has been a decline in the rates for all American infants since about 1965, the key figure is the black/white differential, constant at a ratio of about 2 to 1. This point is driven home when the rates are compared to those of other countries, both industrialized and less-industrialized. In 1984, Japan had an infant mortality rate of 6 per 1,000 live births (World Health Organization 1985) compared to the United States which had an average of about 14 per 1,000 live births (9.4 per 1,000 whites; 18.4 per 1,000 for blacks). The rate for blacks is over three times that of Japan's and is comparable to those found in less-industrialized nations of the world, such as Cuba (18.5 per 1,000 in 1981). Indeed, among major urban centers in the United States with large black populations, the infant mortality rates are comparable to the rates of some of the world's poorer countries. For example, according to the U.S. Census Bureau (1985), Washington, D.C., had a rate of 24.1 per 1,000 live births, and Cleveland, Ohio, had a rate of 23 per 1,000. Comparatively, Panama, Mauritius, and Costa Rica had rates of 20.4 per 1,000, 27 per 1,000, and 24.3 per 1,000 live births, respectively (World Health Organization 1985). Blacks, for all practical purposes, live in a "poor third-world country."

This disparity in health status is consistent when the leading causes of death and disease are examined by race. Blacks suffer disproportionate rates of death from stroke and other cardio-vascular diseases, homicide, cirrhosis, AIDS, and cancer. Heart disease among blacks is proportionately more common than among whites. Hypertension, which leads to heart disease, is more prevalent among blacks; they are more susceptible to the complications of hypertension than whites (*Journal of the American Medical Association* 1989). Among stroke victims, the results are similar: deaths as a result of strokes are usually higher among blacks than whites (Figure 8.3).

Even among non-fatal stroke sufferers, there is a larger proportion of blacks than whites. Some reasons for this are easy to discover. Studies report a correlation between incidence of elevated blood pressure levels and low socioeconomic status (Kiel, et al. 1977). Cases of high blood pressure have been known to be concentrated in areas of high social and economic stress. The urban areas of America, in which 59 percent of blacks live, represent stressful environments.

Homicides and accidents are claiming a greater share of the deaths among the general population. Among African-Americans, however, it seems to be reaching catastrophic proportions. In 1986, African-Americans accounted for 44 percent of all murder victims, while accounting for only 12 percent of the total population (Federal Bureau of Investigation 1987). Homicide is the leading cause of death among young African-Americans aged 15–34; and although less serious, homicide among other African-American age groups is equally disheartening. Some illustrative statistics show that:

FIGURE 8.3

Average Annual Death Rates for Strokes, 1979–1981
(deaths per 100,000 population)

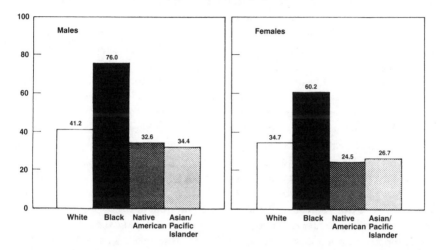

Note: Death rates for Hispanics are not available. Death rates for Native Americans and
Asian/Pacific Islanders are probably underestimated due to less frequent reporting
of these races on death certificates as compared with the census.

Source: National Center for Health Statistics, Bureau of the Census, and Task Force on
Black and Minority Health, 1985.

- Blacks have the highest rates of death by homicide (1981).
  black males   62.2 per 100,000 people
  black females   12.9 per 100,000 people
  white males   10.3 per 100,000 people
  white females   3.1 per 100,000 people
- Black males have a 1 in 21 lifetime chance of becoming a homicide
  victim. For white males, the chance is 1 in 131.
- Black homicide rates are especially high in the largest U.S. cities.
- For black males ages 15–24, the homicide rate (in 1981) was 78.2
  deaths per 100,000 population. In comparison, white males aged 15–
  24 had a rate of 14.4 per 100,000.
- For black males ages 25–34, the rate is about 137 deaths per 100,000
  population; for white males in the same age group, the rate is 17.6
  per 100,000. (U.S. Dept. of Health and Human Services 1985, p.
  160)

No doubt a contributing factor to these alarming numbers is the increasing incidence of drug use in the urban areas. In Washington, D.C., for example, drugs reportedly contributed to an all-time city high of 437 homicides in 1989. Three weeks into 1990, there had been 28 murders, on a pace sure to top the previous year's high (*Time* magazine January 20, 1990).

Drug and alcohol use and abuse lead to other health hazards. With regard to alcohol, "using cirrhosis deaths as an indicator of high alcohol use, cirrhosis mortality rates . . . are still disproportionately high among black Americans, nearly twice that of non-minorities" (U.S. Dept. of Health and Human Services 1985, p. 131). Also, since blacks are perceived as being more likely to be involved in dangerous drugs (such as cocaine, crack, and PCP), their rate of death through drug use is higher than that of whites. Between 1982–84, cocaine-related deaths tripled among blacks while they doubled among whites (U.S. Dept. of Health and Human Services 1985, p. 136).

Intravenous drug users have become increasingly susceptible to AIDS. Since blacks constitute a disproportionately large number of intravenous drug users, they are overrepresented among AIDS sufferers or people who are human immunodeficiency virus (HIV) positive. A study found that over the last 3 years a disproportionate number of persons with AIDS were African-Americans and Hispanics (Friedman, et al. 1989). Over 50 percent of the people who contract the disease through intravenous drug use are black (30 percent Hispanic). In major urban areas, the numbers are especially high. In New York City, for example, among 2,628 intravenous drug-use AIDS cases, 47 percent were black (39 percent Hispanic), and 15 percent white. The 47 percent was made up of direct intravenous drug users, male and female, and mothers who did not use drugs but whose partners were intravenous drug users.

Death rates among blacks and whites from cancer reflect a similar disparity: blacks get cancer at a higher rate and die at a higher rate. Especially among black males, the numbers are disturbingly high. Over a 30-year period (1950–1980), black male cancer rates rose by 77 percent compared to only a 10 percent increase for black females (LeFall 1990). Overall, the cancer incidence rate for blacks rose by 27 percent and only 12 percent for whites. Regarding death rates, there has been a 50 percent increase among blacks but only a 10 percent increase among whites (Table 8.1).

The death rate from lung cancer is 45 percent higher among black males than white males. For prostate cancer, the rate is two times higher. Among women, similar disparities are evident: mortality and incidence rates for cervical cancer are approximately 2.5 times greater among black females than among non-minority females. Non-minority females showed a 20 percent decrease in cervical cancer deaths between 1973–77 and 1979–81, while black females experienced a 27 percent increase in the same period (U.S. Dept. of Health and Human Services 1985).

TABLE 8.1

Cancer Mortality Rates by Primary Site and Race
(rates per 100,000 population)

Selected Primary Sites	Non-Hispanic White	Blacks	Chinese	Japanese	Filipino	Native Hawaiians*	Native Americans*
All sites	163.6	208.5	131.5	104.2	69.7	200.5	87.4
Esophagus	2.6	9.2	3.3	1.9	1.9	6.5	2.1
Colorectal	21.6	22.3	19.3	17.2	8.1	15.0	8.6
Colon	18.1	18.8	15.5	13.6	5.8	11.4	6.8
Rectum	3.5	3.5	3.8	3.6	2.3	3.6	1.8
Pancreas	8.4	11.0	7.4	7.0	3.3	10.9	4.5
Larynx	1.3	2.5	0.7	0.2	0.4	1.4	0.9
Lung							
Male	69.3	91.4	48.2	32.7	20.0	31.5	28.0
Female	20.2	20.1	21.2	8.6	6.8	88.0	8.6
Breast	26.6	26.3	13.0	9.9	8.0	31.5	8.2
Cervix	3.2	8.8	2.9	2.7	1.6	33.0	5.8
Prostate gland	21.0	43.9	7.5	8.8	8.2	11.6	15.5
Multiple myeloma	2.4	5.0	1.2	1.2	1.2	2.8	1.9

Note: *"Hawaiians" refers to Native Hawaiian; "Native Americans" refers to American Indians and Alaska natives.

Source: Adapted from U.S. Department of Health and Human Services, 1985, p. 93.

The health status differential between blacks and whites is sizable and persistent. Table 8.2 summarizes the disparity in terms of mortality rates associated with various causes. Controlling for sex, for all listed causes blacks have a substantially higher risk of death than whites (shown by the "relative risk"[3] statistics in Table 8.2).

Why is this so? What are the reasons that make blacks more susceptible to these diseases?

ANALYSIS OF CAUSES OF BLACK-WHITE HEALTH DIFFERENTIALS

Most of the literature on the health of blacks seems to agree on the reasons why blacks lag behind whites in health. They point to poverty and low economic status of blacks, environment (the social and political climate within which

TABLE 8.2
Death Rates by Selected Cause, Race, and Sex
(rates per 100,000 population)

Total Deaths	Black Male	White Male	Relative Risk*	Black Female	White Female	Relative Risk*
(All causes)	1,112.8	745.3	1.5	631.1	411.1	1.5
Heart disease	327.3	277.5	1.2	201.1	134.6	1.5
Stroke	77.5	41.9	1.9	61.7	35.2	1.8
Cancer	229.9	160.5	1.4	129.7	107.7	1.2
Infant mortality	2,586.7	1,230.3	2.1	2,123.7	962.5	2.2
Homicide	71.9	10.9	6.6	13.7	3.2	4.3
Accidents	82.0	62.3	1.3	25.1	21.4	1.2
Cirrhosis	30.6	15.7	2.0	14.4	7.0	2.1
Diabetes	17.7	9.5	1.9	22.1	8.7	2.5

Note: *Relative Risk is the ratio of black/white death rates.

Source: U.S. Department of Health Services, 1985, Table 5 and p. 67.

Americans live), behavior patterns and lifestyle differences among Americans, and historical bias (the systemic neglect that has characterized the integration of blacks into the larger American society). While all these reasons are related, and in some cases inseparable, it is necessary to attempt to emphasize those that predominate in order to reach some consensus when seeking solutions.

In an often-quoted study by Kitagawa and Hauser (1973), it was established that low socioeconomic status resulted in higher death rates:

> The study found that there was a gradient of mortality rates with steady increases from the highest to the lowest social classes. Mortality rates were higher as a socioeconomic status declined for both whites and blacks, whether that status was measured by family income, educational level or occupation. For people of the lowest status, overall mortality was 80 percent greater than for those at the highest socioeconomic level. In addition to increased mortality, almost every form of disease and disability is more prevalent among the poor (Jaynes and Williams 1989, p. 394).

Thus, given the wealth of information that underscores the relative lower economic level of blacks (see Chs. 2–5), it can be safely surmised that blacks would be overly represented in the population that generally lacks good health care. Income levels for African-Americans have lost ground in comparison with other Americans (Farley 1989; Swinton 1989), and there are serious per capita income differentials between blacks and whites. There is a persistence of high poverty rates among blacks, both in absolute terms and in relation to white poverty rates (Swinton 1989). One out of every 3 blacks is poor, 45 percent of black children live in poverty, and 33 percent of young blacks are unemployed, over 2.5 times the percentage of young whites.

Lacking economic opportunities usually translates into other ancillary concerns: inferior education, poor housing (see Chs. 6 and 7), lack of adequate health insurance, and poor nutritional habits and actual hunger. If one lacks all these, chances of confronting inadequate health are high. Also, economically disadvantaged areas lack amenities such as good medical facilities and adequate social services. This clearly affects the general well-being, particularly health and wellness, of the people who live in such areas.

If the foregoing is combined with the historical bias and systemic exclusion and discrimination that African-Americans have endured since the birth of this nation, a deadly combination is uncovered—race and class—that sheds ample light on the persistent inability of African-Americans to close the health gap—and indeed other gaps—between them and other Americans. From slavery, through Reconstruction and the Jim Crow era,[4] from the civil rights era to the present, African-Americans have had difficulty in becoming an integral part of the society. As Greensberg (1989) states:

> ...theories or explanations of discrimination against blacks have changed from blatant bigotry to claims of biological and psychological inferiority, and more recently to cultural deprivation.
> ... The mixture of laws, practices, customs and attitudes ... cause[d] a disproportionate number of blacks to be poor ... By limiting the access to blacks to political power, education, justice and jobs, ... discrimination and poverty place blacks at a higher risk of illness and premature death.

Legal segregation ensured unequal access to economic opportunities and inadequate social and health facilities for African-Americans. Medical facilities all across the nation were segregated, and the few available to blacks were of lower quality. This effectively put up barriers to adequate health care. As laws were changed, and as society tried to wipe away inequality, efforts were made to upgrade the health status of African-Americans. The statistics presented above suggest, however, that these efforts have been insufficient to close the gap. Figure 8.4 is a diagrammatic representation of the foregoing discussion on the inferior health status of blacks and its causes.

The fundamental construct here is race and class inequality. Race inequality is meant to convey the historical and contemporary biases against, and exclu-

FIGURE 8.4

A Model of Inter-Racial Health Disparities

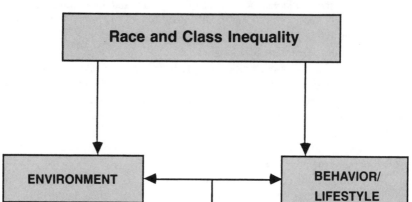

sion of, blacks. Class inequality encompasses many dimensions of socioeconomic status: income, education, occupational prestige, etc. Environment has two components that relate to the places where African-Americans live. One component is the natural environment as modified by human effluents like noise, smoke, toxic wastes; the other is the human-made environment involving social, economic, and political systems. Behavior/lifestyle involves the choices people make in their day-to-day lives as they exist and interact in the environment, such as eating habits, recreational activities, and interpersonal relationship styles.

These aforementioned constructs are interrelated. Environment and behavior/lifestyle are mutually causal; the former clearly shapes how people respond and what constraints are placed on their actions, whereas the latter clearly influences the conditions of the natural environment and how social institutions and norms evolve. In combination, environment and behavior/lifestyle affect health in a variety of obvious ways. Is the air and water polluted or pristine? Are local hospitals and emergency medical services of high quality? Does the neighborhood afford easy access to drugs and drug-trafficking activities? Are there strong familial and institutional support structures? Is there a high level of economic, social, and psychological distress? Is a quality dietary regime followed? Is time afforded for mental and physical relaxation and recreation? Is adequate income or insurance available for both preventative and curative medical attention?

Of most importance, however, are the linkages between environment and behavior/lifestyle and race and class inequality. Race and class inequality shape, inform, and largely determine the environment and the behaviors and lifestyles of the African-American community and, thereby, their relative health status. Race and class inequality, in the final analysis, determine where people live, whether in the inner-city, in the suburbs, in the richest part of town, or near noxious smokestacks. They determine how much power people have in the social system, both in making decisions, or to influence decisionmaking. Race and class inequality, to a large extent, influence behavior and lifestyles—how much and what type of food people can buy, how to deal with all types of stress, and how much space they have to live a decent life. While in reality it may be more difficult to separate them, it is essential to isolate race and class inequality as the most crucial determinants of the persistence of health disadvantages of blacks.

In sum, despite an improved healthier America during the past two decades, there exists a continued disparity between blacks and whites. While there are many reasons for this, it is clear that the two most important reasons are economic status (class) and race. Generally, the poorer a person is, the lower the person's health status. Having African-Americans overly represented in the nation's lower socioeconomic class explains much of the disparity in health between them and the majority of Americans. At the same time, as a result of past practices, African-Americans of every class have been at a relative disadvantage regarding their health status. The combination of class and race places many African-Americans in a precarious position of powerlessness that only contributes to the continuing polarization of the society.

CONCLUSIONS

There is a consensus among many politicians, the administration, private organizations, and other interested parties that the black health disparity vis-à-vis whites is untenable and must be eradicated.

Given the fact that one's economic level to a large extent determines one's health status, it seems obvious that efforts should be made to improve the economic opportunities of African-Americans. Unemployment should not only be reduced, there must be policies towards creating more jobs. Increases in the capacity of African-Americans to live better can only lead to better health. But beyond general economic development, all levels of government—federal, state, and local—must earmark more resources such as money, personnel, and other expertise to the area of health care.

Health insurance must be more readily available and affordable to African-Americans. Indeed, it is time for a commitment to a comprehensive national health insurance for *all* Americans. More hospitals and wellness clinics must be built in inner-city areas, and those that have been allowed to deteriorate or closed altogether must be rehabilitated and reopened. Emergency medical services must be strengthened. Educating more African-American health professionals is key to an improved health status. To this end, medical schools that have traditionally produced the bulk of African-American health professionals—doctors, nurses, researchers, and other medical personnel[5]—must be helped financially by the government. There should be more scholarship money for African-Americans to enter medical schools. After all, "black physicians are more likely to choose primary-care specialists and set up practice in underserved inner-city areas, thus improving access to medical care for less advantaged persons" (*Journal of the American Medical Association* 1989). More resources must also be spent on education to stress prevention of diseases, better eating habits, to inform about special health problems and how to avoid them, and to create programs for mothers about prenatal and postnatal care in order to decrease the atrocious infant mortality rates.

An encouraging sign has been the anti-smoking advocacy efforts of the present Secretary of Health and Human Services, Dr. Louis Sullivan. Dr. Sullivan's active involvement in the anti-smoking campaign epitomizes the use of one's position and power for public policy objectives. Politically, he has been in a position to respond to health hazards that have contributed to the disparity in death rates. However, African-Americans, as a group, do not have enough people in positions of power and authority to be able to get their agendas carried through. Further, the views of African-Americans do not generally reach the corridors of power in the society. If they do, they are only cursorily adhered to. The sense of powerlessness in African-Americans, especially among the urban dwellers, is a combination of "an attitude of self-blame, a sense of generalized distrust, a feeling of alienation from resources of social influence, an experience of disenfranchisement and economic vulnerability, and a sense of hopelessness in the sociopolitical struggle" (*Journal of the American Medical Association* 1989). Empowerment of the African-American community is imperative in efforts to respond to the health crisis.

The polarization in the society is related to lack of economic opportunities, spatial segregation, and lack of power. There is need for a new commitment to make resolving the health crisis in black America a national priority. This is ultimately a political decision. The nation and its leaders must have the *political will* to make those choices that will lead to health parity between blacks and whites. As long as African-Americans suffer social, economic, and political inequalities, their health status will continue to lag behind that of other Americans.

NOTES

1. This, of course, is not to imply that blacks do not occupy positions of authority in American life. There are over 7,000 black elected officials (out of over 500,000 total elected officials), including a state governor (Douglas Wilder, Virginia).

2. These reports include *The State of Black America* (National Urban League 1990) and *A Common Destiny* (Jaynes and Williams 1989).

3. Relative risk is the ratio of black/white death rates.

4. Reconstruction (1865–1877) was the period after the Civil War when the nation attempted to rebuild. Jim Crowism refers to the general idea of legal discrimination and denial and exclusion based on race (segregation). It became so pervasive that even after laws were changed, people still continued to live like that. It became a way of life.

5. These schools make up the Association of Minority Health Professions Schools. They are Charles Drew University of Medicine and Science, Morehouse School of Medicine, Meharry Medical College, and Howard University College of Medicine.

REFERENCES

Congressional Quarterly. 1989. November 25.

Dayal, H., et al. 1982. Race and socioeconomic status in survival from breast cancer. *Journal of Chronic Diseases* 35:675–83.

Devasa, S.S. and E.L. Diamond. 1980. Association of breast cancer and cervical cancer incidences with income and education among whites and blacks. *Journal of the National Cancer Institute* 65(3): 515–28.

Ewbank, D. 1989. History of black mortality and health before 1940. In *Health policies and black americans*, D. Willis, ed. New Brunswick, NJ: Transaction Publishers.

Farley, R. 1989. The quality of life for black americans twenty years after the civil rights revolution. In *Health policies and black americans*, D. Willis, ed. New Brunswick, NJ: Transaction Publishers.

Federal Bureau of Investigation. 1987. *Uniform crime reports of the United States, 1986.* Washington, DC: U.S. Government.

Friedman, S., et al. 1989. Racial dimensions of AIDS: attitudes and policies the aids epidemic among blacks and hispanics. In *Health policies and black americans*, D. Willis, ed. New Brunswick, NJ: Transaction Publishers.

Greenberg, M.R. 1989. Black male cancer and american urban health policy. *Journal of Urban Affairs* 11(2):113–30.

Jaynes, G. and R. Williams, eds. 1989. *A common destiny: blacks and american society.* Washington, DC: National Academy Press.

Journal of the American Medical Association. 1989. 261:2.

Keil, J.E., et al. 1977. Hypertension: effects of social class and racial admixture. *American Journal of Public Health* 67(7):634–39.

Kitagawa, E.M. and P.M. Hauser. 1973. *Differential mortality in the United States.* Cambridge, MA: Harvard University Press.

LeFall, L. 1990. Health status of black americans. *The state of black America*. New York: National Urban League.

Manton, K.G., et al. 1989. Health differentials between blacks and whites: recent trends in mortality and morbidity. In *Health policies and black americans*, D. Willis, ed. New Brunswick, NJ: Transaction Publishers.

Miller, S.M. 1989. Race in the health of America. In *Health policies and black americans*, D. Willis, ed. New Brunswick, NJ: Transaction Publishers.

National Center for Health Statistics. 1988. *Monthly vital statistics report* 37:6. Washington, DC: U.S. Government Printing Office.

National Urban League. 1989. *The state of black America*. New York: Urban League.

Pinkney, A. 1987. *The myth of black progress*. New York: Cambridge.

Swinton, D.H. 1989. Economic status of black americans. In *The state of black america*. New York: Urban League.

Time. 1990. January 29:24.

U.S. Bureau of the Census. 1985. *Statistical abstract of the U.S.* Washington, DC: Bureau of the Census.

U.S. Department of Health and Human Services. 1985. *Report of the secretary's task force on black and minority health*. Washington, DC: U.S. Government Printing Office.

Willis, D.P. 1989. *Health policies and black americans*. New Brunswick, NJ: Transaction Publishers.

World Bank. 1989. *World development report*. Washington, DC: Oxford.

World Health Organization. 1985. *World health statistics*. Geneva: United Nations.

9 Leadership and Race in the Administrative City: Building and Maintaining Direction for Justice in Complex Urban Networks

LAWRENCE F. KELLER

THE RISE OF THE ADMINISTRATIVE CITY

Organizations are the scaffolding of modern urban America. Most daily activities take place in or around complex, formal organizations (for an early recognition of this, see Turk 1977). In the modern city, both the number and size of public and private organizations have increased. These complex organizations sustain high levels of social interactions and a desirable standard of living. However, the diverse and fragmented context of these organizations raises difficult questions of governance. Governance is the coordination of all local organizations to achieve outcomes that are in the interest of the current and future community.[1]

The modern city is an administrative city. Major policy decisions are more likely to be made in an administrative rather than traditional political setting (Keller 1989). Even though the activities of the mayor or city manager, and some of the council, are highlighted in the local news, the everyday life of citizens is only remotely touched by these traditional politicians. Citizens experience government through the activities of public servants, such as the sanitation crews who collect the trash or the inspectors who examine the condition of their houses. The more complex a society, the more critical the governing system; and the more likely the governing system will be dominated by administrative actors, that is, non-elected city officials.

RACE AND OTHER "WICKED PROBLEMS"

Race in the modern city is one of a growing number of problems whose solution requires mobilization of resources within and without the city. Researchers call these "wicked problems."[2] (For some of the consequences, see Yates 1977, and Peterson 1981.) The rise of black politicians in the central city will indeed be a "hollow victory," as Persons sadly notes, if the authority they exercise does not command the resources to deal with the wicked problems. In essence, the nature of the problems that often bring the black politician to power may require political and economic resources far beyond those that exist in their city. Political leadership will only succeed if it effectively governs, that is, mobilizes support and creates politico-administrative systems that solve the wicked problems.

Governance requires coordination of the diverse organizations in the metropolis. Because the metropolis is an administrative city, the coordination will be accomplished more by management than politics. Traditional management offers little guidance. This body of theory is based on the control of a hierarchy, that is, the ability of those at the top to command those below. In essence, management, from this perspective, is the ability to force people and organizations to conform to rather detailed guidelines (Taylor 1947). The modern metropolis with its numerous political jurisdictions and variety of organizations is not a tidy hierarchy. However, more recent research has emphasized both the desirability of decentralizing authority and the impossibility of the type of control that is implicit, if not explicit, in management theory (Peters and Waterman 1982; Kouzes and Posner 1987; Peters 1989). In terms of a community, the key to governance (coordinating diverse sets of organizations and the activities surrounding them) is to nudge the complex networks of organizations and people into desirable policy directions.[3] Not only is this based on a more effective management, it also fosters the diversity that is at the core of a healthy and vibrant community (see Ch. 19).

In essence, community leaders must design and guide interorganizational networks that spatially span the metropolis and tap powerholders (Warren, et al. 1974; Hult and Walcott 1990).[4] They must create and sustain complex systems of people and organizations with efficient and effective policies implemented under an appropriate and "constitutional" arrangement of public authority. The term "appropriate" relates the structure of government and service delivery while "constitutional" requires the basic structures and process to be perceived as political "bedrock," nearly inviolate structures and processes for local politics. The task is exceedingly difficult in the midst of governmental fragmentation, complex formal structures, uncertain economies and often tumultuous politics. More than one researcher (and as civil servants could attest) has underscored the "fragility of the city policymaking system" (Waste 1989). The dimensions of the task can be placed in perspective by looking at the formal setting of local government and its informal dynamics.

THE ADMINISTRATIVE CITY: FORMAL UNITS AND STRUCTURES

Local government in the United States is quite complicated. In fact, the United States has the most complicated governing system in the world. Most of the complexity is at the local level, resulting from several different units of government and types of local agencies. Units of government will be covered first and then different types of agencies. It is best to learn the units and types of agencies at a general level because they vary from one state to another, depending upon their particular constitutional and statutory heritage. Local government is legally controlled, often in excruciating detail, by state government. Also, states often change the basic laws that structure local government. All units of local government are "creatures of the state," an apt phrase used by Judge Dillon (1911) after an Iowa court case almost 90 years ago. In almost every state, the phrase is still an accurate description of the law. With cities, boroughs, villages, etc., their relative independence is a result from amending state law, not replacing the basic doctrine of state control over local governmental units.

In addition to units and agencies, the forms of city government are also important.

Units of Local Government

Some local government units are relatively direct units of state government. They were established to promote local participation in and convenient access to state government. Their boundaries are controlled directly by state government though the state may permit local areas to choose their own boundaries or exercise more discretion in their activities.

Townships

Townships are subdivisions of counties originally established to promote local self-governance in a rural setting. They are rural analogues to towns and were part of Thomas Jefferson's grand design for keeping the United States a republic of independent farmers. In most states, townships cease to exist when a city or similar unit of government is created on the same territory. Townships usually have limited authority, both in terms of what they can do and the revenue they can raise. In many states much of their activities center on roads and similar types of infrastructure. This infrastructure was, and is, very important for farming and related commerce as well as suburban development.

Some states have towns or other similar units rather than townships. Townships are most common in the older midwestern states which were organized under a Jeffersonian, rural democratic ideology.

Counties

When many of the states were created the means of transportation were relatively slow. This inhibited traveling to the state capital to conduct public business. States established administrative subdivisions for the convenience of people needing to go to a state agency. For example, one could get a marriage license from the state by going to a county agency.

As transportation improved many advocated the abolition of counties. However, counties became the basic geographic unit for American political parties and resisted efforts of abolition in most states. In a few states counties were abolished, such as Connecticut, while in many other states counties were transformed into more general units of government, even with the ability to have their own charters. As administrative units, counties lacked any ability to change their structure or be policy making sections. In states where the legislature granted counties the authority to write their own charters, counties could become more policy oriented. With policy powers, counties can alter their structure as well as create basic law.

Councils of Government [COGs]

Many federal grant programs required that any applicants seeking funding have the approval of some type of regional planning agency. The purpose was to coordinate federal funding in a metropolitan area. No grant was to be given to any local government that lacked the approval of the regional planning agency. In some metropolitan areas the planning agencies evolved into more general governing units. Occasionally they could even levy taxes and offer services. The Twin Cities Metropolitan Council is an example of a COG that has assumed significant authority including the levying of local taxes. Most, however, have been minor actors in local politics.

Two other units of local government that are legally circumscribed by state government are special districts and public authorities. These are discussed in the section on local agencies. Special districts and public authorities are both units of governments and types of agencies.

More Self-Governing Units of Local Government

In contrast to the above units of government, which are relatively tightly controlled by state government, cities and other similar classifications of municipalities such as boroughs in Pennsylvania and villages in Ohio possess more authority over their structure and authority.

Around the turn of the twentieth century, a reform movement focused in part on the governing of cities. One of the cornerstones of the reform agenda was providing cities with the ability to create and implement their own charters. In most states, the movement was quite successful. The charter, whether granted by the state or locally created, determines the authority of the city, the structure of its government, the physical boundaries, etc. The boundaries can be changed by annexing surrounding areas according to the relevant state statutes or by merging with another city or cities.

In some states, legislatures passed statutes granting cities the ability to write and adopt their own charters. In other states, the authority was placed in the state constitution. For example, in 1912 the Ohio Constitution was amended and granted cities nearly carte blanche authority to create their charters. Most states grant less authority but nearly all have delegated some control.

Cities

A city is a corporation, legally similar to private companies such as General Motors. American law, however, has carefully and consistently distinguished municipal (city) corporations from the for-profit variety. The distinction recognizes the governing responsibilities placed on city government (Winter 1969).

In some states, cities receive a charter that is specified in state law. Cities may have little or no choice over the content of the charter or even their structure of government. In other states, cities may select a form of government from several different forms of government, which are specified in state law. A municipality must select one of the specified forms and, usually, they cannot vary the specifics of the state statute. Typically, cities select one of three forms of government—commission, council-mayor or council-manager—and operate their governments according to particular state statutes establishing and controlling that form of government. Each of these forms will be explained later.

Finally, in most states cities can decide they prefer "home rule" and write their own charters. Cities can design whatever form of government they desire and thus "customize" government to local conditions. The charters are usually submitted to the voters of the city in a referendum.

Charters are not constitutions even though under a home-rule system they can appear to be very similar. The major difference is the manner in which courts construe them. Constitutions are given the benefit of any doubt. In other words, if a state is sued over a policy in which the party bringing the suit alleges the state lacks the authority to implement such a policy, courts tend to grant the state the authority if the constitution does *not* prohibit it. Interpretations of charters tend to be the reverse, with courts withholding the authority from a city unless the charter specifically grants it because all authority rests with the state and it must be explicitly devolved to the local unit.

Other Types of Municipalities

Many states have categories of municipalities. For example, some states require an incorporated area to be a certain population size to be a city. Ohio, for instance, requires a population of 5,000 for an incorporated area to be a city. Areas with population less than the criterion have a different status, such as borough, village, etc. Cities have the most authority of any municipal structure and other categories have lesser authority, such as an inability to offer certain services or to levy particular types of taxes.[5]

Metropolitan Government

Some metropolitan areas have consolidated local governments into a single government. For example, Jacksonville, Florida, Indianapolis and Nashville merged city governments with their respective counties. Miami, Florida, consolidated some services into a metropolitan government while others were retained by the cities within the county.

TYPES OF GOVERNMENT ORGANIZATIONS

There are several types of governmental organizations. Often examples of each can be found in a single unit of government, especially a city. Each will be briefly reviewed in terms of its structure and use. Figures 9.1, 9.2 and 9.3 illustrate how these appear in organizational charts for the various forms of city government.

Executive Agency

The typical government organization is an executive agency. These have hierarchical structures with all lines of authority leading up to a director (the actual title will vary according to charter and/or ordinance). The director reports directly to the city manager or mayor, depending upon the form of government. Usually the top posts in each executive agency are political appointees of the city manager or mayor, with most charters requiring councilmanic approval of the nominee for the office of director. Most directors serve at the pleasure of the city manager or mayor, that is, they can be fired at any time. They are professionals in their particular policy area or in general management if appointed by a city manager, and even in many cases when appointed by a mayor.

The executive agency receives its authority from the charter, city manager or mayor (executive orders), council and mayor (ordinances)[6] and state statute and/or constitution. The budget for the agency is initially formulated by the mayor or city manager through the staff budget office and then passed as an ordinance by the council. The council can change the budget recommendations of the mayor though the mayor often can veto the ordinance, either in whole or part if he or she disagrees with the councilmanic provisions.

Commission or Board

A favorite organization of the reformers was a commission, sometimes called a board. This is an agency not directly under the administrative direction of the mayor or city manager. Rather, the organization is administered by a commission whose members are typically nominated by the mayor or city manager and confirmed by the council. For example, planning for the city was often granted to a planning commission and civil service, the allocation of public positions on the basis of merit and credentials, was often operated by a civil service board. The budgets of commissions and boards are now usually under the control of the council and mayor but there are many exceptions depending upon local political and legal structures.

Reformers liked Commissions because they thought elected officials would be removed from direct control of governing and thus commissioners could use their expertise without overt political interference (Wiebe 1962; 1967; Schiesl 1977). Planning was placed under a commission so that the planners would not be under the political influence of elected officials. However, it is more accurate to state there is a different political relationship between a commission and elected officials than is the case with an executive agency. In the latter case, the mayor or city manager can usually fire the director. Commissioners normally can only be removed for specified causes and the removing authority may have to follow a particular procedure. The organizational independence can be used to accumulate significant political power as Robert Moses demonstrated in his tenure at the helm of several boards and commissions (Caro 1974). Even if mayors disagreed with Moses, they lacked the legal authority, and certainly the political power, to dismiss him.

Public Corporation

Corporations can be classified as public or private depending on the type of shareholders. Shareholders are those who purchased part of the corporation, a "share" as it is legally called (and thus the name shareholder). Legally a corporation is a separate entity that can be involved in any activity that a person can engage in, such as make contracts, sue, be sued, etc. Conceptually, the shareholders of a municipal corporation, the legal form of a city, are the citizens.

Technically, the shareholders elect the board of directors of the corporation who then appoint a chief executive officer (CEO) to run the corporation according to the mission and policy directions established by the board.[7] A public corporation has all of its stock owned by a government. Members of the board are appointed according to the corporate charter; in the case of a corporation established by a city, typically the city manager or mayor will appoint board members subject to confirmation by the council. Many cities, for example, have established economic development corporations that engage in commercial activities related to increasing the number of jobs. This type of a corporation is illustrated in Figures 9.2, 9.3 and 9.4.

Corporations can be a combination of public and private. The U.S. Bank established in 1797 was part privately owned and part publicly owned (for an account of the politics surrounding the bank, see Peterson 1987). The current Communications Satellite Corporation, which operates most of the communication satellites circling the earth, is also a mixed corporation. Amtrak, which operates all of the intercity passenger trains, and the U.S. Post Office are national public corporations. At the local level, some cities have established development corporations that help to finance rehabilitation of existing, and construction of new, housing.

Public Authority

In some cases, states have opted to establish agencies that are very similar to corporations. These are called public authorities and they usually operate a service much like a corporation. The most famous is the Port Authority of New York and New Jersey. This agency was established by an interstate compact, that is, an agreement between the two states which under the U.S. Constitution had to be ratified by Congress. The agreement determined the boundaries and its functions. The Port Authority operates and coordinates much of the transportation in the Greater New York area.

Authorities raise their own revenues and are more independent than special districts. Many cities use similar authorities to operate their airports and other similar commercial enterprises.

Public authorities are both a unit of government and an organization. As a unit of government their authority is spatially determined. They are legally and structurally similar to corporations, but do not have shareholders. They have a board which selects a director, who can become quite powerful (Caro 1974). The method by which the board is selected is specified in the relevant statute. The board then creates rules and regulations for the agency. They usually possess independent budget authority which frees them from control by other local governmental units.

Special Districts

In recent times, many urban services required units of government larger than individual cities or counties. In response to this need, state government created many special districts, another agency whose authority is spatially determined. Typically, a special district offers a single service over a relatively large area. The area is defined in the state statute creating the district. Examples are transportation agencies, parks, sewage districts, etc.

Districts are established by state laws and are independent of other units of local government. They typically have their own revenue sources, both taxes and user charges. Because they are established under a particular statute each agency tends to have singular authority and structure; that is, special districts vary greatly in how they are structured and what they can do. Legally, in many states they are actually state agencies and can exercise significant authority over local government. For example, when New York City was unable to pay its bills, the state of New York created the Municipal Assistance Corporation [MAC], a state agency that directed the finances of the city.

These are similar to corporations and public authorities. As noted earlier, the structure and processes are specified in state statutes. They are also independent of other local governments both in terms of authority and budget. They typically have less power than public authorities and courts tend to control special districts more closely. School busing is an example where the U.S. Supreme Court required many local school districts to distribute services to students in a more racially balanced manner. States also exercise more control over special districts, such as prohibiting deficit spending and in extreme cases taking over the district. Currently, some state courts are now requiring redistribution of revenue across school districts to equalize state educational expenditures for pupils.

Figure 9.1 illustrates a mythical but typical spatial arrangement of local government. In the figure, there are 3 counties, a city located in one of the counties, a special district whose boundaries include parts of 3 counties, and 2 school districts which bifurcate the city; that is, the city is located in 2 school districts. Even though the boundaries of the city and school district overlap, each of these units are legally, and usually politically, independent. Their relationships are formally controlled by state law and informally by local politics.

Adding to the complexity is the variety of forms of government for cities and other municipal corporations. These can be dramatically different and shape as well as mirror the local politics and culture.

FORMS OF MUNICIPAL GOVERNMENT

A variety of forms of government have developed for the American city. The original form was the council-mayor system. This system reflected the separation of powers embodied in state and national governments. There are two versions of this system.

FIGURE 9.1

Spatial Illustration of
Typical Units of American Local Government

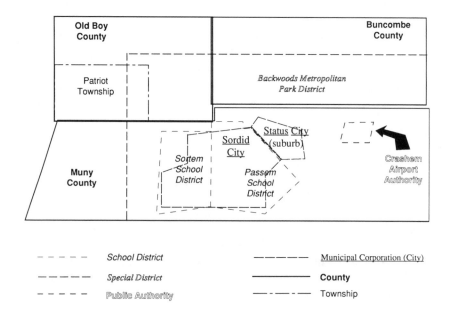

In the council-strong mayor form, the separately elected mayor has significant political authority. Examples are the veto over ordinances of council, hiring and firing of administrative personnel, and drafting and executing the budget. The council tends to be large and partisanly elected from districts or wards. The mayor typically has a 4-year term of office. Figure 9.2 illustrates the classic version of the council-mayor form of government.

In Figure 9.2, the council and mayor are listed side-by-side denoting that each is elected by the voters. The system relied on political parties to form programs and offer them for voter approval. Thus, voters were conceptualized as a partisan electorate, that is, voters who respond to parties. Councilpeople were elected from districts or wards, sections of the city. In many cities, the boundaries of the wards followed neighborhoods, especially those characterized by a specific ethnic group.

The planning commission in Figure 9.2 is only loosely connected to the council and the mayor. This is represented by the dotted line. Members of the commission had terms of office that limited the ability of councilpeople or the mayor to displace them. However, the members were often appointed initially by the mayor and/or council. Also, the budget of the commission had to be approved by the council which usually reacted to the proposed allocation to the commission in an executive budget, that is, the mayor's proposed budget.

The final organization depicted in Figure 9.2 is a development corporation. It, too, is connected only indirectly with the council and/or mayor. Usually the mayor and/or council appoint the board of directors. However, the corporation

FIGURE 9.2

Council-Mayor Form
of Municipal Government

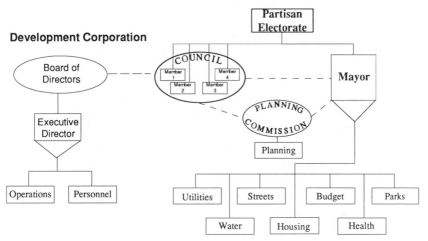

can then conduct its business according to its charter. As a corporation, it possesses the legal ability to make contracts, generate revenue, etc. The actual conduct of its business is controlled by a CEO, an administrator appointed by, and answerable to, the board of directors. In some cases, other city organizations can also make appointments to the board, such as a neighborhood planning group. The charter would contain the details for any particular corporation.

In contrast, the city executive agencies are directly under the authority of the mayor. The agencies are connected by solid lines to the mayor, symbolizing his or her authority over them. Some heads of executive agencies may possess some independence from the mayor. For example, the law director may be empowered by state statute to issue his or her own rulings and be beyond the mayor's removal power. Typical city services are offered through executive agencies.

In the council-weak mayor form, the mayor lacks the *formal powers* granted to the strong mayor. In any particular case, the power of the mayor depends upon several factors. For example, Mayor Richard Daley of Chicago, the father of that city's current mayor, was very powerful, yet he occupied a weak mayoral office. (See the famous biography, *Boss*, by Mike Royko 1971.) His power was derived from his position as chair of the Cook County Democratic Party, the party that rules Chicago politics. Daley illustrates quite nicely the political functions of the county and the possibilities of accumulating power in local politics. (To get a feel for the politics, see Michener 1961 and Reichley 1959.)

The council-mayor form was identified with the political machines characteristic of American cities at the turn of the century. The rampant corruption of political machines motivated reformers of that era to design a new form of government, the commission form (Rice 1977). This form was first used in Galveston, Texas, after a devastating hurricane literally leveled the city. In this form, the city is ruled by a small body (5 to 7 typically) of elected officials who as a collective group are the commission. Each individual commissioner is also an administrator, heading an agency or group of agencies. The commissioners are typically elected at-large, that is, from the city as a whole, in non-partisan elections. Figure 9.3 illustrates a typical commission form of government.

As Figure 9.3 illustrates, commissioners were elected from the city at-large. In contrast to the council-mayor form with its emphasis on parties, the commission form attempted to recruit non-politicians into office. Reformers wanted only those who cared about the city to run for legislative office rather than those who were pursuing a political career. Each commissioner would direct an agency or agencies. In the figure, the control over agencies is shown as a solid line. As with the council-mayor form, relationships with a commission[8] (planning commission in the figure) and a corporation are indirect, indicated by the dotted lines.

FIGURE 9.3
Commission Form
of Municipal Government

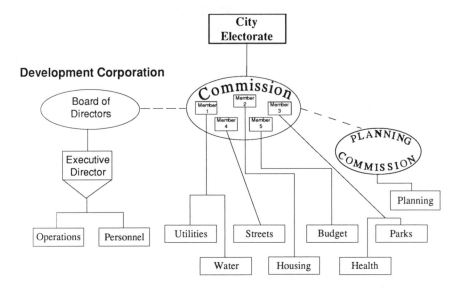

Many cities quickly adopted this form after the successful rebuilding of Galveston. However, problems developed around the coordination of administration because there was no mechanism for requiring the commissioners qua agency heads to cooperate.

The reformers fairly quickly amended the commission form of government and created the council-manager system. In contrast to the separation of powers doctrine implemented in the council-mayor system, commission and council-manager forms of government concentrated authority in the hands of a small, non-partisan council elected at-large.[9] In both forms of government, the council exercised all policy authority. It hired, and could fire at any time, a city manager to administer the city (White 1927; Frederickson 1989).

The city manager has all of the administrative authority of the municipality. He or she hires and fires all administrative personnel, drafts and manages the budget once it is passed by council, and is the executive head of government. There is no mayor in the original system though many cities with this form of government have added an elected mayor. The manager, as noted above, serves at the pleasure of council, meaning he or she could be released at any time.[10]

Figure 9.4 illustrates the classic version of the council-manager form. The solid line between the council and manager denotes the authority of the former

FIGURE 9.4

Council-Manager Form
of Municipal Government

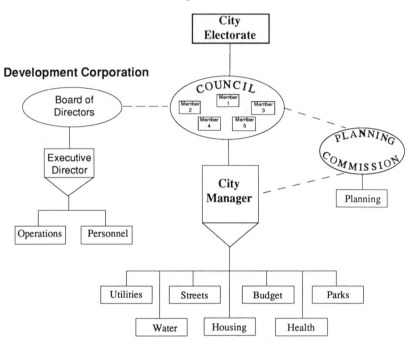

over the latter. Similarly, the council is listed first as it has the basic policy authority of the city. As with the other 2 forms of government, commissions such as the planning commission, and corporations are only indirectly linked to the council or manager. Again the indirect links are indicated by dotted lines.

THE ADMINISTRATIVE CITY: HANDLING THE INFORMAL

Governance of the modern city demands creating and nurturing organizational networks that stretch across jurisdictional boundaries, types of governing units and different forms of city governing systems. Conceptually, the task of governance has two critical dimensions. One dimension is the structure of public authority and the other is the effectiveness of the service delivery system. These can be thought of as interorganizational polities and economies respectively (Benson 1975; Keller 1984). Thus, leadership in the public sector must create appropriate interorganizational polities and effective inter-organizational economies *both within* each political jurisdiction as well as *across all* metropolitan political jurisdictions.

An interorganizational economy ties together diverse actors into a viable pattern for achieving organizational and community goals. (Wamsley and Zald 1973, first applied the concept to public organizations.) The concept of economy notes the existence of rewards for participating in work arrangements that may span the organization in which one works. Furthermore, the concept underscores the primacy of work-related incentives. In contrast, those who approach inter-organizational service delivery from a power perspective are often seen as "playing politics."[11] At the working levels of organizations, participants and clients should be part of an inter-organizational economy, focusing on policies and their outcomes.

For example, a housing inspector should work with homeowners on all aspects of the need to improve their homes. His or her efforts should include alternative methods to achieve compliance with the code, including economic advice as well as explaining technical issues. This requires inspectors who are dedicated to providing service and who work for a department that is linked with other organizations in a functioning interorganizational economy. By being linked to other organizations, the inspector in the field can tap information from the organization.

Unfortunately, all too often housing inspection is a crucial component of local politics. Instead of housing inspection being part of the inter-organizational economy it is an integral component of the inter-organizational polity. In this case, any repairs that an inspector, who is most likely a political appointee of an elected or party official hired because the inspector is a friend of the official, mandates for a house often require the use of a specific contractor who may be an important contributor to political campaigns. A specific contractor may be required regardless of the homeowner's ability to do the repair or the homeowner's financial inability to pay the price the contractor charges.

Polity refers to an arrangement of public authority. Concepts from political science can be relevant guides. For example, an inter-organizational polity should have a functioning "constitution," an agreed on set of fundamental rules prescribing behaviors of significant actors. Adherence to the constitution should create and/or enhance legitimacy. Thus, elected members of council, for example, would behave in particular ways, both in their interactions with citizens and with public employees. For example, the attempt of an elected official to interfere with the legal duties of a public employee, such as attempting to have a housing inspector overlook violations in a rental unit owned by a campaign contributor, should be a violation of the local constitution as well as the law.

Thus, a successful city, one that implements governance, will have an internal inter-organizational network with a viable economy and polity. The network will relate all organizations vested with a public purpose, a broader population of organizations than traditional government agencies. For example, in many states private companies, such as electric utilities, may be empowered by public policy. Utilities can often take land for rights-of-way under state statute. In that case, the local utility is "an organization vested with a public purpose." The economy will tie together services, permitting efficient provision of appropriate services to target groups and even facilitating metropolitan-wide strategic direction over the long run. The polity will relate traditional political institutions such as city councils with administrative units and public management, creating a system of governance. By encompassing relevant organizations beyond just public agencies and focusing on service delivery, the network has ties to the broader community.

In addition, a successfully governed city will have external networks with polities and economies. These networks will tie policies to the larger metropolitan community and even coordinate politics across the fragmented units of current local government. The means of coordination will vary, reflecting institutional history as well as prevailing politics. Leaders will be able to involve citizens and administrators in the creation and implementation of long-term policies. These ties are necessary to deal with the spatially decentralized power in, and the mobilization of resources of, the administrative city. Failure to have working ties spatially will doom efforts of central-city political actors to cope with their increasingly "wicked problems."

RACE AND NETWORKS: INFRASTRUCTURE FOR JUSTICE

By better coordinating networks within and without government as well as within and without the city, the necessary resources can be focused on moral problems such as race. Only viable networks possess both legitimacy and efficiency; both are necessities for coping with "wicked" moral issues. Similarly, only networks involving non-governmental actors who are held publicly accountable, can tackle the critical economic and social issues cities face in a global economy (see Heclo 1978, for an account at the national level).

These networks require institutional infrastructure such as transformational leadership, professional administration, and urban universities. Ideally, legislative bodies will be composed of officials whose primary political ambitions are to serve their community and who have the ability to work with a professional chief executive. If an elected official is primarily interested in a political career at other levels of government, he or she is unlikely to be willing to face the wicked problems. He or she will most likely address issues that have high visibility and short term "political payoffs." For example, a mayor may become the champion of fixing potholes with little regard to an efficient administrative system. The effort can easily be publicized in both the print and visual media. Local television stations may seek the mayor out for coverage and one can easily visualize a gesticulating politician pictured in front of a sizable pothole.[12] Even though some potholes may be fixed more quickly than otherwise, the cost may be quite high, especially in terms of the long-run interference with an effective highway maintenance program. More importantly, the wicked problems of racism, education, community enhancement, etc., are placed on a "back burner."

The strength of reform government is not the professional chief executive but the empowered legislative body. The empowerment permits elected officials to focus on the city as a whole coupled with the ability to fire the chief executive. Reform governments, that is, council-manager systems, tend to elect their councilpeople in at-large elections. The combination of promoting officials with a primary interest in their local situation and being forced to run in the city as a whole tends to make the council a more responsible policy making body.[13] The classical form of reform government lacked an office of mayor, the position most likely to be used as a stepping stone to higher political office. The hope of non-reform government was that political officials could only continue on their political careers if they dealt well with the existing problems. However, the long-term nature of wicked problems unfortunately can induce public officials to avoid dealing with the problems whose solution would be the best test of their true political interests. In contrast to attempting to cope with wicked problems, ambitious politicians will have almost overwhelming incentive to select highly visible, easily solved problems, such as the example of the mayor dealing with potholes noted above.

In the future the same conditions will provide a base for cities to explore their interconnections with other cities in the metropolitan complex. By hiring professional chief executives, cities will be led by those who can conduct effective negotiations with other cities. Being professional, and more often than not from other cities originally, such chief executives can evaluate the city's needs more dispassionately. Given the spatial dimensions of race and power in the modern metropolis, dispassionate leadership will be required to avoid inflaming emotions that could interfere with effective policy making across political jurisdictions divided by race and class.[14]

Without effective networks or viable inter-city connections, moral problems such as race will not be resolved. Race is at root a moral issue, involving rectification of past injustices and implementation of equality. Though political power may force an issue on the public agenda, it will not develop a sure foundation for addressing a moral issue. In fact, if an issue is only sustained by political pressures it will be resolved in the most politically expedient manner. Issues of race go to the core of the "American Dilemma" and a purely political resolution can never generate sufficient rectification or support programs for equality. (See Myrdal 1944, for the original statement on the "American Dilemma.")

Political in this sense relates to what Burns (1978) called "transactional" leadership. In this type of system, issues are resolved through extensive "horse trading." A system of horse trading can work with some degree of fairness if the issues center on splitting a pie that can sustain all types of participants and can be handled by a single unit of government. It works best in periods of growth where issues center on what to do with the next added increment. The system does not work if the issues involve "pain" rather than "gain;" deal with moral concerns which by their nature cannot be resolved by trading favors; or span political jurisdictions. Unfortunately, transactional "games" are the heart of all too many local political systems, pitting group against group in a nearly zero sum game during times of economic adversity.[15] In fact, in a seminal analysis of local politics, Norton Long (1962) called the local community "an ecology of games."

Networks, by mobilizing elected officials seeking a broader, more public interest and who can employ professional chief executives, can induce and support "transformational" leadership. Transformational leadership concentrates on changing the current community for a better future (Burns 1978; in the organizational context see Kouzes and Posner 1987). In contrast, transactional leadership engages in political bargains primarily for short-term gains of the participants. Transformational leadership is not only necessary for directing local government but also for handling moral issues (Elkin 1987). Wicked problems are so wicked because they involve moral choices. Happily, the resolution of moral issues can indeed transform a polity. Even in the most venal transactional systems, political rhetoric extols moral action, painting the actors as statespeople. Unfortunately, performance seldom matches the words but the necessity for such leadership is underscored when dealing with moral issues that go to the very core of political beliefs and daily life. For local America, equality for all is a core belief that can be implemented only by empowered networks led by transformational office holders working with professional public administrators.

CONCLUSION

Effective responses to issues of race and local economy, as well as quality of urban life, require governing networks with viable economies and polities spanning organizations vested with a public purpose within and without individual cities. The task of creating and maintaining such networks requires transformational leadership harnessed to professional administration (Burns 1978; Selznick 1984; Hansell 1988; Moore 1989; Svara 1990).

The administrative city can indeed become a center of empowerment and justice. However, the past indicates that the task will not be easy and will run counter to contemporary systems of transactional politics often laminated with racial overtones. Whether the task will be completed depends on creation of appropriate theories and sustained community leadership.

NOTES

1. Coordination can be achieved by inhibiting outcomes as well as mandating specific policies. Many management theorists do not recognize that removal of obstacles, reduction of reactive forces, etc., can also promote coordination.

Governing is the exercise of public authority over a specified area or territory. Governance is the crafting and implementation of a long-term agenda dealing strategically and constitutionally with the problems besetting the governing system.

2. The public sector can be differentiated from the private sector in many ways. One way is to denote the types of problems that it handles. The public sector often has to deal with the wicked problems, ones with no easy answers because they require making difficult, usually unpopular choices. Often, allegations of the failure of the public sector reflect more the intractability of the problems with which it is attempting to cope rather than the managerial abilities of civil servants.

3. In a study of budgeting, Wamsley and Solomon (1975) analogized the overall movement of policy emanating from a very complex system beyond direct control of any one actor as similar to vectors in physics. In physics, the forces acting on a body have magnitude and direction. The end result of all forces on a body is movement along a "resulting vector." Similarly, the forces acting on local government create "resulting vectors" for all local organizations. The challenge is to align the forces to achieve an overall desired "resulting vector."

4. Researchers tend to lack an agreed-upon definition of network, partially due to the diverse origins of the perspective. However, one useful summary noted that:

Network analysis is essentially a perspective which focuses on structured relationships between individuals and collectivities. As yet there is no commonly agreed definition. We believe that network analysis's salient characteristics are that it gives attention to: (a) structured patterns of relationships and not the aggregated characteristics of individual units, analyzed without reference to their interrelationships; (b) complex network structures and not just dyadic ties; (c) the allocation of scarce resources through concrete systems of power, dependency, and coordination; (d) questions of network boundaries, cluster, and cross-linkages; (e) structures of reciprocal relationships are not just simple hierarchies. (Wellman and Leighton 1988, p. 59n.)

5. There are other categories of local government in addition to the legal classifications in state law. For example, the Bureau of the Census has attempted to capture the demography of the administrative city by creating statistical definitions of urban. A Metropolitan Statistical Area (MSA; formerly, a Standard Metropolitan Statistical Area [SMSA]) is a county with a core city of 50,000 or more in population and all surrounding counties whose population and economy are tied to the core city.

The statistical classifications can be used in law. For example, some federal programs are offered to cities in MSAs or to cities of a certain size. Thus, many cities contest the population count of the census because they not only lose prestige by growing smaller, they also become ineligible for some federal programs.

6.   This is the case in council-strong mayor systems where the mayor can veto actions of council. In these cases, legislation, that is, ordinances, are the joint product of the council and mayor. In council-weak mayor systems, the mayor lacks the veto authority as does the city manager in the council-manager form of government.

7.   In reality, most private corporations have elections controlled by the current board. Most people do not vote their shares and permit current members of the board or the top management to vote their shares. (Legally this is giving a proxy, that is, empowering someone to vote on your behalf.)

8.   Commission here is used as a type of agency. In contrast, the term "commission" in the form of government refers to the structure and authority of the legislative body.

9.   Reformers called for proportional representation [PR] methods of council election. Under this system, candidates were elected if they received a proportion of the vote. Cincinnati used a variation of this system until 1957. In the PR system in Cincinnati, voters ranked candidates from 1, the most preferred, to 9, the least preferred. First preference votes were initially counted, with any candidate receiving one-ninth plus one of such votes elected. If council seats were still available, the second preference votes of those elected were allocated to candidates remaining in the field. The counting continued until all seats were allocated (Straetz 1958). Cambridge, Massachusetts, still employs this system.

This system or some variation may return to some reform systems of government. It would meet requirements for representation of minorities on city councils. Minorities are often excluded in at-large elections in spite of being a significant proportion of the population. At-large elections may have institutional benefits worth preserving by using procedures such as PR.

10.   Many city managers have contracts with their councils. The contracts provide for compensation upon being fired and often permit the manager to remain in office for a few months after the firing.

11.   Many problems in conceptualizing the administrative city spring from the variety of definitions of politics. At a macro level, politics is a system for making value judgments under agreed-upon rules that exclude scientific rationality. At a micro level, politics refers to an orientation around power. A person is described as "political" if he or she approaches relationships in terms of power.

James Thompson (1967) wisely noted that power itself is a slippery concept and substituted notions of dependence. Though his focus was on organizations, it is appropriate at the micro level. One is powerful to the extent he or she is independent of other actors; that is, can act without reference to the views or reactions of others. Conversely, one is powerless if dependent upon others.

Interorganizational networks will, in the long run, be successful to the extent they create *interdependence*, that is, the understanding by relevant organizations that they need to work together to accomplish their goals. Creation of dependence will negate professional discretion as well as citizen participation. In fact, the power of a machine or individual politician is based on their ability to create dependence generally. In this situation, all relationships are perceived as political and service delivery is idiosyncratic, depending upon the political saliency of the immediate service for the service provider and the political status of the client. In other words, a client will only be well served if he or she is important to the service provider and the immediate service need is important to the provider at the time.

12.   A growing problem with modern government is the gap between what is perceived as news and the information on politics that informed citizens need. Increasingly, the information that a citizen must have to make informed judgments is much more complicated than the information that becomes news. As a result, citizens not only lack sufficient information to cast enlightened votes, they may well have a distorted image of government in general and many officials in particular.

For example, Ronald Reagan incurred more public debt at the national level than all of the other presidents combined. However, his presidency was conducted in terms of favorable coverage on televised news regardless of how well government was performed or the long-term consequences. Thus, the ability of cities, especially central cities, to cope with their wicked problems has been greatly diminished with little public attention focused on the causes, such as the amount of public debt (which is still increasing) and the leveraged buyouts of many corporations which were financial anchors to their local communities, e.g., Gulf Oil in Pittsburgh. (See Halberstam 1991.)

13.   A problem with at-large elections is the increased difficulty of minority representatives to be elected. See note 9, *supra*. It may be preferable to have some councilpeople elected from wards and some at-large with most elected at-large.

Conceptually, representation may involve more than the physical appearance of the elected official. It is an indicator of racism that Americans see representation as simply the physical match between voters and elected officials rather than a more useful concern over the ability to guide the community in the future. They key indicator that racism is an issue no longer will be the willingness of non-minority voters to support minority candidates on the basis that the minority candidates do indeed represent well their interests in the future of the community. At present, this is a relatively rare occurrence though greatly increased in the last decades.

The need is to increase the numbers of black administrators and elected officials. This is an area where urban universities, public universities located in metropolitan areas, can play a large role. They can offer programs to educate both pre-service and in-service black officials.

14.   Dispassionate and disinterested do not mean without emotion or interest. Quite the contrary, the commitment of women and men to city management usually reflects an intense belief in cities as communities and public service. These people are not only willing to spend 6 years at the university to obtain a public administration degree, but are also willing more frequently to help as many cities as possible. Without a deep commitment, they soon leave the profession. If they become overly emotional in any one case, they lose their ability to lead a local community effectively.

15.   Zero sum means that the total is constant and thus any gain by one group is a loss to another. They United States is experiencing an economic transition that has made most local economies, especially those in the older industrial areas, closer to zero sum contests. Not since the Great Depression have questions about income distribution been so stark.

In the early days of urbanization, political machines could prosper by running a transactional system. The rapidly growing economy permitted all to gain. In a contracting era the machines have faced a different situation and have found their capacity to rule seriously reduced. The same dynamics may account for the difficulty the Democratic Party has faced in maintaining the coalition of groups initially put together by Franklin D. Roosevelt during the New Deal. Making hard choices strains coalitions if the glue that holds them together is a system of immediate rewards.

REFERENCES

Benson, J. 1975. The interorganizational network as a political economy. *Administrative Science Quarterly* 20:229–50.

Burns, J. 1978. *Leadership*. New York: Harper and Row.

Caro, R. 1974. *The power broker: Robert Moses and the fall of New York*. New York: Alfred A. Knopf.

Dillon, J. 1911. *Commentaries on the law of municipal corporations*. Boston: Little, Brown and Company. (See Vol. 1, sec. 237.)

Elkin, S. 1987. *City and regime in the american republic*. Chicago: University of Chicago Press.

Frederickson, G. 1989. *Ideal and practice in council-manager government*. Washington, DC: International City Management Association.

Halberstam, D. 1991. *The next century*. New York. William Morrow & Company, Inc.

Hansell, W. 1988. The missing ingredient: a credible civic infrastructure. *Public Management* 70:4–5.

Heclo, H. 1978. Issue networks and the executive establishment. In *The new american political system*, A. King, ed. Washington, DC: American Enterprise Institute for Public Policy Research.

Hult, K. and C. Walcott. 1990. *Governing public organizations: politics, structures, and institutional design*. Pacific Grove, CA: Brooks/Cole Publishing Company.

Keller, L. 1984. The political economy of public management: an interorganizational network perspective. *Administration and Society* 15:455–74.

———. 1989. City managers and federalism: intergovernmental relations in the administrative city. In *Ideal and practice in city management*, G. Frederickson, ed., 33–44. Washington, DC: International City Management Association.

Kouzes, J. and B. Posner. 1987. *The leadership challenge: how to get extraordinary things done in organizations*. San Francisco: Jossey-Bass.

Long, N. 1962. *The polity*. Chicago: Rand McNally.

Michener, J. 1961. *Report of the county chairman*. New York: Random House.

Moore, C., ed. 1989. Symposium: leadership that unifies. *National Civic Review* 78:409–64.

Myrdal, G. 1944. *The american dilemma: the negro problem and modern democracy*. New York: Harper Brothers.

Perrucci, R. and H. Potter, eds. 1989. *Networks of power: organizational actors at the national, corporate, and community levels*. Hawthorne, NY: Aldine de Gruyter.

Peters, T. 1989. *Thriving on chaos: handbook for a management revolution*. New York: Alfred A. Knopf.

Peters, T. and R. Waterman, Jr. 1982. *In search of excellence: lessons from America's best run companies*. New York: Harper & Row.

Peterson, M. 1987. *The great triumvirate: Webster, Clay and Calhoun*. New York: Oxford University Press.

Peterson, P. 1981. *City limits*. Chicago: University of Chicago Press.

Reichley, J. 1959. *The art of government: reform and organization politics in Philadelphia*. New York: Fund for the Republic.

Rice, B. 1977. *Progressive cities: the commission government movement in America 1901-1920*. Austin, TX: University of Texas Press.

Royko, M. 1971. *Boss: Richard J. Daley of Chicago*. New York: New American Library.

Schiesl, M. 1977. *The politics of efficiency: municipal administration and reform in America 1800-1920*. Berkeley: University of California Press.

Selznick, P. 1984. *Leadership in administration: a sociological interpretation*. Berkeley: University of California Press (reprint of the 1957 edition with an introduction by Tom Peters).

Straetz, R. 1958. *PR politics in Cincinnati*. New York: New York University Press.

Svara, J., ed. 1990. Symposium: leadership and structure in local and regional governance. *National Civic Review* 79: 302-66.

Taylor, F. 1947. *Scientific management, comprising shop management, the principles of scientific management [and] testimony before the special house committee*. New York: Harper.

Teaford, J. 1984. *The unheralded triumph: city government in the United States 1870-1900*. Baltimore: Johns Hopkins University Press.

Thompson, J. 1967. *Organizations in action: social science bases of administrative theory*. New York: McGraw-Hill.

Turk, H. 1977. *Organizations in modern life*. San Francisco: Jossey-Bass.

Wamsley, G. and L. Solomon. 1975. Sour notes in music city: making budgets in Nashville, 1952-1972. Unpublished paper.

Wamsley, G. and M. Zald. 1973. *The political economy of public organizations*. Lexington, MA: D.C. Heath.

Warren, R., S. Rose and A. Bergunder. 1974. *The structure of urban reform*. Lexington, MA: Lexington Books.

Waste, R. 1989. *The ecology of city policymaking*. New York: Oxford University Press.

Wellman, B. and B. Leighton. 1988. Networks, neighborhoods, and communities: approaches to the study of the community question. In *New perspectives on the american community*, R. Warren and L. Lyon, eds., 57-72. Chicago: Dorsey Press.

White, L. 1927. *The city manager*. Chicago: University of Chicago Press.

Wiebe, R. 1962. *Businessmen and reform: a study of the progressive movement*. Cambridge, MA: Harvard University Press.

_____. 1967. *The search for order, 1877-1920*. New York: Hill & Wang.

Winter, W. 1969. *The urban polity*. New York: Dodd, Mead.

Yates, D. 1977. *The ungovernable city: the politics of urban problems and policy making*. Cambridge, MA: MIT Press.

10 Racial Politics and Black Power in the Cities

GEORGIA A. PERSONS

American society is a democracy that espouses freedom, equality, and full participation for all its citizens. More so than for any other ethnic group, the treatment and status of African-Americans in America have been continuous barometers of success in realizing these goals. While one of the most gripping dramas of American history has been the struggle by African-Americans to obtain their rightful place in the social, economic, and political order of American society, certainly one of the more interesting developments of the past three decades has been their emergence in positions of relative power in American politics. One of the major manifestations of the relative success of African-Americans in obtaining their place in the political order is their presence in high-visibility positions as mayors of big cities. Indeed, as America approaches the dawn of the twenty-first century, the election of black mayors is almost a commonplace occurrence in American politics. However, the apparent routine nature of the election of black mayors at once obscures the arduous political struggles of the past, the significant uncertainty of the future, and most importantly, obscures the critical questions of what has really changed in regard to the status of African-Americans in American society.

The emergence of black mayors came about as part of what political scientists who study the history of the black political struggle in America call "the new black politics." The new black politics is but one of many strategies pursued by African-Americans over time in their efforts to alleviate the burdens of oppression. Analysts generally identify three shifts in black political strategy that have occurred in just the recent past. First, in the mid-1950s, blacks began a shift away from relying on the courts to obtain racial justice, to engaging in activities of direct protest against the injustices of American society. The result was the civil rights movement. Second, impatience with the limited progress and non-violent tactics of the civil rights movement gave birth in the period 1966–67 to the short-lived black liberation movement. The era of the black liberation movement was a mix of strident protest, a somewhat related wave of mass social unrest resulting in urban riots in many American cities, and fiery political rhetoric that incorporated a blend of philosophical notions including among others, black separatism and calls for uniting the black political struggle the world over. Finally, in 1972, another strategic shift occurred with the move to pursuit of electoral politics (Walters 1980). The latter and current period, with emphasis on concerted electoral politics to the exclusion of protest and civil disobedience, has been characterized as the era of the new black politics.

Historically, one of the major pillars in the foundation of political empowerment for different ethnic groups in America has been the strength of their numbers in urban environments. In fact, the path to majoritarian democracy, as America moved towards government based on full participation by members of all racial and ethnic groups, has been one of successive political dominance by various ethnic groups. Each stage of group dominance and succession has brought with it an expanded political participation and changes in the way in which voters are mobilized into victorious groups and coalitions. From the mid-1800s to the present, the political arena of urban America has served as a common stage upon which various groups have in turn starred in politically significant or dominant roles. Each group has engaged in efforts to impose selective notions of civic virtue and social order; to exact political and social recognition for members of their respective groups; and in the case of blacks, finally to seek to ensure the realization of manifold justice from American society. It is from this perspective of urban America as a common stage that one is better able to understand the dynamics of the current drama: the varying degrees of success by African-Americans in achieving political empowerment in America. It is necessary, however, to look back in time to see the unfolding of this process of group political succession.

This chapter focuses on ways in which different racial and ethnic groups have obtained and used different political resources to achieve political empowerment. Particular attention is given to the emergence and experiences of black mayoralities as both the embodiment of a continued dispersion of political power in cities, and as the latest catalyst for ethno-racial conflict. The discussion also focuses on the achievement of black mayoralties and the emergence of new developments within the context of cities, and in regard to strategic efforts pursued by black politicians which pose threats to enhanced black power in cities.

THE EMERGENCE OF MAJORITARIAN DEMOCRACY IN URBAN AMERICA

As the first settler group in America, white Anglo-Saxon Protestants were the earliest custodians of American-style democracy. This group, called Patricians, ruled during the earliest period of city government in America. With wealth, social standing, and political resources, including the right to vote and hold office, all tied together and tightly controlled, early forms of urban politics were indeed a white gentleman's calling. The Patrician class constituted a ruling elite and governed from a broadly shared consensus based on the fact that as Robert Dahl so vividly characterized them:

> They were of one common stock and one religion, cohesive in their uniformly conservative outlook on all matters, substantially unchallenged in their authority, successful in pushing through their own policies, and in full control of such critical social institutions as the established religion, the education system (including not only all the schools but Yale as well), and even business enterprise. Both they and their opponents took their political supremacy as a fact. . . . The elite seems to have possessed that most indispensable of all characteristics in a dominant group—the sense, shared not only by themselves but by the populace, that their claim to govern was legitimate (Dahl 1961, pp. 16–17).

Although Dahl based his observations on the city of New Haven, Connecticut, that city's experience was not unique. Other studies have shown that other American communities were at various times hierarchically ordered social systems, characterized by elite dominance with the intertwining of politics and social standing (Gordon 1973). Indeed, this pattern persisted in some cities such as Atlanta well into the 1950s (Hunter 1953). Early Patrician rule was buttressed by restrictions of the right to vote to those white males who owned real property and also by procedural rules like the "Stand Up Law" which required a man to reveal his choice of candidate in a public town meeting in full view of the ruling elite (Dahl 1961). However, this oligarchical pattern of rule was not to last. In New Haven, the Patricians were supplanted in the early 1840s by the emergence of a group of entrepreneurs, "self-made" men, nouveau riche, who had newly benefitted from growing economic opportunities of an early mercantile economy and who had been inspired by the gradual democratization of politics. These successors to the Patricians were of the same ethnic stock as the Patricians, but they were as a group less well educated, of humbler origins, had come to possess great wealth, but held little claim to high social standing (Dahl 1961). The emergence of entrepreneurs (in New Haven) was the first in what was to become a seemingly perpetual pattern of successive group dominance in urban America. The emergence of entrepreneurs also represented overall, the early and lasting shift from a situation of cumulative inequalities in which one group monopolized the total range of politically relevant resources, to an apparently permanent situation of dispersed inequalities in which different groups retain possession of some political resources, but lack some others.

THE EMERGENCE OF ETHNIC VOTING

Just as the changing nature of the urban economy combined with other forces to drive a shift in political dominance from the Patrician class to the entrepreneurs, economic changes also played a role in the rapid expansion of the urban population base. The industrialization of America required many workers, and they came in large numbers. During the period 1820–1920, 33 million immigrants came to America (Judd 1988). These new immigrants were of different ethnic stock than the Patrician class who were largely British in their origins. The new immigrants were from countries such as Germany, Ireland and Scandinavia, and later in the 1880s, from Italy, Scotland, and Eastern European countries such as Hungary, Poland, and Russia. These groups were generally not treated well by the first settler group of Patricians, thus leading to an enhanced bonding among individuals of common ethnic origins, and resulting in residential settlement patterns in which relatively large clusterings of ethnically homogeneous groups occupied discrete territories in what was overall a rather hetergeneous population.

The process of assimilating these diverse groups, socially and economically, gave rise to new techniques in mobilizing voters, and ultimately to new urban political leadership structures as well. The immediate political manifestation of this process of assimilation was political mobilization based on ethnic appeals. As Dahl described this development: "Any political leader who could help members of an ethnic group overcome the handicaps and humiliations associated with their identity, who could increase the power, prestige, and income of an ethnic and/or religious out-group, automatically had an effective strategy for earning support and loyalty" (Dahl 1961, p. 33). Thus emerged the phenomenon of ethnic voting. Much later, a parallel phenomenon of black bloc voting would emerge in urban America.

Although there is no definitive agreement among analysts as to just what constitutes ethnic voting in its many possible manifestations, generally, ethnic voting is said to occur when ethnic group membership is an important determinant factor in voting behavior. In some instances, members of an ethnic group show a decided preference for one political party over another which cannot be explained solely as a result of other demographic characteristics. The phenomenon of African-Americans voting overwhelmingly for Democrats at both the national and subnational levels is a good example of this. In other instances of ethnic voting, members of ethnic groups respond to appeals made on the basis of their ethnic status, and/or ethnic group support for a political party emerges as the result of historical loyalties and traditions. The early attachment of African-Americans to the Republican party as the party of emancipation was a case of historical loyalty, initially weakened by more class-based voting during the New Deal era, and finally ruptured during the racially charged atmosphere of the early 1960s when African-Americans gave their support to John Kennedy over Richard Nixon. Another manifestation of ethnic voting occurs when ethnic group members cross party lines to vote for or against a candidate belonging to a particular group (Wolfinger 1974). In this latter instance, ethnic group members usually cross party lines in order to vote for a member of their own group. In this form, ethnic voting persists as the group gains recognition as a result of having their members elected to office, and is reinforced by actual or perceived hostilities directed towards the group by other dominant population groups. Like wealth and social standing, ethnicity became a valuable resource in political competition. Thus, by using the strength of their numbers in the population and by engaging in bloc voting based on ethnicity, the second wave of immigrants were able to establish their dominance in elective office and municipal employment in cities of the Northeast and Midwest, thereby translating the power of their vote into particularistic benefits for members of their groups.

The primary embodiment of political power for ethnic groups was the political machine. The political machine was a pyramidal form of political organization that centralized power by organizing and disciplining strong voter support starting at the precinct level, and including the various wards occupied by predominantly working-class immigrant voters. The foundation of the political machine was ethnic voting. The machine mobilized the immigrant electorate and effectively delivered that vote for a select slate of ethnic candidates. These elected officials along with the machine operatives at the precinct and ward levels, in turn distributed jobs and small, but crucial, social welfare favors to the immigrant voters. The machine granted larger favors, such as business licenses, lucrative city contracts and utility franchises, to the up-and-coming ethnic entrepreneurs and the traditional white business elites as well. Generally the political machine subsumed one or more of the local political parties and effectively controlled political appointments, the slating (nomination) of candidates for all posts large and small, a substantial number of jobs in city bureaucracies, and, of course, the outcome of elections. The political machine was headed and directed by a single boss who may or may not have been an elected official holding high political office despite the high reaches of his political grasp (Riordan 1963; Gosnell 1968; Shefter 1976).

THE REFORM MOVEMENT AND RESTRUCTURING OF POLITICAL POWER

The favors on which machine rule thrived led to considerable corruption in city government. This in turn led to successful efforts by Anglo-Saxon middle- and upper-class groups to reform municipal government and thereby reassert their control. The reform movement, which began in the late 1800s with the height of ethnic immigration, was a thinly disguised "good government" move- ment rooted in class tensions. The reform movement sought to bring about a reassertion of political control by the white upper class by altering the structures and procedures of municipal government. As such, the reform movement struck at the heart of machine strength: the ability to mobilize voters; the ability to con- trol local elections; and thereby the ability to dominate local government.

The introduction of the Australian secret ballot in 1890 was aimed at curb- ing fraud in voting. Short ballots replaced long ballots and party labels were removed from ballots. By 1905, voter registration laws were in effect in most states, and voter registration procedures were tightened and enforced by newly established election boards. By 1910, non-partisan at-large elections were grow- ing in popularity and by 1929 were the norm in the majority of large cities. Non-partisan elections removed a major cue from the voting process. Thus, rather than being able to vote for an entire slate of Democratic (and sometimes Republican) candidates who were associated with the machine, the masses of uneducated voters had to now differentiate between candidates and their varying issue positions. At-large elections made the concentration of ethnic voters in defined spatial areas far less potent than had ward-based elections. Municipal elections were scheduled for off-years so as not to benefit from mobilization efforts for state and national elections. In reformed governments, administrative officials in city government were appointed rather than popularly elected, result- ing in the rise to power of professional bureaucrats, experts who acted not so much as agents of the people, but frequently as independent decisionmakers and major contenders for power. By the 1920s, the notion that cities could best be run, without political interference, by city managers had taken hold in a large number of mid-sized cities (Judd 1988). Consequences of the reform movement were a major alteration in the balance of power in American cities and a return of white Anglo-Saxons to a more dominant role in city politics. Although dealt a serious blow by these changes, the political machine did not completely disap- pear (Wolfinger 1972), but remained as a form of entrenched power in many cities.

This early phenomenon of ethnic voting left a substantial legacy in urban politics which in many ways affected the political prospects of African- Americans. Primarily, the ethnic-based political machine embodied the incorporation of early, formally organized black electoral politics in a dependent form. Early black leaders were subordinates of the political machine who, drawing on something of a cult of personality, "delivered" the black vote in support of machine/white candidates. Some very limited benefits, mainly in the form of low-level municipal jobs, accrued to some of the few blacks who actively participated in electoral politics during the height of the machine era. This kind of arrangement characterized the relationship between blacks and the more prominent machine politics in such cities as New York (Katznelson 1973) and Chicago (Wilson 1960; Gosnell 1967), as well as small cities such as Gary and East St. Louis (Nelson and Meranto 1977). These linkages between blacks and political machines spanned the life of the machines, and the machine-like organization of black politics frequently persisted until the era of the new black politics of the late 1970s and arguably beyond in some places. Additionally, the reform movement left a host of obstacles to African-Americans in their later efforts to maximize the political benefits of their concentrated presence in urban populations and thereby seize the reins of urban governance. Some of these obstacles included at-large voting requirements in municipal elections, and non-partisan elections which made it difficult to elect black officials in proportion to the presence of blacks in the population. Varied weak-mayor forms of government imposed under the reform movement limited the possibilities and benefits of having strong and effective black mayoral leadership. Local party organizations were frequently monopolized by political machines, thereby eliminating a basis for mobilizing black voters.

THE RISE OF THE NEW BLACK POLITICS

Like the immigrants before them, blacks came to the cities of the North and Northeast seeking improved economic opportunities and social conditions. The "great black migration" north was driven by three major factors: (1) the push of economic difficulties in the South due to a changing agricultural economy which rendered even the cheap labor of black workers increasingly surplus, (2) otherwise limited employment opportunities, and (3) the human degradation of virulent racism and segregation. This northward movement of the black population from the early 1920s to the late 1960s resulted in the racial and demographic transformation of many northern cities (Judd 1988). For many of the same reasons that millions of blacks moved north, hundreds of thousands moved from rural areas to urban areas within the South, creating over time black population majorities in several southern cities as well (Grant 1972). These population shifts laid the groundwork for eventual black political dominance in many urban areas, North and South.

However, the presence of blacks in cities in large numbers was not sufficient to realize the political resources represented by their numbers. Other developments served as catalysts for converting concentrated population clusters into political resources. Beginning around 1955, the civil rights movement with its demonstrations and other acts of civil disobedience served an early function of spurring a consciousness of defiance and determination among blacks in regard to resisting repressive and discriminatory practices. The nonviolent tactics of the movement gave way to violent riots in cities across the country in the mid- to late-1960s. The civil rights movement and the urban riots served to awaken the entire nation to the more oppressive forms of racism. The report of the Kerner Commission on civil disorders issued in the wake of the riots called attention to the "two Americas, one black, one white; separate and unequal" (National Advisory Commission on Civil Disorders 1967). These developments served to mobilize the black community around efforts to elect new urban political leadership. The Voting Rights Act, passed in 1965, served to eliminate legal and informal barriers to voting by blacks in Southern states, and spawned the major presence of blacks in elective office (Barker and Barker 1982; Williams 1982; Lawson 1985). From the mid-1960s to the late-1970s, specially targeted voter education and registration drives in southern and northern cities resulted in adding millions of blacks to the eligible voter rolls. The foundations of the new black politics were thus laid.

Perhaps because the struggles to obtain the right to vote and efforts to elect members of their own group to office were so intense, the expectations among blacks about the power of the vote were exaggerated. These expectations were captured by Nelson (1982, pp. 188, 189):

> The new black politics represents an effort by black political leaders to capitalize on the increasing size of the black electorate; the strategic position of black voters in many cities, counties, and congressional districts, and the growing political consciousness of the black population. . . . The new black politics would become an instrument of social change, permanently eradicating obstacles to the upward mobility and continuing progress of the entire black community.

THE ELECTION OF BLACK MAYORS

Perhaps the most important achievement of the new black politics has been the election of black mayors in many of the major cities in the United States as well as in hundreds of small cities. There were some 293 black mayors in early 1990 with the majority to be found in small cities (Joint Center for Political

Studies 1990). Prior to the election of L. Douglas Wilder as governor of Virginia and the first black to be elected governor in the United States, big-city black mayors were the most visible black elected officials. Their responsibilities to their constituencies are much greater and more comprehensive than that of most other black elected officials at the local level, and their political influence is less subject to dilution than black representatives in Congress. Thus, the election of a black mayor, particularly in a big city, constitutes a major socio-political achievement. It is a highly symbolic achievement, symbolizing the political upward mobility of African-Americans, and it is highly visible evidence of the payoffs of black strategic efforts.

In regard to big-city (population 150,000 and above) black mayors, there have been roughly five electoral waves. The first wave occurred with the election of black mayors in Cleveland and Gary in 1967, and Newark in 1970. Cleveland lost its first black mayoralty in an unsuccessful effort to elect a second black mayor in 1972. The second wave occurred with the election of black mayors in Atlanta, Detroit, and Los Angeles in 1973, and the District of Columbia in 1974. Prior to receiving home rule in 1973, the mayor and city council of the District of Columbia had been appointed by the President of the United States. Thus Lyndon Johnson appointed the first black mayor of the District of Columbia in the mid-1960s. The third wave brought black mayors to New Orleans and Oakland in 1977, and Birmingham in 1979. The fourth wave occurred in 1983 with the election of Harold Washington in Chicago, Wilson Goode in Philadelphia, and Harvey Gantt in Charlotte, North Carolina. The black mayoralty in Chicago was lost in 1989 subsequent to the death of Washington during his second term in office. In Charlotte, Harvey Gantt was defeated for reelection by a white female Republican. Baltimore was added in 1987, initially by default with the election of then-Mayor Schaeffer to the state governorship and automatic ascendancy of the black deputy mayor to the position of mayor. Harvard-trained attorney and Rhodes Scholar, Kurt Schmoke became the first elected black mayor of Baltimore in 1987. The fifth and most recent wave occurred in November 1989 with the election of black mayors in Durham, North Carolina; New Haven; New York City; Seattle; and again in Cleveland, Ohio.

Most black mayors have been elected in cities with a majority or near-majority black population. Roughly 63 percent of black-mayor cities with populations of 50,000 or more have black populations of 40 percent or more (see Table 10.1). This means that African-Americans have used the strength of their numbers in political jurisdictions where their presence has been in concentrated clusters. Most such jurisdictions are located in the southern states, but in small cities. Alabama has over 30 black-mayor cities, the largest number of black mayors of any state though only one black-mayor city, Birmingham, can be characterized as a big city. Alabama's smallest black-mayor city, Emelle in

TABLE 10.1

Black Mayors of Cities with Populations over 50,000, 1990

Name	City	Population	Percent Black
David Dinkins	New York City	7,071,000	25.0
Thomas Bradley	Los Angeles, CA	3,259,000	17.0
W. Wilson Goode	Philadelphia, PA	1,642,000	40.2
Coleman Young	Detroit, MI	1,086,000	63.1
Kurt Schmoke	Baltimore, MD	763,000	54.8
Marion Barry	Washington, DC	626,000	70.0
Michael White	Cleveland, OH	573,800	45.0
Sidney Barthelemy	New Orleans, LA	554,000	55.3
Norman Rice	Seattle, WA	493,800	9.5
Maynard Jackson	Atlanta, GA	421,000	66.6
Lionel Wilson	Oakland, CA	356,000	46.9
Sharpe James	Newark, NJ	316,000	46.9
Richard Arrington	Birmingham, AL	277,000	55.6
Richard Dixon	Dayton, OH	181,000	37.0
Jessie Ratley	Newport News, VA	154,000	31.5
Carrie Perry	Hartford, CT	137,000	33.9
Thomas Barnes	Gary, IN	136,000	70.8
John Daniels	New Haven, CT	129,000	31.0
Chester Jenkins	Durham, NC	110,000	47.0
Edward Vincent	Inglewood, CA	102,000	57.3
Noel Taylor	Roanoke, VA	100,000	22.0
Walter Tucker	Compton, CA	93,000	74.8
Melvin Primas	Camden, NJ	82,000	53.0
John Hatcher, Jr.	East Orange, NJ	77,000	83.6
George Livingston	Richmond, CA	77,000	47.9
Edna W. Summers	Evanston Township, IL	72,000	21.4
Walter L. Moore	Pontiac, MI	70,000	34.2
Ronald Blackwood	Mt. Vernon, NY	68,000	48.7
E. Pat Larkins	Pompano Beach, FL	66,000	17.2
Carl E. Officer	East St. Louis, IL	51,000	95.6

Sources:　Joint Center for Political Studies, Washington, DC; U.S. Bureau of the Census, 1986 population estimates.

Sumter County, has a population of only some 98 citizens. Due to media attention, and the directions of scholarly research, Americans are much more familiar with big-city black mayors. Almost all big-city black mayors have been elected with some level of white-voter support, including those cities where the size of the black population made such support unnecessary for the election of a black mayor. Blacks have also been elected mayors in cities with majority white populations. The 1973 election of Thomas Bradley in Los Angeles was an early case. Recent examples include New Haven, New York City, and Seattle.

RACE AND POLARIZATION

When blacks were initially elected mayors in big cities, they pursued elective office against a range of different power structures. In some cities such as Cleveland and Detroit, blacks faced remnants of old-line, white-ethnic political machines which had traditionally dominated the politics of these respective cities. In these cities, the Democratic party machinery was, in fact, controlled by the political machine, and blacks were either locked out of these organizations or were relegated to distinctly subordinate roles (Nelson and Meranto 1977). This meant that black mayoral contenders could not count on using the party apparatus as a vehicle for mobilizing voters in their campaign efforts. It also meant that in addition to their mere presence being a challenge to the prevailing racial order, their candidacies posed a serious threat to the patronage jobs and city contracts on which the political machines thrived. The latter threat was as great or even greater than the former.

In cities such as Atlanta and Birmingham, black mayoral contenders confronted the twin southern legacies of racial segregation, still widely in place in the early 1970s and the total domination of local politics by the white business community. In both Atlanta and Birmingham, mayoral elections were conducted on a non-partisan basis, thus in the absence of partisan loyalties, individual personalities and racial issues quickly rose to the forefront of political campaigns. As a city that very early in its existence started to emerge as a regional city in terms of business locations and the location of regional offices of the federal government, Atlanta had long promoted itself both as "a city too busy to hate," and as a city whose politics was characterized by a biracial coalition. The biracial coalition was real, but mainly operated only at the level of white business elites and a small group of black civic and social leaders. Many of the latter group dominated the black business community which in the early days thrived primarily because of racial segregation. The white business community effectively monopolized expression of the political interests of the white middle class. Both parties to the Atlanta biracial coalition were able to call on the support of the respective groups that they represented in an election day alliance. The Atlanta biracial coalition effectively served to keep working-class whites out of political power. Working-class whites always supported candidates who made strident racist appeals to white voters, thereby being offensive and threatening to blacks, and generally undermining the image of the city that the

white business community so carefully developed, primarily for outside consumption. Thus for years, the biracial coalition worked well to defeat white-
working class, racist candidates and to always elect the white middle-class candidate preferred by the white business community. When blacks sought to lead
the Atlanta biracial coalition and elect one of their own to the position of mayor,
the coalition quickly broke down, and racial polarization ensued.

With very few exceptions, the early elections of a first black mayor (as
opposed to subsequent elections of second and third black mayors) in big cities,
has resulted in severe racial polarization (Nelson and Meranto 1977; Levine
1974). Generally, such polarization was attendant to the mayoral campaigns and
the nature of the campaign themes utilized. Black candidates not only had to rely
primarily on a black voter base for any hope of success, they also had the arduous task of mobilizing a primary support base which in many cases was not
registered in large numbers, and had not previously been encouraged to register.
Many were not accustomed to city government serving their needs and interests
and were therefore apathetic about politics. Thus particularly in the early days,
black mayoral candidates had to adopt campaign themes that emphasized social
and political change. Such campaign themes also embodied strong appeals to
blacks as a racial group in opposition to continued dominance by whites. By
adopting such political postures, black mayoral candidates were able to appeal
to the very strong desire on the part of black citizens to change their subordinate
status in urban society. Black mayoral candidates also benefitted from a rather
strong racial solidarity forged by a common state of oppression more so than by
anything else. White contenders in these situations frequently resorted to "save
our city" campaigns, beseeching white voters to band together against "a black
takeover." In some cases, more moderate white contenders publicly pursued a
race-neutral stance of wanting to represent "all of the people" though they too
primarily focused on mobilizing white voters by using code words such as "law
and order" for racist sentiments. Such dynamics were not only attendant to early
black mayoral campaigns that took place during the "fever pitch" of black political mobilization nationwide. As recently as 1983, America witnessed severe
racial polarization with the election of Harold Washington as the first black
mayor of Chicago, primarily due to the way in which Washington's candidacy
explicitly challenged the prevailing order of Chicago politics.

With the early black mayors, there was also the tendency for racial polarization to develop in the aftermath of the election when a first black mayor began
engaging in the routine activities of mayoral prerogatives and daily governance.
For example the appointment process, an area of mayor prerogative was almost
always highly controversial for early black mayors. The removal of a white police chief and the appointment of a black chief generally sparked the most ran-
corous conflict and in some instances provided racial polarization. As the first
black mayor of Atlanta, Maynard Jackson provoked a prolonged and severe

crisis, including a challenge to the constitutionality of the city charter, when he appointed a black police chief (Persons 1985). This was primarily due to the fact that in Atlanta as in most other cities at the time, the police had come to symbolize the embodiment of white control over the black population. Thus, the appointment of a black police chief struck at the heart of white power. Also, for the first time in the history of the city, the local Atlanta newspapers published the salaries of all top city appointees, many of whom were, for the first time, black. This action served to exacerbate resentment among some whites about the "coming to power" of African-Americans. In such a racially polarized atmosphere, there was a strong tendency by both whites and blacks to view most developments in city politics as benefitting one group over the other.

Racial polarization did not occur in all cases with the election of first black mayors. Los Angeles was an exceptional case, and in 1973, this was not unrelated to the facts that blacks comprised such a small percentage of the city's population, or the manner in which Bradley waged his campaign so as not to provoke a white backlash. In a later exceptional case of Philadelphia, which has a sizable black population, the critical factor was the refusal of the black mayoral candidate to make special appeals to blacks, relying instead on the symbolic significance of a black candidate to sufficiently stir black voting solidarity. Also over time, in most cases, whites have come to at least tacitly accept the reality of black political dominance in many big cities (Eisinger 1980). In the end, black political dominance has not been a major setback to the political influence of whites, and certainly has not been a threat to their positions of social and economic dominance.

Except for the predominant, though not exclusive, pattern of a reliance on a sizable black population base, particularly in the early years, the dynamics surrounding the election of black mayors are very diverse with few commonalities across time and place. However, the potential for racial polarization continues in many cities. In cases with significant black populations and wherein black candidates mount social reform campaigns, voting largely continues along racial lines with black candidates rarely getting more than 20 percent of the white vote. This was the case in the mayoral elections of 1983 and 1987 in Chicago as well as in the 1989 election to succeed the late Harold Washington. In some locales where blacks are in a clear majority, elections frequently occur without the presence of a single white candidate and thus the racial dynamics of the campaigns change. In such cases, white voters tend to support the least "radical" black candidate. This has occurred in some elections in Atlanta and Detroit. In some similar cases such as the New Orleans election of 1986, a black candidate may make an explicit appeal to white voters, making this group the pivotal voting block. In a range of locales, but particularly in some locales where blacks comprise a critical but not decisive voter base, or wherein blacks do not comprise a significant portion of the population at all, some black candidates have chosen to mount campaigns based on issues that clearly transcend racial concerns or concerns about social reform. The 1989 black mayoral elections in New Haven, Seattle, and to a lesser degree, New York City and Cleveland are examples of what some analysts call the new black crossover politics which emphasize a deracialized strategy. The success of such black mayoral candidacies make clear that the limits of race as a descriptive condition can be overcome. As discussed later in this chapter, such successes do not necessarily augur well for the advancement of a social reform agenda.

WHAT DID BLACK MAYORS INHERIT?

Since the mid-1960s, African-Americans have increasingly taken their turn at center stage in the governance of big cities. In an interesting turn of events, they have been able to use the results of their social ostracism, i.e., forced residential segregation, to create political resources. Partly due to migration and natural population growth, but also due to white flight from the cities to the suburbs, the political power balance was altered along with the population dynamics of big cities. The important question is what difference has black political power made in big cities? There are no easy answers to this question, and no consensus on any one answer among scholars or lay observers.

In terms of electoral successes, the new black politics has been rather successful (at the subnational level). In addition to significant increases in their total numbers, most black mayors have been reelected and a number of first black mayors—in Detroit, Los Angeles, Washington, D.C., and until recently in Gary and Newark—have enjoyed long-term incumbencies. In Atlanta, Gary, New Orleans, and Newark, first black mayors have been succeeded in office by other black mayors, primarily reflecting the dominance of African-Americans in the local populations. However, a rather mixed picture emerges if other questions are raised about: (1) the strength of the economic base of black-mayor cities, (2) relative changes in the distribution of economic power, or (3) the ends towards which political power has been directed by elected political leadership. Even without attempting specific answers to these questions for specific cities, it can easily be discerned that while not all black mayors have inherited the "hollow prizes" of economically bankrupt cities, declining populations, and inadequate public services so direly predicted some two decades ago (Feemstra 1969), some clearly have. Those cases of economically distressed cities reflect the dynamic forces of wealth in a capitalist society, a realm of power not readily accessible through voting, the major resource in the black political arsenal. The cases of Gary and Newark are good examples of how a combination of forces, many beyond the control of elected officials, black or white, and some provoked by racial considerations, have combined to determine the fate of some cities.

Within the span of a 12-month period, 2 of the nation's longest serving black mayors were defeated in reelection bids: Gibson in Newark in May 1986, and Hatcher in Gary in May 1987. Although both long-term incumbents were succeeded by other black mayors, succession was not the real story. Gibson was initially elected mayor of Newark in 1970, winning with 60 percent of the vote in the heady and hopeful period following the Newark riots. He was reelected in 1974 with 55 percent of the vote in a bitter, racially charged contest against Anthony Imperial (the former mayor of Italian descent, whom Gibson had initially defeated), and reelected again in 1978 with 68 percent of the vote. Gibson faced a black challenger in his fourth race in 1982, winning with 52 percent of the vote despite the fact that he and his major challenger were under federal indictments on charges of corruption. In 1986, the deficiencies in Gibson's record became a liability, coupled with the generally continuing decline of the Newark economy. Unfortunately, Gibson's tenure in office paralleled the general decline in the city's economy.

Much to Gibson's disadvantage, his 16 years in office provided a convenient timeframe for assessing the economic well-being of the city. Between 1970 and 1985, the city had a population loss of 68,050 residents, a decline of 17.8 percent. The steel fabrication plants, breweries, and other factories which once boosted the local economy had closed or declined. Unemployment in Newark in 1986 was 11.2 percent overall, and triple that for some segments of the black community. During the period 1970 to 1986, the number of movie theaters in Newark had declined from 14 to 6; hotels from 32 to 6; bowling alleys from 15 to 0; restaurants from 937 to 246; and food stores from 377 to 184 (*New York Times*, May 14, 1986). Interestingly, *The Times* asserted that Newark's economy had begun to rebound with a burgeoning downtown and plans for major corporate relocations from Manhattan to Newark. However, many of Newark's neighborhoods remained blighted and the office real estate boom was not expected to aid the poor.

Over the years, Gibson had risen to national prominence as a politician. He had twice, but unsuccessfully, sought the Democratic nomination for governor of New Jersey. He had achieved considerable stature in national Democratic party circles, a necessary and beneficial achievement during Democratic presidential regimes. Those ties had facilitated the rewarding of the low-income black voter base so crucial in the calculus of national Democratic party politics. However, under the Reagan regime, the city of Newark, like most major cities, had lost substantial federal funds previously provided under the Community Development Block Grant program, the Comprehensive Employment and Training Act program, and other federal programs. Thus, Gibson was rendered vulnerable and defeated by a strong black challenger, Sharpe James, who emphasized economic revitalization, improving the image of the city, increasing the housing stock, and more effectively combating crime. Ironically, in many respects, the issues were very much the same as had been emphasized by Gibson in his first campaign in 1970. James carried all 5 of the city's wards, garnering 55 percent of the total vote to Gibson's 40 percent. It is, of course, highly unlikely that Gibson's successor will be able to substantially reverse the economic decline of Newark. Although the city may rebound over the next 2 decades or so as it shifts to a different economic base, it is not clear that the city's poorest citizens will reap substantial benefits of any such resurgence.

In relationship to the Newark succession election of 1986, the outcome of the Gary succession election in 1987 was very much one of *déjà vu*. Richard Hatcher was the longest serving black mayor in America, initially elected in 1967. Like Gibson, Hatcher had the misfortune of presiding over a city that declined along with the steel industry on which its economy depended. Gary had also lost substantial population, 60,000 or 27 percent, since 1967. Gary had also lost its taxi service, movie houses, many restaurants, and many other businesses (*Indiana Crusader*, Mar. 14 1987). Hatcher, too, was indisputably a black politician of national prominence and stature and was widely respected beyond Gary for his efforts on behalf of the national struggle for black political empowerment. Many national-level black politicians campaigned on his behalf, but to no avail. Hatcher lost to a black challenger who promised to improve the functioning of the city government and the general welfare of its citizenry.

In part, Hatcher's embattled position significantly reflected the consequences of the long-standing refusal of major components of the white power structure to accept the transition to black mayoral governance. Hatcher had never won the support of the white business community or the white ethnic-dominated Democratic party which previously dominated the city's politics. In the case of the business community, their split with city hall had actually preceded Hatcher in that they had earlier objected to mayoral efforts in support of striking steel workers (Lane 1979). They were, of course, not satisfied with Hatcher's initial election and when Hatcher faced reelection in 1971, in a last-ditch effort to forestall their political displacement, the white business community and the party machine endorsed a black moderate candidate in opposition to Hatcher. Apparently in response to the prospects of an extended period of insurgent black mayoral leadership in Gary, the business community moved to abandon the city by building a mall in the adjacent suburb of Merrillville. Within less than 10 years after Hatcher's initial election, all 4 department stores, over 100 smaller businesses and 2 major banks had closed operations in Gary and moved to the suburban mall (Lane 1979).

Moreover, Gary was in many ways a company town, originally established as the locus of a major U.S. Steel operation and surrounding corporate-owned housing areas for its employees. Subsequently, for decades, U.S. Steel and ancillary industries dominated the economy of Gary and the Lake County region. Thus, the fortunes of the Gary economy waxed and waned with the fortunes of U.S. Steel. Unfortunately, the latest waning of the local steel-based economy in Gary paralleled much of Hatcher's later years in office. For example, during the period of 1979–1982, employment at U.S. Steel in Gary dropped from 25,000 to 8,000, and by 1987 had declined still further to 6,000 (Chicago *Post Tribune*, Jan. 17 1986). Although Hatcher had not initially inherited a hollow prize as some analysts predicted that black mayors would, he was left, in the end, to preside over one.

While black political power in Gary had not come exclusively at the price of a loss of economic vitality as there was no causal relationship between black political dominance and the decline of the U.S. steel industry, ironically, blacks in Gary were forced to entertain the option of trading off political dominance for the prospect of improving the economic lot of the city. Thus, when the state legislature proposed a consolidation of the many separate governments in Lake County into a single political entity of Metrolake, which would have subordinated Gary residents politically and racially, many blacks in Gary speculated that such consolidation was perhaps what the city needed for economic rejuvenation. Metrolake would have excluded Merrillville, and would have consolidated some 70 governmental entities into a single metropolitan government serving a population of 405,000, with whites making up 60 percent and blacks comprising 40 percent of the population. This new governmental entity would have diluted black voting strength. Although the consolidation proposal was dropped, Mayor Hatcher had been able to garner only minimal black support at public rallies organized in opposition to the consolidation (Chicago *Post Tribune*, Oct. 28 & Nov. 3 1986).

There were other forces external to the city of Gary that undermined the success of black mayoral leadership. Hatcher had not been able, or necessarily willing according to some, to establish influential ties with the Republican-dominated state legislature. In early 1986, the state taxation board granted U.S. Steel of Gary a reduction in its property tax assessments of $16 million, leading to a 10 percent shortfall for the city of Gary and its school system. The state taxation board had previously refused to allow the city to raise taxes (Chicago *Post Tribune*, Oct. 28 & Nov. 3 1986). Hatcher was faulted by many with not seeking support from the state legislature until 1986, far into his mayoralty, when it was, some argued, effectively too late. Others understood that Hatcher was distrustful of whites in the state legislature and in the county suburban areas. In contrast, Hatcher's successor had worked to build support among whites in suburban areas and, as a result, enjoyed considerable popularity among this group. Hatcher was hampered in part by his record of insurgency-style politics and apparently by his own conception of the dictates of independent black political leadership. During all of the political empowerment in Gary, Hatcher's primary support base of black voters had become ambivalent about his leadership. In 1987, he had great difficulty in mobilizing his supporters and Barnes won the

Gary mayoralty with 56 percent of the vote, carrying all but 1 of the city's voting districts. Although Hatcher had overstayed his political welcome as mayor, the larger scenario clearly reflects the highly dependent status of American cities—and their political leadership—within the context of the larger political and economic systems.

Clearly not all black-mayor cities have experienced the economic downturns that have characterized Gary and Newark. Many other black-mayor cities, such as Atlanta and Los Angeles, have thrived economically, though nowhere has there been a transformation in the economic status of their African-American citizens. The very basis for black political empowerment—the concentration of blacks in large numbers in urban areas—also translates into the presence of a sizable population of poor and needy citizens, as African-Americans continue to be disproportionately represented among the poor in America. The important thing to remember is that the plight of black-mayor cities and their citizenry is tied to larger economic forces over which African-Americans simply have no control. This is a profound economic reality that frequently drives the political path pursued by black mayors; and that path may offer only minimal, if any benefits to the African-American community. Indeed, the demands of governing are frequently very conflicting ones and frequently black mayors in their governing roles actually serve to reinforce the prevailing economic and social order that they were expected to aid in changing.

The case of Detroit under Coleman Young presents a somewhat different illustration of the conflicting convergence of race, larger economic forces, and the demands of governance. In 1975, a year after his initial election Young and his primary support group of black voters were forced to make some very tough decisions, including a hiring freeze and laying off of municipal workers. Young had inherited a city treasury with a deficit of $16.5 million for 1 year alone. The fiscal crisis was largely due to a declining tax base resulting from the loss of population and jobs to the surrounding suburbs. Detroit's economy was also entering a downturn in as much as it was tied to the U.S. automotive industry, whose world-market position was being battered by foreign competition. Young was able to resolve the 1975 crisis by making major cuts in city services and by enlisting the help of the local business community, which in turn assisted in obtaining fiscal assistance from the state of Michigan (Rich 1989). In 1981, the city again faced fiscal crisis. To avoid having the city go into receivership, Mayor Young had to plead for an income tax increase from an already economically strapped citizenry. Despite the support of the white business community with which the mayor had forged an alliance, the tax increase was won exclusively in the black wards of the city with white voters opposing it 7–1 (Rich 1989). In a most contradictory and controversial action, Young later used city funds to finance the land acquisition for a new General Motors plant inside the city rather than see General Motors relocate the plant to a suburban jurisdiction (Hill 1983). As the world's largest privately held corporation, one could not readily argue that General Motors needed a bail-out from the largely poor and black citizens of Detroit. In the end, Young's tenure as mayor has been distinguished by one major accomplishment. He has held onto that which has defined Detroit as an economic entity: its image and position as the center of the U.S. automobile industry. However, one might conclude that the black citizens of Detroit have paid a high price in shouldering the responsibilities of governance.

THE IMPACT OF BLACK MAYORS

Originally it was expected by many black voters and some analysts that black mayoralties would establish a new social, economic, and political order within urban America. Their mere presence was expected to be significant in providing symbolic gratification to black citizens. Many black mayors have vigorously adopted the political posture of social reformers and all share the image of social reformers. If one focuses on discrete indicators of social reform, their collective image has a sound basis in reality. Many black mayors have appointed black chiefs of police to, in the early days, quell reports of police brutality and to generally transform local police departments from a white-occupying force in relationship to the African-American community. Black mayors have increased employment of blacks in municipal jobs generally and have as well increased the appointment of blacks to high-paying and high-level administrative positions (Eisinger 1980).

Black mayors have increased spending by their cities for social services (Karnig and Welch 1980). Black mayors were the first to adopt policies providing black businesspeople with access to the considerable amounts of monies spent by cities in contracting with the private sector for goods and services ranging quite literally from paper clips and toilet paper to leasing office space and construction of major facilities. While these minority set-aside programs admittedly benefited only a small portion of the black community, they gave black businesspeople opportunities to make money in ways that white businesspeople had long enjoyed. However, minority set-aside policies were dealt a serious blow by the Reagan Supreme Court case of *City of Richmond* v. *Croson* (1989). The *Croson* decision overturned the minority set-aside program initiated by the city of Richmond, Virginia, and severely restricted the scope and efficacy of similar programs adopted by other cities (Drake and Holsworth 1990).

The election of black mayors has generally resulted in a change in the kind of issues that dominate the urban political agenda. Certainly in the early years, issues of importance to low-income blacks such as the equitable distribution of urban public services, low-income housing, jobs and police brutality, were especially salient. While mayors can easily affect changes in provision of municipally provided public services, mayors have less control over jobs and the local economy, and must operate within considerable budgetary constraints which do not permit extensive efforts in providing housing for the poor. Housing has traditionally, and appropriately, been a federal government responsibility, but one that was effectively eliminated during the Reagan years.

Even in the absence of substantial tangible benefits, the symbolic gratification that attends the election of a black mayor is very significant for all African-Americans, and for many whites as well. The election of black mayors represents major strides in the realization of full participatory and majoritarian democracy in America, and in turn makes local government more open and accessible to a broader range of interests.

THE FUTURE OF BLACK POWER IN THE CITY

Several developments have the potential for significantly altering the foundations of black power in American cities. They are: (1) the changing place, and thus a likely changing nature of politics in urban areas, (2) the changing demographics or racial/ethnic population mix in many big cities, and (3) the changing philosophical thrust of black politics as represented by the new black crossover politics.

The important issue in politics is the representation of interests. Representation of interests requires political empowerment, which is dependent upon the availability of resources and access to political processes. For African-Americans, like the ethnic groups before them, the city has served as the primary place of political empowerment. The city has been the place where they have been present in concentrated numbers which, with access to the franchise, have provided the pivotal resource of majority or near-majority black population settings, any significant dispersion of the population beyond the boundaries of central cities poses a threat to black political empowerment in many cities. The movement of blacks to the suburbs has trailed that of whites and has occurred on a much smaller scale (Schnore, et al. 1986), constrained first by overt housing discrimination, and later, and just as effectively, by exclusionary zoning practices and related high costs of housing (Danielson 1976). There are, however, growing numbers of middle-class blacks moving from central cities to the suburbs in search of better housing, schools, and other amenities. The imperfections of American democracy become poignantly clear when one has to contemplate a tradeoff between place of residence and effective representation of one's political interests.

As the primary place of politics shifts for many blacks, there is not necessarily an accompanying shift in representation of their interests. The politics of suburbia is both strongly anti-city and heavily racially tinged, with these two characteristics being simply two sides of the same coin in many places. The jurisdictional place of suburban politics is primarily the county and many suburban counties have at-large voting systems. Thus, aside from the relative smallness of their numbers in suburban settings, blacks are disadvantaged by at-large voting systems (Davidson and Korbel 1984) and are less likely to win elections in suburban settings. There are exceptions, such as Fulton County (Atlanta) where the city is effectively the county and district-based election systems maximize the impact of a large, concentrated black population. In a somewhat different case, black suburban presence may be largely a spillover from the central city as in Prince George's County, Maryland, a suburb of Washington, D.C. In both cases, blacks dominate the government of the central city and are well represented in the government of a single county within a multi-county metropolitan area.

Many cities are now serving as the primary place of political empowerment for more recent immigrant groups, particularly Hispanics, and to a lesser degree, Asian and Pacific Islanders (API). Hispanics are defined as Spanish-speaking individuals who may be of any race, and who come from many different countries. The Hispanic community has grown dramatically over the past two decades, exceeding the 20 million mark in 1989 and totalling 8.2 percent of the U.S. population (U.S. Census Bureau 1989). The Census Bureau combines APIs as a common population grouping. This grouping includes more than 30 different ethnic groups that differ in origins, culture, language, and recentness of immigration. The API population numbered 3.7 million in 1980 and comprised 1.6 percent of the total population (U.S. Census Bureau 1980). While the API population is highly concentrated in California, Hawaii, and Washington State, the Hispanic population is widely dispersed. Increasingly, the bigger cities across the country are becoming populated by African-Americans and Hispanics. Relations between these two groups may be plagued by social conflict as has been seen at various times in many cities, or these groups may engage in political cooperation as was seen in the election of Harold Washington in Chicago (Stark and Preston 1990; Akalimat and Gills 1984), and in the 1989 Dinkins victory in New York City (McCormick 1990). Relations between blacks and members of the API population have frequently been strained in many cities, with hostilities primarily emanating from the growing presence of APIs in small but vital businesses throughout the black community.

Finally, the politics of deracialization or black crossover politics threaten to transform the nature of political discourse in regard to what issues constitute the agenda of city politics. The 1989 mayoral elections in Cleveland, New Haven, New York City, and Seattle can be characterized as black crossover victories. Each successful black candidate won in a predominantly white jurisdiction, and each articulated a political message that cannot be easily defined as a black agenda or an agenda for social reform. Black crossover politics seeks to neutralize the race of the candidate and the appeal of the campaign issues, instead basing voter appeals on partisanship or transcendent, "city-wide" issues. While black crossover politics may overcome the limits of race in determining electoral success in the politics of some cities, it may do so by abandoning efforts to change the political system in ways of substantive benefit to the black underclass in particular.

CONCLUSIONS

As America enters its third century, it can be concluded that a political revolution of sorts has taken place. The gap between the ideals of freedom, equality, and full political participation, and the prevailing reality has closed substantially. There has been a definite dispersion of political resources, driven first by the efforts of white ethnics and later by African-Americans. These efforts have made American society more inclusive and more democratic. This political transformation has not been without considerable social conflict, and at times has induced severe racial polarization. Black political empowerment has had mixed benefits, substantively and symbolically, constrained in many ways by the limits of change in a capitalist society. However, the future of black power in American cities is at least potentially threatened by some ominous developments that threaten to undermine or dilute the long-term benefits of the political gains realized over the past several decades.

REFERENCES

Akalimat, A. and D. Gills, 1984. Chicago: black power vs. racism. In *The new black vote, R.* Bush, ed. San Francisco: Synthesis Press.

Barker, L. and T. Barker. 1982. The courts, section 5 of the voting rights act, and the future of black politics. In *The new black politics: the search for political power* (first ed.), M. Preston, et al. eds., 55–69. New York: Longman.

Dahl, R.A. 1961. *Who governs?* New Haven, CT: Yale University Press.

Danielson, M.N. 1976. *The politics of exclusion.* New York: Columbia University Press.

Davidson, C. and G. Korbel. 1984. At-large elections and minority group representation: A reexamination of historical and contemporary evidence. In *Minority vote dilution,* C. Davidson, ed. Washington, DC: Howard University Press.

Drake, W.A. and R. Holsworth. 1990. Electoral politics, affirmative action and the supreme court: the case of Richmond v. Croson. *National Political Science Review* 2.

Eisinger, P.K. 1980. *The politics of displacement: racial and ethnic transition in three american cities.* New York: Academic Press.

Feemstra, L.P. 1969. Black control of central cities. *Journal of American Institute of Planners* 4:75–79.

Gordon, D.N. 1973. The bases of urban political change: a brief history of development and trends. In *Social change and urban politics,* D.N. Gordon, ed., 2–18. Englewood Cliffs, NJ: Prentice Hall.

Gosnell, H. 1967. *Negro politicians: the rise of negro politics in Chicago.* Chicago: University of Chicago Press.

————. 1968. *Machine politics: the Chicago model.* Chicago: University of Chicago Press.

Grant, R.B., ed. 1972. *The black man comes to the city: a documentary account from the great migration to the great depression, 1915–1930.* Chicago: Nelson-Hall.

Hill, R.C. 1983. Crisis in the motor city: the politics of economic developming in Detroit. In *Restructuring the city,* S. Fainstein, et al., eds., 80–125. New York: Longman.

Hunter, F. 1953. *Community power structure.* Chapel Hill, NC: University of North Carolina Press.

Joint Center for Political Studies. 1990. *Roster of black elected officials.* Washington, DC.

Judd, D. 1988. *The politics of american cities: private power and public policy* (third ed.), Glenview, IL: Scott, Foresman.

Karnig, A. and S. Welch. 1980. *Black representatives and urban policy.* Chicago: University of Chicago Press.

Katznelson, I. 1973. *Black men, white cities.* New York: Oxford University Press.

Lane, J. 1979. *City of the century: Gary from 1900–1975.* Bloomington, IN: Indiana University Press.

Lawson, S. 1985. *In pursuit of power: southern blacks and electoral politics, 1962–82.* New York: Columbia University Press.

Levine, C. 1974. *Racial politics and the american mayor: Power, polarization, and performance.* Lexington, MA: Lexington Books.

Massotti, L. and J. Hadden. 1974. *Suburbia in transition.* New York: Franklin Watts.

McCormick, J.P. 1990. The November elections and the politics of deracialization. *New Directions* 17(1) (January).

National Advisory Commission on Civil Disorders. 1967. *Report.* Washington, DC: Government Printing Office.

Nelson, W.E. and P. Meranto. 1977. *Electing black mayors: political action in the black community.* Columbus, OH: Ohio State University Press.

Nelson, W.E. 1982. Cleveland: the rise and fall of the new black politics. In *The new black politics: the search for political order* (first ed.), M. Preston, et al. eds., 187–208. New York: Longman.

Persons, G.A. 1985. Reflections on mayoral leadership: the impact of changing issues and changing times. *Phylon* 46 (September):205–18.

Rich, W. 1989. *Coleman Young and Detroit politics: from social activist to power broker.* Detroit: Wayne State University Press.

Riordan, W. 1963. *Plunkitt of Tammany Hall.* New York: Dutton.

Schnore, L., C. Andre and H. Sharp. 1976. Black suburbanization 1930–1970. In *The changing face of the suburbs,* B. Schwartz, ed. Chicago: University of Chicago Press.

Shefter, M. 1976. The emergence of the political machine: an alternative view. In *Theoretical perspectives on urban politics*, W.D. Hawley, et al., eds., 14–44. Englewood Cliffs, NJ: Prentice Hall.

Stark, R. and M. Preston. 1990. The political legacy of Harold Washington: 1983–1987. *National Political Science Review* 2:161–68.

U.S. Bureau of the Census. 1980. *Census of population*, asian and pacific islander population by state: 1980, Suppl. Report, PC80-S1-12. Washington, DC.

_____. 1989. *Current population reports*, the hispanic population in the United States, March 1989, Series P-20, No. 444. Washington, DC.

Walters, R.W. 1980. The challenge of black leadership: an analysis of the problem of strategy shift. *The Urban League Review* 5(Summer):77.

Williams, E.N. 1982. Black political progress in the 1970s: the electoral arena. In *The new black politics: the search for political power* (first ed.), M. Preston, et al., eds. New York: Longman.

Wilson, J.Q. 1960. *Negro politics*. New York: Free Press.

Wolfinger, R.A. 1972. Why political machines have not withered away and other revisionist thoughts. *Journal of Politics* 34(May):365–98.

_____. 1974. *The politics of progress*. Englewood Cliffs, NJ: Prentice-Hall.

PART III

Policy Prescriptions

11 A Cumulative Causation Model of the Underclass: Implications for Urban Economic Development Policy

GEORGE C. GALSTER

In his 1944 monumental work, *An American Dilemma*, Gunnar Myrdal introduced the notion of "cumulative causation" as the central principle for analyzing race relations:

> Throughout this inquiry, we shall assume a general interdependence between all the factors in the Negro problems. . . . The mechanism that operates here is the "principle of cumulation" . . . . Behind the barrier of common discrimination, there is unity and close interrelation between the Negro's political power; his civil rights; his employment opportunities; his standards of housing, nutrition, and clothing; his health, manners and law observance; his ideas and ideologies. The unity is largely the result of cumulative causation binding them all together in a system and tying them to white discrimination. It is useful, therefore, to interpret all the separate factors from a central vantage point. (pp. 75–77 passim)

Four decades after Myrdal's path-breaking work, the "Negro problem" has assumed a particularly odious form in urban America: what has been dubbed the "black underclass."[1] Their plight has been rightly labelled "the real dilemma for urban America" (Ledebur 1981, p. 11).

This chapter analyzes the black underclass phenomenon from a "neo-Myrdalian" perspective. More precisely, it extends, updates, and provides detail to Myrdal's general principle of cumulative causation by developing a conceptual model of the underclass that synthesizes contemporary concepts and evidence from a variety of social scientific disciplines. The succeeding section presents the model and brings to bear supporting empirical evidence. Implications are drawn from the model for development of effective policies aimed at ameliorating the underclass problem. Several contemporary proposals for urban economic revitalization will be critiqued in the context of this analytical framework.

CUMULATIVE CAUSATION MODEL

The underclass phenomenon is comprised of seven elements that may be categorized under three general rubrics: people, place, and labor market. Under the *people* category are two groups of people: the underclass (ghettoized African-American poor) and everyone else compared with (the white poor and the non-poor of all races). The former group exhibits numerous disadvantageous *material* conditions and behaviors (lower income and education, higher criminal activity, welfare dependency, chemical dependencies, and illegitimate births) unlike the latter group (element 1). The two groups also possess crucial *psychological* distinctions: underclass attitudes are characterized by pessimism about prospective economic opportunities (element 2), and non-underclass attitudes are characterized by prejudices against the underclass (element 3). Beneath the *place* category is the segregation of the underclass in deteriorated central city neighborhoods (element 4) and the existence of a pervasive set of individual and institutional practices that serve to exclude them from suburban communities (element 5). Below the *labor market* heading are the bifurcation of employment opportunities into secondary and primary sectors and the presence of a variety of individual and institutional practices that hamper the entry of the underclass into the more desirable primary sector (element 6) and relegate them to the secondary sector (element 7).

In simplest form, the basic interrelationships between these elements can be seen as a series of circular causations. As such, there is no single "cause," but rather a web of mutually reinforcing connections in which elements serve both as causes and effects. In Figure 11.1, the seven elements of the model are portrayed diagrammatically as rectangles. Interrelationships between elements are portrayed as arrows showing causal directionality.

For the sake of this exposition, the element of *people* is described first. This is not meant to imply that this element is the ultimate cause of the underclass phenomenon or that it is any more important than other elements. The conditions, behaviors, and attitudes of the underclass (elements 1, 2) spawn and intensify the prejudices of non-underclass people (element 3), thus encouraging the non-underclass to erect and maintain both legal and social exclusionary barriers in housing and labor markets (elements 5, 6). Spatial segregation of the

FIGURE 11.1

A Cumulative Causation Model of the Underclass Phenomenon

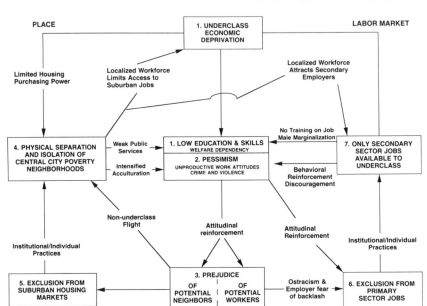

underclass (element 4) constrains their labor market opportunities, confines them to political jurisdictions that provide limited public resources for human capital acquisition, and encourages formation of distinct subcultural traits. Confinement in a segment of the labor market characterized by low-skill, low-pay, no-advancement jobs (element 7) perpetuates underclass economic insecurity by increasing chances for unemployment, provides few chances for skill-enhancement, reinforces unproductive work habits, and discourages future aspirations. These feedback effects, in turn, further circumscribe future possibilities of breaking through spatial and labor market barriers and intensify the initial material, behavioral, and attitudinal characteristics of the underclass (elements 1, 2).

The elements and their interrelationships are described and empirically supported in the following section.

Elements and Relationships of the Model

The categories of people, place, and labor market effectively describe the three key dimensions that collectively portray the underclass reality. The *people* dimension encompasses the current economic, social, and psychological attributes of the typical underclass individual. Economic features include minimal formal education or vocational skills (low "human capital"), unstable work histories punctuated by frequent and extended periods of unemployment or nonparticipation in the labor force, and chronically low incomes. Socially, the underclass is characterized by exceptionally high rates of female-headed households, illegitimate births, welfare dependency, substance abuse, and participation in quasi-legal and illegal activities. The psychological attribute consists of unproductive attitudes toward work, alienation, apathy, criminality, and violent tendencies (Glasgow 1980; Auletta 1982; Wilson 1987; Ch. 3 in this volume).

The *place* dimension represents urban poverty neighborhoods in which the underclass is concentrated. These neighborhoods are preponderantly located in the distressed, larger central cities of the Northeast and Midwest (Ricketts and Sawhill 1988). Several indicators suggest that the incidence and concentration of the underclass in such areas has steadily risen during the past two decades (U.S. Department of Housing and Urban Development [HUD] 1980 pp. 4–5; Massey and Eggers 1990).

The *labor market* dimension represents employment opportunities divided into "secondary" jobs that are available to the underclass and "primary" jobs from which the underclass are typically excluded. The "dual labor market" model used herein, unlike the neoclassical economic view, recognizes two distinct sectors of the labor market and that there are significant barriers between them and that each has dramatically different types of jobs and each has different formal and informal requirements for its workers (Fusfeld 1973, Ch. 3; Gordon, Edwards and Reich 1982). As formulated by Piore:

> The primary market offers jobs which possess several of the following traits: high wages, good working conditions, employment stability and job security, equity and due process in the administration of work rules, and chances for advancement. The secondary sector has jobs that ... involve low wages, poor working conditions, considerable variability in employment, harsh and often arbitrary discipline, and little opportunity to advance. The poor are confined to the secondary labor market. (1970, p. 55)

The key factor in creating this duality of job characteristics is the job's relationship to technology. The primary sector is distinguished fundamentally by its relative capital-intensiveness and its need to train workers on the job for skills that are unique to a specific firm or industry. Its structure which emphasizes job security, seniority, work rules, etc., though beneficial to workers, is established primarily to aid firms in training and then retaining personnel (Piore and Doeringer 1971). Seniority systems, for example, promote informal training activities among workers and encourage experienced workers to stay with the firm. Workers with seniority should not be reluctant to transmit skills to new recruits since the new recruits cannot compete for the senior-level jobs; and workers should be loath to forfeit accumulated seniority privileges by quitting. The emphasis on trainable, stable workers places a high premium on an employer's ability to screen out unsuitable applicants from jobs that provide access to the ladders of advancement within a primary sector firm. Credentials and other readily discernable traits are the main vehicle for accomplishing exclusion of applicants from these "port-of-entry" jobs (Thurow 1975; Braddock and McPartland 1987).

These three key dimensions, reinforcing people, place, and labor market, are interconnected through a complex array of *relationships*. The relationships not only manifest themselves through tangible institutional practices and individual behaviors but, perhaps more importantly, through modification of perceptions, attitudes, and beliefs both held by underclass and non-underclass individuals. This will be made clear by describing in more detail each of the model's elements and their interrelationships, beginning with the labor market and proceeding to place and then people elements. As a starting point, take as given the current economic, social, and psychological condition of underclass people described above. These characteristics, behaviors, and attitudes spawn and reinforce the prejudices of the non-underclass elements. The ramifications in the labor market are first considered. (See the middle and right-hand portions of Figure 11.1 for an illustration.)

Labor Market

Prejudiced primary sector workers are more likely to resent, or at best benignly ignore, any potential underclass co-workers, since they would view them as "inferior," "unworthy," or even "dangerous." In turn, underclass workers' informal acquisition of appropriate work habits and on-the-job training is inhibited. Thus, as Piore notes, the performance of the few secondary-sector workers who have initially succeeded in obtaining primary-sector employment:

> may have been seriously affected by a backlash among the line supervision and rank-and-file of hourly employees. It is these people who serve as instructors in on-the-job training. Without their cooperation, the new workers progress more slowly at best. . . . The presence of strong backlash among white employees is clearly indicated by comments of black workers. . . . Some of their comments suggest the instruction has been completely withheld. Limited acceptance by the work group appears to be virtually universal. (1969, p. 109)

In other words, the prejudicially based behaviors of co-workers are likely to frustrate underclass workers' attempts to gain on-the-job training, more productive work habits, and social acceptance in the primary sector.[2] Under these circumstances it is easy to understand why underclass workers' behavior reflects the high rates of employment terminations, absenteeism, apathy, and disciplinary problems on the job. Such underclass behavior becomes, of course, a self-fulfilling prophecy and serves to further strengthen the stereotypes held by primary sector workers.

Primary sector employers, likewise, often deal with the underclass prejudicially. In this sector a job applicant's "skills" are typically not objectively evaluated on the basis of current ability to perform certain technical or intellectual tasks. Rather, they are subjectively judged on the basis of a set of readily discerned physical, behavioral, and attitudinal traits that the employer believes reflect the applicant's potential to learn skills and advance through on-the-job training (Thurow 1975, Ch. 4), as well as reflect the likelihood that the applicant will remain on the job long enough for the employer to recoup the training investment (Piore and Doeringer 1971). In such a context, a cheap and tolerably efficient means of screening applicants becomes the process of "statistical discrimination." Readily assessed traits like race, educational attainment, demeanor, speech patterns, job experience, and criminal record are used to predict an individual applicant's job performance based on statistical averages for the previously employed group having those same traits (Braddock and McPartland 1987).[3]

And what of the applicants fitting the "underclass statistical profile"? Employers can typically cite data indicating that such previously hired applicants *have* been harder to train, *have* been less productive, *have* created workplace disruptions, *have* been more frequently fired, and *have* quit more often. Of course, as seen, the refusal of non-underclass workers to associate with and help train underclass employees on the job explains why employers' previous experiences with the group may have produced these data. Employers' opinions of underclass hirees may be even more negative if non-underclass employees' morale and productivity drop, say, due to their personal distaste for class heterogeneity in the workplace or their suspicion of employer favoritism toward the underclass (Piore 1969, pp. 109-10). In any event, once employers' stereotypical judgments about underclass workers' potential job performance become ingrained, they severely limit the subsequent access of the underclass to primary sector employment, whether these judgments continue to be based on current statistical data or not (Reich, Gordon and Edwards 1973; Kalleberg and Sorensen 1979).

Understandably, typical experience with primary sector barriers discourages potential underclass workers (Glasgow 1980, Chs. 1, 5). Those who may, in fact, possess the ability to be trained and become productive in the primary sector are often never given the chance due to the hiring barrier of statistical discrimination. Even if they manage to overcome this barrier, they are still faced with co-worker ostracism, which limits their actual acquisition of productive attributes, minimizes their chance for advancement, and creates an unpleasant social atmosphere on the job. Deteriorating labor force participation in underclass neighborhoods due to "discouraged workers" is a symptom of the underclass' assessment of the reality confronting them (Committee on National Urban Policy 1982, Ch. 3; Ch. 5 of this volume).[4] Pessimism, anger, alienation, and apathy are predictable psychological reactions.

For those who continue trying to work, the characteristic option is secondary sector employment. Yet, employment of the underclass in the secondary sector provides no immediate means of escaping economic deprivation and over time reinforces the very traits that are used to screen the underclass out of primary sector jobs. Since secondary work is short term, labor intensive, and unskilled, there is no need for general or vocational education, no need for extensive on-the-job training, and no need for workers to adhere to rigid rules or even to show up regularly. Because secondary jobs pay low wages, provide no skills, and are unstable, other sources of income such as welfare and illegal activities often become relatively attractive options. Young African-American men, in particular, are severely marginalized in the labor market (Freeman and Holzer 1985; Ch. 5 in this volume). William J. Wilson (1987) has argued that this male marginalization has created a shortage of marriageable partners for young African-American women. This, in turn, reduces the chances of long-term, stable relationships and often forces women who bear children to exclude the economically marginal father from the household in order to qualify for welfare.

Thus, the character of secondary sector jobs alters the underclass' perceptions of the relative merits of legitimate employment, regular and orderly work habits, education, welfare, and crime, resulting in the underclass attitudes and behaviors discussed previously.[5] Perversely, legitimate (but secondary sector) employment opportunities available to the underclass tend to perpetuate their economic deprivation. (See the feedback arrows from labor market to people components in Figure 11.1.)

Place

Underclass attitudes and behaviors not only reinforce prejudices held by potential co-workers and employers in the primary labor market but, likewise, reinforce prejudices held by potential neighbors. (See the middle and left-hand portions of Figure 11.1.) Non-underclass households would most likely react with distaste or even alarm at the prospect of underclass households moving into their neighborhood. Inmigration could occur if there was a declining demand by non-underclass households for a specific neighborhood. Landlords might defer building maintenance and lower rents in an attempt to attract customers and thereby permit underclass immigration. Or, inmigration could occur in less marginal neighborhoods if underclass households were given rent subsidies to reside there (Struyk 1990), if public housing were built there (Galster 1989a), or if single-family dwellings were acquired by local public housing authorities for underclass residents (Olion Chandler 1990). Opinion polls have demonstrated a direct relationship between a respondent's income, or the socioeconomic status of the community, and the expressed preference for neighborhood income-class homogeneity (HUD 1978, Section E). Significant numbers of households cite their main reason for previously changing residences as a decline in the status of their neighborhood (Birch, et al. 1979); this is especially likely if race and class transition are simultaneous (Pettigrew 1973). Undoubtedly, part of the reason why some people engage in these behaviors is the fear of property value depreciation (Birch, et al. 1979).[6] What all this means is that "flight" of non-underclass residents can be anticipated if, for one reason or another, an area was "invaded" by members of the underclass; this flight would result in the eventual resegregation of the neighborhood on the basis of socioeconomic status (Yinger, et al. 1979; Grigsby, et al. 1987).

Avoidance of the accompanying psychological, social, and economic costs of the neighborhood transition provides a potent motivation for the erection of exclusionary barriers in the housing market (Downs 1973, 1981; Galster 1990b). Exclusion may be promulgated against an underclass individual by another individual.[7] For instance, they may be told by a landlord that no apartment is available when, in fact, one is; or they may be directed by leasing agents to show only the most decrepit apartments in the heart of poverty neighborhoods. Exclusion may also be collectively imposed on the underclass through the auspices of a political jurisdiction. As stated by the President's Commission for a National Agenda for the Eighties:

> Middle-class whites—and middle-class blacks—guard their social and physical separation from the urban underclass. An array of political forces (zoning regulations, building codes) supports an approach that keeps the poor where they are. (1980, p. 59)

Institutionalized exclusionary practices make it financially impossible for the underclass to reside in many suburban jurisdictions by forcing up the price of private housing. Prohibitions on scattered-site subsidized housing also serve to maintain class homogeneity in the suburbs (Downs 1973; Hirsch 1983). In addition, many whites fail to recognize class distinctions within the African-American community, and equate "blackness" with poverty. This serves to intensify all sorts of individual and institutional forms of racial discrimination in housing markets.

The net result of prejudice in its spatial manifestations—non-underclass flight, individual and institutional exclusionary practices in housing—is the physical isolation of the underclass, in a few neighborhoods of the largest Northern center cities (HUD 1980, Ch. 4; Massey and Eggers 1990; Ch. 1 in this volume). A panoply of exclusionary acts by individual rental agents inhibits underclass entrance into areas they might otherwise be able to afford. Flight of non-underclass people of all races ensures that any areas entered into by the underclass will not remain economically mixed for long. And institutionalized exclusion renders attempted underclass suburban relocations economically infeasible by limiting the number of low-cost dwellings in these areas.

People

Although the physical isolation of the underclass, primarily in decaying central-city neighborhoods, is partially caused by their economic deprivation, it also compounds the likelihood of their continuing deprivation for at least three reasons. First, a spatially segmented labor market is created. Some underclass workers may have the traits that might permit their acceptance and effective participation in the secondary or even the primary labor market. Yet, jobs in both sectors are increasingly becoming spatially separated from underclass neighborhoods (Kasarda 1985, 1990). The resultant reduction in the underclass' information about, and/or transportation access to, these burgeoning suburban job opportunities precludes their taking advantage of them (Kasarda 1985; Wilson 1987; Braddock and McPartland 1987). In other words, limited income, combined with poor information and high commuting costs, creates a "localized" spatial labor market for the underclass (Gastwirth and Haber 1976; Cheshire 1979). Several empirical analyses have found that such localization plays an important role in explaining labor market outcomes (Reid 1983; Alexis and DiTomaso 1983; Galster 1987; Leonard 1987; Ihlanfeldt and Sjoquist 1989). Moreover, the spatial segmentation of labor further encourages the spatial segmentation of employment (Mills 1985). According to Clark and Whiteman:

> Given that labor market segmentation creates a distinctive income distribution based upon group attributes, these same attributes coupled with journey-to-work budget constraints can in fact "build" a dual labor market in urban space. . . . If employers (of the underclass) locate to utilize the spatially segmented labor the system becomes reinforced. (1981, p. 16)

Thus, the restricted residential pattern of the underclass not only perpetuates their economic deprivation by reducing their access to suburban secondary and primary jobs, but also encourages further evolution of the geography of urban jobs along lines that are disadvantageous to the underclass.

Second, confinement in center-city neighborhoods creates a host of problems for the underclass because of the typically weak fiscal capacity of the political jurisdiction in which they reside. The older housing stock, the concentrations of fire and health hazards, the decaying municipal physical facilities, and (particularly in older Northern cities) strong municipal unions, entrenched bureaucracies, and an exodus of middle-class population combine to produce a problem of a weakening local tax base in the face of rising service costs (Baumol 1963; President's Commission 1980). This nexus forces the underclass into the unenviable tradeoff between the reduction of public services to affordable levels and the increase of services until they are adequate but impose a heavy tax burden. Studies have found that those in central-city jurisdictions pay a larger portion of their income in local taxes (Peterson 1976) yet appear still to be receiving comparatively inferior services, especially in public education (Jencks, et al. 1972; Ch. 7 in this volume). The underclass' acquisition of human capital that might allow them to overcome statistical discrimination in the primary labor market is thereby hindered.

Finally, the spatial concentration of the underclass both permits and encourages development of distinct sociological and psychological subcultural traits that inhibit economic opportunities. Some of the traits, though distinctive, are innocuous as far as potential labor force performance. Here such attributes as brightly colored clothing, rhythmic walking, loud, often profane bantering, and a proclivity for rap music come to mind (Anderson forthcoming). Other behaviors associated with "street corner life" are more harmful to potential productivity (Brown 1965; Liebow 1967). A milieu of "hanging around" punctuated by brief intervals of secondary work, illegal activities, and episodic adventures involving sex, drugs, alcohol, or violence, reinforces a lifestyle that is irregular, immediate, and sensational. Further psychological reactions to confinement in deprived neighborhoods, such as mistrust, escapism, and difficulty in controlling aggression, have been well documented (Clark 1965; Bullough 1967; Wilson 1971; Kardiner and Ovesey 1972). Of course, these underclass traits brand them as distinct and undesirable in the eyes of many potential employers (Braddock and McPartland 1987). Nevertheless, these traits are perfectly rational adaptations to an environment in which five role models predominate: the street-wise dudes, workers moving from one dead-end job to another, derelicts destroyed by drug abuse, permanent welfare dependents with illegitimate children, and those engaged in illegal activities that, while dangerous, hold the potential for wealth, glamor, and status—no matter how transitory (Magnum and Seninger 1978, Ch. 4; Glasgow 1980, Chs. 1, 6; Ch. 13 in this volume).

Thus, the physical separation and social-psychological isolation of neighborhoods inhabited by the underclass create spatial constraints to their attainment of good primary-sector jobs, limit their ability to obtain quality public services that potentially could enhance their future chances of attaining such jobs, and encourage the development of traits that abet statistical discrimination against them in the primary sector. (See the feedback arrows from the place component to the people component in Figure 11.1.) It is, of course, precisely these underclass deprivations, attitudes, and behaviors that represent the objective reality that began the presentation of the model.

The foregoing discussion has focused on the *endogenous* (i.e., those originating within) linkages between the seven elements in the underclass model. But, before proceeding, it must be noted that there are numerous significant exogenous (i.e., those originating from without) relationships between these elements and the larger society. Although not explicitly portrayed in Figure 11.1, it must be recognized that changes in such factors as macroeconomic conditions, technologies, political ideologies, religious beliefs, laws, and public policies at national, state, and local levels can impinge at various points on the elements of the model. The connections between these endogenous and exogenous linkages are analyzed in the next section.

Cumulative Causation in the Model

The previous analysis of the individual relationships between the various elements comprising the underclass phenomenon only hinted at the dynamic nature of the entire *system*. This section considers the dynamic properties explicitly.[8]

Unfortunately, what has undoubtedly occurred in recent decades is a combination of exogenous forces and endogenous linkages that has produced an ever-worsening self-reinforcing "vicious circle" (see Myrdal 1944, pp. 75–78). The exogenous culprits are several and well known (Chs. 3–5 in this volume). The heralded entrance of the post-industrial society has brought with it altered demands for worker attributes (Kasarda 1985, 1989, 1990; Squires 1988). New transportation and manufacturing technologies and the rise of international capitalism have changed the amount and spatial configuration of port-of-entry jobs that have traditionally served as stepping stones for the urban poor. These same forces have contributed to the deteriorating fiscal capacity of central cities in which underclass people reside. National public policies, especially with regard to the construction of interstate highways and inner-city public housing projects, and subsidized mortgages for the middle class, have unwittingly served to physically segregate the underclass and non-underclass segments of society. More recently, the rekindling of "rugged individualist" ideologies have exacerbated and justified prejudices against the underclass.

The consequences of these predominantly negative exogenous forces have, in turn, been intensified by the endogenous linkages of the underclass phenomenon. The seven elements in the system have interrelated in mutually reinforcing ways so that the whole of the phenomenon has become greater than the sum of its parts.

The worsening material, behavioral and attitudinal traits of underclass people have intensified prejudices of non-underclass members of society against those who had the potential of being co-workers, employees, or neighbors. These prejudices have manifested themselves in the creation of an interlocking array of barriers that has increasingly impaired both underclass mobility and their ability to obtain employment in the primary-sector labor market. Spatial barriers have constrained underclass access to burgeoning primary-sector and better-paying secondary-sector suburban job opportunities and have encouraged a concentration of the worst secondary-sector jobs in the center cities. Those who surmount these spatial barriers have been confronted with additional prejudicial obstacles to their hiring and subsequent success in the primary labor market. Underclass perceptions of limited legitimate economic opportunities have encouraged their pursuit of illegal activities and have discouraged labor force participation. The labor participation that has occurred has been principally confined to the secondary sector of the labor market.

Unfortunately, due to the nature of the jobs involved, secondary-sector employment provides no training and reinforces the very underclass behaviors and attitudes that are viewed as counterproductive by mainstream society. These influences have been intensified by the underclass' spatial concentration and isolation. The pervasiveness of welfare dependency and illegitimacy, illegal activities, and frustrated working poor have helped create acculturation forces that further discourage legitimate, habitual labor force participation and the acquisition of education, training, behaviors, and attitudes appropriate for primary-sector employment. The deteriorating fiscal capacity of the central-city jurisdictions in which the underclass have been confined has further worsened these trends, enhancing spatial isolation and neighborhood deprivation.

Finally, it is precisely this potent combination of criminal record, unstable job history, illegitimacy, low educational attainment, poor work habits, and chemical dependencies that has legitimized stereotypical images of the underclass. These intensified prejudices, of course, have led to a further strengthening of the geographic and labor market constraints. The self-fulfilling prophecy has become manifest. In the absence of any potent exogenous interventions, such as extreme labor shortages, there is no reason to suspect that this downward spiral of cumulative causation will not continue indefinitely, with the odious social consequences perversely intensifying over time.

Some Final Clarifications

Before employing the previous model in a policy analysis, some final clarifications of potential misunderstandings must be made. For simplicity in the foregoing presentation, the linkages in the cumulative causation framework were implicitly treated as if they were universal, mechanistic, and of equal significance. Obviously, such an interpretation would be improper. Certainly, all underclass individuals are not inevitably and perpetually trapped within the snare of vicious circles, nor are all linkages necessarily operative in all situations. Undoubtedly, all linkages are not of equal importance. (In fact, as emphasized below, the lack of quantification of the magnitude of these linkages is the most pressing need of future research in this area.) Nevertheless, this analysis does not retreat from the central claim of the conceptual framework: there is a complex set of mutually reinforcing linkages between people, places, and labor markets that is currently driving the system downward in a vicious spiral and making the plight of the underclass ever more desperate. Finally, some of the linkages described above adversely affect non-underclass people as well and have caused an upsurge of urban poverty generally. Furthermore, not all low-income people are to be considered underclass. The point is that poverty can readily be converted into underclass status if one becomes enveloped by the web of social, psychological, economic, and spatial interrelationships presented earlier.

IMPLICATIONS FOR URBAN ECONOMIC DEVELOPMENT POLICY

The cumulative causation model of the underclass not only provides a means for better understanding the underclass phenomenon but also can be used as a tool for analyzing alternative public policy approaches to the problem. This section outlines three distinct categories of policy approach suggested by the analysis, namely: "break the linkages," "reverse the cycle," and "establish a parallel system." For each category, I will examine the implicit empirical assumptions about endogenous and exogenous forces operating on the elements and the assumptions of the magnitude of the linkages between those elements that must be made if the given policy is to work. Finally, I will discuss and critique past and proposed urban economic development policies in light of this analytical framework.

The Break the Linkages Policy Approach

The break the linkages strategy attempts an intervention that severs one or more of the connections between the elements of the underclass model portrayed in Figure 11.1, hoping to alter the dynamics of the vicious cycle. Many past and proposed policies fall under the breaking the linkages category: anti-"snob-zoning" legislation, affirmative action, job training programs, federal funding of central-city public service employment, assistance for public transit access to suburban work sites, and anti-discrimination laws for jobs and housing.

These approaches involve central empirical assumptions: (1) that the most significant linkages in the phenomenon can be broken effectively through public policy intervention, and (2) that by breaking such linkages the condition of the underclass will be markedly improved, as opposed to merely decreasing its rate of deterioration. Put differently, this approach assumes that there are both exogenous forces tending to improve the underclass' situation and public policy interventions that could effectively isolate the exogenous forces from other forces that tend to worsen the situation. Little evidence supports either assumption.

First, many key links probably can be altered by public policy, but others cannot. Undoubtedly, there are some policies that hold potential for severing a few linkages. For example, special public transit routes could be devised to increase underclass access to suburban jobs; intergovernmental transfers could be expanded so as to strengthen the fiscal capacity of the jurisdictions in which underclass people reside; central-city school districts could be reorganized and subsidized (see Ch. 17); affirmative action could open some doors into primary sector jobs (Heckman and Payner 1989); and additional resources and new techniques involving matched interracial parts of testers or "checkers" could aid the fight against discriminatory acts in housing and labor markets (Galster 1988). One fundamental difficulty, however, would remain: how to break the central linking element of attitudinal reinforcement. It is hard to imagine how even a concerted campaign of "information/persuasion" could significantly alter the fundamental stereotypes and opinions held by both underclass and non-underclass individuals if the reality on which such stereotypes and opinions are based remains essentially correct. Without incontrovertible evidence to the contrary, the underclass may be skeptical about public appeals claiming that education will benefit rather than crime and that they will be accepted into primary-sector jobs and suburban neighborhoods. Conversely, without clear improvements in the material, social, and psychological state of the underclass, non-underclass prejudices will not likely be tempered and will continue to provide a potent motivation for the maintenance of prior exclusionary barriers in addition to the creation of newer, more impregnable devices. Second, even if policies could effectively sever linkages between elements of the underclass phenomenon, this might serve only to reduce the rate at which the vicious circle spirals downward, and not to reverse the cycle. Unless it can be shown that there are strong, positive exogenous forces affecting the system, merely isolating some elements from the negative reinforcement of others will only slow the further erosion of the underclass' relative position. Perhaps the projected labor shortage early in the next century will provide such an influence, but for now it can only be viewed as speculative (Hill and Rock 1990).

The Reverse the Cycle Policy Approach

Another strategy involves altering the type and magnitude of forces that affect one or more elements in the underclass phenomenon, while leaving the linkages between them intact. The goal in this strategy is to provide sufficient ameliorative impacts so that cumulative causation begins to operate in a positive, corrective direction.

This strategy is founded on the key assumption that the positive impact of a given public policy on a particular "target" element would be strong enough to outweigh *all* other negative exogenous forces on the system.[9] This assumption cannot command convincing empirical support. The arguments presented here can be made more specific by considering three alternative reverse the cycle policy proposals that are currently predominant in political and academic circles: enterprise zones, dispersed subsidized housing, and retraining subsidies.

The enterprise zone approach (Butler 1981; Wilder and Rubin 1989) tries to deal with the underclass *place* dimension by providing a variety of capital and labor tax credits and deregulatory concessions to firms that locate in designated center-city poverty areas. But even if enterprise zones attracted enough firms so as to ameliorate the spatial constraints on the underclass' employment opportunities, would it be sufficient to counter the forces of the labor market dimension?

The answer lies in what *kind* of jobs the enterprise zone employers would provide and who is hired to fill these jobs (Wolf 1990). Obviously, the greater the degree to which the predominant exclusionary barriers in the primary labor market are not eroded but merely geographically rearranged, the less will be the salutary impact on the underclass. There are reasons to believe that such a scenario would be the result.

First, many enterprise zone jobs created for the underclass might be of the archetypical secondary sector type (Walton 1982; Clark 1981). One could infer this from the glowing prognostications made by the plan's supporters concerning the zone's ability to compete with low-wage, labor-intensive production in the Third World. But even more directly, it can be concluded from the nature of the proposed employment subsidies themselves. Current plans call for tax credits (wage subsidies) to encourage the *hiring* of "hard-core unemployed." Presumably, the profit-maximizing enterprise zone firms would restructure their production processes so as to more efficiently use this low-skill (but now cheaper) input. But there are no proposed subsidies for *training* or *maintaining* (let alone *promoting*) these new underclass hirees. Thus, the possibility of encouraging the creation of "revolving-door," secondary-type job slots is rife.

What if, however, non-trivial numbers of primary-type jobs were created in the zones and nominally opened to underclass trainees? There still might be little long-term underclass participation and success. The concessions in hiring standards and work rules needed to accommodate underclass trainees are likely to intensify non-underclass worker backlash, given the strong customary and union-enforced norms against favoritism (Piore 1969, pp. 111–12; Bonney 1971). This fear of backlash has been responsible for the reluctance of employers in earlier manpower programs to "mainstream trainees" (Piore, 1969, p. 113; Iacobelli 1970) and for the resulting creation of "trainee jobs" isolated from the regular workforce which merely catered to existing behaviors of the underclass (Piore 1969, pp. 123–24; 1970, pp. 56–57). This workplace segregation provides explanation for Harrison's inability to find a significant statistical relationship between underclass participation in past training programs and their unemployment rates, occupational status, or incomes (1972, pp. 66–68). Additionally, dropout rates in such programs have been high, precisely because underclass trainees perceived their new placements as low-wage, dead-end jobs, and sensed both co-worker hostility and a lack of commitment on the part of primary-sector employers to any long-term upgrading efforts (Green and Faux 1969; Harrison 1972, pp. 173–77). Williams (1982) found that primary-sector management had a goal of restricting black workers to a number below some "critical mass" in the more prestigious, better-paying job categories. This goal was accomplished by eliminating training programs that would have given the highest relative benefits to black trainees.

To the degree that secondary or "quasi-secondary" jobs would be forthcoming in enterprise zones, the plan might contribute more to the problem than its solution. The underclass would likely perceive little marked change in the opportunities available to them. Their participation in the plan consequently might be minimal,[10] as would the changes in their economic, social or psychological situation. In turn, little alteration in the prejudices of mainstream society could be expected. There, thus, would be little prospect of reversing the cycle.

The dispersal of subsidized housing is another policy for altering the *place* dimension of the underclass phenomenon. In non-poverty areas, public housing could be built in small-scale, low-density clusters, existing housing could be purchased for use by public housing tenants, or rent vouchers could be given to underclass households to enable them to rent apartments at market rates. Experiments with such dispersal attempts have met with mixed results (Hogan and Lengyel 1985; Olion Chandler 1990). The model suggests why: key attitudinal and discriminatory barriers would remain.

Given the underclass' (correct) perceptions of the hostility awaiting them in most non-underclass neighborhoods (McGrew 1981; Galster 1989b), many would be loath to abandon the social networks of their own neighborhoods (Edel 1972; Farley, et al. 1978; HUD 1978, Sec. E). For those who would be willing, and able to disperse into non-underclass neighborhoods, the consequences would ultimately be counterproductive. Non-underclass prejudices may only be intensified since interclass contact would not be of the "equal-status" variety (Gans 1968; Yinger 1986). That is, middle-class whites would be confronting lower-class blacks, thereby reinforcing these middle-class whites' stereotypes about the inseparability of race and class. Finally, dispersal does not necessarily enhance job opportunities for the underclass if discriminatory labor market practices remain (Kain and Zax 1983; Braddock and McPartland 1987).

Retraining policy approaches the *people* dimension of the underclass phenomenon by supplying a personal trait (skills) that will supposedly be demanded in the labor market (President's Commission 1980, Ch. 5; Cottingham 1982b; Sawhill 1988). The first question is whether the key type of training needed—long-term behavioral and attitudinal transformation—will occur through the envisioned policy (Piore 1969, pp. 104, 122–25). If, for example, the proposed training is "public-institutional," that is, separated from an actual work context in some school-like situations run by the government, the key work habits and norms that can only be learned on the job will not be developed. If the training is "private on-the-job," that is, conducted by and within primary sector firms, similar problems as those noted for enterprise zones will be encountered. Perceptions of training payoffs by the underclass thus might not be augmented substantially in either case.

The Parallel Institutions Policy Approach

The final conceptual approach involves the establishment of a variety of institutions (mainly economic) located in and controlled by the underclass community (Browne 1979; Squires 1988; Pierce and Steinbach 1987).[11] The goal is to create a *new set* of *people* and *labor market* elements and linkages that can establish a distinct and positively reinforcing cumulative causation cycle, while leaving the original *place* element virtually intact.

There are basic assumptions in this approach as well. First, indigenous institutions can be structured and operated in such a way that they avoid the shortcomings of mainstream institutions yet do not create equally severe handicaps of their own. This implies that there is both the will and the incipient expertise and leadership in the community to affect such changes. Second, the exogenous forces acting upon the new, parallel institutional structures will not overwhelm them or completely negate their efforts. Third, the consequences of these institutions on underclass people will be salutary enough both to induce their widespread participation in programmatic activities and to begin erosion of the prejudices of non-underclass elements of society. In a related vein, these institutions will not serve to socio-psychologically isolate these two groups such that mutual distrust, fear, and resentment are intensified. Fourth, members of the underclass will "graduate" to the mainstream economy at some point.

The cornerstone of any parallel institutions strategy would need to be the creation and long-term maintenance of a variety of community owned and operated economic enterprises, located within underclass neighborhoods. In order to avoid the shortcomings of the current labor market, these enterprises must be structured in such a way that they impart productive work habits, attitudes, and technical skills to the underclass on the job and that non-market spin-offs that augment the community's physical and social infrastructure are equal in importance to the production of the given good or service.[12] Indigenous control of the enterprises would be crucial to the proposal so as to abet the underclass' sense of personal efficacy (both individually and through collective action) to develop nascent leadership potential and to encourage the perception that they would reap substantial programmatic payoffs.[13]

In order to compensate for shortfalls in the purchasing power of the local community and supply some insulation from exogenous macroeconomic and technological forces, these enterprises would probably need to be assisted (initially and over time) by some sort of public support. A variety of direct supports is possible: loans, tax abatements, contract set-asides, technical assistance, etc. Indirect supports could involve the establishment of community owned and directed, but federally guaranteed, institutions for providing seed capital to the community enterprises (Browne 1979; Taub 1988), or the rebuilding of crucial physical infrastructure in the area.

First, if the new economic institutions are to be community controlled and operated, serve a training function, and operate in labor-intensive industrial sectors, there is reason to believe that productivity may not be as great as firms in the mainstream. Furthermore, if the new parallel institutions cater to a neighborhood clientele, the potential flow of sales revenues will be limited. In combination, these factors suggest that the enterprise is doomed to economic failure. In order to avoid such failures (and further erosion of self-image within underclass communities), there would likely need to be substantial, ongoing infusions of public and private assistance. This raises the question of whether such organizations could indeed be community controlled, or whether *de facto* power would belong to the grantors of assistance.

Second, even if new parallel institutions were able to maintain control and become economically successful, irresistible political forces might arise to thwart their progress. Imagine the lobbying reactions of mainstream businesses whose profits were being eroded by the competition from new parallel institutions who were the beneficiaries of public subsidies! Political pressures from within underclass communities might also spawn inefficiencies, such as featherbedding and cronyism.

Finally, there is some question whether the reputed economic success of parallel institutions would be met by approval or resentment from mainstream society. The reaction might depend in part on the degree to which such success was perceived to come at the expense of mainstream institutions. In a related vein, the *place* aspect of the underclass phenomenon would be reinforced, as the new parallel institutions solidify a nearby group of worker-participants. This, too, could lead to exacerbated misperceptions between those in parallel mainstream and erstwhile-underclass institutions structures.[14]

CONCLUSIONS

This chapter has attempted to demonstrate that the cumulative causation principle presented by Myrdal four decades ago can be fruitfully applied to the contemporary urban phenomenon of the black underclass. The model formulated describes the mutually reinforcing interrelationships between the conditions of the underclass people, the places in which they live, and their labor market opportunities. The central conclusion to be drawn from this analysis is that the underclass is mired in a "vicious circle" that progressively worsens their plight, and that there now appears to be no forthcoming exogenous forces on the horizon that will reverse this cycle.

The cumulative causation model also enables one to evaluate comparatively three distinct strands of policy approaches toward the underclass: breaking the linkages, reversing the cycle, and building parallel institutions. Particularly, within the context of the model, one can more easily perceive the implicit empirical assumptions that each approach must make if it is to presume to offer the best solution.

The obvious implication one is forced to draw after reviewing existing empirical evidence is that vastly more research needs to be done that attempts to quantify the linkages and the magnitudes of exogenous and endogenous forces described in the model. Until such rigorous evidence is provided, evaluation of policy proposals must, in large part, rest on logical and theoretical inferences. Nevertheless, such theory-based critiques of. policy proposals are valuable because they serve to clarify whether the debate is over conceptual framework, empirical evidence, or ideological underpinnings.

A final word: the above criticisms of policies should not be interpreted as a justification for "benign neglect." On the contrary, the social need for intervention is urgent and unquestionable. The conclusion is inescapable: limited, piecemeal approaches to the underclass problem are bound to fail. Unfortunately, in the past Americans have been unable to mobilize the political will to try little more than fragmentary efforts. Their (predictable) failure has, ironically, engendered a widespread, if fallacious, sentiment that the problem is insoluble. It is hoped that the model and pointed challenges presented in this chapter will lead not to inertia, but to an aggressive formulation of the most efficacious, comprehensive package of policy interventions possible.

NOTES

1. For more details on the size, composition, and distribution of the urban underclass, see Housing and Urban Development 1980, Chs. 2–3; Wilson 1987; Magnum and Seninger 1978, Chs. 1–3; Committee on National Urban Policy 1982. Ch. 3; and Ch. 3 in this volume.

2. Documentation that African-Americans receive very little informal on-the-job training when hired by white firms and that *de facto* discrimination in interpersonal job relations persists is provided by Cottingham (1982a). Such documentation is provided by Cottingham (1982a). Such documentation offers an explanation for the empirial finding that on-the-job training does not benefit African-Americans as well as whites (Taylor 1981).

3. Surveys of those employers, who were pre-selected as being the "most economically progressive," have revealed that even they retain tacit acceptance of barriers to economic opportunity fostered through statistical discrimination (Rossi 1968). One clear symptom of such was uncovered by Myers and Phillips (1979), who found that Comprehensive Employment and Training Act applicants who interviewed for jobs in census tracts of the same racial composition as their own neighborhood of residence had a higher probability of being offered a job.

4. One indicator of the magnitude of this reaction is that in declining central cities, nearly 60 percent of poor blacks do not participate in the labor foce. For more data on participation rate trends and its relationship to employment opportunities, see Magnum and Seninger 1978, Chs. 2–3; Newman 1979; HUD 1980, Ch. 4; Ch. 5 in this volume. Other studies have shown that workers' attitudes concerning work change when they perceive they have been discriminated against and that such changes, in turn, are statistically related to subsequent lower likelihood of employment (Becker and Krystofiak 1980; Becker and Hills 1981). Glasgow's case study of Watts showed that 95 percent of potential workers never even attempted to apply for jobs which had traditionally been closed to them via discrimination (1980).

5. For further explanation and documentation of members of the underclass' negative perceptions of work versus alternative sources of income, see Fusfeld (1973, Ch. 4), Task Force on Employment Problems of Black Youth (1971), and Magnum and Seninger (1978, Ch. 4).

6. Statistically significant relationships between residents' perceptions of property values and the socioeconomic status and racial composition of neighborhoods, controlling for housing structural features, have been identified by Galster (1982).

7. The pervasiveness and severity of these exclusionary tactics have been documented nationwide (Wienk, et al. 1979; Galster 1990a, b).

8. In principle, it is possible for the model described to be in "equilibrium" (see Myrdal 1944, Appendix 3). That is, the exogenous impacts of the various elements in the system, plus the magnitude of the endogenous interrelationships between the elements, might be such that the conditions embodied in each element are temporarily static. In such an instance the degree of underclass deprivation, non-underclass prejudices, and spatial and labor market exclusionary barriers would, on the whole, remain constant over time.

9. Recall that these negative forces affect the target element both directly and indirectly by their impact on *other* elements in the system and subsequent transmission of that impact to the given element through the linkages. Therefore, both direct and indirect effects must be overcome if the plan is to be successful; that is, if a policy is to improve condition A of the underclass, it must overcome the effects of other conditions associated with the underclass (say, B and C) that are causally linked to A, because the linkages themselves are not being broken.

10. The underclass' perception that, in spite of their training, there will be little payoff in terms of surmounting barriers in the primary labor sector provides an explanation for their historically low rates of participation in previous attempts at manpower training (Harrison 1972, pp. 29–38; Perlman 1976, pp. 176–79).

11. The approach is also related to earlier schemes titled "green-house industries" (Vietorisz and Harrison 1970) and "feeder factories" (Tabb 1970), and is consistent with, though not as sweeping, some of the proposals forwarded by black socialists (Ofari 1970; Marable 1981, Ch. 11).

12. Emphasis on restructuring the "internal labor market" (Piore and Doeringer 1971) within these new institutions distinguishes the proposal from those that merely try to fit the underclass hiree into a pre-existing private job structure. As stated by Green and Faux (1969, p. 27): "in addition to creating the skills necessary to work at a particular occupation, programs will need to have to create the occupations themselves in an environment free from the pressures of pro-white bias so that the 'hard-core' ghetto adult can develop into a confident, competitive worker. This means creating an economic foundation within the ghetto itself to provide jobs and opportunities where the people are."

13. The crucial need for local involvement in the planning of such redevelopment activities is argued in more length by Green and Faux (1969), Henderson (1979), and Marshall and Swinton (1979). The principle of community control need not be limited only to the new enterprises, but could productively be extended to other institutions operative in underclass neighborhoods (Labrie 1971; Browne 1979; Clark 1981).

14. Green and Faux (1969) have argued that to obtain true racial integration America needs to develop black institutions that can interact with white ones on an equal basis. Historically, for other minorities these economic enterprises have provided group support for individual minority contacts with majority groups and have forced a respect for the former that formed the basis for subsequent productive interracial contacts. As Green and Faux conclude, "rather than being an obstacle to integration, the growth of black economic power has as a major goal the building of meaningful links between the races" (1969, p. 39).

REFERENCES

Alexis, M. and N. DiTomaso. 1983. Transportation, race and employment. *Journal of Urban Affairs* 5 (Spring): 81–94.
Anderson, E. n.d. *Streetwise*. Philadelphia, PA: University of Pennsylvania Press (forthcoming).
Auletta, K. 1982. *The underclass*. New York: Vintage Books.

Baumol, W. 1963. Urban services: interactions of public and private decisions. In *Public expenditure decisions in the urban community.* Washington, DC: Resources for the Future.

Becker, B. and S. Hills. 1981. Youth attitudes and labor market activity. *Industrial Relations* 20 (Winter): 60–69.

Becker, B. and F. Krzystofiak. 1980. *Some evidence on the effects of labor market discrimination on work attitudes.* Buffalo, NY: SUNY, Department of Economics.

Bederman, S. and J. Adams. 1974. Job accessibility and underemployment. *Annals of the American Association of Geographers* 64 (September): 378–86.

Birch, D., et al. 1979. *Behavioral foundations of neighborhood change.* Washington, DC: HUD.

Bonney, N. 1971. Unwelcome strangers: a study of manpower training programs in the steel industry. Ph.D. dissertation, University of Chicago.

Braddock, J. and J. McPartland. 1987. How minorities continue to be excluded from equal employment opportunities. *Journal of Social Issues* 43(1): 5–39.

Brown, C. 1965. *Manchild in the promised land.* New York: Macmillan.

Browne, R. 1979. Institution building for urban revitalization. *Review of Black Political Economy* 10 (Fall): 34–43.

Bullough, B. 1967. Alienation in the ghetto. *American Journal of Sociology* 72 (March): 469–78.

Butler, S. 1981. *Enterprise zones.* Washington, DC: Universe.

Cheshire, P. 1979. Inner areas as spatial labor markets. *Urban Studies* 16 (February): 29–43.

Clark, G. 1981. The employment relation and spatial division of labor. *Annals of the American Association of Geographers* 71 (September): 412–24.

Clark, G. and M. Gertler. 1983. Local labor markets: theories and policies in the U.S. during the 1970s. *Professional Geographers* 35 (August): 274–85.

Clark G. and J. Whiteman. 1981. *Why poor people do not move.* Cambridge, MA: Harvard University, Kennedy School Discussion Paper D81-3.

Clark, K. 1965. *Dark ghetto.* New York: Harper and Row.

Clark, S. 1981. Enterprise zones: seeking the neighborhood nexus. *Urban Affairs Quarterly* 18 (September): 53–71.

Committee on National Urban Policy, National Research Council. 1982. *Critical issues for national urban policy.* Washington, DC: National Academy Press.

Cottingham, C. 1982a. Introduction. In *Race, poverty, and the urban underclass,* C. Cottingham, ed. Lexington, KY: D.C. Heath/Lexington.

———. 1982b. Conclusion: the political economy of urban poverty. In *Race, poverty and the urban underclass,* C. Cottingham, ed. Lexington, KY: D.C. Heath/Lexington.

Downs, A. 1973. *Opening up the suburbs.* New Haven, CT: Yale University Press.

———. 1981. *Neighborhoods and urban development.* Washington, DC: Brookings Institution.

Edel, M. 1972. Development versus Dispersal. In *Readings in urban economics,* M. Edel and J. Rothenberg, eds. New York: Macmillan.

Farley, R. 1977. Residential segregation in urbanized areas of the U.S. in 1970. *Demography* 14 (November): 497–518.

Farley, R., et al. 1978. Chocolate city, vanilla suburbs: will the trend toward racially separate communities continue? *Social Science Research* 7 (December): 319–44.

Freeman, R. and H. Holzer, eds. 1985. *The black youth employment crisis*. Chicago: University of Chicago Press.

Fusfeld, D. 1973. *The basic economics of the urban racial crisis*. New York: Holt, Rinehart, and Winston.

Galster, G. 1982. Black and white preferences for neighborhood racial composition. *American Real Estate and Urban Economics Journal* 10 (Spring): 37–68.

_____. 1987. Residential segregation and interracial economic disparities. *Journal of Urban Economics* 21 (January): 22–44.

_____. 1988. *Federal fair housing policy in the 1980s*. Cambridge, MA: MIT Center for Real Estate Development, Housing Policy Paper #5.

_____. 1989a. Subsidized housing and racial change in Yonkers, NY. Paper presented at the Association of Collegiate Schools of Planning Conference, Portland, Oregon.

_____. 1989b. Denver PHA dispersal plan controversy. *Trends in Housing* 28(1): 1, 8.

_____. 1990a. Racial discrimination in United States housing markets: a review of the audit evidence. *Journal of Planning Education and Research* 9(3): 165–75.

_____. 1990b. Racial steering by real estate agents: mechanisms and motivations. *Review of Black Political Economy* 18 (Winter): 105–29.

Gans, H. 1968. *People and plans*. New York: Basic Books.

Gastwirth, J. and S. Haber. 1976. Defining the labor markets for equal employment standards. *Monthly Labor Review* 99 (March): 32–36.

Ginzburg, E. 1980. Youth unemployment. *Scientific American* 242 (May): 43–49.

Glasgow, D. 1980. *The black underclass*. San Francisco: Jossey-Bass.

Gordon, D., R. Edwards, and M. Reich. 1982. *Segmented work, divided workers*. New York: Cambridge University Press.

Green, G. and G. Faux. 1969. Social utility of black enterprise. In *Black economic development*, W. Haddad and G. Pugh, eds. Englewood Cliffs, NJ: Prentice-Hall.

Grigsby, W., M. Baratz, G. Galster and D. Maclennan. 1987. *The dynamics of neighborhood change and decline*. London: Pergamon.

Harris, J. 1979. State government and urban policy planning. *Review of Black Political Economy* 10 (Fall): 30–33.

Harrison, B. 1972. *Education, training, and the urban ghetto*. Baltimore, MD: Johns Hopkins University Press.

Heckman, J. and B. Payner. 1989. Determining the impact of federal anti-discrimination policy on the economic status of blacks. *American Economic Review* 79 (March): 138–77.

Henderson, L. 1979. Policy and administrative challenges of community economic revitalization. *Review of Black Political Economy* 10 (Fall): 68–78.

Henderson, W. and L. Ledebur. 1972. *Urban economics: processes and problems*. New York: John Wiley.

Hill. E. and H. Rock. 1990. Education as an economic development resource. *Environment and Planning C: Government and Policy* 6: 53–68.

Hirsch, A. 1983. *The making of the second ghetto*. New York: Cambridge University Press.

Hogan, J. and D. Lengyel. 1985. Experiences with scattered-site housing. *Urban Resources* 2(2): 9–14.

Iacobelli, J. 1970. A survey of employer attitudes toward training the disadvantaged. *Monthly Labor Review* 92 (June): 51–55.

Ihlanfeldt, K. and D. Sjoquist. 1989. The impact of job decentralization on the economic welfare of central city blacks. *Journal of Urban Economics* 26 (July): 110–30.

Jencks, C., et al. 1972. *Inequality*. New York: Basic Books.

Kain, J. and J. Zax. 1983. Quits, moves and employer relocation in segregated housing markets. Unpublished paper, Department of Economics, Harvard University.

Kalleberg, A. and A. Sorenson. 1979. The sociology of labor markets. *Annual Review of Sociology* 5: 351–79.

Kardiner, A. and L. Ovesey. 1972. *The mark of oppression*. New York: World Publishing.

Kasarda, J. 1985 Urban change and minority opportunities. In *The new urban reality*, P. Peterson, ed, 33–68. Washington, DC: Brookings Institution.

———. 1989. Urban industrial transition and the underclass. *Annals of the American Academy of Political and Social Science* 501: 26–47.

———. 1990. Jobs and the underclass in large and mid-size metropolitan areas. Paper presented at New Perspectives on Racial Issues Conference, University of Wisconsin-Madison, May.

Labrie, P. 1971. Black central cities. *Review of Black Political Economy* 1 (November): 78–79.

Ledebur, L. 1981. Cities and economic development. *Urban Institute Policy and Research Report* 11 (Spring): 10–13.

Leonard J. 1987. The interaction of residential segregation and employment discrimination. *Journal of Urban Economics* 21 (May): 323–46.

Levitan, S. 1975. Job corps experience with manpower training. *Monthly Labor Review* 95 (October): 3–11.

Liebow, E. 1967. *Tally's corner*. Boston, MA: Little, Brown and Company.

Magnum, G. and S. Seninger. 1978. *Coming of age in the ghetto*. Baltimore, MD: Johns Hopkins University Press.

Marable, M. 1981. *Blackwater*. Dayton, OH: Black Praxis Press.

Marshall, S. and D. Swinton. 1979. Federal government policy in black community revitalization. *Review of Black Political Economy* 10 (Fall):11–29.

Massey, D. and M. Eggers. 1990. The ecology of inequality: minorities and the concentration of poverty 1970–1980. *American Journal of Sociology* 95 (March): 1153–88.

Mayer, S. and C. Jencks. 1989. Growing up in poor neighborhoods: how much does it matter? *Science* 243 (March): 1441–45.

McGrew, J. 1981. Resistance to change continues to restrict public housing choices. *Journal of Housing* (July): 375–80.

Mills, E. 1985. Open housing laws as stimulus to central city employment. *Journal of Urban Economics* 17 (March): 184–88.

Myers, S. and K. Phillips. 1979. Housing segregation and black employment: another look at the ghetto dispersal strategy. *American Economic Review* 69 (May): 298–302.

Myrdal, G. 1944. *An american dilemma*. New York: Harper and Row.

National Commission for Manpower Policy. 1978. *C.E.T.A.: an analysis of the issues*. Washington, DC: U.S. Government Printing Office.

Newman, M. 1979. Labor market experience of black youth, 1954–78. *Monthly Labor Review* 102 (October): 19–27.

Ofari, E. 1970. *The myth of black capitalism*. New York: Monthly Review Press.

Olion Chandler, M. 1990. Dispersed public housing. Paper presented at Urban Affairs Association meetings, Charlotte, North Carolina.

Perlman, R. 1976. *The economics of poverty*. New York: McGraw-Hill.

Peterson, G. 1976. Finance. In *The urban predicament*, W. Gorham and N. Glazer, eds. Washington, DC: Urban Institute Press.

Pettigrew, T. 1973. Attitudes on race and housing. In *Segregation in residential areas*, A. Hawley and V. Rock, eds. Washington, DC: National Academy of Science.

Pierce, N. and C. Steinbach. 1987. *Corrective capitalism*. New York: Ford Foundation.

Piore, M. 1969. On-the-job training in the dual labor market. In *Public-private manpower policies*, A. Weber, et al., eds. Madison, WI: Industrial Relations Research Association.

———. 1970. Jobs and training. In *The state and the poor*, S. Beer and R. Barringer, eds. Cambridge, MA: Winthrop.

Piore, M. and P. Doeringer. 1971. *Internal labor markets*. Lexington, KY: D.C. Heath.

President's Commission for a National Agenda for the Eighties/Panel on Policies and Prospects for Metropolitan and Non-Metropolitan America. 1980. *Urban America in the eighties: perspectives and prospects*. Washington, DC: Government Printing Office.

Reich, M., D. Gordon and R. Edwards. 1973. A theory of labor market segmentation. *American Economic Review* 63 (May): 359–65.

Reid, C. 1983. The effect of residential location on the wages of black women and white women. Paper, Industrial Relations Section, Princeton University.

Ricketts, E. and I. Sawhill. 1988. Defining and measuring the underclass. *Journal of Policy Analysis and Management* 7 (Winter): 316–25.

Rossi, P. 1968. Between white and black: the facts of american institutions in the ghetto. In *Supplemental studies of the national advisory commission on civil disorders*. Washington, DC: U.S. Government Printing Office.

Sawhill, I. 1988. Poverty in the United States. *Journal of Economic Literature* 26 (September): 1073–1119.

Squires, G. 1988. *Deindustrialization, economic democracy and equal opportunity*. Milwaukee, WI: Working paper, Department of Sociology, University of Wisconsin-Milwaukee.

Struyk, R. 1990. Race and housing: affordability and location. Paper presented at New Perspectives on Racial Issues Conference, University of Wisconsin-Madison.

Tabb, W. 1970. *Political economy of the black ghetto*. New York: W.W. Norton.

Task Force on Employment Problems of Black Youth. 1971. *The job crisis of black youth*. New York: Praeger.

Taub, R. 1988. *Community capitalism*. Cambridge, MA: Harvard Business School.

Taylor, D. 1981. Education, on-the job training, and the black-white earnings gap. *Monthly Labor Review* 104 (April): 28–32.

Thurow, L. 1975. *Generating inequality*. New York: Basic Books.

U.S. Department of Housing and Urban Development. 1978. Survey of the quality of community life. Washington, DC: HUD.

———. 1980. President's national urban policy report. Washington, DC: HUD.

U.S. Department of Labor. 1968. *Finding jobs for negroes*. Washington, DC: U.S. Government Printing Office.

Vietorisz, M. and B. Harrison. 1970. *Economic development of Harlem*. New York: Praeger.

Walton, J. 1982. Cities and jobs and politics. *Urban Affairs Quarterly* 18 (September): 5–18.

Wienk, R., C. Reid, J. Simonson and F. Eggers. 1979. *Measuring discrimination in american housing markets*. Washington, DC: Office of Policy Development and Research, HUD.

Wilder, M. and B. Rubin. 1989. Urban enterprize zones. *Journal of American Planning Association* 55 (Autumn): 418–32.

Williams, B. 1982. Internal labor markets and black suburbanization. In *Race, poverty, and the urban underclass*, C. Cottingham, ed. Lexington, KY: D.C. Heath/ Lexington.

Williams, L. 1979. Fire destroys Bronx home after blacks move in. *New York Times*, March 9.

Wilson, R. 1971. Anomie in the ghetto. *American Journal of Sociology* 77 (November): 66–87.

Wilson, W. 1987. *The truly disadvantaged*. Chicago: University of Chicago Press.

Wolf, M. 1990. Enterprise zones: a decade of diversity. In *Financial economic development*, R. Bingham, E. Hill and S. White, eds. Newbury Park, CA: Sage.

Yinger, J. 1986. On the possibility of achieving integration through subsidized housing. In *Housing desegregation and federal policy*, J. Goering, ed., 290–312. Chapel Hill, NC: University of North Carolina Press.

Yinger, J., G. Galster, B. Smith and F. Eggers. 1979. The status of research into racial discrimination and segregation in american housing markets. *HUD Occasional Papers in Housing and Community Affairs* 6 (December): 55–175.

12 The Underclass: Causes and Responses

EROL RICKETTS

It is often assumed that there is a direct relationship between knowing what the cause or causes of social problems are and resolving them. However, some social problems cannot be resolved by simply reversing their causes or by reestablishing the conditions that prevailed prior to the onset of the problems. Often this is because social problems operate on the basis of a cumulative causation model. A problem may have had a predominant cause, but other factors interplay to give rise to a complex set of problems that cannot easily be resolved. For example, depression may cause drug abuse and drug abuse may lead to a host of other problems—thievery, neglect of family, imprisonment, joblessness, homelessness, etc.,—all reinforcing depression, and all creating a situation where it becomes difficult to identify a "cause" to reverse or resolve the problems.

Moreover, what often stands between understanding the causes of social problems and resolving them in the policy arena is the willingness to resolve them. The willingness to resolve problems is often itself dependent on the societal understanding of problems within the context of the society's values as well as consensus that the problems ought to be resolved and that they should be given priority above other pressing problems.

It is perhaps naive then to discuss the causes of social problems and policy responses without taking into consideration the social climate as the context within which the problem is conceptualized and understood and policy responses formulated. The perfectly thought-out and conceived policy response is not particularly useful in a social context where it is unlikely to be accepted and implemented. One then has to focus on the social context as an enabling element in the resolution of social problems.

For example, the legalization of hard drugs may be the perfectly conceived solution for much of the violence and crime in inner-city areas; however, so far, that solution has been unacceptable to the American public because it would require some level of distribution and control of hard drugs by the federal government and that clashes with a societal value that the federal government should not be in the business of disbursing drugs that can contribute to increasing addiction. Further, many social problems such as the drug problem generate different worries in different sectors of the population, so that while legalization could result in reduction of violence and crime (costs to society), it most likely would lead to some increase in addiction which offends those who are more concerned about increasing addiction (the personal welfare of addicts). Yet, many people approach the resolution of social problems solely as an issue of identifying and understanding causes or having a set of policy interventions.

The point of departure for this chapter then is not a review of the many programs that work or could work. That issue is receiving attention by an increasing number of authors such as Schorr and Schorr (1988) and Ellwood (1988). Knowing which programs work is not the most critical factor in legislating and implementing social policy. Very little attention is paid to the social climate and the compromises that must be obtained before meaningful change in policy can occur. Moreover, an adequate review of the programs that work to reduce any single social problem could be lengthy enough to fill volumes. Instead, this chapter focuses on some of the major agreed on causes of the underclass and the expected directions that the responses motivated by subscription to these causes would take. It argues that the various arguments about causes of the underclass can be accommodated within a single framework that posits the problems of the underclass to the post-industrial transformation of the American economy and society and the adaptation to this by marginal members of society. This is followed by a very general discussion of the circumstances that would have to be obtained for any significant attempt at resolution of the underclass problem. The chapter concludes with a very topical discussion of some of the necessary components a national initiative to resolve the problems of the underclass would entail.

CAUSES OF THE UNDERCLASS

As stated above, social problems that are associated with the underclass usually occur in bunches so that the welfare dependent is often the school dropout who is often the teen parent, the drug addict and so on. It is therefore very difficult to discuss the causes of the underclass separately because the underclass is characterized by problems that mutually reinforce each other and that have the cumulative effect of marginalizing members of the underclass from society, a process which itself reinforces the other problems. The argument made here is that solving any one problem of the underclass in isolation is fairly pointless.

In addition, research on the underclass is still relatively underdeveloped and so far has not unambiguously established the causal primacy and sequencing of the various factors at play in the emergence and growth of the underclass. This section is, therefore, concerned with the "predominant" causes of the underclass. Obviously these are highly correlated and in some cases one could argue the obverse of assumed causal directions.

The emergence of the underclass has been viewed as: (1) a result of the marginalization of the poor brought on by postindustrialization, as well as an adaptation by the poor to their superfluity (e.g., Kasarda 1983; Wilson and Aponte 1985; McLanahan, et al. 1986; Wilson and Neckerman 1986); (2) a result of mass migration by minorities to major urban areas coinciding with deindustrialization (see Kasarda 1983; Lieberson 1980); (3) a result of federal government social programs (e.g., Loury 1984; Murray 1984; Wilson 1984; Nathan 1986); (4) a consequence of the acting out of entrenched cultural values (e.g., Kaus 1986; Lehman 1986), and (5) a consequence of racial discrimination (Ellwood 1986; Massey and Denton 1989; Massey 1990).

POSTINDUSTRIAL MARGINALIZATION AND ADAPTATION ARGUMENT

Advocates of what may be called the "postindustrial marginalization and adaptation argument" view the emergence of the underclass both as a consequence of deindustrialization and as a reaction or adaptation to it. This is because the transition to postindustrial society causes decreasing participation in the labor force because of the mismatch between the growth in jobs requiring high levels of education and skills and the absence of education and skills among the poor. The spatial reorganization of production away from inner-city areas where the poor are concentrated compounds the problem (see, for example, Bluestone and Harrison 1982; Kasarda 1983; Wilson 1983; McLanahan, et al. 1986).

Kasarda (1983) argues that America's urban areas have been going through what appears to be an irreversible structural transformation—from centers of production and distribution of material goods to centers of administration, information exchange, finance, trade, and government services. This process has eliminated millions of manufacturing, wholesale, and retail jobs in central cities and has greatly accelerated since about 1967. At the same time there has been an increase in occupational positions requiring levels of training and education that are typically beyond the reach of disadvantaged city residents.

Kasarda notes that these economic changes have been matched by demographic changes. The out-migration of affluent whites from central cities cou-

pled with the recent arrival of blacks and Hispanics have weakened the infrastructure of inner-cities and have deepened ghettoization. The declining quality
and quantity of schooling among inner-city youths make them unsuited for
newly created occupation positions. As Kasarda argues, job opportunities that
match the skill levels and educational background levels of central-city minorities especially in manufacturing have disappeared from the inner-city and are
now prevalent in the suburbs. At the same time, there has been an increase of
white-collar jobs in central cities. Kasarda argues that this mismatch between
the location of workers and appropriate jobs manifests itself daily on urban
expressways in the heavy stream of white collar workers commuting into central
cities and the increasingly heavy counter stream of inner-city residents commuting to blue-collar jobs in outlying areas.

Early skepticism about the theory of skill and geographic mismatch
between workers and jobs among some observers (see Ellwood and Summers
1986; Jencks 1988) has given way to at least guarded acceptance of the theory as
it is increasingly supported by research. Even observers such as Ellwood, who
in the past argued that race and not place was the significant factor determining
access to jobs by black youths, now accept the importance of the spatial
mismatch between jobs and poor inner-city minority workers (see Suro 1991).

The second part of the argument, the adaptation hypothesis, views the
behaviors associated with the underclass—criminal activity, dependence on welfare and so on—as adjustments or adaptations by people among the redundant to
their structural isolation or marginalization (see Glasgow 1980; Kasarda 1983;
Currie 1985; McLanahan, et al. 1986; Wilson and Neckerman 1986; Van
Haitsma 1989). McLanahan, et al. (1986) argue that direct and indirect attachment to the labor force carry a right to income. The common denominator for
all the subgroups that have been included in the underclass is detachment from
the labor force and low wage or salary income. Hence, members of the underclass must find other ways to supplement their income. Welfare, crime, and the
underground economy are all means of supplementing or attaining income.
McLanahan, et al. argue that it is the common need of subgroups in the underclass to find additional sources of income and the social stigma associated with
their position that allow these diverse groups to be lumped together as the
underclass (see also Glasgow 1980; Kasarda 1983).

THE TIMING OF MASS MIGRATION TO MAJOR URBAN AREAS

Some observers have argued that because of the transition to postindustrial
society, more recent low-skilled migrant groups may be at greater risk for
experiencing underclass conditions because of declining job opportunities. For
example, because the mass migration of blacks and Hispanics, particularly

Puerto Ricans, to major central cities was ill-timed to match economic restructuring, members of those groups would tend to have a higher probability of being redundant and, hence, in the underclass (see Lieberson 1980; Kasarda 1983; Katznelson 1983).

Some evidence in support of this argument can be gleaned from the experience of blacks and Puerto Ricans in the Northeast. Puerto Ricans migrated to major urban centers in the Northeast en masse after the Second World War, about the same time of black mass migration from the South. Puerto Ricans are significantly overrepresented among the low-income population and live in close proximity to blacks in depressed areas of major northeastern cities. Although rates of social ills for the Puerto Rican population were substantially less than comparable rates for the black population in 1960, the incidence of many social problems among the Puerto Rican population is now higher, suggesting that common experience in the Northeast may partly explain the problems. For example, the rate of female-headed households among Puerto Ricans grew from 15.8 to 43.9 percent between 1960 and 1985 compared to growth from 20.6 to 43.7 percent for the black population (see Sandefur and Tienda 1988).

The departure of the black and Puerto Rican mobility experience from the classic model of successful intergenerational mobility of other immigrant groups may result from the fact that the migration of blacks and Puerto Ricans was ill-timed, coinciding with shifts in the economy from goods producing to service producing (c.f. Kasarda 1980; 1983; 1985; Glazer and Moynihan 1970; Waldinger 1983; see also Lieberson 1980; and Blau and Duncan 1967). The good blue-collar manufacturing jobs that formed the basis for the mobility of previous cohorts of immigrants and their children were no longer around when blacks and Puerto Ricans arrived.

Moreover, barriers to intergenerational mobility of first-generation migrants may reinforce the isolation of subsequent generations. Piore (1979) notes that the culture of poverty is usually associated with unstable migrant communities which remain cut off from mainstream society. He points out that first-generation immigrant communities are inherently unstable, reflecting the transience of the migrants and their existence outside a structured social context of family networks and stable jobs. The mind-set and values of migrants may be conditioned by the kinds of employment opportunities provided by the market (see also Liebow 1966) and the migrants' expectations. The present orientation of migrants may be a manifestation of the temporary character of migration, including migrants' expectations to return home or the inability to find stable jobs. Second-generation migrants are likely to resemble first generation migrants in their behavior and motivations, if they grow up in communities dominated by first-generation migrants who have not been able to make the transition to stable jobs and lifestyles (Piore 1979).

In this sense, second- and more recent generations of migrants who have grown up in communities where assimilation has been prevented for one reason or another are likely to be overrepresented in the underclass (Swinton and Burbridge 1981). As recent migrants to urban areas undergoing economic change, the conditions of blacks and Puerto Ricans and their association with the underclass seem to support this argument (see also Liebow 1966; Gans 1962).

Anecdotal evidence of the success of some recent immigrant groups, Asians and Cubans for example, does raise some questions about the timing of migration and the postindustrial marginalization arguments. However, the success of those groups can partly be explained by the selectivity of their migration. The well-known demographic "law" that the greater the distance migrated, the higher the skill level of migrants, can explain the success of Asians, and the selectivity of Cuban "political" migration which results in Cuban immigrants being more highly skilled and motivated can explain Cuban success.

Other observers such as Katznelson (1983) point out that the social and economic attainment of migrant groups may also vary depending upon whether or not their migration is censored. For example, the curtailing of Japanese and Chinese migration allowed those groups to develop certain mobility niches—the Japanese in truck farming and the Chinese in the laundry business—which formed the basis for the movement of both groups into the social and economic mainstream. Native blacks and Puerto Ricans may have fared poorly because their migration was unrestricted and, therefore, contributed to a climate of hostility and discrimination without the development of any particular socioeconomic niche.

GOVERNMENT SOCIAL POLICY

Some observers have argued that government social policy has contributed to the emergence of underclass conditions (e.g., Loury 1984; Murray 1984; Wilson 1984; Nathan 1987). However, there are differing views regarding the reasons why government policy has had an adverse effect on the poor and one must be careful not to confuse the various positions. Murray (1984), a major advocate of this position, argues that social problems, such as welfare dependency, teen pregnancy and dropping out of high school, which are usually associated with the underclass, are a consequence of misguided federal policy. He argues that anti-poverty programs, by providing alternative sources of income to working, led to the growth of social ills because they reduced the costs of social nonconformity. Hence, he views the emergence of behaviors associated with the underclass as a rational response to government-induced changes in the rules of the game governing the life of the poor.

Other observers, such as Nathan (1987), Wilson (1984) and Loury (1984), have pointed to the role that government social programs have played in the process of bifurcated social stratification among the black population and, consequently, the emergence of the black underclass. Nathan argued that the emergence of the black underclass is a consequence of the "success," not failure, of American social policy, including the civil rights revolution and the "big-spending social programs" of the last two decades. Civil rights legislation opened up suburbia, and anti-poverty programs provided the means for more able blacks to escape the ghetto leaving the underclass behind.

In addition, both Wilson (1984) and Loury (1984) argued that affirmative action programs have not really helped the truly disadvantaged. What has happened is that, because of the race-specific nature of affirmative action programs, more-able blacks have been able to take greater advantage of the opportunities created by affirmative action requirements. The upshot of this is that more able blacks who benefited from those programs were able to move out of black neighborhoods, leaving the lower class without traditional role models and consequently contributing to the greater isolation and pathology of the lower class. Moreover, in contrast to Murray, Wilson argued that the solution to the problems of lower-class blacks does not require a hands-off policy by government. On the contrary, what is needed is greater government involvement and class-specific policies, such as full employment, which are designed to assist all poor Americans.

These are two very different causal arguments about the relationship between government social programs and the emergence of the underclass. Murray's argument is that anti-poverty programs reduced the cost of social nonconformity and this in turn allowed the poor to engage in underclass behaviors. Wilson, Loury, and Nathan propose that because affirmative action programs required racial quotas, they mostly helped more-able blacks who used the opportunities offered by these programs to migrate out of traditional black communities. This increased the social isolation and pathology of the residual group of poor blacks because they no longer had traditional role models to emulate. In short, the programs worked, and now America is left with an unintentional and fairly intractable consequence of those programs.

Those critical of Murray's argument that anti-poverty programs have contributed to the emergence of the underclass have pointed out that were it not for anti-poverty programs, levels of social dislocation and poverty would be much higher (e.g., Wilson 1985; Danziger and Gottschalk 1985; Ellwood and Summers 1986). Ellwood and Summers, for example, cite a variety of evidence to show that Aid to Families with Dependent Children [AFDC] is not primarily responsible for growing dependency or for family instability. Family dissolution increased over the 1970s while the real value of AFDC benefits declined, and variations in benefit levels across states are not associated with corresponding variations in the incidence of single-parent families, divorce, or out-of-wedlock births. Second, for one presumed subgroup of the underclass—unemployed black youths—trends in unemployment are unlikely to be related to welfare benefits since, in general, youths are ineligible for those benefits.

Also, contrary to Murray, Danziger, et al. (1986) argue that anti-poverty programs have not had a significant negative impact on work effort. And Danziger and Gottschalk (1985) show that even when spending for AFDC and food stamp programs declined in the 1980s, the percentage of female-headed families continued to rise. Unemployment also rose over the period.

The Wilson, Loury and Nathan hypothesis, although highly plausible, remains untested. Without a doubt, there has been significant out-migration of the more advantaged blacks and increasing levels of pathological behavior among inner-city blacks. But the causal relationship of the out-migration of more able blacks to changing attitudes and the relationship of attitudes to increased pathological behavior among the residual population (see Wilson 1985) remain untested because of the absence of the required retrospective data on attitudes (for a good discussion of this see Danziger and Gottschalk 1987).

THE CULTURE OF POVERTY

The culture of poverty argument is that socially deviant behaviors of the underclass are an expression of an entrenched and enduring culture among the underclass as opposed to a rational response to the adverse conditions members of the underclass face. The argument is made that the underclass is beset by distinct values and aspirations that weaken the motivation to achieve and that are transmitted intergenerationally. This is somewhat different from Lewis's (1966) rendition, because Lewis viewed the culture of poverty as a proximate adaptation or reaction to social structure, while current culture of poverty advocates credit the culture of poverty to more distant events such as slavery or sharecropping in the South.

In some ways, the culture of poverty thesis is the converse of the Protestant ethic thesis of Max Weber (1930), which has been discredited. Weber argued that capitalism emerged among Calvinist Protestants because of their values—in other words, they had values other people did not have. Of course, as capitalism has flourished among other cultures, including Buddhist Japanese, the thesis became discredited. Likewise, the culture of poverty thesis emphasizes the absence of Calvinist values and the presence of opposite ones among the poor.

Lehman (1986), for example, ties the emergence of welfare dependency and the underclass to the post-slavery culture of sharecropping that emerged in the South. This culture was characterized by dependency on white authority figures, family instability and out-of-wedlock births, and a low value for education (see also Dash 1989). He argues that the emergence of the underclass in Northern cities is really a consequence of ex-sharecroppers and their descendants migrating and transporting this culture to the North.

Auletta (1982) credits the emergence of the underclass to patterns of inner-city living and parenting. He argues that the underclass is mostly a consequence of poor youths growing up in female-headed households, where there is no father figure in the family to add stability to their development.

Although some observers credit the origin of family breakdown among blacks to the slavery or sharecropping culture of the South (see, for example, Lehman 1986), research evidence supports Auletta's view that family breakdown among blacks is a recent phenomenon that is associated with the urbanization of blacks since the late 1950s (see Ricketts 1989).

To some extent even the proponents of the culture of poverty argument contradict themselves about the determinacy of culture. For example, Lehman's argument that the culture of poverty among the black underclass arose out of the sharecropping in the South only shows that culture and behavior reflect adjustment to specific objective circumstances and is changeable. Moreover, the fact that sharecropper background is what determines underclass status among blacks, suggests that blacks have overcome the harsher effects of slavery. Even Auletta questions the intergenerational transmission of the culture of poverty because he notes that among the underclass he witnessed behavior patterns and values reminiscent of the culture of poverty among people from two-parent families as well as middle-class values among those raised in one-parent families.

Whether the socially dysfunctional behaviors of the underclass are a rational response to objective conditions or whether they are a result of entrenched cultural values will continue to be debated. It is obvious that the information content of a culture has a limiting effect on the range of options available to adherents of the culture. It is also quite likely that there is some contagion or demonstration factor at play among the underclass that will tend to prolong an underclass culture due to the geographic clustering/social and cultural isolation of the group (see Wilson 1990). Individuals residing in underclass areas may also engage in deviant behavior because they perceive that the personal costs of their behavior are lowered due to the significant number of others engaging in similar behavior. What is more debatable, however, is the degree of determinacy of culture.

DISCRIMINATION

Until recently, the significance of discrimination as a factor in development of the underclass was discounted mostly because of how the underclass debate developed. In response to the civil rights revolution and affirmative action programs, college educated blacks made considerable socioeconomic progress during the 1970s. The progress of more able blacks affirmed that discrimination had lessened, and scholars such as Wilson focused on explaining why a sizable proportion of the black population did not exploit opportunities to make the transition. This discussion naturally focused on the social and class characteristics as a disabling factor since the upward mobility of many blacks suggested that discrimination was no longer as significant a barrier to advancement.

After the euphoria that followed the early successes of the civil rights revolution, the significance of discrimination has received a more sober reassessment (see, for example, Massey 1990; Massey and Denton 1989). Massey (1990), for example, argues that racial segregation is the crucial factor explaining the emergence of the black underclass in the 1970s. This occurred primarily because increasing rates of poverty combined with residential segregation to create greater concentrations of the underclass in segregated inner-city areas.

The tendency to downplay discrimination as an important causal factor in discussions about the underclass may also underestimate how well entrenched the more subtle forms of discrimination are (see, for example, Culp and Dunson 1986), as well as what might be a growing reemergence and acceptance of racial intolerance (see, for example, Nathan 1987). The consequences of less severe forms of discrimination, such as statistical discrimination (e.g., when employers use stereotypes in employment decisions in the absence of concrete information) and consumer discrimination (e.g., when hiring practices anticipate consumers' preferences for certain kinds of workers), may have devastating consequences for the underclass, because members of the underclass tend to fit undesirable stereotypes.

In addition, to the extent speech, dress, and work habits come into consideration, members of the underclass may fare poorly in the growing service sector, where jobs tend to require interaction with the public. On the other hand, more educated minorities may do well in the labor market, even where there is intolerance of some minority modes of dress and behavior, because higher education embodies behavior patterns that are more consonant with mainstream norms. Therefore, subtler forms of discrimination against cultural nonconformity may partially explain the success of highly educated minorities and the plight of the less educated minorities in the underclass.

OTHER FACTORS

One underrated factor, although it has received some consideration, is alienation. It is possible that alienation among blacks and Hispanics may partly be a carryover from the 1960s and 1970s when it was cultivated by the more radical civil rights groups because of their vision of impending revolution. Once brought into being, continued widespread alienation among disadvantaged minorities may also reflect their disadvantaged status as well as their growing detachment from society's mainstream—although alienation and apathy are usually considered aspects of the culture of poverty.

Another factor that may partially explain the emergence of the underclass is increased competition from immigrant workers, given the weak performance of the economy over the last two decades (see Reischauer 1986, 1987). For example, more-able blacks made substantial inroads into the economic mainstream during the early 1960s when the economy was strong. The inability of less-able blacks to make the transition into the mainstream may be partially due to the slowdown in the economy during the 1970s and early 1980s coupled with increased competition from immigrants. Besides, more liberal changes in the immigration laws in 1965 and increasing levels of "illegal immigration" suggest there has been greater competition for entry-level jobs. A weak economy and increased competition mean less-able blacks, particularly young uneducated blacks entering the labor force, may have found it more difficult to secure decent jobs that would help them move into the mainstream. However, recent research has not supported this view (see, for example, Muller and Espenshade 1985). Instead, recent research in this area generally shows the effect of immigrants on native workers is innocuous.

Nonetheless, some observers such as Lieberson (1980) posit the existence of an American ethnic occupational hierarchy in which blacks occupy the lowest position. The implication of this argument is that blacks do better when more preferred ethnic labor is scarce. There is some historical evidence supportive of this argument (see Marks 1983; Wilkie 1976). For example, blacks fared better during World Wars I and II when immigration was curtailed and there was a very tight labor market.

While the underclass debate has rejuvenated discussion of the importance of these factors, there is still little research that can help to adjudicate between them. Currently, there is more consensus for the argument that skills and/or geographical mismatch between workers and jobs is a significant cause of the underclass than for the other arguments (see, for example, U.S. Government Printing Office 1991).

POLICY IMPLICATIONS OF ARGUMENTS FOR EMERGENCE OF THE UNDERCLASS

As argued earlier, it is not easy to translate an understanding of the causes of the underclass into policy action. Nonetheless it is important to distinguish between the various arguments for the emergence and growth of the underclass—postindustrial marginalization and adaptation, government intervention, ill-timed mass migration, the culture of poverty, and discrimination—because they suggest the general thrust of policy prescriptions that are likely to be advanced as solutions for the problems of the underclass.

If the problems of the underclass are viewed as consequences of redundancy and marginalization brought on by postindustrial change, then proposed solutions could involve a fairly broad set of policy initiatives ranging from macroeconomic growth policy to upgrading skills and education, and perhaps include policies to relocate members of the underclass to where job opportunities are. Basically, if the issue is one of mismatch between the education and skills available and those needed by a postindustrial society, or if it is a mismatch between the number of jobs that are available in certain areas and the number of workers that are needed, then policy makers could either improve the performance of the macroeconomy or the individual to improve the match or relocate the underclass.

Those who argue that the problems of the underclass result from past social policies may well advocate a hands-off policy by government as Murray has suggested (see U.S., Congress, House 1986). Their laissez-faire policy would leave the resolution of the underclass' problems to the workings of the market. In the extreme case—in the absence of government assistance—the underclass would be faced with the dilemma of working under any condition or starving.

On the other hand, those who believe the problems are caused by insufficient or misdirected government intervention may suggest greater involvement or redirection of government efforts. In general, policy making is usually motivated by this perspective.

Those who believe that the problems of the underclass result in part from the ill-timing of the mass migrations of blacks and Puerto Ricans to major northeastern industrial centers in the throes of postindustrial transformation may prescribe macroeconomic, skills training, and cultural initiatives. This is because the mass migration argument can be seen as a special case in which migration aggravates the skills and geographic mismatch problem. Those subscribing to this argument may also advance policies aimed at cultural integration because of the sense that the children of migrants can become mired in the culture of poverty to the extent their parents are not integrated into mainstream society and, hence, fail to become good models of mainstream behavior.

Those who see the problems of the underclass as a result of well-entrenched cultural values would perhaps suggest two kinds of initiatives—do nothing or resocialization. If culture is as enduring and deterministic as some authors suggest, then little can be done to change it. The more deterministic view of the culture of poverty is often seen as ideological because it credits the problems of the underclass, particularly the black underclass, to an immutable culture that is beyond policy intervention. Some observers who support this position tend to view social problems as genetically determined. On the other hand, those who believe in a less deterministic version of the culture of poverty may support resocialization or, more generally, cultural enrichment programs.

Because the culture of poverty is viewed as a conservative ideological ploy, most liberals are inclined to throw out baby and bath water when it comes to assessing the role of the culture of poverty, yet most acknowledge the importance of culture in the emergence and growth of the underclass. Scholars such as Wilson (1990) now recognize the importance of culture or "concentration effects" in the maintenance of the underclass. Concentration effects are the cumulative effects of living in underclass neighborhoods where the prevalence of disadvantaged and socially dysfunctional behavior among one's social contacts encourage similar behavior. Others such as Ogbu (1978, 1983) acknowledge the importance of the development of a reactive anti-education culture among disadvantaged minorities, particularly blacks, that accepts white stereotypes and is self-replicating in the vein of Lewis's theory.

Acknowledgement of the importance of culture among liberals is most evident in the popularity of the "Eugene Lang" type of experiments and programs that show children from very disadvantaged neighborhoods can achieve at significantly higher rates if they are provided with the same kind of cultural enrichment resources middle-class children have. There is room here for common ground between conservative and liberal policy makers on a mix of initiatives that are likely to include workfare-like proposals, involving an acculturation or resocialization component such as day care. Emphasis by both conservatives and liberals on work and re-socialization suggests they believe the norms and values of the culture of poverty are not immutable, and the culture of poverty argument is not as extreme a position on the underclass as it appears. The culture of poverty perspective simply places more emphasis on the relative effects of culture.

Those who believe the problems of the minority underclass stem from continued discrimination are likely to support efforts at social and economic integration and equal opportunity and desegregation efforts particularly in the workplace and in housing. Until recently discrimination was not a prominent argument for explaining the underclass because the underclass model chiefly arose out of the need to explain why lower-class blacks were not as successful as upper-class blacks in exploiting the opportunities for socioeconomic mobility that arose out of the decline of racial discrimination and segregation that accompanied the civil rights revolution. In short, the underclass model turns on an acknowledgement of the declining significance of racial discrimination. However, analysts have recently pointed out that discrimination is more well entrenched than previously thought and may, in fact, be increasing.

RELEVANCE OF ARGUMENTS FOR THE EMERGENCE OF THE UNDERCLASS

Although the various arguments for the emergence and growth of the underclass appear as competing arguments, they can be integrated within the postindustrial marginalization and adaptation framework.

The argument that the ill-timing of mass migration by blacks and Puerto Ricans to major northeastern cities experiencing postindustrial change contributed to the prevalence of those groups among the underclass, can be seen as a qualifier for the postindustrial marginalization argument. This is because mass migration aggravates the mismatch between the number of jobs and need among disadvantaged workers and can lead to substitution of more skilled in-migrants for native workers.

In addition, the effects of culture and behavior can plausibly be integrated into the adaptation thesis of the postindustrial marginalization argument more so than current renditions of the culture of poverty argument, which stress the independent determinacy of culture.

Although observers such as Murray argue that government intervention contributed to development of the problems of the underclass, others have provided more convincing evidence that without the intervention of government, conditions among the underclass would be worse, because of postindustrial change. The idea is that the transformation of the economy must be viewed as the interpretive context against which to evaluate forms of government intervention.

Finally the importance of discrimination mainly stems from the fact that it traps the minority poor in the inner-city. Discrimination accentuates skills and geographic mismatch between inner-city residents and available jobs, by limiting access to increasing job opportunities in the suburban ring.

The coincidence of a number of factors does give weight to the postindustrial marginalization argument. There is consensus that since World War II there has been a transition towards a postindustrial economy. Second, there is some consensus that, in recent years, there has been a trend to locate production away from central cities as well as in foreign countries. Third, immigration has increased rapidly since the immigration laws were changed in 1965. Fourth, during this period, the baby-boom generation also entered the labor market. Fifth, the labor force participation of women increased steadily since World War II. This combination of factors suggests that there is a growing mismatch between the increasingly scarce "good" low-skilled jobs and the supply of low-skilled workers.

CONDITIONS NECESSARY FOR A SEMINAL POLICY CONSENSUS ON THE UNDERCLASS

This chapter has emphasized the importance of an enabling social environment as a prerequisite for meaningful initiatives on the underclass. This section addresses the question: What is the set of social circumstances that would have to be obtained in order to create the elemental conditions for a federal policy initiative on the underclass? This section is, therefore, speculative and seeks to accomplish no more than a broad outline of the kind of policy environment believed conducive to significant policy action on the underclass.

The following conditions are perhaps basic to such a scenario: (1) the emergence of a consensual understanding of the underclass that attributes the problem primarily to social as opposed to individual causes, (2) a consensus that the underclass problem requires urgent policy attention, (3) a realization that resolution of the problem is beyond the capacity of local communities and government, and (4) a realization that the federal government must take leadership in resolving the problems of the underclass.

Continued controversy about the nature and the causes of the underclass is evidence of a lack of consensual understanding of the underclass among the general public. The predominant societal explanation for the problems of the underclass is that they are caused by personal failings. This understanding arose out of the perception that the War on Poverty was adequate for eradicating poverty and those among the poor whose poverty problems were not solved by it were beyond the reach of social programs, or that the social programs themselves caused the problems (see Murray 1984). This perspective seems to be declining and it is being challenged increasingly by the postindustrial marginalization argument, partly based on results from increasing research activity on the underclass.

Arguably there is some consensus that the problems of the underclass require urgent attention. One can argue that such policies as the Family Support Act of 1988 and the War on Drugs are urgent responses to problems of the underclass, and as such, provide evidence that the problems are perceived as needing urgent attention. However, few observers would argue that these responses are adequate for a problem that is perceived as being fairly intractable and experiencing rapid growth. There is no doubt that the underclass will need greater policy attention and higher elevation on the policy agenda.

Yet in an era of increasing budget deficits, the federal government has abrogated its role to redress the problems of the poor and the underclass to state and local government. In part because the problems of the underclass have been seen as resulting from personal failings, they are seen as solvable at the state and local levels. If one accepts that the problems of the underclass are caused by postindustrialization, then it is doubtful that the problems of the underclass can be solved at the local level. Regardless of what communities can reasonably be expected to do in the way of solving the problems of their residents, it is doubtful they can resolve problems such as significant loss of jobs that are due to plant closings or plant relocations. One simply needs to visit a steel town in which the predominant mill has closed in order to realize this. The current epidemic of drug abuse also shows the limitation of community responses.

The magnitude and severity of the problems of the underclass suggest that resolving them is beyond the capacity of most communities. Therefore, they are likely to be resolved only by a well-coordinated effort at the federal level. Because of the difficult choices that such an effort would require, more than the customary commitment from a president would be needed in order to assure success. To be successful, it would require the commitment of a president who would be willing to sacrifice a second term in office in order to make significant progress resolving these issues.

BASIC COMPONENTS OF A NATIONAL INITIATIVE ON THE UNDERCLASS

Meaningful action to resolve the problems of the underclass will require compromise and cooperation by liberals and conservatives. Since it is unlikely that the nation will resolve the budget deficit any time soon, support for a major initiative to address the problems of the underclass will require a significant shift in prioritizing among the many national causes that compete for attention. The most likely way a compromise between conservatives and liberals can be effected is around an understanding that the poor are obligated to work as a condition for receiving public assistance. Liberals and conservatives must agree that all able-bodied individuals must work or be actively preparing to work in order to receive assistance from the state.

This means that conservatives would have to accept that the state must be responsible for providing gainful employment to all in cases where the market fails to do so. In return, liberals would have to agree that social assistance go only to those who abide by the social contract to be gainfully employed or to those who are disabled. Any initiative along these lines would have to be accompanied by comprehensive programs to train members of the underclass for jobs if it is to succeed.

A comprehensive overhaul of the anti-poverty infrastructure with the aim of getting more resources directly to the poor by eliminating the bureaucracy and by combining the delivery of services is also essential. Currently, much of the resources intended for the poor is consumed by middle-level bureaucracy. For example, John McKnight has argued that if all the federal funds spent on anti-poverty activities in the city of Chicago were cashed out, each poor person could receive $6,209 and each family of three, $18,600 (see Peirce 1990).

This is a significant sum of money and ways must be sought to put it to productive use that increases the multiplier effect of this money in poor communities rather than simply handing it over for consumption to the poor.

Comprehensive reform of drug policy is the *sine qua non* of any serious initiative to resolve the problems of the underclass. Because of the multi-faceted ways in which drug trafficking and drug abuse are tied to other problems of the underclass, resolving the drug problem is pivotal to resolving the many other problems that are its second-order consequences. Finding a means to make hard drugs quasi-legal is imperative if profit from drug trafficking is to be removed. Only then will disruptive and destructive violence around drug selling cease in poor communities. At the same time, comprehensive treatment programs will need to be instituted.

Another indispensable factor in any initiative on the underclass is a housing policy. For any serious anti-underclass initiative to be successful it would have to include a comprehensive housing policy. Either members of the underclass must be provided with housing vouchers or housing must be developed in underclass neighborhoods.

Perhaps the most significant need is for the federal government to rethink its laissez-faire policy with regard to creating employment opportunities in industry. If macroeconomic transformation and attendant dislocation are fundamental to the emergence and growth of the underclass, then what is needed is federal involvement in economic development. The federal government must approach helping the underclass and poor communities the same way it approaches helping poor third-world countries—it must tie aid to sound management and investment. Nothing short of a comprehensive, well-coordinated effort led by the federal government will even begin to make a dent in the underclass problem.

REFERENCES

Auletta, K. 1982. *The underclass*. New York: Random House.
Blau, P.M. and O.D. Duncan. 1967. *The american occupation structure*. New York: John Wiley.
Bluestone, B. and B. Harrison. 1982. *The deindustrialization of America*. New York: Basic Books.
Corcoran, M., G. J. Duncan, G. Gurin and P. Gurin. 1985. Myth and reality: the causes and persistence of poverty. *Journal of Policy Analysis and Management* 4: 516–36.
Culp, J. and B.H. Dunson. 1986. Brothers of a different color: a preliminary look at employer treatment of white and black youth. In *The Black Youth Employment Crisis*, J. Culp and B. Dunson, eds., 233–60.
Currie, E. 1985. *Confronting crime*. New York: Pantheon.
Danziger, S.H. and P. Gottschalk. 1985. The poverty of loosing ground. *Challenge* (May–June):32–38.
_____. 1987. Earnings inequality, the spatial concentration of poverty and the underclass. *AEA Papers and Proceedings* 77:211–15.
Danziger, S.H., R.H. Haveman and R.D. Plotnick. 1986. Anti-poverty policy: effects on the poor and nonpoor. In *Fighting poverty: what works and what doesn't*, S.H. Danziger and D.H. Weinberg, eds. 50–77. Cambridge, MA: Harvard University Press.

Dash, L. 1989. *When children want children*. New York: William Morrow.

Ellwood, D.T. 1988. *Poor support: poverty in the American family*. New York: Basic Books.

_____. 1986. The spatial mismatch hypothesis. Are there teenage jobs missing in the ghetto? In: *The Black youth employment crisis*, R.B. Freeman and H.J. Holtzer, eds. Chicago: University of Chicago Press.

Ellwood, D.T. and L.H. Summers. 1986. Poverty in America: is welfare the answer to the problem. In *Fighting poverty: what works and what doesn't*, S.H. Danziger and D.Weinberg, eds. Cambridge, MA: Harvard University Press.

Gans, H. 1962. *The urban villagers*. New York: Free Press.

Glasgow, D.G. 1980. *The black underclass: poverty, unemployment, and entrapment of ghetto youth*. San Francisco, CA: Jossey-Bass.

Glazer, N. and D.P. Moynihan. 1970. *Beyond the melting pot*. Cambridge, MA: MIT Press.

Jencks, C. 1988. Deadly neighborhoods. *New Republic* (June 13): 23–.

Kasarda, J.D. 1980. The implications of contemporary redistribution trends for national urban policy. *Social Science Quarterly* 61:373–400.

_____. 1985. Urban challenge and minority opportunity. In: *The new urban reality*. P. Peterson, ed. Washington, DC: Brookings Institution.

_____. 1983. Caught in the web of change. *Society* 21:41–47.

Katznelson, I. 1983. Slicing the political pie. *Society* 21:48–53.

Kaus, M. 1986. The work ethic state. *The New Republic*, (July):22–33.

Lehman, N. 1986. The origins of the underclass? *The Atlantic* (June): 31–55 and (July): 54–68.

Lewis, O. 1966. The culture of poverty. *Scientific American* 215:19–25.

Lieberson, S. 1980. *A piece of the pie: black and white immigrants since 1880*. Berkeley, CA: University of California Press.

Liebow, E. 1966. *Tally's corner*. Boston, MA: Little, Brown and Company.

Loury, G. 1984. The need for moral leadership in the black community. *New Perspectives* 16:14–19.

Marks, C. 1983. Lives of communication, recruitment mechanisms, and the great migration of 1916–1918. *Social Problems* 31 (October): 73–83.

Massey, D.S. 1990. American apartheid: segregation and the making of the underclass. *American Journal of Sociology* 96(2).

Massey, D.S. and N.A. Denton 1989. Hypersegregation in U.S. metropolitan areas: black and hispanic segregation along five dimensions. *Demography* 26(3).

McLanahan, S., I. Garfinkel and D. Watson. 1986. Family structure, poverty and the underclass. Paper prepared for Workshop on Contemporary Urban Conditions sponsored by the Committee on National Urban Policy of the National Research Council, Washington, DC, July 16–17.

Muller, R. and T. Espenshade. 1985. *The fourth wave: California's newest immigrants*. Washington, DC: The Urban Institute Press.

Murray, C. 1984. *Losing ground: american social policy 1950–1980*. New York: Basic Books.

Nathan, R. 1987. Will the underclass always be with us? *Society* (March-April): 57–62.

Ogbu, J. 1978. *Minority education and caste: the american system in cross-cultural perspective*. New York: Academic Press.

_____. 1983. Minority status and schooling in comparative perspective. *Comparative Education Review* 27(2): 168–90.

Peirce, N.R. 1990. John McKnight's new war on poverty. *National Journal* (December 1).

Piore, M.J. 1979. *Birds of passage: migrant labor and industrial societies.* New York: Cambridge University Press.

Reischauer, R.D. 1986. A comment on 'the underclass—will it always be with us'. Paper prepared for Symposium at the New School for Social Research, November 14.

_____. 1987. The size and characteristics of the underclass. Paper presented at the annual conference of the Association for Public Policy Analysis and Management, Bethesda, Maryland, October.

Ricketts, E. 1989. The origin of black female-headed families. *Focus* 12 (Spring/ Summer): 1.

Sandefur, G.D. and M. Tienda. 1988. *Divided opportunities: minorities, poverty and social policy.* New York: Plenum Press.

Schorr, L.B. and D. Schorr 1988. *Within our reach: breaking the cycle of disadvantage.* New York: Anchor Press.

Suro, R. 1991. Where have all the jobs gone? Follow the crab grass. *New York Times,* March 3,4:5.

Swinton, D.H. and L. Burbridge. 1981. *Civil rights and the underclass.* Urban Institute Research Paper.

U.S., Congress, House. 1986. Select committee on hunger, poverty, and the welfare system, 99th Cong., 2d Sess. (Aug. 5).

U.S. Government Printing Office. 1991. *Budget of the United States government,* fiscal year 1991.

Van Haitsma, M. 1989. A contextual definition of the underclass. *Focus* 12 (Spring/ Summer):1. Madison, WI: University of Wisconsin, Madison Institute for Research on Poverty.

Waldinger, R. 1983. The occupational and economic integration of the new immigrants. *Law and Contemporary Problems* 45: 197–222.

Weber, M. 1930. *The protestant ethic and the spirit of capitalism.* London: Allen & Unwin.

Wilkie, J.R. 1976. Urbanization and de-urbanization of the black population before the civil war. *Demography* 13 (August):311–28.

Wilson, W.J. 1983. Inner-city dislocations. *Society* 21:81–6.

_____. 1984. Race-specific policies and the truly disadvantaged. *Yale Law and Policy Review* 2:272–90.

_____. 1985. Cycles of deprivation and the underclass debate. *Social Science Review* 59:541–59.

_____. 1990. Social theory and public agenda research: the challenge of studying inner-city social dislocations. Presidential address, Annual Meeting of the American Sociological Association, August 12.

Wilson, W.J. and R. Aponte. 1985. Urban poverty. *Annual Review of Sociology* 11:231–58.

Wilson, W.J. and K.M. Neckerman. 1986. Poverty and family structure: the widening gap between evidence and public policy issues. In *Fighting poverty: what works and what doesn't*, S.H. Danziger and D.H. Weinberg, eds, 232–59. Cambridge, MA: Harvard University Press.

13 From Caste to Class to Caste: The Changing Nature of Race Relations in America

CHARLES WASHINGTON

Living in America's inner-cities are millions of people who are beset by high teenage birthrates, crime, drugs, prostitution, homelessness, and poverty that persists from generation to generation (Auletta 1982; Wilson 1985, 1987a, 1987b, 1989). These people are collectively known as the "underclass." The term is nearly synonymous with the large African-American population of the inner-city ghettos (Kasarda 1985; and Wacquant and Wilson 1989). The underclass, however, is not the sole province of African-Americans; other minorities and poor whites are members as well (Auletta 1982).

The underclass represents the hard inner core of poverty (Wilson 1985) and should be distinguished from the transitional poor, many of whom flow in and out of poverty along with swings in the economy.[1] What distinguishes the underclass from the transitional poor is the "hope" the transitional poor have for a better future (Hochschild 1989).[2] For the underclass, all hope may be lost failing government help.

One of the major causal factors in the development and maintenance of the African-American underclass is racism. Racism imposes social, legal, political, and economic barriers on the cultural, and structural integration of African-Americans. This results in the disproportionate representation of African-Americans in the underclass. Aside from a brief period, the history of race relations in America has been characterized by the maintenance of these barriers. The net effect has been creation of castelike socioeconomic divisions based on race, the clearest manifestation of which is the underclass. Any solution to this problem will have to take race explicitly into account. In America, color has been and continues to be the conspicuous mark of caste status, a status determined by birth. Membership is ascribed and is difficult to overcome. African-Americans, who occupy the lowest racial caste, have long been considered inherently inferior and relegated to a disadvantaged position regardless of their behavior.

This chapter argues that the history of race relations in America can be broken down into three distinct periods: the first period (1619–1953) was characterized by an exclusionary, castelike system based on race that served to lock all African-Americans first into slave status and later into second-class citizenship.[3] This period gave way to a short-lived period of class-oriented inclusiveness (1954–1979) that outlawed *de jure* political and legal discrimination and allowed some middle-class African-Americans to escape poverty and the inner city, thereby leaving behind their lower-class brethren. Finally, there is evidence that America has entered a third period, which began in 1980. The current period is characterized by a retreat from class-oriented inclusiveness, an erosion of the legal and political gains of the second period, and potentially a *de facto* reinstitution of portions of the castelike exclusionary system of the first period.

DISTINCTION BETWEEN CASTE AND CLASS

Systems of social stratification are of many kinds: slave, estate, class, caste, etc. (Heller 1987). This chapter limits the discussion to caste and class. A caste system is defined as a hierarchy of endogamous societal divisions. Membership in these divisions is hereditary and permanent and characterized by inequalities in status, wealth, and access to goods and services. In contrast to a caste system, class systems are based on egalitarianism; they de-emphasize political, legal, and social prohibitions to upward mobility and place greater emphasis on economic determinants—individual talent and efforts are the primary delimiting factors. As defined, these are "pure" or "ideal" constructions of caste and class; they do not exist in the real world. In the real world, stratification systems dominate and contain elements of both caste and class systems.

Caste and class are often viewed as polar extremes on a continuum, with class-based social systems being more open to upward mobility and caste-based systems being more closed. Societies move along this continuum. Most see this movement as linear, progressing from caste to class (Yinger 1965; Fischer 1982; and Wilson 1987a). Movement along the continuum is determined by time and circumstance. When a society is dynamic and demands for change are great, it moves toward the class end of the continuum; inclusiveness is enhanced as interstrata barriers weaken and mobility mechanisms increase in number and pervasiveness. Conversely, when a society is in a more conservative state, it moves toward the caste end of the continuum; inclusiveness is minimized, interstrata barriers ossify, and mobility mechanisms become less numerous and pervasive. An example of a class-dominated society would be one that is experiencing a labor surplus versus one that is experiencing a shortage of workers where castelike structures would be expected.

Both caste and class systems have similar characteristics. The following is a list of the systemic characteristics that define a caste system:

1.   Affiliation is by descent and a degree of endogamy is expected.
2.   There are normative forces that justify and legitimate the status quo.
3.   There is institutionalized inequality in the society.
4.   There are few socioeconomic mobility mechanisms.
5.   There is general disbelief and skepticism about the efficacy of efforts toward upward mobility.

Affirmative responses to these descriptors indicate that the society is more caste-like; negative responses to these descriptors indicate that a society is more class-like. Figure 13.1 illustrates how these forces function in dynamic fashion to define caste and class systems. These forces are described in more detail below.

In both caste and class systems affiliation is by descent, meaning that one is born into a given caste or class. In caste systems, one is expected to remain for life in the caste in which one is born. Castes function under the principle of endogamy, thereby making sex and intermarriage between castes unacceptable and, thus, contributing to the permanency of inequalities inherent in that system of social stratification. Conversely, in class systems permanent membership in the class of one's birth is not expected or necessarily desirable; endogamy is not expected and fewer prohibitions against interclass associations exist.

Norms play an important role in the stratification system because they serve to justify and legitimize the status quo. Normative forces are rooted in the religious institutions, values, and mores of the society. The normative forces contribute to a collective belief in the inherent "rightness" of the system. The rigid inequalities of caste systems could be destabilizing in the long term were it not for the generally accepted belief that the system is right and/or the upper castes have the power to impose the system over the objections of those who disagree with it. The same is true for class systems: societal norms reinforce the rightness of egalitarianism and inclusiveness. Change from one system of social stratification to another is impossible without fundamental changes in the societal norms.

How a society's institutions are structured and function is important in terms of societal stratification. As the major institutions of society come to embody the norms of society, their structure and function come to serve that logic and, therefore, society's values and norms become institutionalized.

FIGURE 13.1

Comparison of Caste and Class Dynamics

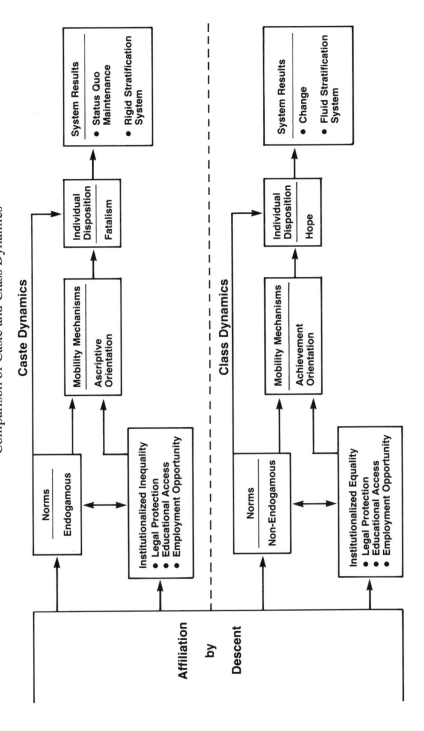

Institutional arrangements help to determine the level of rigidity in a given society. Their ability to facilitate upward mobility may be assessed according to the following criteria:

1. Political: freedom to vote and hold public office, etc.
2. Legal: the right to enter into contracts, equal protection under the law, etc.
3. Social: equal access to mainstream education, freedom of movement, association, and settlement, etc.
4. Economic: equal employment opportunity, and equal access to the goods and services of society, etc.

When societies have more of the foregoing characteristics, its institutions can facilitate upward mobility; where there is less, its institutions can inhibit upward mobility. Because caste systems are based on the principle of institutionalized inequality and differential access to society's goods and values, its institutions inhibit upward mobility.[4] Class systems are based on the principle of egalitarianism and their institutions facilitate upward mobility.

Mobility mechanisms are the acceptable methods by which people move up the socioeconomic ladder within societies. They are part and parcel of the structure and function of society. The acceptability of these mechanisms depends upon the society's norms. The degree of mobility in a given society is determined by the ease with which lower castes or classes can take advantage of the opportunities offered by existing mobility mechanisms.

Mobility in caste systems is based on ascriptive determinants—kinship, friendship, ethnic affiliation—and, thus, it is limited. Mobility in class systems is based on achievement—education and skills attained—and, thus, it is potentially open to all.

Societal norms and the height of institutional barriers to advancement combine to influence beliefs about the efficacy of efforts to improve one's socioeconomic position. This is true regardless of whether there is general agreement on the "rightness" of the social stratification system or not. The inherent rigidity of the caste system makes one believe that any effort would be fruitless. Therefore, it can lead to fatalism, a lack of effort by members of lower castes, and ultimately to a maintenance of existing inequalities. The fluidity of the class system would make one believe that upward mobility is possible and, therefore, leads to hope and action, which, in turn, spur mobility.

APPLICABILITY OF THE CASTE CONCEPT TO THE UNITED STATES

There are those who are unconvinced as to the applicability of "caste" to the United States (Cox 1948). They believe that the caste principle is only applicable to India and the lack of a religious justification for it in the United States negates its applicability. There are other social scientists who believe that the caste principle is applicable to the United States (Myrdal 1944; Yinger 1965; Ogbu 1978; Fischer 1982; Wilson 1987a, 1987b; Williams 1989; and Ogbu 1990). They define a caste system as a hierarchy of endogamous divisions in which membership is hereditary and permanent (where hierarchy includes inequality both in status and access to goods and services). Using this definition, nearly all are in agreement that social stratification in the antebellum South was characterized by the existence of two different castes—one white and the other African-American—and that this stratification resulted in the institutionalized inequality of the latter.

This chapter seeks to show that race relations in the United States have some elements that give them a castelike quality: institutionalized inequality for African-Americans (and others), *de facto* norms that support their inequality, unequal access to mobility mechanisms, and unequal access to society's goods and services.

THE CASTE SYSTEM AND THE BEGINNING OF THE UNDERCLASS: 1619–1953

The caste system was established in the antebellum South when African-Americans were kept as chattel slaves. American slavery was a caste system in all major respects: legal, political, social, and economic. African-Americans had no rights under the law and could, therefore, be disposed of in any way that whites saw fit. The system of slavery was characterized by the physical segregation of the races and the relegation of African-Americans to the lowest socioeconomic strata. African-American families were dismembered, thereby destroying any sense of belonging and reinforcing their position as chattel. They were subject to physical torture and even death at the whim of their white masters. Conscious efforts were made to stifle African-American intellectual attainment and entrepreneurial spirit so as to limit their ability to function independently, thereby strengthening the bonds of servitude. The system of slavery was augmented by philosophical and moral justifications of African-American racial inferiority and the "rightness" of their servitude. This helped to lend legitimacy to the institution (Stampp 1956; Logan 1965; Simpson and Yinger 1965; Franklin 1980; Fischer 1982; Bloom 1987; Ogbu 1978; Williams 1989; and Ogbu 1990). Thus, the caste confinement of African-Americans was complete.

In 1863, President Lincoln signed the Emancipation Proclamation freeing the slaves. Slavery had a bitter legacy, however. As a result of 150 years of dehumanization and brutal exploitation, few African-Americans had made much educational or economic progress. Many African-Americans suffered the psychological damage of self-hate, a belief in their own racial inferiority, and a fear of whites—what Fischer calls the "caste mentality" (1982, p. 45; and Ogbu 1990).

The North imposed Reconstruction on the South in an attempt to rectify the status of former African-American slaves. The Thirteenth, Fourteenth, and Fifteenth Amendments to the Constitution and a number of federal legislative initiatives were enacted to ensure the rights of African-Americans. The federal government forced Southern states to reconstruct their laws and regulations so that they were consistent with the new federal mandates granting citizenship and equal rights to African-Americans. Union troops were posted in the South to hold the forces of white supremacy in check and to ensure Southern compliance.[5]

During Reconstruction, African-Americans experienced tangible social, economic, and political gains. Demonstrable gains included the formation of educational institutions and religious and civic organizations in African-American communities. Before the end of the Civil War, African-Americans rarely owned property or engaged in business. After the Civil War, African-American participation in trades, investment in business, and ownership of property rose substantially. In 1865 an estimated 100,000 of the 120,000 artisans in the South were African-American. In 1872 an African-American-owned savings and trust company had 70,000 depositors; in 1873 the Freedman's Bank of Charleston had $350,000 in deposits and 5,500 depositors; and African-Americans in Williamsburg, Virginia, invested $151,000 in new businesses. In Mississippi, 1,800 African-Americans were settled on confiscated plantations, which, in 1866, showed profits of $159,000; also in 1866, African-Americans had secured homesteads in Florida totaling 160,000 acres; and in Georgia in 1874 African-Americans owned more than 350,000 acres of land (Fischer 1982, pp. 46–47).

The most notable gains for African-Americans, however, were political. African-American registration, voting, and holding of political office rose sharply during Reconstruction. In 1867 South Carolina voting records showed 78,982 African-American and 46,346 white registrants. Mississippi's voting records showed 60,167 black and 46,636 white registrants (Fischer 1982, p. 47). This pattern of African-American voting majorities was duplicated in the other Southern states and it altered the racial makeup of state legislatures. Prior to 1865, there were no African-Americans in Southern state legislatures. After 1867, the percentages of African-Americans rose to 27 percent in Alabama, 11.3 percent in Arkansas, 17.4 percent in Georgia, 28 percent in Mississippi, 1 percent in North Carolina, 60 percent in South Carolina, 9 percent in Texas, and 15.3 percent in Virginia. African-American representation was 21.5 percent of the total of all Southern state legislators (Fischer 1982, p. 47).

African-American gains, however, were short-lived. Before the end of Reconstruction, the forces of white supremacy sought to stem the tide of African-American social and economic advancement. Militant white organizations were formed and bent on putting the African-American "back in his place" and keeping him there. Some, such as the Ku Klux Klan and the Knights of the White Camellia, used the most violent methods to accomplish their purposes. As a result, African-Americans throughout the South were intimidated, lynched, and murdered in the hundreds. Their homes and churches were burned and they were denied legally won seats in state legislatures (Fischer 1982, p. 48).

Northern liberalism retreated in the wake of the revival of militant white supremacy. The Period of the Redemption (1879–1944) saw a betrayal of African-Americans by the federal government, beginning with the withdrawal of the Union troops which had kept white racists at bay. At the start of this period in history, the federal government abandoned its commitment to ensure the rights of African-Americans (Logan 1965; Fischer 1982).

During the period of Redemption, the gains that African-Americans had made during Reconstruction were brutally rolled back and the legal and structural barriers to African-American upward mobility were reformulated in new and virulent forms. Whites sought to reinstate African-American inequality through the development of the Jim Crow Laws, which were passed between 1890 and 1910. These laws continued the separation of the races in schools and public facilities (Palen 1987, p. 218). African-American political participation was curtailed by the usage of grandfather clauses, literacy tests, poll taxes, and the white primary.[6] As a result of these policies, the number of African-Americans registered to vote, and who actually voted and held political office dropped to near zero by 1900 (Fischer 1982, p. 51).

Socially, African-American and white relations came to be defined by an inaccurate term embodied in the legal principle of "separate but equal." This principle was established by the Supreme Court in its ruling on *Plessy* v. *Ferguson* in 1896. The legacy of this ruling was the recreation of two societies—one African-American and the other white—and the reformulation and legitimation of the caste system begun during slavery (U.S. Commission on Civil Rights 1982a).

By 1900 many African-Americans migrated from the rural South to the urban North. African-American migration was driven by both push and pull forces. They were pushed by increasing racial intolerance in the South, the failure of Southern agriculture due to the boll weevil's destruction of the cotton fields, and the redundancy of African-American labor associated with the mechanization of Southern agriculture (Palen 1987). They were also pulled by labor recruiters trying to attract new sources of labor to the factories of the North. The recruiters were initially stimulated by the labor shortages triggered by World War I.

As a result, the African-American population of Northern cities grew dramatically. By 1900, Chicago had 30,150 African-Americans; New York,

60,666; St. Louis, 35,516; Philadelphia, 62,613; Washington, D.C, 86,702; and Baltimore, 79,258 (Fischer 1982, p. 82). The North offered better economic opportunities than did the marginal rural economies of the South.

Prior to 1914, problems of race relations were largely a Southern problem. The migration of African-Americans to the North transplanted the problem there. Upon arriving in the Northern cities, African-Americans were immediately subjected to intensified racism. From 1915 to 1920, a series of race riots and other forms of violence against African-Americans occurred in Northern cities. Two notable examples took place in 1917: in East St. Louis 9 whites and 29 African-Americans died, and in Chicago 15 whites and 23 African-Americans died as a result of racial disturbances (Drimmer 1969, p. 373).

Discrimination in its many forms—housing, education, employment, political participation—worked in synergistic fashion to keep African-Americans out of the American mainstream. Discrimination in housing forced African-Americans into overcrowded, decaying, unsafe, unhealthy slums. Discrimination in education forced them to attend schools that ill-prepared them to compete in the marketplace, thereby relegating them to the most menial jobs. Thus began the cycle of urban poverty wherein minorities became locked in the ghetto and out of the American mainstream (Ogbu 1990). Labor unions conspired to keep African-Americans out of desirable trade and craft occupations and in low-paying jobs. The development of the urban underclass began with the urbanization of African-American migrants (Bloom 1987).

THE DECLINE OF CASTE AND RISE OF CLASS-ORIENTED INCLUSION: 1954-1979

During the Redemption, the plight of African-Americans suffering under the weight of racism was largely ignored in America. After World War II, this was to change. The year 1944 saw the beginnings of a new era in race relations characterized by class-oriented inclusion. In that year, in the case of *Smith* v. *Allwright*, the Supreme Court declared unconstitutional the white primary laws and rules that had excluded Southern African-Americans from political participation since the beginning of the Redemption. And in the 1954 landmark Supreme Court decision rendered in *Brown* v. *Board of Education of Topeka*, the Supreme Court struck down public school segregation and the "separate but equal" principle on which it was based. Once again, legal changes began to open the political process up to African-Americans.

Attempts to break down caste barriers were advanced when Congress passed the Civil Rights Act of 1964. The act made overt discrimination in employment illegal and was the springboard of subsequent civil rights legislation. The act was reflective of a new liberal mood that was sweeping the country, a growing national perception of the plight of the African-Americans in general (and those living in America's inner-cities in particular), and a growing national commitment to do something about their plight.

The new mood led to massive social intervention by the federal government. President Johnson initiated numerous programs under the The Great Society and through them conducted his War on Poverty. The original intent of these policies was to keep the poor from slipping further into poverty and, hopefully, to help them escape it altogether. During this period, "race" was no longer a criteria for the allocation of society's benefits. Discrimination was discredited and political and legal castelike structures, which had divided America along racial lines and had been the basis for allocating societal goods and values since the Redemption, were systematically dismantled.

The War on Poverty was conducted along a broad front. It included social, economic, political, and legal efforts. Among its programs were: means-tested income transfers (welfare, supplemental security income, Medicare, and unemployment insurance), special education and training programs, Model Cities funds to combat poverty in neighborhoods, Title I Compensatory Education, minority contracting programs, enforcement of the 1964 Civil Rights Act, and associated affirmative action programs (see Green 1977; Bloom 1987; Hamilton 1988; Jacobs 1988, p. 4).

During this period, African-Americans made significant progress. After the Civil War, African-Americans made remarkable progress in education. Just consider the fact that during slavery it was illegal for African-Americans to learn or for someone to teach them to read (Ogbu 1990). From 1940 to 1960, more African-Americans attended school at all levels—grade school, middle school, secondary school, and post-secondary school—than in any previous period (Jaynes and Williams 1989, pp. 332–40).

From a political standpoint, African-American voter registration, voting, and holding of political office increased. As whites left the inner-city, it gave African-Americans enough of an electoral majority to elect African-American mayors in many of America's cities, such as Coleman Young in Detroit, Richard Gordon Hatcher in Gary, and Carl Stokes in Cleveland, and to elect African-American congressmen from many urban districts (see Ch. 10). On the legal front, numerous Supreme Court rulings, laws, and regulations made overt individual and organizational discrimination against minorities and women illegal. Related equal opportunity and affirmative action programs allowed those minorities who could meet the education and skills requirements to enter the American mainstream. Socially, this was a period of class revolution for African-Americans in America. The Great Society, coupled with the civil rights movement, began the process of dismantling the racially-oriented caste system that had existed since the Redemption and began a period of class-oriented inclusiveness. The Great Society, in short, began the process of establishing a broader class structure within the African-American community (Landry 1987).

The liberalization of social, educational, economic, political, and legal aspects of society created new opportunities for those African-Americans in a position to take advantage of them. Because of these changes, a new African-American middle class was allowed to move up the socioeconomic hierarchy, out of the ghetto, and into the American mainstream. Affirmative action and equal employment opportunity laws began to solve the economic problems for the emerging African-American middle class by lowering legal barriers to employment. In little more than a generation, the proportion of African-Americans holding professional, technical, and craft positions grew from 11 to 21 percent of the occupational distribution of the African-American community. Between 1964 and 1969, the African-American middle class grew between 7.9 percent and 12.4 percent annually. The African-American middle class continued to improve its position relative to whites until the beginning of the 1973–1975 recession. As a consequence of the recession, the African-American middle-class growth rate fell to 2.3 percent. Whites experienced just the opposite growth rate. The African-American middle class did not recover their pre-recession growth rates until 1978 (Landry 1987).

Between 1976 and 1979, the African-American middle class achieved a growth rate of 6.7 percent to 9.9 percent (Landry 1987, pp. 194–96). Many of the new African-American middle-class individuals were blue-collar individuals working in manufacturing and construction. These industries were hit hardest by the recession. In addition, many never recovered from losing their jobs, as equivalent employment opportunities were not available. (For post-1979, see Ch. 4.)

Evidence shows that the percentage of African-Americans below the poverty line was growing during the decade from 1973 to 1983. It rose from 31.4 percent in 1973 to 35.7 percent in 1983 (Meltzer 1988, p. 146). In addition, new and disturbing rifts in the fabric of the African-American nuclear family structure were becoming apparent. There was a startling increase in female-headed households—now called the "feminization of poverty" (Bernstein 1986; Kemper 1988; Anderson 1989; McLanahan and Garfinkel 1989; and Sullivan 1989)—and a rise in aberrant behavior, prostitution, drugs, and crime (Auletta 1982; Wilson 1985, 1989). As normal family support structures weakened, members of the underclass became more susceptible to the social ills of society and they adopted an alternative lifestyle to one considered normal and acceptable (Ogbu 1990).

Equal employment opportunity and affirmative action mainly benefited the new African-American middle class. It is conceivable that they could have benefited the underclass if allowed to remain in place long enough; however, they did not. It is questionable whether anti-poverty programs designed to aid the poor ever gave the poor what they really needed to break the grip of poverty and take advantage of the new mobility mechanisms available—regular, decently paying jobs (Meltzler 1986, pp. 96–97).

What the poor got instead were welfare benefits targeted at specific symptoms of poverty; not a comprehensive, coordinated program designed to eliminate poverty. Therefore, their economic problems were not solved during the period of class-oriented inclusiveness. Ironically, while the African-American middle class and underclass drifted apart, their fates remained linked. It is the perceived plight of the underclass that sustains the affirmative action and equal employment opportunity movements that primarily benefit the new African-American middle class (Landry 1987).

Because of changes in the legal system, in the dominant philosophy (moving from conservative to liberal), in federal government activism, and in the mobility mechanisms (from ascription to equal opportunity and social inclusiveness), caste and race declined as the major determinants of social stratification in America. They were replaced by a more egalitarian class system (Fischer 1982; Wilson 1987a).

The beginning of the end of the period of class-oriented inclusiveness was signaled by the Supreme Court cases, *DeFunnis* v. *Odegard* (1971) and *Regents of the University of California* v. *Bakke* (1978). The two helped to establish the principle of "reverse discrimination." Reverse discrimination maintains that conscious efforts to rectify past discrimination against African-Americans by targeting recipients of society's goods and values based on their race discriminated against whites and was, therefore, illegal. Increasing acceptance of the legitimacy of reverse discrimination began to contribute to the erosion of the mobility mechanisms that equal employment opportunity and affirmative action had offered African-Americans.

It is arguable that had the national consensus to correct the problems of African-Americans held together longer, more could have been done for the poor and the underclass. Unfortunately, in the 1980s, before the new African-American middle class or the underclass could completely solve their assimilation problems, the period of class-oriented inclusion seemed to come to an end as a new conservative administration swept into the White House in 1980. The Reagan administration's policies reflected a change in the norms of the nation.

Reagan came into office with a new agenda, to shift national policy to the pursuit of economic growth at the expense of social equity. This new policy focus would entail: increasing the defense budget and lowering taxes on the one hand and dismantling affirmative action and the Great Society on the other (Blaustein 1982; Browning 1988; Smeeding 1988). While members of the Reagan administration did not state it directly, the net effect of these policy changes would be to roll back the gains of the new African-American middle class and to permanently trap the poor in the ghetto, in poverty, and out of the

American mainstream. With the simultaneous collapse of Northern blue-collar manufacturing, the conditions were ripe for creation of an underclass.[7]

DISMANTLING CLASS-ORIENTED INCLUSION AND REINSTITUTION OF CASTELIKE STRUCTURES: 1978 TO THE PRESENT

With Reagan in office, the forces of white supremacy had a friend in the White House. Reagan was committed to scaling back, or terminating, much of the federal social welfare effort (Browning 1988; Smeeding 1988). Reagan sought to shut down the social programs of the Great Society that had helped keep the poor afloat and sought to erode the political and legal framework that constituted the mobility mechanisms that allowed African-Americans to attain middle-class status.

Reagan's dismantling of the Great Society was done in the name of political decentralization—getting the federal government off the people's backs and empowering the states so decisions could be made closer to the people. Reagan maintained that the loss felt by poor and moderate-income people would be made up by the private sector, altruistically filling the void left by the federal government. Unfortunately, the private sector did not step in and the poor slipped further into poverty.

The 1980s marked the second time that the federal government had betrayed African-Americans. It was a time of increasing hardship for inner-city communities. They began to be decimated by crime, crack, and poverty; yet, the national government withdrew their efforts to help them. In *The State of Black America 1988*, John Jacobs found that during the Reagan administration the numbers of poor increased by 4 million; and real income of the lowest one-fifth of the population (adjusted for inflation) declined by $663 per family between 1979 and 1986, while the top one-fifth gained $12,218 in real income per family. During this period, programs especially benefiting African-Americans were cut drastically: federal government subsidies for housing were slashed by 79 percent, training and employment programs by 71 percent, compensatory education for the poor by 12 percent, Community Development Block Grants by more than 33 percent (Jacobs 1988, pp. 27–28).

For the majority of the 1980s, federal programs and policies that had fought to ensure the rights of minorities and women were subverted. Reagan made political appointments to the Justice Department who "... strongly supported his anti-civil rights views and aggressively strove to transform those views into the policies of the Justice Department" (Ball and Greene 1987). He appointed ideologues to the Civil Rights Commission whose purpose was not only to lower the commission's profile but to redefine the nature of civil rights itself (Thompson 1987). Reagan also appointed judges who were openly unsympathetic to civil rights and who seemed intent on dismantling the product of a national consensus—a commitment to equality for African-Americans—that had taken more than 100 years to develop.

The Reagan administration sought to block affirmative action and equal employment opportunity enforcement efforts by crippling the agencies responsible for that enforcement. The crux of any regulatory policy lies in the vigor with which it is enforced; affirmative action and equal employment opportunity have never been enforced very vigorously. Nevertheless, the Reagan administration struck at the heart of these two mechanisms by cutting the budget for 5 federal agencies with responsibility for enforcing anti-discrimination laws: the Departments of Education, Health and Human Services, Justice, and Labor, and the Equal Employment Opportunity Commission. The enforcement budgets for these agencies were cut by 25 percent between 1980 and 1983 after correcting for inflation (U.S. Commission on Civil Rights 1982b).

Over the first 7 years of his tenure in office, Reagan was able to cripple most of the institutions responsible for implementing the nation's civil rights laws. He was, however, unable to alter the laws fundamentally or the principles on which they were based. His placing of Arthur Kennedy on the Supreme Court created a conservative majority (5–4 conservative to liberal) that finally allowed an assault on those principles to proceed. Following the appointment of Kennedy, the new Court consistently ruled that socially inclusive laws made during more liberal times were unconstitutional. Beginning in January 1989, the Supreme Court made several rulings that are likely to have a devastating impact on affirmative action and equal employment opportunity.

In *City of Richmond* v. *Croson* (1989), it was declared that set-asides of state and local funds for minority contractors was unconstitutional. In *Wards Cove Packing Co.* v. *Antonio* (1989), the Court declared that statistical evidence was not sufficient to prove discrimination. In *Martin* v. *Wilkes* (1989), the Court declared court-approved consent decrees open to legal challenge by whites who were not party to the original decision. It now seems that many of the battles that the civil rights community thought it had won are open to contention again.

Eleanor Holmes Norton, a Georgetown University law professor, now predicts that the Supreme Court will cease to be the champion for African-American rights that it was in the 1960s and 1970s (Poinsett 1990). African-Americans ". . . will have to seek civil rights enforcement through Congress and state legislatures," adds Mary Barry, a U.S. Civil Rights Commission member (Poinsett 1990). Congress passed legislation that might have undone all of the recent anti-civil rights Supreme Court decisions. However, George Bush, Reagan's successor as president of the United States, vetoed that legislation.[8]

MACROECONOMIC CHANGES AND THE FUTURE OF AMERICAN BLACKS

In the past, overt racism was used to hold African-Americans in lower social strata. Centuries of systematic exclusion, their allocation to the lowest-paying and least-skilled jobs, ensured that African-Americans were ill-prepared to take advantage of the possible opportunities for upward mobility. The current conservative state and severe economic dislocation caused by the restructuring of the American economy from 1979 to 1983 increase the prospects for intensified burdens in the future.

America is in a precarious position. Global economic changes, the onset of the "information age" and the service economy, are heightening education and skills requirements. This threatens to make the underclass even more economically redundant and dysfunctional than it has ever been. America finds itself being outcompeted by the countries in Europe, the Pacific Rim, and elsewhere. Asian countries are beginning to dominate in automobiles, machine tools, heavy industries, microchips, and consumer electronics. Textiles are being taken over by Asian and Latin American competitors. American firms, in order to take advantage of lower labor costs and thus become more competitive, are setting up subsidiaries in countries where the costs of labor are lower. All of this hurts the job prospects for all African-Americans. Middle-class African-Americans are disproportionately hurt by these events because the areas of the American economy being affected the most by foreign competition are the industries that employ the majority of African-Americans.

As bad as things are for the African-American middle class, they are worse for the underclass. Global economic restructuring and America's trillion-dollar debt dominate the domestic policy agenda. Even during the best of economic times, the underclass is ill-served. Great Society programs helped to keep many from sinking further into poverty, but these programs were not the springboard for the poor. Even those programs are gone now and the current economic crisis does not augur well for the prospect of changing America's policy priorities to include new massive government programs to help the underclass.

CONCLUSIONS AND POLICY IMPLICATIONS

Racism still powerfully affects the quality of life and, indeed, the life-chances of the underclass and the incipient African-American middle class. As the number of programs designed to prevent the underclass from slipping further into poverty decline and as vehicles for upward mobility diminish in number and effectiveness, the chances of salvaging the millions mired in poverty in U.S. inner-cities and of maintaining and building on the gains of the African-American middle class will diminish.

Currently, there is reason to fear for the worse. For most of America's history, race relations have been characterized by the existence of rigid, endogamous castes. Caste-type race relations, enforced by white supremacy and the institutionalized inequality of African-Americans, have resulted in two separate Americas. There have been two efforts to lower caste barriers and encourage the upward mobility of African-Americans. Both occurred during times of a generally expanding economy and a national liberal mood: during post-Civil War Reconstruction and during the civil rights era. The resulting changes in race relations were fueled by a national commitment to do something about the plight of African-Americans.

Despite a more liberal mood in both periods, it took massive federal programs (and even federal troops) to ensure the rights of African-Americans, lower caste barriers, and hold the forces of white supremacy at bay. Many systemic changes were wrought during these periods that eased the rigidity in the system of social stratification. African-Americans benefited socially, politically, economically, and legally from these inclusionary efforts. But in both cases, gains were short-lived, as the federal government lost its commitment and left African-Americans at the mercy of white supremacists who proceeded to re-erect caste barriers.

America seems to be on the verge of returning to a period wherein race relations will be determined by race-based caste exclusion rather than class inclusion. The present era is different from the earlier era of retrenchment after Reconstruction. Then the federal government lost interest in helping African-Americans, but did not seek *de facto* reenslavement of African-Americans; state governments in the South did that. Today the federal government, long the last recourse for African-Americans, has taken an active part in rolling back African-American gains.

During the period of class-oriented inclusion (1944–1978), the change in the national mood and institutions (political, economic, social, and legal) yielded a two-pronged attack on the plight of African-Americans. Great Society programs provided a social safety net under the poorest and most vulnerable, and affirmative action and equal employment opportunity programs produced increased opportunities for upward mobility for some African-Americans, thus creating a new middle class. The new liberal mood was short-lived, however, as recession in the early 1970s and again in the 1980s produced a change toward conservatism. This change culminated in the election of a conservative president, whose policy agenda included dismantling both programs.

These political changes are coupled with growing economic problems. Conservatives and liberals alike believe that overall economic growth plays a part in solving the problems of the chronically poor. Growth without equity, however, will only maintain the status quo, further enrich those already well-to-do, and further impoverish those already poor. This is especially unfortunate because by the year 2000 the majority of America's labor force will be comprised of women and minorities, groups that historically have been discriminated against. If America is to remain competitive with the rest of the world, it cannot afford to raise barriers to the advancement of these groups.

Racial (and gender) caste barriers must be lowered and new avenues of upward mobility must be found. It is in America's best long-term interest to rekindle the fires of class-inclusion by mounting a national effort to end racism, once and for all. The alternative is too devastating to contemplate. The forces of white supremacy may see advantage in raising caste barriers to limit the amount of domestic competition for societal goods and values. The ramifications of having more than 50 percent of the American workforce crippled by the ravages of discrimination will mean, however, that winning the battle of short-term economic advantage will come at the loss of America's long-term war of global economic competition.

Antidiscrimination policies should be focused in both short and long term. In the short term, it is necessary to pass the Civil Rights Bill of 1990 that is aimed at undoing the effects of recent Supreme Court rulings: *Croson, Martin v. Wilkes*, and *Wards Cove*. More money is needed for the enforcement of affirmative action and equal employment opportunity; both the budgets and staffing of federal agencies responsible for enforcement of these policies need to be increased to pre-Reagan levels. More guidance is needed from the federal government in the area of affirmative action and equal employment opportunity to prevent further drift toward race relations characterized by castelike exclusion and discrimination; George Bush's "kinder, gentler nation" will be impossible to achieve otherwise. Mechanisms for class-oriented inclusion are essential in the coming pluralistic workforce of the year 2000.

In order to keep the urban underclass from slipping further into poverty, it will be essential to spend more, not less, money on social overhead capital. The dismantling of the Great Society, with its programs aimed at addressing the problems of the poor and providing a safety net, seems simply wrong-headed.

It is necessary to reverse the trend of withdrawing money from training and employment programs, income transfers, housing, and Community Development Block Grants. For example, more money is needed in training and employment programs as these programs could help to enhance the skills and education of African-Americans, bringing more people in line with the requirements of the information and service economy and helping to reduce unemployment. More money is needed in income transfer programs because these programs represent the core of the social safety net; they help to bridge the gap between the earning capacity of African-Americans and the cost of living. More money is needed in the area of housing in order to ensure reasonable accommodations for the underclass. More money is needed in the Community Development Block Grant programs, specifically those that are targeted toward benefitting low- and moderate-income persons and on preventing inner-city blight.

While the Great Society programs may not have solved the problem of poverty, they cushion the impact of poverty on many. Without a fully funded safety net, many will sink to depths from which they may not recover. This could recreate a stratification system wherein socioeconomic divisions parallel ethnic and racial divisions, creating "castes" defined on racial lines—a relatively well-to-do, white upper caste and a lower caste comprised of minorities. Such a situation is explosive. Rather than spending less on the welfare of the poor, America needs to spend more.

It is not too late to reaffirm the commitment to end racism; to live up to the national creed of democracy, justice, and equality; and to complete the process of class-inclusion begun during Reconstruction and carried further during the civil rights era. This will require the same level of national commitment and government involvement as was evidenced during those eras. This means that hard policy choices have to be made in the near future. Absent continued positive governmental efforts to eliminate racism and insulate those most vulnerable to its ravages, the seemingly neutral forces of global economic change will serve to reinforce the already extensive inequality, poverty, and segregation that characterize America.

NOTES

1. While the literature on the underclass makes distinctions between it and the rest of the poor, it treats poor as if it is a monolithic grouping. It fails to appreciate that there are segments among the poor that have not lost all of its social mobility. Those with hope for social mobility continue to play the game. Those without social mobility opt out of the system. It is these people who represent the hard inner core of poverty—the underclass.

2. According to the thesis presented here, "underclass" may not be the appropriate name for the subject of this chapter; "undercaste" is better. To facilitate understanding, however, this chapter adopts the convention of referring to these people by the generally accepted term.

3. See, for example, D.C. Cox (1948); W.J. Wilson (1973); and J.U. Ogbu (1990).

4. W.J. Wilson and M. Harrington would call this structural discrimination "economic discrimination." It is still the cycle of pathology thesis, wherein the discrimination in the various sectors react in cycles of mutual causation to create patterns of self-reinforcing, self-perpetuating discrimination that is difficult to counteract. See Wilson, (1987b) and Harrington (1984). See also Friedman (1975); Feagin and Feagin (1986); and U.S. Commission on Civil Rights (1981).

5. The Thirteenth Amendment to the Constitution, ratified in 1865, was meant to abolish slavery and to ensure the "practical freedom" of former slaves by placing them on equal footing with whites. Vehement opposition and punitive legislation (in the form of the infamous Black Codes) from the states made it necessary to further amend the Constitution in an effort to ensure the rights of newly freed blacks. The Fourteenth Amendment, ratified in 1868, was intended to prevent the abridgement of privileges and immunities of national citizenship, the deprivation of "life, liberty, and property, without due process of law" of any person, and the denial of "equal protection of the laws." The Fifteenth Amendment, ratified in 1869, guaranteed blacks the right to vote. See U.S. Commission on Civil Rights (1982a, pp. 3–5). The federal government enacted several laws to prevent the abridgement of rights given to blacks by the amendments to the Constitutions. Among them were: (1) The Civil Rights Act of 1866, which declared all persons born in the United States to be citizens and to have all rights commensurate with citizenship regardless of previous condition of servitude; (2) the Civil Rights Act of 1870, which was enacted to carry out the mandates of the Thirteenth, Fourteenth and Fifteenth Amendments; (3) the Klu Klux Klan Act of 1871, which provided civil and criminal penalties for the abridgement of the right to vote; and (4) the Civil Rights Act of 1875, which prohibited discrimination in the full and equal enjoyment of public accommodations and jury selection and provided civil and criminal penalties for violations. See U.S. Commission on Civil Rights (1981, pp. 5–7).

6. During the Redemption, Southern states employed a number of devices designed to limit the incidence and impact of African-American voting. One of the most widely used were grandfather clauses which prohibited anyone from voting whose grandfather did not have the right to vote. Obviously, newly freed slaves, whose grandfathers had no such right, were themselves prevented from voting. Literacy tests, which required proof of one's ability to read and comprehend complex documents such as the Declaration of Independence and the Constitution of the United States, effectively prevented many newly freed slaves from voting because few could read. During slavery, they had been forbidden to learn to read and write on pain of torture and even death. Poll taxes were fees exacted at the polls for the right to vote. Though often nominal, these fees exceeded the means of newly freed slaves, who were thus prevented from voting. Finally, the white primary prevented all but whites from voting in a primary election, where candidates for general elections were chosen. Even if African-Americans could circumvent all of the above prohibitions, they could not choose who ran for office which was tantamount to making their votes null and void.

7. One of the most fundamental changes that Reagan administration appointees sought was a move away from the notion of "group reparation" to "individual reparation" in cases of discrimination. This meant that minorities and women, as a group, were not due reparation for the centuries of discrimination they had undergone. Under this new definition, reparation could only be sought on an individual basis, where the discriminatory act and its perpetrator could clearly be identified. Such a definition ignores the history of discrimination against minorities and women in this country and it strikes at the heart of the notion of protected classes. It also makes it impossible to ever solve the larger problem of discrimination—institutional discrimination in its various forms. See Friedman (1975).

8. The Congress put forth legislation that will undo the effects of all the recent Supreme Court rulings except *Croson*. Nearly identical bills have been introduced in the House of Representatives and the Senate that will, in the manner of *Grove City*, "...amend the Civil Rights Act of 1964 to restore and strengthen civil rights laws that ban discrimination and for other purposes." See *S. 2104*, 101st Cong., 2nd Sess. (1990). The *Croson* case, however, will not be affected by this legislation.

REFERENCES

Anderson, E. 1989. Sex codes and family life among poor inner-city fathers. *Annals* 501:59–78.

Auletta, K. 1982. *The underclass*. New York: Random House.

Ball, H. and K. Greene. 1987. The Reagan justice department. *The Reagan administration's record on human rights* in 1986. New York: Lawyer's Committee for Human Rights Watch Committees.

Bernstein, B. 1988. *Saving a generation*. New York: Priority Press Publications.

Blaustein, A. I. 1982. *The american promise: equal justice and economic opportunity*. New Brunswick, NJ: Transaction Books.

Bloom, J. 1987. *Class, race, and the civil rights movement*. Bloomington, IN: Indiana University Press.

Brown v. Board of Education of Topeka, 347 U.S. 483 (1954).

Browning, R. 1988. Priorities, programs, and presidents: assessing patterns of growth in U.S. social welfare programs, 1950–1985. In *The distributional impacts of public policy*, S. Danziger and K. Portney, eds. New York: St. Martin's Press.

City of Richmond v. Croson, 488 U.S. 469 (1989).

Cox, D.C. 1948. *Caste, class and race: a study in social dynamics*. New York: Doubleday.

Defunnis v. Odegard, 416 U.S. 312 (1971).

Drimmer, M., ed. 1969. *Black history: a reappraisal*. Garden City, NY: Doubleday & Company.

Feagin, J.R. and C.B. Feagin. 1986. *American style: institutional racism and sexism*. Malabar, FL: Robert E. Krieger Publishing Company.

Fischer, S. 1982. *From margin to mainstream: the social progress of black Americans*. New York: Praeger.

Franklin, J.H. 1980. *From slavery to freedom*. New York: Alfred Knopf.

Friedman, R. 1975. Institutional racism: how to discriminate without really trying. In *Racial discrimination in the United States*, T. Pettigrew, ed. New York: Harper & Row.

Green, R.L. 1977. *The urban challenge-poverty and race*. Chicago, IL: Follett Publishing Company.

Hamilton, C.V. and D.C. Hamilton. 1988. Social policies, civil rights, and poverty. In *Fighting poverty*, S. Danziger and D.H. Weinber, eds. Cambridge, MA: Harvard University Press.

Harrington, M. 1984. *The new american poverty*. New York: Rinehart and Winston.

Heller, C.S. 1987. *Structured social inequality: a reader in comparative social stratification*. New York: Macmillan Publishing Company.

Hochschild, J. 1989. Equal opportunity and the estranged poor. *Annals* 501:143–55.

Jacobs, J.E. 1988. America, 1987: an overview. In *The state of black America 1988*, J. Dewart, ed. New York: National Urban League, Inc.

Jaynes, G.D. and R.M. Williams, Jr., eds. 1989. *A common destiny: blacks and American society*. Washington, DC: National Academy Press.

Kasarda, J.D. 1985. Urban change and minority opportunities. In *The new urban reality*, P. E. Peterson, ed. Washington, DC: The Brookings Institution.

Kemper, V. 1988. Sexism keeps women poor. In *Poverty: opposing viewpoints*, W. Dudley, ed. St. Paul, MN: Greenhaven Press.

Landry, B. 1987. *The new black middle class*. Berkeley, CA: University of California Press.

Logan, R.W. 1965. *The betrayal of the negro: from Rutherford B. Hayes to Woodrow Wilson*. New York: Collier Books.

McLanahan, S. and I. Garfinkel. 1989. Single mothers, the underclass, and social policy. *Annals* 501:92–104.

Martin v. *Wilkes*, 488 U.S. 810 (1989).

Meltzer, M. 1986. *Poverty in America*. New York: William Morrow & Co., Inc.

———. 1988. Racial discrimination affects poverty. In *Poverty: opposing viewpoints*, W. Dudley, ed. St. Paul, MN: Greenhaven Press.

Myrdal, G. 1944. *An american dilemma*. New York: Harper & Row.

Ogbu, J.U. 1978. *Minority education and caste: the American system in cross-cultural perspective*. New York: Academic Press.

———. 1990. Minority status and literacy in comparative perspective. *Daedalus* VII (Spring):101–68.

Palen, J.J. 1987. *The urban world*. New York: McGraw-Hill Book Company.

Plessy v. *Ferguson*, 163 U.S. 537 (1896).

Poinsett, A. 1990. What blacks can expect in the '90s. *Ebony* (January).

Regents of the University of California v. *Bakke*, 438 U.S. 265 (1978).

S. 2104. 101st Cong., 2nd Sess. (1990).

Simpson, G.E. and J.M. Yinger. 1965. *Race and cultural minorities*. New York: Harper & Row.

Smeeding, T.M. 1988. Reagan, the recession, and poverty: what the official estimates fail to show. In *The distributional impacts of public policies*, S.H. Danziger and K.E. Portney, eds. New York: St. Martin's Press.

Smith v. *Allwright*, 321 U.S. 649 (1944).

Stampp, K.M. 1956. *The peculiar institution, slavery in the ante-bellum south*. New York: Vintage.

Sullivan, M.L. 1989. Absent father in the inner city. *Annals* 501.

Thompson, R.J. 1987. The commission on civil rights.*The Reagan Administration's record on human rights in 1986*. New York: Lawyer's Committee for Human Rights Watch Committees.

U.S. Commission on Civil Rights. 1981. *Affirmative action in the 1980s: dismantling the process of discrimination*. Washington, DC: Government Printing Office.

_____. 1982a. *Civil rights: a national, not a special interest.* Washington, DC: Government Printing Office.

_____. 1982b. *The federal civil rights enforcement budget: fiscal year 1983.* Washington, DC: Government Printing Office.

Wacquant, L.J.D. and W.J. Wilson. 1989. The cost of racial and class exclusion in the inner city. *Annals* 501:8–25.

Wards Cove Packing Co. v. *Antonio,* 490 U.S. 642 (1989).

Williams, V.J., Jr. 1989. *From a caste to a minority: changing attitudes of American sociologists toward Afro-Americans, 1896–1945.* New York: Greenwood Press.

Wilson, W.J. 1973. Power, Racism and Privilege. New York: Macmillan.

_____. 1985. The urban underclass in advanced industrial society. In *The new urban reality,* P. Peterson, ed. Washington, DC: The Brookings Institution.

_____. 1987a. The declining significance of race: from racial oppression to economic class subordination. In *Structured social inequality,* C.S. Heller, ed. New York: Macmillan Publishing Company.

_____. 1987b. *The truly disadvantaged: the inner city, the underclass, and public policy.* Chicago, IL: The University of Chicago Press.

_____. 1989. The underclass: issues, perspectives, and public policy. *Annals* 501:182–91.

Yinger, J.M. 1965. *A minority group in american society.* New York: McGraw-Hill.

14 New Directions in Housing Policy for African-Americans

PHILLIP L. CLAY

The housing problems of African-Americans are best understood in the context of larger national trends. Given the significant progress in housing status for all Americans that occurred over the last 50 years, it is tempting to view the nation's current housing problems, especially affordability, as just a "bump in the road." Some changes can be expected such as reduction in interest rates, containment of housing speculation, more flexible regulation, or a new federal initiative to address the housing difficulties faced, including those of blacks identified in Chapter 6.

In order to assess whether America is dealing with a "bump in the road" or something more permanent and serious, it must be determined why the old mechanisms in the market and in public policy, which promoted the progress in the past, no longer seem to work. While the inequality between blacks and whites was not eliminated and problems were not solved, some progress did take place in recent decades.

As pointed out in Chapter 6, the 1980s, by contrast, were marked by a growing interracial gap, most especially in increasing homelessness, with black families constituting more than half of the total population, and declining homeownership after three decades of steady increase. Two questions seem pertinent. First, given there have been recessions before and racism has been more active and virulent at times in the past, why is there the sense that there is no momentum now and indeed some loss of progress? Second, what policy initiatives are appropriate given the problems described in Chapter 6 and environmental shifts detailed in sections below?

WHY CAN'T AMERICANS MAKE HOUSING PROGRESS
THE WAY THEY USED TO?

The first part of the answer to this question is that public policy has not directly addressed housing problems during the 1980s. Prior to 1990 and, in fact, not since the mid-1970s have Congress and a national administration taken a serious look at housing and attempted to address problems by creating or updating programs. A few demonstration and pilot efforts represent the only initiatives offered in recent years, while in previous periods—going back to 1937—a rich array of program initiatives have been available (Sternlieb and Hughes 1983).[1] Congress and various administrations pushed housing policy in specific directions to address housing policy goals.[2]

Three distinct phases of U.S. housing policy can be identified. In these phases—which go back to the 1930s—America sought to remove roadblocks to expanding the nation's housing supply of affordable housing or to assist families in affording private housing opportunities. Historically, while never directed toward and often harmful to blacks, housing production programs nevertheless provided significant benefits to blacks. These benefits were partial at best since the housing was still segregated.

In Phase I (1937-1965), a federal public housing program was undertaken that would eventually produce 1.3 million units by the 1970s. A national mortgage system and secondary market were developed.[3] Homeownership benefits were offered to young families and veterans through the Federal Housing Administration (FHA) and Veterans Administration programs which provided low downpayments, more favorable interest rates and more uniform underwriting standards. Tax incentives were created to encourage housing development by the private sector and consumption by families.

Programs created and implemented during this initial period did not help blacks very much. They either discriminated against blacks directly or were not available in areas where blacks lived or where they could move. Indeed, the nature of the system was such that discriminatory schemes were official policy. For example, FHA rules suggested effectively that loans not be given in areas with changing racial composition.

When public housing projects were built for blacks, they established or reinforced segregation. It was accepted practice that blacks would not be moved into white projects and vice versa. These publicly initiated, racist policies went unchallenged until the late 1960s when fair housing laws and court challenges were mounted (Goering 1986).

In Phase II (starting in the mid-1960s and ending with the moratorium on housing programs instituted by President Nixon in 1973), America involved the private sector with housing policy by making production its responsibility. This was accomplished by programs—such as Section 221 and Section 236—to produce what is now known as federally assisted housing.[4] The focus in housing for this period was on those whose incomes were too low to afford decent private housing but too high to qualify for public housing—the so-called moderate-income family (about 80 percent of area median income.) Over time as more and more whites moved out of the big cities to the suburbs, core city neighborhoods and public housing in such areas came to be majority black. This trend expanded segregation.

This was also an era characterized by a very modest effort at rebuilding urban communities with new housing and non-housing projects on land cleared for renewal. While some blacks did benefit from redevelopment and new housing, many more were victims of a process in which whole neighborhoods were demolished and their residents forced to look for a new place to live in an increasingly segregated market.

Section 235 of the 1968 Amendments to the Housing Act of 1949 program was designed to help poor families buy homes. To the extent that blacks benefitted from this low-income homeownership program, this, too, was in the context of a segregated market and older housing.

The major point about this period—when almost 700,000 federally assisted units were built—is that many blacks did acquire better housing, albeit mainly segregated housing. Housing progress, coupled with other efforts such as the anti-poverty programs, fostered hope that kept community institutions (e.g., settlement houses, fraternal groups, service agencies and churches) active. Some of the neighborhoods in which these efforts of community development occurred have since become underclass enclaves; the housing is in physical or financial distress, and the institutions have lost their capacity to be effective at community enrichment. Many agencies have fallen by the wayside as the programs that underwrote their activities have dried up. Other agencies and groups have taken on narrow service roles rather than the broader community-building functions.

In Phase III (1974 to 1980), the federal government, under Section 8 funding, subsidized the development or rehabilitation of nearly one million units of housing for poor families. The government also focused attention on neighborhood restoration and conservation by spending more than half the subsidy resources on rehabilitation rather than new construction. Housing certificates and vouchers, which are forms of direct aid to tenants, were elements of this period. Housing development in this period was done in connection with an assessment of area housing needs.

Also during the period, the nation increased local discretion in program development in housing and community development programs. The administration and Congress started the deregulation of financial institutions in the hope (or with the expectation) that high return in a free market would make housing more competitive for capital. New legal authority to challenge lending discrimination against individuals and communities was granted to communities.[5]

With all of the program initiatives in this period and in the years before, the share of eligible poor households receiving housing assistance rose from 12 percent in 1970 to 28 percent by 1987. Blacks shared in this progress, though as indicated in Chapter 6, the benefits were mixed because both the design and implementation of programs did not produce desegregated housing opportunities and was often not intended to be fair.

The inauguration of Ronald Reagan in 1981 marked the end of Phase III. Every administration since President Hoover and before President Reagan tried to assist in meeting the nation's housing goals or at least not undo progress already made. Reagan opposed a government role in housing generally and failed to propose any new production or related program. He attempted to cease funding housing programs and succeeded eventually in cutting funds by 80 percent (Struyk, et al. 1982).

Past Progress and Future Prospects

If America had policies in the past that were somewhat effective, except that racism limited benefits to blacks, the nation might simply restore and reform the past initiatives and thereby make further progress, this time benefitting blacks. Unfortunately, times have changed and mere reform will not be sufficient. For all the reasons discussed in Chapter 6 and below, not only has the policy environment changed (i.e., persistently less federal interest, limited state and local capacity, polarization of incomes, rising housing costs against declining real income, etc.), but also attitudes and expectations of policy.

In addition, there used to be a floor that prevented large numbers of people from falling to the destitute state of homelessness. The way the system seems to have worked was that as housing quality improves, the floor was raised so that it was possible for nearly all families to improve their housing over time. The section below looks at options available to families in the past, how these options worked, and where America stands with each of them today. These include: (1) savings and family assistance; (2) filtering down of good quality older units of declining value; (3) subsidized housing; and (4) if none of these work, and as a temporary solution, families could change their consumption goals (i.e., accept smaller units, etc.) and housing preferences (i.e., cheaper housing or units in a poorer neighborhood, etc.). Blacks have always been at a relative disadvantage in all these dimensions.[6] Yet these options, at different times and in different combinations over the last half century, have helped most families, including many black families, obtain better if not always affordable housing.

These four options are no longer available in sufficient degree to improve housing for poor people whose race constrains choice. First, saving at the scale required to purchase a first home is not feasible for most households of any race.

In 1986, only 16 percent of all young (25–34 years old) renters could qualify to purchase at even a modest 10 percent downpayment threshold. Only 4 percent of blacks in that cohort could pay this amount (Joint Center for Housing Studies [JCHS] 1990). Not only has the cost of housing risen faster than income in recent years, but families have had less real income from which to save. Moreover, the ability to finance home purchases with low downpayments runs up against the more conservative realities of housing finance policy which now require higher downpayments and have more stringent underwriting standards.

In recent years, the metaphor for urban families has not been "building a nest egg to get the dream house," but "getting on the (housing) train before it leaves the station." This has been especially true in those areas where prices have escalated quickly. Those who could play this speculative game did and those who could not have been left behind. Overconsumption and speculative purchases tend to inflate prices, dramatically in some areas, and make it difficult for those who might have succeeded in getting a downpayment by reducing consumption, working two jobs, or leveraging family help. For all but upper middle-income and upper-income households, this led to declining ownership rates—from 60 percent in 1973 down to 54 percent in 1990 for 30–34 year olds. This a 10 percent decline in one decade at a rate that had climbed steadily for 40 years.

Second, families used to be able to improve their housing situation by occupying units that were sold by higher-income people moving into newly constructed housing. The older housing fell more in price than in quality, providing lower-income households an opportunity for affordable upgrading. Eventually, as successive waves of income groups moved into dwellings vacated by the next higher-income group even the least well-off families would improve their housing within limits of their income. Low-income blacks, even under the worst situations, obtained units that were either surplus to whites or units that filtered down from upper-income blacks. While this improved the quality of housing for blacks, the fact that the housing included units left by whites who moved to the suburbs meant that there was often little or no net permanent desegregative benefit. In fact, some communities became more segregated as whites moved from mixed areas.

The situation is quite different now. The demand for housing which used to be met, in net terms, almost entirely by new construction increasingly has been met (almost 20 percent) in the 1970s and 1980s by existing housing (Apgar 1982). In other words, low-income families have had to compete with the non-poor for older units that used to be both affordable and available (Berry 1985). Upgrading now comes at a steep real cost. This cost rise (16 percent between 1980 and 1987 against a decline in real income for low- and moderate-income groups since 1973) results in shortages of affordable units (JCHS 1990).

Third, families used to have access to a variety of new public and subsidized housing units. The programs described in the above section were critical as temporary way stations for upwardly mobile families and to others as permanent housing. The units—greater than 150,000 additions a year in the 1970s—not only were a direct response to need, but indirectly helped to relieve pressure on the non-subsidized stock, which in some urban neighborhoods was being disinvested or abandoned, and gentrified in others. As Table 14.1 shows, declining resources define a sharply declining contribution to meeting the nation's housing needs in the 1980s. New construction or substantial rehabilitation of subsidized housing is no longer available to a significant degree and the poor have had to rely on the existing supply with housing certificates and vouchers as the principal subsidy.

The loss of this source of housing has come at a time when the loss in the numbers of affordable rental units has escalated sharply. While there has been an increase in rental units, it should come as no surprise that all the net growth has been in expensive units—$400 or more per month. Rental units that a poor family can afford (in current dollars) declined from just over 9 million units in

TABLE 14.1

New Budget Authority for Assisted
Housing, FY 1977–1988
(in billions of dollars)

Fiscal Year	New Budget Authority
1977	28.0
1978	31.5
1979	24.4
1980	26.7
1981	19.8
1982	13.3
1983	8.7
1984	9.9
1985	10.8
1986	10.0
1987	7.5
1988	7.0

Source: Housing and Urban Development,
Annual Budgets, 1977–88 (Washington, DC:
Department of Housing and Urban
Development).

1980 to 7.1 million in 1987. During the same period there was an increase in the number of families needing such housing (JCHS 1990).

Finally, households in the past have been willing to change their preferences by lowering their expectations for housing, at least temporarily. While this technically is not a means of meeting housing needs, it is a coping strategy until other more permanent solutions are found. This forbearance took a variety of forms. Some households waited in place, others doubled with family or friends, some settled for smaller or poorer quality units, and some households did not form (i.e., married couples remained in a spouse's family home).

Changing preferences or forbearance are temporary and are only acceptable options when some real progress is likely. It is now more an option for single individuals than for families. A family pays a potentially high price when it chooses bad housing in order to save. The anxiety about housing as well as the actual problems (i.e., poor quality public service, exposure to violence and poor schools, etc.) have escalated as it became clear that no relief was in sight. Because there are fewer resources to meet housing problems and fewer choices to offer victims of these trends, the reality of persistent difficulty has been altogether more apparent and nowhere better illustrated than the emergence of family homelessness in the 1980s for the first time since the Depression. More than half of these newly destitute families were black (Committee on Ways and Means 1990).

In short, the old tools for upward mobility in housing do not work effectively today. Few low-income families are in a position to engage in self-help and little is available at the federal level to assist them or others.

Some cities and states have been creative in finding new ways to use limited resources to fill partially the void left by the federal government. Only a small number of families in about a dozen states have benefitted, however, because state programs benefit the poor mainly by supplementing federal programs. With the federal void firmly in place, "affordable housing" in many state programs is really housing for young middle-class families, those earning $35,000 to $40,000 per year or more. State programs are also more often targeted to suburban first-time buyers for whom the downpayment, transaction costs (i.e., financing fees, legal expenses, and moving costs), or the payment burden in the early years are relieved (Terner and Cook 1990).

NEW DIRECTIONS FOR NATIONAL HOUSING POLICY

It is not appropriate and space does not permit detail here about specific housing programs to address the broad policy issues. Part of the anguish in Washington and elsewhere in the country stems from an awareness of problems and concerns on the part of analysts and advocates but no existing way to address them. In an earlier section, three historic phases of American housing policy were outlined. America now needs a set of policies to usher in Phase IV, a phase that gets past the old problems as well as new realities. Where none of the other three phases was aggressive in articulating the needs of blacks, a new policy that is responsive to the dimensions of the problems outlined here, is implemented with justice in mind, and takes full account of the issues discussed in this chapter and in Chapter 6, will aid the mal-housed within the black community. Without a race-sensitive national housing policy, the progress blacks have made will continue to be eroded, as it was in the 1980s.

The initiatives that are undertaken should be pursued in partnership among government (federal, state, and local), the private sector, and the nonprofit sector. America has learned two things from the history of housing policy and from recent developments. First, a single, nation-wide grant program will not work. While the federal government is the best source of dollars, local design of program elements and strategies is needed. Housing problems are too diverse and too sensitive to the local market. America has also learned a great deal about the non-cash resources of state and local government that are so critical (Terner and Cook 1990).

The major elements of a housing policy for the 1990s—incorporating mainly federal elements but also companion initiatives of state and local government—might include the following:

- A housing production program for public and assisted housing that offers the prospect of incremental increases in the stock of permanent and affordable housing units. A production program of at least 100,000 units per year would be targeted to tight markets and to areas where new supply is needed. The housing produced here should be in small projects and scattered in a way that promotes racial and class integration.

- Continuing use of vouchers for the poor in markets where there are available decent units and to help close the gap of affordability in privately developed new housing. A voucher for homeless and other populations with special needs should be available even where a production program exists.

- Increased fair housing enforcement to prevent discrimination in the rental, sale, financing, siting and insuring of housing. In addition, state and local fair housing initiatives should address regulatory barriers that prevent affordable housing production. The barriers include, for example, exclusionary zoning, that effectively requires a limited number of expensive units rather than allows a larger number of more affordable units.

- An effective strategy to preserve the supply of public and subsidized housing (currently totals about 4 million units) which will be at increasing risk of loss over the next decade as 20-year-old contract and subsidy provisions to help the poor expire. Preservation is far cheaper than building new housing to replace housing that might be lost.
- Incentives and programs to encourage private production and maintenance of affordable housing. The Tax Reform Act of 1986 includes strong disincentives against private rental housing where three-quarters of poor renters live. Investors have even fewer incentives to develop or maintain housing in the black community.
- Programs to develop greater capacity for nonprofit and community-based housing initiatives that can, in addition to housing development, tap community spirit, promote self-help, and facilitate public-private partnerships.
- Programs to support homeownership for the poor, including those who have limited income. The potential for opening up many communities is only possible if there is the means for blacks to overcome the more severe barriers to home purchase that exist today compared to the past when prices (relative to income) were lower and when interest rates were 25 percent less.

The political power that blacks have mustered can be an important force in shaping local housing and development policy. This can result in policies that are more fair and could broaden the black community's stake in how cities take advantage of urban revitalization and the restructuring of downtowns. While mayors may have little to do directly with unemployment rates or welfare levels, they have several powerful levers on the development process for housing as well as for other types of development.

America should also be mindful of the potential benefits of resident involvement in community housing initiatives. Self-help is where residents play a central role in defining housing and community development initiatives. Empowering individuals and community groups to take more responsibility for their own lives and thereby increase their personal confidence and control greatly improves the chance that the housing and community development policy will work and make the community more willing to accept diversity. There are some communities where the opposite is true, that is, where community initiative *is* resistant to diversity. In such cases, public education on the benefits of diversity and enforcement become central.

Community-based initiatives and self-help programs are important because they ensure that the local community both initiates and accepts programs that will reinvest in their neighborhoods (Clay 1990). Externally imposed programs either lack the involvement or the understanding of the population they intend to serve, or they fail to take into account the subtle dynamics of targeted neighborhoods. Chances for success increase dramatically when programs are either undertaken by, or in partnership with the community.

If self-help is to work and community-based organizations are to be effective, much more attention needs to be paid to capacity-building of local institutions, such as community development corporations and social agencies that operate in the black community. While community-based organizations have demonstrated potential for making significant contributions, there is a very uneven record. Some areas are rich in the capacity represented by these organizations; others are not (National Congress for Community Economic Development [NCCED] 1988).[7]

If the approach is taken where policies toward housing in communities are addressed by federal, state, and local government and community-based organizations, America will have a chance not only to meet the housing needs of blacks but build better communities as well.

The decade of the 1990s offers the opportunity to make the most substantial progress in this century. Some of the racial barriers have been lowered. There is a growing number of blacks who can take advantage of a wider range of opportunities. There are more effective tools to fight discrimination.

The decade also has potential for replicating the decade of the 1980s, during which many black households continued to experience housing problems and some new problems emerged. The current deliberations in Congress and the willingness of the current administration to participate positively are encouraging signs that such replication may be avoided.

NOTES

1. Over the years, there have been a host of housing bills, programs and initiatives, including major bills in 1949, 1954, 1958, 1965, 1968, and 1974 (Sternlieb and Hughes 1983). While 1988 and 1989 were marked by a flurry of activity, the first result in 1988 was that some programs were established, a low-income homeownership program, for example, and then funded only at minimum or demonstration levels. Included here is the implementation of the McKinney Bill for the homeless and the Nehemiah program on low-income homeownership. As this is written both the House and the Senate have passed housing bills. There were housing related tax measures in 1981 and 1986.

2. Actually the Tax Reform Act of 1986 should be considered as an anti-housing initiative since it removed many of the financial incentives for private investors to produce rental housing and reduced moderately the advantages of homeownership.

3. Prior to this period buyers had to make a substantial payment toward the price of the house; mortgages were for a short time and subject to the call of the lender. The new system made long-term and low-downpayment mortgages possible and created

mechanisms (secondary market institutions) for lenders to sell loans in order to replenish their capital.

4. Sections 221 and later Section 236 were sections of the Housing Acts of 1961 and 1968 through which the federal government subsidized the development of private rental housing. The private apartments were for moderate-income families (about 80–110 percent of the local median income).

5. The Community Reinvestment Act of 1975 and the Home Mortgage Disclosure Act of 1976 gave standing to communities to call to account local lenders for their lending and community investment activity (or lack of activity). In some communities, lenders then set about to do more urban lending than they might have. Recent studies have indicated that this effort not been entirely successful as widespread discrimination in underwriting continues (Fishbein 1989).

6. Because of low income, blacks have few savings compared to whites, and in recent years with declining real income, saving in general is harder to do. Discrimination limits the options for upgrading to the best units left by those with higher income, and as noted in previous sections, the siting of subsidized housing often reinforced segregation.

7. The organization has produced an estimated 125,000 units over the past decade (NCCED 1988).

REFERENCES

Apgar, W. 1982. The changing utilization of the housing inventory: past trends and future prospect. Cambridge, MA: Joint Center for Urban Studies of Harvard and MIT.

Berry, B. 1985. Island of renewal in seas of change. In *The new reality*, P. Peterson, ed., 33–68. Washington, DC: Brookings Institution.

Clay, P. 1990. *Mainstreaming the community builders: the challenge of expanding the capacity of nonprofit housing development organizations*. Cambridge, MA: MIT.

Committee on Ways and Means, U.S. House of Representatives. 1990. *The 1990 green book: background material and data on programs within the jurisdiction of the committee on ways and means*, Appendix G. Washington, DC: U.S. Congress.

Department of Housing and Urban Development. *Annual budgets* (various volumes 1977-88). Washington, DC: Department of Housing and Urban Development.

Fishbein, A. 1989. Testimony before the subcommittee on consumers and regulatory affairs of the committee on banking, housing and urban affairs of the United States Senate, October 24.

Goering, J. 1986. *Housing desegregation and federal policy*. Chapel Hill, NC: University of North Carolina Press.

Joint Center for Housing Studies [JCHS]. 1990. *The state of the nation's housing 1990*. Cambridge, MA: Harvard University.

National Congress for Community Economic Development. 1988. *Against all odds*. Washington, DC: NCCED.

Sternlieb, G. and J. Hughes. 1983. Review of past policies and assumptions: what worked and what didn't. A paper prepared for the Lavenburg Housing Conference, Harrison, New York.

Struyk, R., et al. 1982. Housing and community development. In *The Reagan experiment*, J. Palmer and I. Sawhil, eds., 393–418. Washington, DC: The Urban Institute.

Terner, I.D. and T. Cook. 1990. New directions for federal housing policy: the role of the states. In *Building foundations*, D. DiPasquale and L. Keyes, eds., 113-36. Philadelphia: University of Pennsylvania.

15 The Case for Racial Integration

GEORGE C. GALSTER

What should be the public policy response to separate or isolated racial communities in U.S. metropolitan areas? As seen earlier in Part II of this book, the African-American community is a place characterized by polarization and powerlessness. Twenty years ago the Kerner Commission recognized this but waffled on the central questions related to possible policy responses (Ch. 2). Should America respond by maintaining this community as a spatial entity and attempting to improve the economic, housing, health, educational conditions there—"gilding the ghetto," as it has been called? Or, should America respond by attempting to desegregate metropolitan areas, thereby minimizing the spatial aspect of race? Should America try to eliminate only that portion of segregation attributed to illegal, discriminatory practices in housing markets or attain an even more desegregated outcome? If so, which personal freedoms and preferences may justifiably be infringed upon in the name of the larger social goal of integration?

Many urban policy analysts (including those in the Bush administration) believe that widespread racial integration is neither necessary, feasible, nor even particularly desirable. Developing the African-American community economically, socially, and politically as it now stands as a spatial entity is their focus. Policy responses such as enterprise zones and resident-owned public housing projects are representative. Indeed, many of the housing and educational reforms offered in this book implicitly take place as given (Chs. 14 and 17).

The alternative approach is proposed in this chapter, based on the premise that the place component of the place-power-polarization triad must be significantly weakened if Americans as a society are seriously to affect racial disparities. As such, the proposals forwarded here represent examples of the "breaking the linkages" policy strategy presented in Chapter 11. The first section proposes and describes an operational policy goal: the attainment of a stable, integrative process. The second reviews the reasons why meeting this goal is crucial for moving toward racial equality, as well as reducing enormous social costs borne by all Americans. The third argues that achieving a stable, integrative process is also necessary for providing true freedom of housing choices for all households. The final sections turn from the desirability of the integrative goal to a discussion of the means of attaining it. The fourth section explores the dynamics of racial segregation processes and shows why a stable, integrative process is unlikely to occur without aggressive, coordinated policies. The fifth section presents specific programmatic means of achieving this process and reviews the results of recent attempts to do so. It argues that these policies need not result in limiting African-Americans' housing choices, but potentially could expand choices for all households.

A POLICY GOAL: STABLE, INTEGRATIVE PROCESS

As a goal of urban policy, all levels of government should actively strive to desegregate racially isolated communities and encourage stable, racially diverse ones. The goal should be to achieve a *stable integrative process* in all metropolitan areas. A stable integrative process should be thought of as a particular kind of market *dynamic*, rather than a particular kind of residential *outcome*. It is a dynamic in which homeseekers representing two or more races actively seek to occupy the same vacant dwellings in a substantial proportion of a metropolitan area's neighborhoods over an extended period.[1]

To illustrate, a stable integrative process would involve a continuous stream of black and white homeseekers inspecting, bidding for, and presumably occupying single-family homes and apartments in neighborhoods formerly occupied only by whites. It would also involve such a flow of racially diverse housing demanders in now racially-mixed and mostly black-occupied neighborhoods. Such a stable integrative process in a housing market could well be consistent with a variety of racial occupancy outcomes in neighborhoods and changes in those outcomes over time. Thus, it would be mistaken to view a stable integrative process in terms of precise percentages of various racial groups living in neighborhoods that constituted an outcome of "integration." All that can be said about the outcomes of a stable integrative process is that they would tend to desegregate racially homogeneous neighborhoods and promote racially diverse neighborhoods.

Perhaps a stable integrative process can be more clearly understood by contrasting it to its opposite: a process in which only homeseekers of one race actively seek to occupy vacant dwellings in any given neighborhood within a metropolitan area. Such a segregative process leads to one of two alternatives. If the race of the in-movers perpetually matches that of the out-movers, stable racial segregation results. If the race of the in-movers differs over an extended period from that of the out-movers, temporary racial integration results, followed inevitably by transition and resegregation of the area as an exclusively black-occupied one. A stable integrative process would avoid producing these two outcomes. It provides an alternative to a society characterized either by perpetually segregated neighborhoods or by neighborhoods that are only temporarily integrated while they resegregated.

It is also important to distinguish a stable integrative process from a related, but distinct term frequently used when fair housing issues are discussed: "freedom of choice." Freedom of choice in housing refers to a situation where any household is free to occupy any residence they desire and can afford, regardless of their race, ethnicity, religion, sex, handicap, or family status. Freedom of choice does not necessarily imply a stable integrative process because whites may be freely moving out of racially mixed areas *en masse* and into white-occupied ones, and blacks may be freely looking for housing only in ghetto areas. Thus, these two terms are not synonymous, although as demonstrated below they can be complementary goals for a national urban policy.

A STABLE, INTEGRATIVE PROCESS IS CRUCIAL FOR REDUCING INTERRACIAL DISPARITIES

As detailed in other chapters of this book, place is a crucial determinant of racial disparity. The main arguments are briefly reviewed here. A stable integrative process is a desirable alternative to the *status quo* for one simple reason: equal opportunity is a sham in a segregated society. Segregation means restricting blacks from opportunities for social and economic advancement and full participation in the American Dream (Yinger, et al. 1979; Leadership Council 1987; Galster 1987a; Galster and Keeney 1988).[2] Segregation forms the key link in a vicious circle of self-perpetuating racial prejudice and inequality. Although this set of interrelationships has particularly devastating consequences for the black poor (as explained in Ch. 11), its effects extend to all classes and all races. This vicious circle is portrayed diagrammatically in Figure 15.1.

Segregation limits blacks access to appropriate public education, health, and social service resources. (Chs. 4 and 11 amplify these points.) Segregation also limits their information about, and access to, jobs that hold the promise of stability, good training and benefits, and advancement. By limiting access to work and the means by which people become productive workers, segregation helps create and perpetuate economic and social inequalities between racial groups. (See arrow A in Figure 15.1). In other words, segregation is the pri-

FIGURE 15.1

The Vicious Circle of Prejudice and Inequality

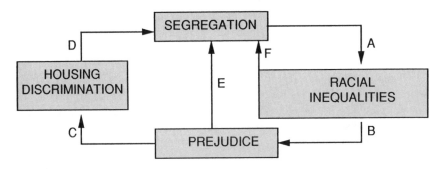

mary cause of the litany of depressing black-white disparities presented in Chapters 1–7 in terms of poverty and unemployment, housing costs and quality, school dropouts, mortality and morbidity, welfare dependency, out-of-wedlock births, crime, and drug and alcohol abuse.

Together, these inequalities produce two effects. First, they make it less likely that blacks can afford to live in the sorts of neighborhoods occupied by many whites. (See arrow F in Figure 15.1). If blacks accumulate less wealth for downpayments and command less monthly income to defray rent or mortgage costs, where they buy or rent property will be more limited than the areas attainable by whites.[3] Thus, inter-racial economic disparities feed back and abet segregation (Galster 1987a; Galster and Keeney 1988).

Second, these economic and social inequalities reinforce the stereotypes held by some whites. Whites look at the urban black and too often see someone unemployed, poor, ill, minimally educated, single-parenting, engaging in crime, and/or doing drugs. These images, of course, legitimize these prejudices against the "undesirable characteristics" supposedly possessed by all blacks. (See arrow B.)

Such reinforced prejudices make it more likely that white households will want to perpetuate segregation. "Who would want to live with them?" they might ask. Some whites may be unwilling to remain in neighborhoods once blacks begin to move in. When seeking different accommodations they may be reluctant to search in areas where blacks live. These actions by whites directly reinforce segregation. (See arrow E.)

But there are other actions by whites that also reinforce segregation. Their aforementioned prejudices can motivate them and their agents to discriminate in order to keep blacks out of exclusively white-occupied areas. (See arrow C.) White real estate brokers steer black homeseekers away from vacancies in such areas and toward those already having substantial numbers of blacks (Galster

1990b, c). White landlords of apartments in all-white areas refuse to rent to blacks, excluding them through the use of ruses such as saying, "Oh, the apartment already is rented" (Galster 1990a). Blacks who do succeed in moving into erstwhile white-occupied areas can be so harassed by their prejudiced white neighbors that they are soon forced to leave. Such discrimination provides another mechanism through which prejudice indirectly intensifies segregation. (See arrow D.)

Black households bear crushing costs from the perpetuation of this vicious circle. Think what it means for people's life-chances for personal fulfillment and economic security if they are consigned to inferior schools and health care facilities, faced with frequent unemployment or underemployment, frustrated in their attempts to buy homes or accumulate wealth in other legitimate ways, and relegated to an environment where violence, crime, drugs and alcohol abuse are prevalent. It is impossible, of course, to quantify fully this burden of segregation (Leadership Council 1987). If America could reduce residential segregation by 25 percent the median income of black families would rise 12 percent, presumably through a weakening of the vicious circle (Galster and Keeney 1988).

Majority race households pay for this vicious circle as well. They pay through higher transportation costs caused by the spatial distortion of where they work and where they believe they must reside due to racial considerations. They pay higher housing prices through the bidding up of exclusively white-occupied areas by whites who, based on their prejudices and stereotypes and integrated living, avoid racially mixed neighborhoods (Galster 1982). They pay through higher taxes needed to battle crime and to support a needlessly dependent minority population. They pay through fear and inter-group animosity.

Not only do households of all races pay for the maintenance of a segregated society, there are additional costs incurred by those living in neighborhoods that rapidly change from predominantly white- to predominantly black-occupied. Many households prefer to live in a racially diverse neighborhood, and this desire is thwarted by processes of resegregation (which is described more fully below). A national poll showed that 60 percent of blacks and 17 percent of whites preferred a neighborhood that was about half black and half white; another 5 percent of blacks and 42 percent of whites preferred one that was mostly (not exclusively) white (U.S. Department of Housing and Urban Development [HUD] 1978). As households of both races are forced to leave an area whose racial composition is rapidly changing in an undesirable manner, substantial out-of-pocket and psychological costs are incurred. Finally, the racial transition process hastens the physical decay of the area. Many white residential and commercial property owners view racial change as equivalent to reducing the socioeconomic status and safety of the area (Taub, Taylor and Dunham 1984). They become pessimistic about the future marketability of the area and cut back on property maintenance and improvements (Galster 1987c, Chs. 2, 10).

Segregation costs all urbanites—black and white alike. Encouraging a stable integrative process would remove substantial burdens from all members of society by breaking the vicious circle that now perpetuates inter-group inequalities and prejudices.

A STABLE, INTEGRATIVE PROCESS IS NECESSARY TO ACHIEVE FREEDOM OF CHOICE IN HOUSING

A controversy has begun to swirl around fair housing policy that centers on the prospective pursuit of two goals. One goal is the desegregation option articulated above in terms of a stable integrative process; the other goal is freedom of choice. The controversy is twofold. Is a stable integrative process an important goal? Is the pursuit of a stable integrative process consistent with the pursuit of freedom of choice?

It is clear that the framers of Title VIII of the Civil Rights Act of 1968, the first federal fair housing law, would have answered both these questions with a "yes." They saw the achievement of freedom of choice as promoting a stable, integrative process (Lake 1986; North 1986, pp. 8–9; Smolla 1986). In the succeeding 11 years after 1968, the actions of both the Department of Justice [DOJ] and the Department of Housing and Urban Development [HUD] were reasonably consistent in their support of the twin goals of freedom of choice and a stable, integrative process (Citizens' Commission 1983, pp. 28, 49; Orfield 1986; Newman 1986).

Federal policy over the past decade suggests that both implicit answers have changed. The value of a stable integrative process has been downplayed, consistent with the Reagan-Bush administrations' laissez-faire approach to social policy. HUD requirements for communities to consider in their Community Development Block Grant applications the housing needs of minority residents "expected to reside" in the area have been relaxed. Low-income housing policy has switched from scattered-site construction to vouchers which have proven to stimulate little geographic expansion of housing choice (Sutker 1986; Ch. 6 in this volume). Requirements for collecting data on the racial characteristics of HUD-assisted dwellings have been eliminated. Although a HUD effort to desegregate public housing projects began in 1985, this seems less the result of commitment to desegregation *per se* than to the avoidance of further disruptive lawsuits.[4]

Not only has the value of a stable integrative process been questioned, but its pursuit has been seen in some circles as antithetical to the pursuit of freedom of choice.[5] Events of the past 20 years provide the context for this view. Individual suburban communities that have vigorously enforced fair housing laws have frequently witnessed an upsurge in demands by minority homeseekers. In order to stabilize this initial burst of demand, some have enacted a wide variety of what unfortunately have been called "integration maintenance" policies (North 1986; Polikoff 1986a, b). All of these policies attempt to provide information, change attitudes, and encourage behaviors of both white and black homeseekers so as to attain a stable integrative process. A subset has gone beyond these steps and has rigidly limited occupancy through racial quotas, thereby allegedly restricting freedom of choice. The DOJ received such a finding from the federal courts in recent years regarding the racial quota schemes for the apartment complexes at Starrett City in Brooklyn[6] and Atrium Village in Chicago.[7]

This counterposing of freedom of choice and a stable integrative process is unnecessary and obfuscating. The rhetoric has drowned out the reality that freedom of choice and a stable integrative process can be *complementary* in both principle and practice. In *principle*, true freedom of choice is only possible in the presence of a stable integrative process; in *practice*, an *appropriate* set of policies designed to promote a stable, integrative process is *necessary* for the achievement of freedom of choice. The current controversy is thus turned on its head: instead of worrying about doing away with pro-integration efforts so America can get on with the business of freedom of choice, it is argued that the only way to effectively get on with the business of freedom of choice is to worry about achieving a stable integrative process.

In practice, progress in achieving a stable integrative process aids in the battle against choice-restricting housing market discrimination by reducing the motivation for such discrimination. The crux of the argument is this: assuming that "equal-status" inter-racial residential contact is a fundamental means by which prejudices are eroded, and prejudices of white real estate agents and/or their clientele are the root motivators for discriminatory acts in the housing market, attaining a stable integrative process becomes a means for promoting freedom of choice.

Social scientists have documented how all peoples' racial stereotypes wither when they have the opportunity to live with neighbors of other races who have roughly equal socioeconomic status . . . precisely the sort of outcome that should be produced by a stable integrative process (Yinger 1986a; Helper 1986). Recent studies also have reached a consensus that most discriminatory behavior in the housing market is founded on either the personal prejudices of agents or their belief that it is in their financial interest to cater to the presumed prejudices of their white customers (Yinger 1986b; Galster 1987b, 1990c; Newburger 1989). Thus, insofar as a stable integrative process can be achieved and such prejudices thereby reduced, the pursuit of freedom of choice can be enhanced. Empirical support for this contention has been provided by a recent study showing that, after controlling for other factors, metropolitan areas with less segregation also have lower rates of housing discrimination (Galster and Keeney 1988). Unlike the current strategy embodied in the Fair Housing Amendments Act of 1988, which tries to eliminate discrimination through *deterrence*, the stable integrative process approach tries to eliminate it by removing its root *cause*: prejudice spawned by lack of inter-racial exposure.

But even if all housing market discrimination was eliminated, in principle a stable integrative process would still be a necessary condition for freedom of choice. Consider what freedom of choice in housing really means. Does housing mean merely a dwelling, or is it a more comprehensive package of attributes?

It is clear that freedom of choice as a goal of Title VIII means the expansion of potential housing choices for minority homeseekers *outside* traditional ghetto neighborhoods. Proponents of the legislation believed that breaking down discriminatory barriers would be a sufficient condition for substantial desegregation (Polikoff 1986b). Implicit in this view is the expansion of choices of not only *dwelling* type and quality, but also of *neighborhood* characteristics like schools, public services, physical environment, proximity to employment, and, presumably *racial composition*.

This broader view of "housing" as a *package* consisting of *both* dwelling and neighborhood attributes is not only commonsensical but has consistently been the foundation of federal policy since the Housing Act of 1949 articulated the goal of "a decent home and a *suitable living environment* (emphasis added) for all Americans." Indeed, social science research has shown that the neighborhood affects households' residential choices and their residential satisfaction as much as the dwelling structure.[8]

It follows from this definition of housing as a package that freedom of choice means the expansion of options for black (as well as white) households to live in stable, racially diverse neighborhoods, an option clearly desired by many.[9] But for freedom of choice to be more than a sham, this presumes that there actually are such neighborhoods from which to choose. Unfortunately, given longstanding prejudices and practices, which are discussed more below, a stable, integrative process rarely occurs in metropolitan housing markets without active public policy intervention. This means that the goal of freedom of choice cannot be achieved *in principle* without simultaneously achieving the goal of a stable, integrative process.

A STABLE, INTEGRATIVE PROCESS IS UNLIKELY WITHOUT AGGRESSIVE, COORDINATED PUBLIC POLICIES

A stable integrative process is rare today in metropolitan America, as witnessed by the preponderance of racially isolated resegregating neighborhoods. Conventional indexes of residential segregation in 1980 show that, on average,

79 percent of black households would need to move from their current location in order to achieve complete racial mixing of larger U.S. metropolitan areas (where most blacks live). By comparison, the comparable percentages are only 48 and 43 for Hispanics and Asians, respectively (Farley 1986; McKinney and Schnare 1986). Recent studies have found that this segregation of blacks within large metropolitan areas has hardly changed since 1970 (Massey and Denton 1987). In the largest U.S. cities only about one-fifth of the census tracts may be classified as racially mixed, and of these only one-fourth remained stable during the 1970–80 period (Lee 1985).

Why is a stable integrative process seemingly so hard to achieve? First, illegal acts of housing discrimination continue to be perpetrated at an alarming rate. Recent audits which have utilized interracial pairs of "testers"[10] have found, on average, that minority homeseekers face at least a one-in-three chance of being discriminated against each time they confront a housing agent (Galster 1990a,b). Such acts inhibit the stable integrative process by precluding the active participation of all races in the competition for particular dwellings and/ or neighborhoods, as explained above.

Second, and perhaps more fundamentally, a stable integrative process would be unlikely in the foreseeable future *even if all discriminatory acts were to cease*, due to the legacy of discrimination. The cumulative effect of a host of private and public acts of discrimination perpetrated over generations has been to create negative stereotypes about desegregation in the minds of many households.

For many whites the stereotype is that any desegregation of a formerly all-white neighborhood *inevitably* leads to racial transition, resegregation, declining property values, and physical deterioration. This stereotypical dynamic has often been demonstrated because of the concerted effects of discrimination. Discrimination by housing agents and racial restrictive covenants conspired to overcrowd minority households into the oldest, most decrepit portions of the central cities. Such areas are always prone to decay and abandonment in response to new housing construction on the suburban fringe and commercial expansion of the central business district. Deterioration and property value depreciation were further abetted by the "redlining" practices of lenders, which greatly restricted flows of mortgage and home improvement loans into these neighborhoods. Mass migration of minorities into cities, especially during and after the two world wars, also provides important historical context. These migrations produced intense, prolonged pressures on metropolitan areas to expand the supply of housing available for minority occupancy. But discriminatory barriers closed most communities to potential minority expansion. The resultant channeling of minority housing demand into relatively few neighborhoods, and the concomitant steering away of potential white homeseekers by real estate agents, precluded a stable integrative process. Unscrupulous "blockbusting" and "panic-peddling" activities accelerated the process of transition and resegregation.[11]

History has provided ample evidence to reinforce the common belief that desegregation is synonymous with inevitable resegregation and decay. But this historical pattern is contingent upon a backdrop of pervasive discrimination and a total absence (until recently) of any concerted public efforts to promote a stable integrative process.

From the perspective of the minority homeseeker, the historically derived stereotypes are equally pervasive. Generations worth of experiences with explicit and implicit forms of discriminatory impediments to freedom of choice in housing have convinced many that most neighborhoods occupied predominantly by whites do not want to be desegregated. Well-publicized incidents of harassment of minorities in such areas have provided vivid reinforcement to these beliefs. These beliefs translate into a reluctance on the part of many minority homeseekers to search for, or occupy, dwellings outside of neighborhoods where they have traditionally looked: Those already having substantial minority proportions and adjacent to ones located in the path of the historical expansion of the minority community (Birch 1979; Lake 1981).

Thus, many households of all races hold stereotypes about desegregation that have been legitimized and reinforced over generations. Yet these beliefs do not correctly ascribe *necessary* attributes of desegregation; rather, those that have arisen because of a legacy of discrimination. The way desegregation has worked in the past is not a guide for how it will work in the future. But as long as these stereotypes predominate a stable integrative process will be rare, even if discriminatory acts magically were to vanish instantaneously. In terms of Figure 15.1, even if linkage D were eradicated linkage E would suffice to perpetuate the vicious circle.

The momentum of discriminatory history cannot be stopped merely by ceasing to discriminate. Pro-integrative policies must aggressively intervene to encourage a process of residential choice that confounds the conventional stereotypes and promotes neighborhoods that are racially diverse, stable, high-quality, and hospitable to all.

ACHIEVING INTEGRATIVE PROCESS IN WAYS THAT
EXPAND HOUSING CHOICES FOR ALL HOUSEHOLDS

This raises the question about how society should pursue the goal of a stable integrative process. Must it be done in such a way that, ironically, constricts freedom of choice? The oft-heard response of "yes" is based on a misapprehension about what means necessarily must be employed in the pursuit of a stable integrative process (North 1986; National Association of REALTORS

1987; Kearny-King and Marquis 1990). Put differently, pursuit of a stable integrative process need not employ (indeed should not employ) quotas for racial occupancy and other choice-restricting methods

There is no doubt that the use of racial quotas as a means of maintaining a particular racial mix in a community or housing complex typically restricts the choices of minority homeseekers. Because it thereby imposes undue burdens on the protected class, its use has been judged illegal (Polikoff 1986b).

Other devices for encouraging a stable integrative process do not, however, create limitations on choice. Limitations on the size and placement of "For Sale" signs and bans on solicitations by real estate agents of homeowners who have officially requested not to be solicited, for example, have been upheld in federal court.[12] The questions raised by these cases are what sorts of information do these prohibited activities convey, and are substitute courses readily available? From the perspective of those trying to promote a stable integrative process, a forest of signs on the lawns and a flurry of unwanted solicitations convey much more than factual information: they pander to fear and rumor and thus help create self-fulfilling prophecies of neighborhood racial transition and resegregation. Are there other, readily available means of blacks and whites obtaining real estate services in a manner that does not convey these psychological messages damaging to a stable integrative process? Surely, reputable brokers are only a phone call away from prospective homebuyers and homesellers who wish an assessment of current market potential.

Still other means for attaining a stable integrative process are actually choice-expanding. For example, the provision of additional information to homeseekers of all races about options in neighborhoods in which traditionally they would not have searched expands housing choices clearly. Illustrations of such services are provided by the Leadership Council in the Chicago area, the Center for Integrated Living in the Milwaukee area, and the East Suburban Council for Open Metropolitan Communities in the Cleveland area (see Ch. 16). These three organizations try to encourage blacks to move into predominantly white suburban areas by, for example, supplying listings of available suburban vacancies, personally showing units and explaining attributes of the communities, providing follow-up counseling and supportive services, and teaching seminars on homeowning skills.

Similarly, the provision of financial incentives to *all* homeseekers who make pro-integrative moves (i.e., into areas where their race is underrepresented) provides extra resources for defraying the higher housing market search costs that such non-traditional moves might entail. As examples, the Ohio Housing Finance Agency has set aside a portion of its below-market interest rate mortgage funds (raised by general obligation state bond issues) for use by first-time homebuyers making pro-integrative moves (see Ch. 16). The Philadelphia-based Fund for an Open Society offers low-interest, deferred repayment loans to homebuyers making pro-integrative moves. Oak Park (a suburb of Chicago, Illinois) is experimenting with a plan that provides financial incentives to apartment owners who maintain racially integrated buildings.[13] Not only are homeseekers encouraged to expand their range of housing options, but real estate brokers are similarly encouraged because financial incentive plans provide them an additional means of marketing particular areas to particular customers. They also are a palpable symbol of commitment by the community to the goal of a stable integrative process, and thereby reassure current and prospective residents that historical patterns of neighborhood change will be resisted.

Thus, although one means for achieving a stable integrative process clearly restricts freedom of choice, others are neutral, and still others expand the range of choices. The question arises as to whether a stable integrative process can be pursued effectively without recourse to the restrictive means.

The answer is yes. Oak Park and Park Forest, Illinois, have had successes with their programs. But, undoubtedly, the most nationally prominent case is the comprehensive plan for a stable integrative process operating in the eastern suburbs of Cleveland. Sponsoring entities include the cities of Cleveland Heights, Shaker Heights, University Heights, and the two school districts encompassing these three jurisdictions.[14] The plan takes a unique, area-wide, multifaceted approach. Housing information offices provide homeseekers of all races with additional options in neighborhoods where their race is currently underrepresented. Homebuyers are given incentives to undertake pro-integrative moves by providing home mortgages (typically of several thousand dollars) at below-market interest rates. The real estate industry is regularly monitored by testers, educated about fair housing law and practice if necessary, and encouraged to cooperate. Brokers consistently found not to discriminate are placed on a listing of preferred agents that is given to homeseekers by the housing information offices. Existing residents (predominantly whites) are encouraged to remain in the community. Elementary school districts are adjusted to avoid racially isolated schools and significant resources are committed to maintaining a superior level of educational quality. Public infrastructure, housing codes, and housing rehabilitation subsidies work in concert to preserve an attractive physical environment.

The plan works. There appears to be active participation in the housing market by all races in virtually all areas of the communities involved. This is suggested by a recent statistical analysis of changes in these communities' racial composition (Galster 1990d). It showed that formerly all-white neighborhoods had much larger increases in the numbers of minority residents than would have been predicted based on patterns elsewhere in Cuyahoga County. Similarly, neighborhoods already having substantial numbers of minority residents at the beginning of the study period witnessed larger numbers of new white homeseekers than would have been predicted otherwise. In other words, a stable integrative process was created in both stable segregated neighborhoods and in racially mixed neighborhoods that normally would have been unstable and transitory.

Of course, as yet little evidence is available that the Heights experience may be generalized to other communities. Others having a different socioeconomic status, municipal resource base, and mixture of locational amenities may find that they cannot overcome the momentum of segregation. The effects of the combination of racial and class integration (through, for example, scattered-site public housing or housing vouchers being used in the suburbs) on the performance of Heights-like policies is also unknown. Nevertheless, the potential gains from policy experiments aimed in this direction seem to outweigh by far the costs.

Conclusion

True freedom of choice in housing for all races implies the presence of a stable integrative process. Furthermore, this process removes the major motivator for illegal discriminatory acts (i.e., prejudice), thereby making attainment of freedom of choice that much easier. A stable integrative process can be effectively pursued in ways that expand housing choices, not restrict them. Finally, the alternative to a stable integrative process, a racially segregated society, imposes enormous social and economic costs on all citizens, regardless of race. For these reasons a stable integrative process should be established as an explicit goal of urban policy. Unfortunately, it will not likely arise of its own accord in the foreseeable future, even if housing discrimination were instantaneously eradicated, due to the historical legacy of discrimination. It follows that an aggressive means to encourage a stable integrative process be developed that goes beyond merely hoping that it will occur as a by-product of enforcing fair housing laws.

Notes

1. What a "substantial portion" means depends, of course, on the particular metropolitan area in question. Those having relatively few minorities might expect that a stable, integrative process would mean a lower fraction of their neighborhoods would be characterized by active demands by two or more races.

2. The value of integration has been affirmed in numerous court cases (Smolla, 1986).

3. It must be stressed, however, that economic disparities are not the primary cause of segregation (see Galster 1988, 1989).

4. See, e.g., *Client's Council* v. *Pierce* 1983 (No. 82-1383, CA-8, 6-28-83) and *Maimes* v. *Lucas Metropolitan Housing Authority, HUD, et al.* 1093 (CA-20, c. 74-86; N.D. Ohio).

5. See Lake 1986; North 1986, pp. 10-14. HUD Secretary Samuel Pierce has, however, articulated that there is no conflict; see, e.g., his letter to Rep. Steward McKinney (June 3, 1985). The debate is summarized in the *Realtor News* (April 20, 1987), p. 2: "The confusion which exists concerning what the fair housing laws require is in large measure the result of the disagreement over fair housing objectives. It is a disagreement between those who understand the fair housing laws as mandating 'free housing choice' . . . and those who understand those laws as mandating an 'integrated society.' "

6. *Mario, et al.* v. *Starrett City Assoc.* 1979 (79 C.V. 3096; E.R.N.) and *USA* v. *Starrett City Assoc.* 1984 (C.V. 84-2793). For summaries of the case, see Newman (1986); *TRENDS In Housing* (1987a) and Leedy (1987). This lower court decision was upheld without comment by the Supreme Court in September, 1988 (*TRENDS In Housing* 1988). Starrett City, located in the East New York section of Brooklyn, consists of 46 high-rise buildings and almost 6,000 apartments. Some 20,000 middle-income people live there. The management sought to maintain an ethnic mix of 62 percent white, 23 percent black, 8 percent Hispanic, and 5 percent Asian through the use of quotas, because of the disproportionate minority demands generated by the proximity of the nearly all-minority East New York and Brownsville neighborhoods.

7. See *TRENDS In Housing* (1987b). Atrium Village is a 309-unit complex located on the near-north side of Chicago. It had been integrated economically by mixing subsidized and market-rent units, and racially by a quota limiting black occupancy to 50 percent. Other court cases involving quotas are analyzed by Smolla, 1986.

8. For a review of the evidence, see Galster 1987c, Chs. 6-7.

9. The Supreme Court has held, for example, that white residents who were not directly harmed by a discriminatory policy nevertheless had standing to challenge such a policy because it denied them the benefits of interracial association; see *Trafficante* v. *Metropolitan Life Insurance Co.,* 409 U.S. 205 (1972).

10. Testing is a research and investigative device that involves pairs of trained investigators who play roles as homeseekers. Both members of each tester pair are carefully matched for age and sex, and are given comparable roles to play that specify desired housing, economic assets, family characteristics, etc. The only characteristic that differs significantly between the testers is their race. Both members respond to an advertisement about a vacancy (typically with several hours of separation) and record everything that transpired during their contacts with the real estate agent or landlord. Because the testers only differ in their race, any consistent patterns of differential treatment are assumed to be evidence of racial discrimination.

11. These practices, which are prohibited by law, typically involved agents playing on the racial fears of white homeowners, thereby inducing them into selling their homes at a discount. The agents then sell these homes to blacks at inflated prices, thereby generating arbitrage profits as well as commission income.

12. *Greater South Suburban Board of Realtors* and *NAR* v. *South Suburban Housing Center* 1984 (No. 83 C8149) and Goering 1986.

13. For further details and discussion, see Silverman (1977).

14. The plan recently won the national competition in the Ford Foundation's prestigious Innovations in State and Local Government program. For more details, see Walters (1988).

REFERENCES

Birch, D. 1979. *The behavioral foundations of neighborhood change*. Washington, DC: HUD/PDR.
Citizens' Commission on Civil Rights. 1983. *A decent home*. Washington, DC: Center for National Policy Review, Catholic University.
Farley, R. 1986. The residential segregation of blacks from whites. In *Issues in housing discrimination*, Washington, DC: U.S. Commission on Civil Rights.
Galster, G. 1982. Black and white preferences for neighborhood racial composition. *American Real Estate and Urban Economics Association Journal* 10 (Spring): 39–46.
_____. 1987a. Residential segregation and interracial economic disparities. *Journal of Urban Economics* 21: 22–44.
_____. 1987b. On the ecology of racial discrimination in housing. *Urban Affairs Quarterly* 23: 84–107.
_____. 1987c. *Homeowners and neighborhood reinvestment* Durham, NC: Duke University Press.
_____. 1988. Residential segregation in american cities: a contrary review. *Population Research and Policy Review* 7: 93–112.
_____. 1989. Residential segregation in american cities: a further response. *Population Research and Policy Review* 8: 181–92.
_____. 1990a. Racial discrimination in housing markets during the 1980s. *Journal of Planning Education and Research* 9: 165–75.
_____. 1990b. Racial steering by real estate agents: a review of the audit evidence. *Review of Black Political Economy* 18:105–129.
_____. 1990c. Racial steering by real estate agents: mechanisms and motivations. *Review of Black Political Economy* 19: 39–63.
_____. 1990d. Neighborhood racial change, segregationist sentiments and affirmative marketing policies. *Journal of Urban Economics* 27: 344–61.
Galster, G. and M. Keeney. 1988. Race residence, discrimination and economic opportunity. *Urban Affairs Quarterly* 24: 87–117.
Goering, J. 1986. Introduction. In *Housing desegregation and federal policy*, J. Goering, ed. Chapel Hill, NC: University of North Carolina Press.
Helper, R. 1986. Success and resistance factors in the maintenance of racially mixed neighborhoods. In *Housing desegregation and federal policy*, J. Goering, ed. Chapel Hill: University of North Carolina Press.
Kearny-King, J. and H. Marquis. 1990. Freedom of choice vs. integregation maintenance. *TRENDS in Housing* 28 (December-January): 15–16.
Lake, R. 1981. *The new suburbanites*. New Brunswick, NJ: Center for Urban Policy Research, Rutgers University.
_____. 1986. Postscript. In *Housing desegregation and federal policy*, J. Goering, ed. Chapel Hill: University of North Carolina Press.

Leadership Council for Open Metropolitan Communities. 1987. *The costs of housing discrimination and segregation*. Chicago: LCOMC.

Lee, B. 1985. Racially mixed neighborhoods during the 1970s. *Social Science Quarterly* 66: 346–64.

Leedy, M. 1987 Federal court rules against quotas. *Realtor News* (May 8): 1.

Massey, D. and N. Denton. 1987. Trends in the residential segregation of blacks, hispanics and asians, 1970–1980. *American Sociological Review* 52: 802–25.

McKinney, S. and A. Schnare. 1986. *Trends in residential segregation by race, 1960–1980*. Washington, DC: Urban Institute.

National Association of REALTORS. 1987. *Statement of policy*. Chicago: NAR.

Newburger, H. 1989. Discrimination by a profit-maximizing real estate broker in response to white prejudice. *Journal of Urban Economics* 26: 1–19.

Newman, O. 1986. Fair housing: the conflict between integration and non-discrimination. In *Issues in housing discrimination*, Washington, DC: U.S. Commission on Civil Rights.

North, W. 1986. *Passwords and prejudice*. Chicago: National Association of REALTORS.

Orfield, G. 1986. The movement for housing integration. In *Housing desegregation and federal policy*, J. Goering, ed. Chapel Hill: University of North Carolina Press.

Polikoff, A. 1986a. What's in a name: the diversity of racial diversity programs. In *Issues in housing discrimination*, Washington, DC: U.S. Commission on Civil Rights.

_____. 1986b. Sustainable integration or inevitable resegregation: the troubling questions. In *Housing desegregation and federal policy*, J. Goering, ed. Chapel Hill University of North Carolina Press.

Silverman, R. 1977. Subsidizing tolerance for open communities. *Wisconsin Law Review* 19: 375–501.

Smolla, R. 1986. Racial occupancy controls and integration maintenance. In *Issues in housing discrimination*. Washington, DC: U.S. Commission on Civil Rights.

Sutker, J. 1986. Race and residential mobility. In *Housing desegregation and federal policy*, J. Goering, ed. Chapel Hill: University of North Carolina Press.

Taub, R. G. Taylor and J. Dunham. 1984. *Paths of neighborhood change*. Chicago: University of Chicago Press.

TRENDS in Housing. 1987a. Court bans quotas at Starrett City. 26 (June-July): 1.

_____. 1987b. Justice sues complex for using racial quotas. 26 (August-September): 5.

_____. 1988. Update on Starrett City. 27 (October-November): 12.

U.S. Department of Housing and Urban Development. 1978. *The HUD survey on the quality of community life*. Washington, DC: U.S. Government Printing Office.

Walters, J. 1988. Three suburbs scale the heights of integration. *Governing* 2: 34–35.

Yinger, J. 1986a. On the possibility of achieving racial integration through subsidized housing. In *Housing desegregation and federal policy*, J. Goering, ed. Chapel Hill: University of North Carolina Press.

_____. 1986b. Measuring discrimination through fair housing audits. *American Economic Review* 76: 881–93.

Yinger, J., G. Galster, B. Smith and F. Eggers. 1979. The status of research into racial discrimination and segregation in American housing markets. *HUD Occasional Papers* 6: 55–175.

16 Obstacles to Housing Integration Program Efforts

MITTIE OLION CHANDLER

Programs to promote housing integration arouse philosophical debate and encounter political, as well as situational, obstacles to their implementation. The deeply rooted existence of racially segregated housing caused by discrimination creates a formidable challenge to the aspirations of integration programs. The philosophical debate, centering on the relationship between integration and the intent of the federal fair housing law, is discussed below. The political fragmentation among municipalities leads to disjointed integration efforts and permits segregated enclaves to persist. The discussion of several integration programs in this chapter illustrates this point.

The situational barriers—attitudes of blacks and whites, institutional discrimination by real estate agents and mortgage lenders—are major factors in the perpetuation of segregation. Some integration programs attempt to address these situational barriers, as discussed below, but the barriers remain largely intact. Integration programs are not designed to combat the causes of segregation on a large scale. In the final analysis, therefore, the eradication of segregated living patterns will be incremental and modest. The chapter concludes with a discussion of the implications of the program design issue on achieving integration.

PERSISTENCE OF SEGREGATION: THE ROLE OF ATTITUDES AND DISCRIMINATION

In their present form, integration programs are limited in their ability to modify segregated living arrangements. The federal fair housing legislation was enacted in 1968 after the Kerner Commission Report on Civil Disorders had warned of separate societies populated by blacks and whites. Almost 20 years later, major cities in the United States remain locations of segregated housing (Massey and Denton 1988; Lake 1986; Galster 1986; Ch. 2 of this volume). Studies on the status of segregation between 1960 and 1980 reveal that very little change has occurred in the levels of racial residential isolation, particularly in large metropolitan areas of the Midwest and Northeast. Part of the separation occurs between central cities and their suburbs, where blacks are concentrated in central cities and whites are dispersed throughout the suburbs. The separation is also evident within cities and suburbs where specific blocks or neighborhoods are racially homogeneous.

There has been a marked change in migration patterns with the growth of black suburbanization. The number of blacks living in suburbs increased by nearly 50 percent in the 1970s. By 1980 about one-fourth lived in suburbs, accounting for 6.1 percent of the suburban population. This did not, however, signal a big decrease in segregation. Most black suburbanization took place in suburbs adjacent to black neighborhoods in big central cities, and most blacks continue to live in segregated central-city neighborhoods (Harrigan 1989). The suburbanization of middle-income blacks, therefore, has resulted in only modest levels of residential integration (Massey and Denton 1988).

Juxtaposition of Black and White Attitudes

While an increasing number of white persons indicate support for integrated neighborhoods, they not only tend to live in segregated neighborhoods but their conception of integration differs dramatically from that of black persons. A 1985 opinion poll on race relations in Greater Cleveland, conducted by Gordon S. Black for the *Cleveland Plain Dealer*, found that 54 percent of whites favored integration for their neighborhood; and 23 percent opposed it (see Table 16.1). Sixty-five percent of black persons felt that a neighborhood with an even distribution of blacks and whites was the ideal racial balance, while 25 percent of whites thought so (Lynch 1985). The majority of whites (56 percent) thought that a mostly white neighborhood was ideal while 9 percent of blacks held this viewpoint. Furthermore, perceptions regarding integration are at variance with empirical findings. A 1990 public opinion poll of Cuyahoga County (where Cleveland is located) reported that 71 percent of Greater Clevelanders would consider their neighborhoods as being racially integrated. The rate was 87 percent among blacks and 69 percent among whites. The Cleveland area, however, is considered to be one of the most segregated areas in the country.

Differing perceptions about the pervasiveness of housing discrimination may partially account for disparate views about fair housing enforcement. The aforementioned poll found that 60 percent of blacks and 40 percent of whites

TABLE 16.1

Racial Attitudes Survey
(in percent)

Disposition Regarding Integration	Blacks	Whites
Favor	86%	54%
Oppose	10	23
Neither	3	18
Don't know/refused	1	5
Ideal Racial Balance	*Blacks*	*Whites*
Even	65%	25%
Predominantly or overwhelmingly white	9	56
Predominantly or overwhelmingly black or Hispanic	18	0
Don't know	8	19

Source: Cleveland Plain Dealer, December 1985.

considered racial discrimination a serious problem in Cleveland. On the question of increased enforcement of fair housing laws, 87 percent of blacks while 52 percent of whites were in favor. Similarly, a *Washington Post/ABC News* survey found that only 16 percent of whites believed that blacks still faced discrimination in the housing market (1981). A University of Michigan study showed that white Americans indicated a continuing, though modest, gain in support for local open housing laws (Schuman, et al. 1985). In 1983, 46 percent of whites supported open housing laws, up from 34 percent in 1973. Historically high levels of resistance to fair housing initiatives may be weakening, but they still pose a barrier today.

The actual housing choices of some blacks and whites are rather inconsistent with the preferences for integrated housing reported in several polls. These polls apparently do not tap the underlying attitudes that guide behaviors. These behaviors, however, are important factors in explaining the persistence of segregation. Some black people are choosing housing in more segregated neighborhoods rather than in more integrated neighborhoods. The efforts of the Ohio Housing Finance Agency [OHFA] illustrate this point.

OHFA ran two mortgage subsidy set-aside programs—one for minority first-time buyers and the other for blacks and whites making pro-integrative moves. The former program was more popular among black buyers and the funds were quickly depleted. The majority of black buyers chose homes in areas deemed segregated under program guidelines discussed later. These choices may not be wholly voluntary due to apprehensions held by some blacks about prointegrative moves.

Based on a long history of violent incidents and negative reactions to neighborhood transition, blacks demonstrate some reluctance to move into potentially hostile environments. Farley and Colasanto found that the fear of prospective discrimination and hostility from white neighbors appeared to be a much larger impediment to black suburbanization than ignorance of the opportunities (1980). Farley, Bianchi and Colasanto reported that the reluctance of Detroit-area blacks to pursue residency in integrated settings was due to concern about white reactions that may be unfriendly and make them feel unwelcome, anticipated physical violence, and danger of physical harm to selves, families, or homes (1979). Neither perceptions of costs in white areas nor reactions of other blacks was found to be a barrier to the willingness of blacks to live in white neighborhoods.

Whites generally hold beliefs about the processes of neighborhood change and instability that have fed the notion that black neighbors are undesirable. Reynolds, Bianchi, and Colasanto (1979) found that the barriers to acceptance of integration by individual whites were: the perception that other whites are opposed to integration; a belief that they will suffer personally if they do not move out of their neighborhood shortly after blacks enter; a belief that blacks would be undesirable neighbors because of differences in social class and behavior; and a failure to realize that blacks who enter will resemble them in social and economic standing. The concept of racial tipping (when the black presence in an area reaches an estimated 10 to 30 percent of the neighborhood population) has come to convey the prediction of an inevitable and rapid transition from white to black residential dominance. Polikoff, for example, discusses a "conundrum of race relations in the United States: blacks move into previously all-white neighborhoods, but the resulting integration does not persist and the neighborhoods eventually lose virtually all their white residents" and resegregate (1986). This set of beliefs has given rise to contentious research about the tipping point and to controversial programs aimed at maintaining racial proportions below that point (each will be discussed more fully below).

The two sets of attitudes and associated behavior patterns noted above practically ensure that racially balanced neighborhoods will become all or predominantly black in time (Schermer 1979, p. 31). The entire resegregation process may be immune to anti-discrimination enforcement techniques, since a majority of whites are still panicky and will attempt to escape if they find themselves a racial minority. Conversely, most blacks, given a chance, will elect not to be the first to integrate a neighborhood and tend to search for homes where a modicum of racial mixture has been established. The notion of neighborhood tipping has arisen based on these types of actions.

Role of Institutionalized Discrimination

Real estate and lending institutions are frequently mentioned as major contributors to the segregation of neighborhoods and to instability in racially mixed neighborhoods (Helper 1986; Kain 1985). As for the real estate industry, research has determined that steering black and white households, which results in segregated living, did not end with the passage of fair housing legislation (Massey and Denton 1988; Galster 1990b). The channeling of black and white homeseekers to certain neighborhoods is partially attributable to segmentation in the housing industry such that black and white agents are familiar with and have their primary listings in different markets. At one time, black real estate agents were excluded from membership on real estate boards. In 1948 black realtors responded to this exclusion by establishing their own boards and a National Association of Real Estate Brokers (Brown 1971). The resulting dual housing market affects the information available to black and white sales agents and, therefore, to the clients they serve. Some steering, moreover, is intentionally conducted.

A major national study released in 1989 by the Department of Housing and Urban Development found that 59% of black homebuyers were discriminated against in 25 metropolitan areas. A review of 69 fair housing audits found that racial discrimination continues to be a dominant feature of metropolitan housing markets in the 1980s (Galster 1990a).

The real estate agent is one of several "gatekeepers" in modern society who channel and control the activities of individuals seeking certain goals. This control may be exercised in the withholding of services as well as their direct application (Palmer *as cited in* Barresi 1968). The private real estate market controls housing opportunities by distributing information concerning available housing and providing access in accordance with class and racial neighborhood patterns that reflect the inclinations of the majority of housing consumers (Piven and Cloward 1980). If a majority of housing consumers prefer segregated housing, the real estate industry is likely to respond to that preference. In an earlier study of racial practices of real estate agents, Helper reported that the agents justified their residential control practices on the basis of social pressures exerted by neighborhood residents, other brokers, and mortgage financiers. She found that many real estate agents believe that they do the community a service by preventing minority groups from entering white neighborhoods. The agents, guided by the belief that non-whites cause neighborhoods to deteriorate and property values to decline, feel that they are acting in the best interests of the white homeowner (Helper *as cited in* Barresi 1968).

In addition to real estate agents, financial institutions have a powerful role in housing provision and the residential patterns that occur. A 4-month investigation by *Money* magazine concluded that widespread institutional racial discrimination still prevents middle-class black families from earning as much as whites, lowers their access to mortgages, business loans and other financial services, and retards their homes' rate of appreciation (Updegrave 1989). In 1988 and 1989 alone, studies were released that document redlining of predominantly nonwhite neighborhoods in Baltimore, Boston, Chicago, Louisville, Washington, D.C., and elsewhere. The *Atlanta Journal-Constitution* reported high levels of racial disparity in mortgage rejection rates in the nation's largest cities (Dedman 1989). Another researcher noted that racial discrimination in mortgage lending and housing generally has long been a fact of life in Milwaukee and other cities around the country (Squires 1990).[1]

Integration programs are impeded in attaining their objectives by their inability to change these patterns in the real estate and finance industries. The dispositions of these institutions suggest that integration programs should: first, counter the financial benefit of maintaining a discriminatory, segregated market by making integration profitable to the real estate industry; and, second, include integrated neighborhoods among the options considered by the homeseeker.

INTEGRATION PROGRAMS

The implementation of integration programs poses a dilemma for supporters of fair housing legislation because they often resurrect the debate over the initial intent of the national fair housing law: Title VIII of the 1968 Civil Rights Act. The stated purpose of Title VIII is "the achievement of fair housing throughout the United States." Two major contrasting interpretations emanate from that purpose. In one interpretation, Title VIII is intended to eliminate discrimination by assuring that all housing is accessible to all persons regardless of the resulting racial residential patterns (also known as the "freedom of choice" position). Therefore, households could be segregated by race as a matter of choice. A second interpretation holds that the promotion of stable integration is the ultimate purpose of Title VIII. While some consensus has been reached that the initial expectation of Congress was that open housing would lead to integrated housing, no unanimous agreement exists among policy analysts on this point (Polikoff 1986). The programs discussed in this chapter are based on the second interpretation, which clashes with the freedom of choice position (an alternate view is presented in Ch. 15).

The lines of this debate are drawn primarily, though not absolutely, along racial lines. Black fair housing advocates are more inclined to favor the freedom of choice position, while white fair housing advocates are more likely to support integration promotion efforts. The components of local and state programs to initiate or manage integration illustrate the intricacies of this debate, the fragmentation among fair housing advocates, and the continuing discord in the United States over racially sensitive issues.

Pro-integration programs that are designed to *initiate* racial integration are more difficult to construct and implement than those designed to *maintain* integration, and are subject to different problems. Yet, the two related efforts overlap because integration must occur on a broad scale to avoid the resegregation of integrated communities. The same organizations are often involved in running both types of programs. These agencies employ a number of strategies intended to reduce segregation or to prevent resegregation. Table 16.2 presents the major elements of integration programs across the county and their means of affecting integration. Like the programs discussed below, agencies use a variety of techniques.

Case Study: The OHFA Set-Aside Program

In 1982, Ohio followed a national trend and created a state-wide entity, the Ohio Housing Finance Agency [OHFA], to assist first-time homebuyers of low- and moderate-income by offering below-market rate mortgages through participating lenders. OHFA creates revenue for the loans by floating tax-exempt bonds. A 9-member board, composed of representatives of banking, labor, real estate, and the public interest, oversee the agency. OHFA was not conceived of as having a fair housing mission and its legislative history reflects a desire not to subsidize suburban integration (Husock 1989). Until 1985, OHFA functioned without regard to fair housing issues.

In 1985, The Cuyahoga Plan of Ohio, a Cleveland-based fair housing organization, released its analysis of 1983–84 OHFA financing distribution, challenging the impact of the program on racial residential patterns. The Cuyahoga Plan charged that OHFA was contributing to the segregation and resegregation of neighborhoods by not undertaking an effective marketing program. As a consequence, whites tended to buy in predominantly white areas and blacks tended to buy in predominantly black or transitional neighborhoods. They argued that affirmative marketing would attract more black buyers, who were underrepresented, to the program; and encourage them to move into non-black areas.[2]

In the aftermath of the criticism, OHFA adopted a proposal to set aside 10 percent of the 1985 Cuyahoga County (Cleveland area) share of the low-interest mortgage funds for pro-integrative moves. The lone dissenter on the OHFA board was the executive vice president of the Ohio Association of Realtors, who voiced opposition to the development of a new social program with mortgage-revenue bonds. This program was the first of its kind in the country and has since been replicated and expanded upon in Wisconsin. In order to participate,

TABLE 16.2

Key Elements and Objectives of Integration Programs

Program Element	Objective
1. Financial incentives	Limited information available to homebuyers about uncustomary options.
2. Affirmative marketing to promote integration by matching clients with rental listings	Resegregation that occurs when black demand or search in an area exceeds white demand while whites continue to seek out other predominantly white areas.
3. Commitment from realtors to promote integration in housing	Realtors who play a major role in providing and guarding access to neighborhoods.
4 Strong building code enforcement	Prevention of deferred maintenance and the visible decline of property which has been associated with neighborhoods undergoing racial transition.
5. Diversity counseling	Issues and adjustments facing persons in integrated or potentially integrative neighborhoods.
6. Equity assurance to guarantee a certain housing resale value	Thwarting homeowner concerns about the decline in property values often associated with racially changing neighborhoods. These concerns have led to panic selling and blockbusting.
7. For-sale signs ban and real estate solicitation regulation	Dispelling outward indicators of neighborhood change by preventing the use of mechanisms that can create a panic atmosphere.
8. Monitoring or testing for discrimination	Detection of differential treatment inflicted upon persons which violate fair housing statutes.
9. Federal Section 8 rental assistance program to promote pro-integrative moves.	Economic and racial integration of low-income minority households to enhance opportunities for upward mobility.

Source: Author.

homebuyers must purchase in census tracts where their race is under-represented, in accordance with established numerical guidelines. Eligible census tracts could diverge no more than 15 percentage points from the 25 percent county-wide ratio of blacks to whites (see Table 16.3 for the guidelines).

Following an unsuccessful challenge from a Cleveland-based state legislator about the legality of using mortgage-revenue funds to promote integration, OHFA announced another state-wide pro-integration set-aside of $9.5 million for 1988. Additional opposition surfaced from black persons associated with 3 main organizations (Professional Housing Services,[3] National Association for the Advancement of Colored People [NAACP], and Cleveland Area Real Estate Board). They charged that numerical ceilings serve to further limit the choices and participation of black homeseekers (the freedom of choice argument) and that implicit in the numerical guidelines is an assumption that predominantly black neighborhoods are inferior or undesirable.

In response, OHFA divided the pro-integration set-aside to provide a separate allocation of funds for minority homebuyers who could purchase homes wherever they chose, including predominantly black neighborhoods. No additional funds were appropriated to accommodate the expanded population of eligible buyers. The program guidelines also were changed to reflect school zone percentages, which were considered better indicators of potential resegregation than census tract percentages. Because the percentage of blacks attending a neighborhood school tended to be higher than the representation of blacks in the overall population, pro-integration proponents felt comfortable increasing the percentages of blacks in neighborhoods targeted for the OHFA set-aside (Husock 1989). (See Table 16.4.) Under both the old and new standards for qualification, the freedom of choice contingent maintained that the net effect was to reduce the cost of borrowing for whites while denying blacks the opportunity to buy.

TABLE 16.3
OHFA Integration Assistance Loan Guidelines, 1985

Census Tract Racial Percentage	Loan Guidelines
0–10 percent black	Blacks qualified for loans
10–40 percent black	Neutral. No one can qualify
40–100 percent black	Whites qualified for loans

Source: Husock, "Integration Incentives" in Suburban Cleveland, 1989.

TABLE 16.4
Revised Integration Assistance Guidelines, December 1988

School Zone Racial Percentage	*Loan Guidelines*
0–25 percent black	Blacks qualified
25–50 percent black	Neutral. No set-aside loans
50–100 percent black	Whites qualified

Source: Husock, "Integration Incentives" in Suburban Cleveland, 1989.

In August 1989, $10 million was made available for both the minority set-aside and pro-integration set-aside programs; other metropolitan areas began to participate. The major program implementors were located in the Akron, Cincinnati, and Cleveland areas.[4] The level of participation was almost evenly split approximately between blacks and whites.

By January 1990, 53 Cleveland area households had received the pro-integration loans from the 1989 allotment; 24 were black and 19 were white. The black and white families moved largely in keeping with patterns established by previous pro-integrative loan programs: to the eastern suburbs where the bulk of the implementing agencies were located. A noteworthy variation saw some black buyers locate on the near west side of Cleveland, a predominantly white stronghold. Another exception occurred when some white buyers moved into a small gentrified enclave within a low-income area near west side neighborhood. Few of the moves were "pioneering" in the sense that they deviated from prior trends noted in other pro-integrative unassisted moves.[5] In January 1990, $6 million remained in the pro-integration pool, while the non-targeted mortgage funds and the minority set-aside funds were completely expended by that time.

The $10 million set-aside for minority first-time homebuyers was totally exhausted within 6 weeks of its availability. The majority of buyers moved into Cleveland and nearby integrated suburbs. The comparative experiences of this and the pro-integration program indicate that integration must be marketed to blacks and whites if it is to occur. They also suggest that making traditional moves to segregated areas is perceived by homebuyers as easier, if not more desirable, than making non-traditional moves to unfamiliar communities. The changes resulting from the OHFA mortgage subsidy or similar programs depend on the efforts undertaken by the implementing agencies, such as those described in an upcoming section.

Milwaukee: State-Supported Comprehensive Program

Milwaukee has the only other state-funded program to provide mortgage money to promote integration. The order to establish a housing counseling and recruitment center that would facilitate residential racial integration was part of the 1987 settlement of a suit by the Milwaukee Public Schools and the NAACP against the state of Wisconsin and 24 suburban school districts. The Center for Integrated Living [CIL] was launched in 1989 to provide special assistance to persons of all races interested in making pro-integrative moves within the 4-county Milwaukee metropolitan area. A pool of special mortgage funds ($5 million) was set aside by the Wisconsin Housing and Economic Development Authority [WHEDA] for use by persons making pro-integrative moves. This is one of many services that the CIL offers which include rental assistance and aid to developers of low- and moderate-income housing.

ESCOC: A Targeted Pro-Integration Program

The East Surburban Council for Open Communities [ESCOC] opened a housing service in 1983 for the purpose of introducing integrated living to the predominantly white Hillcrest area of Cuyahoga County, Ohio. ESCOC was dismantled at the end of 1990 but its demise tells the story of how differing goals can frustrate a pro-integration program.

The local units of government in the Hillcrest area were not members of ESCOC. ESCOC was created by integration forces operating in the nearby integrated Heights suburbs, who saw geographically expanding the search of black buyers as a way to relieve the demand on their neighborhoods. As such, ESCOC used strategies employed by the Heights suburbs to influence black buyers to make pro-integrative moves: counseling, conferring with real estate salespersons, and offering financial incentives. Incentive loans of between $3,000 and $5,000, at an interest rate of 3 percent, were offered to black home-buyers in Hillcrest. ESCOC also participated in the OHFA pro-integrative mortgage program.

Despite the disadvantage of not having full governmental support of the target communities, the ESCOC 1988 annual report indicates that 117 black families moved into the Hillcrest area with assistance from the program during 1987 and 1988. Without the endorsement and support of local governments, ESCOC did not achieve its maximum potential. A favorable component of the program was the inclusion of five municipalities, rather than one, in the Hillcrest area. Since the target area consists of multiple communities, the perceived threat of resegregation is diminished. Nonetheless, the effects of the

ESCOC pro-integration were limited by the relatively small size of the target area.

A major disagreement arose within ESCOC regarding the extent of services provided to renters versus buyers. The executive director chose to emphasize ownership rather than tenancy contrary to the preference of some board members. In a subsequent letter of resignation as executive director, Winston Richie was pessimistic about ending segregation under the existing scope of ESCOC operations saying he was tired of "feeling like I'm beating my head into a brick wall" (Morrison 1990). The ESCOC board of directors dissolved the organization commensurate with his resignation at the end of 1990.

In 1991, the Heights communities contracted with the Cuyahoga Plan of Ohio to operate Hillcrest Housing. It renders pro-integration services to the previous ESCOC target area. Richie has since established the Center for Equal Housing Services to perform a similar function countywide pending the receipt of operating funds.

INTEGRATION MANAGEMENT PROGRAMS

Concerns that racial balance in integrated areas will be jeopardized by the continual immigration of black households into them has given rise to integration management programs. Integration management generally describes two similar, and often, interrelated processes. First, the management of integration implies efforts to control or direct the means by which integration occurs. The means may include setting up a housing service, as was done in Shaker Heights, Ohio, where sellers and landlords were encouraged to list the availability of their properties. The objective of this program was to selectively direct white and black homeseekers to certain areas to avoid resegregation.[6]

Second, integration management refers to attempts to maintain integration at certain levels. In this instance, desired ratios of black and white households are established. The objective of this strategy usually is to make areas acceptable to white homeseekers by keeping the number of black households at a "tolerable" level. The private owners of the Starrett City apartment complex in Brooklyn, New York, established quotas to alleviate community fears of a predominantly minority project. This race-conscious tenant selection plan set a distribution of 64 percent white, 22 percent black, and 8 percent Hispanic. The U.S. Court of Appeals for the Second Circuit subsequently found that the use of racial quotas to maintain integration in the complex violates the Civil Rights Act of 1968. The court ruled that even though the quotas promoted integration in effect, they contradicted the law's anti-discrimination policy.

Other programs that use race-conscious calculations to establish criteria for program eligibility also have been controversial. It has been alleged that black homeseekers are denied freedom of choice when they do not fit the designated classification. By their efforts to maintain specific racial proportions, integration management programs assent to perceptions about the adverse outcome of racial transition. This implicit element of these programs was revealed by an integration management program official as he attempted to explain that program publicity avoids integration themes which whites will not accept:

> Most people think of integration as wholesale racial change: whites moving out, blacks moving in, property values don't hold up, problems occur in schools—things that actually happen. (Detroit *News*, August 19, 1990).

Integration management programs entail a variety of mechanisms designed to direct underrepresented groups into racially isolated neighborhoods, to control the process of integration and to restrain the process of resegregation in a given geographical area, such as a housing development or a municipality. By design or coincidence, these mechanisms can operate simultaneously within a metropolitan area to create perplexing outcomes. The fragmentation among municipal governments in most metropolitan areas typically means that integration programs are limited to particular communities, but have impacts outside their boundaries. Persons who prefer segregated neighborhoods are able to flee to other areas unaffected by integration efforts. Further, pressure builds in the integrated area to retain its character; this is helped by expanding opportunities for integrated living. Promoting integration in other communities is a strategy employed to avert resegregation. Integration efforts must be universal or most suburbs are likely to remain segregated (Keating 1988).

Integration management can only occur where some modicum of integration has already occurred. Pro-integration efforts, in this sense, and integration management efforts augment each other. Encouraging integration in a segregated area aids the process of preserving integration and avoiding resegregation. Expanding integration goals increases the options available to homeseekers and reduces the pressure on smaller areas where some integration has occurred.

The Heights Communities

A major challenge facing integration management advocates is to maintain integration in areas like Shaker Heights, Ohio, a Cleveland suburb estimated to be 29 percent black in 1990. Before any significant number of black families moved into Shaker Heights, instances of rapid resegregation had occurred in two other eastern Cleveland suburbs, East Cleveland and Warrensville Heights. Persons in Shaker Heights acted to prevent the recurrence of this experience.

Shaker Heights opened the agency that is now known as the Shaker Heights Community Services Department [CSD] in 1967. It is a department within the city of Shaker Heights government.

Integration management efforts of the department take the approach of encouraging whites to move into the area through the use of a fairly elaborate affirmative marketing program. The CSD provides homeseeker tours, locates rental units for prospective tenants, and distributes information on community services, schools, recreational facilities, and other amenities. Black families are not displayed in this marketing program in proportion to their population because program officials contend that whites will not buy integration themes.

The CSD also participates in a program, Fund for the Future of Shaker Heights, which offers incentive loans of $3,000 to $4,800 to buyers making pro-integrative moves. By November 1990, just 7 of 106 loans through this program had been awarded to black buyers; the balance was granted to white buyers. OHFA funds are available in some parts of Shaker Heights depending on the racial composition of the neighborhood and the interested buyer. To date, all loans have been utilized by white buyers. Targeting its marketing efforts toward whites has achieved the intended results in Shaker Heights. Shaker Heights had a black population of 1 percent in 1960; 24 percent in 1980; and 29 percent in 1990. It appears that resegregation has been abated in Shaker Heights.

Oak Park: Targeted, Comprehensive Approach

A situation similar to that in Shaker Heights faced Oak Park, Illinois. The village of Oak Park, Chicago suburb, adopted a policy establishing a commitment to racial diversity and developed a comprehensive plan of action in 1973. The apparent success of the Oak Park plan for racial diversity is due to strong community and governmental commitment combined with the support of realtors, landlords, and financial institutions. The approach is a fairly comprehensive attack on segregation on all fronts.

The Oak Park Housing Center [OPHC], established in 1972, is a component of the plan. OPHC deals almost exclusively with rentals in seeking to encourage and assist prospective renters to make moves that will increase or maintain racial diversity in the community. Among the means pursuant toward that end are affirmative marketing, working with realtors to promote integration, and an advertising and public relations program, all working in conjunction with the village government to inspect units. The village government provides diversity counseling aimed at prospective home purchasers and tenants. Another component of the Oak Park plan is an equity assurance program created in 1978. This program guarantees that owners will not suffer any capital losses even if home prices declined. An ordinance banning "For Sale" signs and regulating solicitation by real estate agents has also been passed.

The range of activities undertaken in Oak Park exemplifies a broad-based approach to the pursuit of integration that contrasts with some of the less expansive efforts provided by the OHFA set-aside, for example. Further, the complementary efforts of the local government and the nonprofit OPHC are not always present in integration programs. The extent of such cooperation, however, contributes to the ability of officials to maintain racial integration at the levels desired. If local government is not supportive of the integration concept, the efforts of the nonprofit organization are more complicated and the goals more difficult to achieve.

PRO-INTEGRATION AND INTEGRATION MANAGEMENT PROGRAMS:
CAN SIP BE ACHIEVED?

Chapter 15 introduced the notion of stable integrative process (SIP): a particular kind of market dynamic in which homeseekers representing two or more races actively seek to occupy the same vacant dwellings in a substantial proportion of a metropolitan area's neighborhoods over an extended period. Galster attempts to distinguish the SIP from its outcomes. Presumably, SIP would produce integrated neighborhoods. This presumption could be valid since the differences in information available to black and white buyers is a contributor to housing segregation (see Rosser and White 1975).

SIP, however, assumes a state of affairs that does not currently exist. The impediments to integrated outcomes discussed earlier in this chapter are essentially impediments to SIP. Integrated outcomes have been achieved in selected neighborhoods as the result of deliberate actions on the part of groups and individuals. These groups do not function in large parts of all metropolitan areas. In fact, greater Chicago, greater Cleveland, greater Milwaukee, and other metropolitan areas are largely unaffected by integration efforts in spite of unusually intensive integration maintenance and pro-integration programs in these areas, as outlined above.

SIP is an ideal circumstance that could occur if there was not the pervasive history of discrimination and segregation discussed earlier in this chapter. There is no example of a true SIP that operates freely, that is, without some programmatic intrusion, to achieve an integrated outcome.

Beyond the idealism associated with SIP, its utility is questionable unless it is examined in terms of outcomes. The process is less important than the outcomes. The mere act of a diverse group of potential buyers seeking housing in the same area will not ensure that the accompanying moves will result. It is the consequences of the searches by black and other minority homebuyers that, in large part, explain segregated residential environments. These homeseekers encounter or anticipate that they will encounter discrimination or other actions that reveal opposition to their housing choice; hence, an integrated environment is not chosen or a segregated choice is made.

If black homeseekers encounter or perceive discrimination by individual home sellers, real estate agents, or financial institutions, the SIP would not insure the anticipated integrated result. "Integration," however defined, must be based on the outcomes of the search for housing. The outcome determines whether a stable integrative process is taking place.

Pro-integration programs seek to attain desired proportions of white and black residents by altering the stream of housing demand that contributes to segregation or resegregation. The less intrusive programs, like the OHFA set-aside, rely on a demand-side approach which requires that individual home-buyers make buying decisions in keeping with integration objectives but do not seek to correct any systemic maladies that account for segregation and resegregation: discriminatory actions of individuals and real estate agents.

Integration management efforts, particularly those that employ numerical guidelines or ratios, are likely to be more effective in achieving their desired results because they are more intrusive than pro-integration programs. Integration management programs do not operate in a SIP mode (with people of different races seeking the same housing in the same community); they construct limits or conditions that operate against that happening. So, not only do the intended beneficiaries not get helped, they may get harmed, and integration may still not be achieved. The choices provided through integration management programs may not expand the options available to all prospective buyers. In a study of the renowned Oak Park integration maintenance strategy, Goodwin found that the goals of completely open housing and stable racial integration were mutually exclusive (1979).

Integration is an extremely powerful reform when properly implemented and requires a concerted intervention into the housing market (Orfield 1986). Integration efforts must correct the fundamental dualism of the market from within or previously established patterns will prevail and yield the same results. In order for this to happen, a unitary marketing system that provides equal access to housing opportunities and meets the needs of all people is needed (discussed by Rosser and White 1975). The unitary marketing concept prescribed opens up the entire real estate market transforming it from one that is fragmented and monopolistic. The establishment of a well-publicized metropolitan-wide housing service, and the use of state licensing and regulation of real estate brokers as an anti-discrimination tool are two major reforms needed to allow integration to occur more freely (discussed in Polikoff 1986).

CONCLUSION

The net effects of integration programs are difficult to measure. While segregation continues, there have been some obvious cases where resegregation has been held in check. The levels of segregation might be higher without them (see Galster 1990c). The impact of integration programs is determined by two sets of issues discussed in this chapter which can be summarized as: (1) how comprehensively the program or implementing agency addresses the range of issues that create segregated or resegregated communities and (2) how supportive key actors are, particularly local government officials and residents. The Milwaukee Center for Integrated Living [CIL], for example, operates a relatively comprehensive program in one of the most supportive environments. It covers a four-county area, provides a range of services, and has state funding for integration activities. The elements of segregation, integration, and resegregation are complex and must be tackled on many fronts.

The approach of the integration maintenance programs, particularly, needs to be reexamined. The contentious element of these programs responds to negative perceptions that people hold about racially changing or predominantly black neighborhoods. The perception needs further exploration. The question concerning racial shifts in mixed neighborhoods no longer appears to have a single answer, with compositional stability and changes in both directions now being observed. Rapid increases in black population in racially mixed neighborhoods oversimplify the experiences in the largest U.S. cities, where significant percentages of census tracts underwent declines in proportions of black residents or remained racially stable during the decade (Lee 1985). A greater understanding of the processes of neighborhood stability and change could result in programs that deal with the impediments to integration or SIP.

Vigorous enforcement of the laws that prohibit unlawful discrimination is of the utmost importance. In order for integration programs to fulfill their objectives, governmental entities with enforcement responsibilities must fulfill their mandates and remove the obstacles they encounter. Persistent impediments to open housing provide the impetus for both integration and freedom of choice policies. If lawful access to all housing could be eventually achieved, the contrast between freedom of choice and integration goals would be lessened. Greater equality of housing opportunity is a worthy public policy goal regardless of its impact on integration. Significant increases in integration, however, would almost certainly accompany such policy achievements.

NOTES

1. In response to its number one ranking in this study, Milwaukee and Wisconsin officials created a Fair Lending Action Committee in April 1989 to identify reasons for

racial disparity and make recommendations to increase mortgage lending for blacks and other racial minorities. Six months later a report recommended several steps to address their findings. Nine months later, no loans had been made to implement the report.

2. The Cuyahoga Plan report found that of 2,131 loans during 1983 and 1984, in Cuyahoga County, which includes Cleveland, 11.2 percent went to blacks while blacks made up 21 percent of the county's total population.

3. Formed in 1985, the stated mission of Professional Housing Services is to facilitate access to adequate housing and eliminate discrimination in housing for all homeseekers.

4. One shortcoming of the OHFA set-asides was the lack of funds to certify applicants for the programs. Implementing agencies in the Cleveland area have sought and received grants from local foundations and area lenders to carry out such certification on a restricted basis.

5. Cleveland Heights, Shaker Heights, and University Heights had been engaged in integration maintenance for over 15 years before the OHFA program began. ·

6. Customarily, resegregation occurs when a neighborhood that was initially predominantly white goes through an interim period of integration as the white families are replaced by black families to the point where the neighborhood eventually becomes predominantly black.

REFERENCES

Barresi, C.M. 1968. The role of the real estate agent in residential location. *Sociological Focus* 1:59–71.
Berry, B. 1979. *The open housing question*. Cambridge, MA: Ballinger Publishing Co.
Bradburn, N., S. Sudman and G. Gockel. 1970. *Racial integration in american neighborhoods*. Chicago: National Opinion Research Center.
Brown, W.H., Jr. 1971. Access to housing: the role of the real estate industry. *Economic Geography* 48: 66–78.
Clark, W.A.V. 1986. Residential segregation in american cities: a review and interpretation. *Population Research and Policy Review* 5:95–127.
Cuyahoga Plan of Ohio. 1989. Municipal approaches to fair housing. Unpublished report. Cleveland, OH: February.
Dedman, B. 1989. The color of money. *Atlanta-Journal Constitution* (January).
Downs, A. 1981. *Neighborhoods and urban development*. Washington, DC: Brookings Institution.
Farley, R. and D. Colasanto. 1980. Racial and residential segregation: is it caused by misinformation about housing costs? *Social Science Quarterly* 61: 623–37.
Farley R, S. Bianchi and D. Colasanto. 1979. Barriers to the racial integration of neighborhoods: the Detroit case. *Annals of the American Academy of Political and Social Sciences* 441 (January): 97–113.
Farley, R., et al. 1978. Chocolate city, vanilla suburbs: will the trend toward racially separate communities continue? *Social Science Research* 7: 319–44.
Galster, G. 1988. Residential segregation in american cities: a contrary review. *Population Research and Policy Review* 7:93–112.

———. 1986. More than skin deep: the effect of housing discrimination on the extent and pattern of racial residential segregation in the United States. In *Housing desegregation and federal policy*, J. Goering, ed. Chapel Hill, NC: University of North Carolina Press.

———. 1990a. Racial discrimination in housing markets during the 1980s: a review of the audit evidence. *Journal of Planning Education and Research* (April 11).

———. 1990b. Racial steering in urban housing markets: a review of the audit evidence. *Review of Black Political Economy* (February 17).

———. 1990c. Neighborhood racial change, segregationist sentiments, and affirmative marketing policies. *Journal of Urban Economics*.

Goering, J. and S. Sacks. 1985. Civil rights enforcement in a federalist system: an analysis of policy formation and implementation. In *Public policy across and communities*, D. Judd, ed. Greenwich, CT: JAI Press, Inc.

Goodwin, C. 1979. *The Oak Park strategy: community control of racial change*. Chicago: University of Chicago Press.

Harrigan, J.J. 1989. *Political change in the metropolis*. Boston: Little, Brown and Company.

Helper, R. 1986. Success and resistance factors in the maintenance of racially mixed neighborhoods. In *Housing desegregation and federal policy*, J. Goering, ed. Chapel Hill, NC: University of North Carolina Press.

Husock, H. 1989. 'Integration incentives' in suburban Cleveland. Kennedy School of Government Case Program.

Kain, J.F. 1985. Black suburbanization: a new beginning or false hope. In *American domestic priorities*, J.M. Quigley and D.L. Rubinfield, eds. Berkeley: University of California Press.

Keating, W.D. 1988. Suburban Cleveland's 20-year integration struggle. *Planning* (September): 18–19.

Lake, R. 1986. Unresolved themes in the evolution of fair housing. In *Housing desegregation and federal policy*, J. Goering, ed. Chapel Hill, NC: University of North Carolina Press.

Lake, R. and J. Winslow. 1981. Integration management: municipal constraints on residential mobility. *Urban Geography* 12: 311–26.

Lamb, C.M. 1984. Equal housing opportunity. In *Implementation of civil rights policy*, C.S. Bullock III and C. Lamb, eds. Monterey, CA: Brooks/Cole Publishing Co.

Lee, B.A. 1985. Racially mixed neighborhoods during the 1970s: change or stability. *Social Science Quarterly*.

Leigh, W.A. and J.D. McGhee. 1986. A minority perspective on residential racial integration. In *Housing desegregation and federal policy*, J. Goering, ed. Chapel Hill, NC: University of North Carolina Press.

Lieberson, S. and D.K. Carter. 1982. A model for inferring the voluntary and involuntary causes of residential segregation. *Demography* 19 (November):511–26.

Lind, K. 1982. Maintaining residential integration: municipal practices.

Lynch, M.L. 1985. Races split on housing integration. *Cleveland Plain Dealer*, 23 December.

Massey, D. and N. Denton. 1988. Suburbanization and segregation in U.S. metropolitan areas. *American Journal of Sociology* 94(3): 592–626.

McGrew, J.L. 1981. Resistance to change continues to restrict public housing choices. *Journal of Housing* (July): 375–81.

Morris, W.R. 1980. The black struggle for fair housing: 1900–1980. *The Urban League Review* (excerpted from *The Crisis*) (December): 518–24. New York: NAACP.

Morrison, B. 1990. Housing advocate leaves post in 'frustration' over segregation. *Cleveland Plain Dealer*, c-1.

Orfield, G. 1986. The movement for housing integration: rationale and the nature of the challenge. In *Housing desegregation and federal policy*, J. Goering, ed. Chapel Hill, NC: University of North Carolina Press.

Piven, F.F. and R.A. Cloward. 1980. The case against urban desegregation. In *Housing urban america*, J. Pynoos, R. Schafer and C.W. Hartman, eds. Hawthorne, NY: Aldine Publishing Co.

Polikoff, A. 1986. Sustainable integration or inevitable resegregation. In *Housing desegregation and federal policy*, J. Goering, ed. Chapel Hill, NC: University of North Carolina Press.

The Public Policy Forum. 1989. Housing in metropolitan Milwaukee: programs designed to achieve racial diversity. Unpublished report. (November).

Rosser, L. and B. White. 1975. An answer to housing discrimination: the need for a unitary marketing system. *Civil Rights Digest* (Winter).

Rubinowitz, L.S. and E. Trosman. 1979. Affirmative action and american dream: implementing fair housing policies in federal homeownership programs. *Northwestern Law Review* 74(November): 496–621.

Schermer, G. 1979. Steering: realtors as gate-keepers. Michigan Advisory Committee to the U.S. Commission on Civil Rights (July 9).

Schuman, H., C. Steeh, and L. Bobo. 1985. *Racial attitudes in America: trends and interpretations*. Cambridge, MA: Harvard University Press.

Squires, G.D. 1990. Biased lending. *Journal of Housing* 47(4): 182–85.

Updegrave, W.L. 1989. Race and money. *Money* 18(12)(December).

U.S. Commission on Civil Rights. 1979a. *The federal fair housing enforcement effort*.

U.S. Department of Housing and Urban Development. 1979. *Measuring racial discrimination in American housing markets*. Washington, DC: Government Printing Office.

———. 1984. Recent evidence on discrimination in housing. PD&R-786 (April).

Washington Post. 1981. March 24:A2 (from Orfield).

Wienk, R.D., C.E. Reid, J.C. Simonson and F. Eggers. 1979. *Measuring racial discrimination in American housing markets: the housing markets practice survey*. Washington, DC: Department of Housing and Urban Development, Office of Policy Development and Research.

17 Policy Prescriptions for Inner-City Public Schooling

HEIDI MARIE ROCK and EDWARD W. HILL

Urban public schools, by most accounts, are failing. A disproportionate number of former students of inner-city public school districts of all races falter in the workplace. Current and former students are not learning, which is a failure in achievement; and too many students drop out or do not complete their post-secondary education, which is a failure in attainment. This is a rather roundabout way of saying that, even if a student graduates from an inner-city high school, he or she may not have learned enough to succeed at either a job or in more advanced learning.

Even after considering gains in the National Assessment of Educational Progress (NAEP) test scores, on average, students in urban school districts continue to perform poorly. A 22 percentage point disparity in the 1984 NAEP reading scores exists between disadvantaged urban 17-year-old students and the average for all 17-year-olds (Ch. 7). Nearly one-half of students in urban public schools cannot attend institutions of higher learning, unless they obtain a General Equivalency Degree, because they do not graduate from high school (Council of Great City Schools 1987). The percent of black youths who enrolled in institutions of higher education dropped from 48.0 percent in 1977—when it nearly equaled the white rate—to 36.5 percent in 1986; the white rate has increased since 1977 to 57.0 percent (Jaynes and Williams 1989, pp. 338–39).

Comments made by Kenneth Wong and George Galster were particularly helpful in developing the arguments presented in this chapter. This chapter was prepared with partial funding from the Urban University Program of the Ohio General Assembly and Ohio's Board of Regents.

Appraisals of the effectiveness of inner-city school systems are typically based on measures of the end product of schooling—achievement. Those measures are output measures, and in the case of inner-city schools they do not depict success. Yet these measures do not tell why school systems are failing because they do not examine educational inputs.

In fact, the focus on end-point testing that has been reinforced by the excellence-in-education controversy has led to dictums from the top—most often a state's educational bureaucracy or legislature—ordering all schools to do better (National Commission on Excellence in Education 1983). This approach assumes that the basic structure of the educational system is fine and that the problem lies in the inappropriate or wasteful use of resources in the classroom (Boyd and Kerchner 1988). Unfortunately, a top-down approach that orders improvement and focuses almost exclusively on competency testing of students in secondary schools is largely irrelevant for inner-city school systems. The top-down approach does not focus on the adequacy of educational inputs and does not determine if the necessary preconditions for educational excellence—or, more realistically, competence—are present in central-city schools. All too often they are not.

The first portion of this chapter discusses the relationship between nine aspects of public education. These aspects consist of the two fundamental preconditions that must exist in school buildings and among students before education can take place and seven other aspects of education that can be grouped into three goals: educational, economic and social/cultural. This framework is required to answer two questions: (1) Are the preconditions for educational success present in inner-city schools? and (2) Why has the system not reformed itself? These questions are discussed in the second and third sections of the chapter. Public education's policy environment is the focus of the fourth section. The chapter concludes by discussing a reform proposal offered by Michael W. Spicer and Edward W. Hill (1990).

FOUR STANDARDS FOR PUBLIC EDUCATION

Public schools are publicly supported institutions and as such they respond to a number of different sources of influence. Weiss (1990) identifies five sources: professional norms, administrative actions, political and legal processes, market forces, and societal values and ideas, and she discusses which actors are most likely to exercise each type of control. Each of these sources makes separate demands on public educational policy and resources. Each source is used by different stakeholders in the system, such as taxpayers without children in the system, parents, teachers, politicians, non-teaching employees and vendors, school administrators, and local firms that employ the system's graduates. Each stakeholder emphasizes distinct aspects of public education as a social and economic activity, and all use different combinations of the five sources of influence.

Despite the wide range of stakeholders and their various sources of influence, there has been a long-held societal consensus on nine aspects of public schooling that are important to policy makers and the public (Hill and Rock 1990).[1] These nine aspects can be simplified into a fundamental set of preconditions that nurture the learner and the three goals: academic, social/cultural, and economic (Table 17.1). Each of the goals is composed of several aspects of education and form a hierarchy, so that each preceding goal becomes a necessary, but not sufficient, precondition for the following goal. This forces distinction between the fundamental preconditions and the precondition for each specific aspect of education. For the sake of simplicity, the three goals and the preconditions are referred to as the four standards for public education. Four standards are referred to because the fundamental preconditions to learning are not goals *per se*, but they must be provided for by either the home, community, or the school if learning is to take place.

All schools are expected to achieve the three goals of public schooling. Schools situated in neighborhoods with extreme levels of non-employment and poverty, unstable family structure, high crime rates, youth gangs, and drug addicts, however, must address the standards differently than schools in socially stable communities. Public schools in stable communities have a luxury that

TABLE 17.1

Four Standards and Nine Aspects of Public Schooling

Standards	Aspects
Fundamental preconditions	Secure learning environment Social safety net
Academic goals	Basic skills Life-long learning Intrinsic learning
Social /cultural goals	Assimilation Participatory democracy
Economic goals	Employability Economic development

Source: Author.

most inner-city schools do not have—they can assume that the fundamental preconditions are met, while urban schools must first focus resources on attaining the preconditions. In short, each of these two types of schools has a different starting point. The relationship between the four standards and nine aspects of public education are depicted in Figure 17.1.

Fundamental Preconditions

The fundamental preconditions are a secure learning environment and social safety net. Addressing the fundamental preconditions is paramount because the assumption that the family and the society outside of the school building will resolve social dysfunctions that children bring to school is too often not valid. If a school is not successful in attaining the preconditions of providing a secure learning environment or mending holes in the social safety net, it is not likely that the other aspects of public education will be successfully

FIGURE 17.1

The Relationship Between the Four Standards and
Nine Aspects in Public Schooling

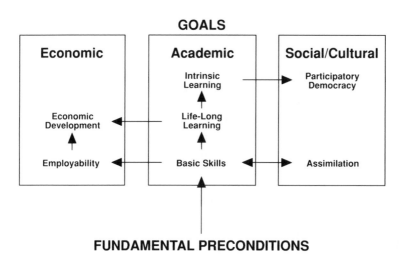

achieved. This point is emphasized in the Figure 17.1 by the fact that the fundamental preconditions undergird the three goals.

Secure Learning Environment

A school must provide a secure learning environment. There are four components to providing a secure learning environment: fiscal security, physical security, administrative consistency, and stability within student and teacher populations. Students, teachers, and school building administrators must be assured that the school year will begin with the necessary materials and end without interruption due to monetary difficulties. Secondly, schools must provide an environment that is personally safe, physically secure, and encourages learning for all participants. Finally, a secure learning environment depends upon consistent and stable political and administrative leadership, as well as a stable population of students and teachers.

Inner-city schools are marked by extreme instability on the part of both students and staff. Students move frequently—it is not uncommon to have at least one-third of the student body change school buildings during the course of a calendar year (Chicago Panel 1990). The change in student population is caused by parents moving from apartment to apartment over the course of a year, by alterations in the student's custodial arrangements, or by court-mandated moves if the system uses busing extensively as part of a court-supervised desegregation plan. At the same time, staff in large urban systems also change schools frequently through the exercise of contract-protected seniority rights, personal request, or mid-year staffing changes to match enrollment fluctuations throughout the system.

Instability among the student body and staff undermine both the learning environment in the system as a whole and the safety net of the child. Large systems usually attempt to deal with these problems by trying to standardize the curriculum across their system, however, they cannot standardize the staff's familiarity with the student or the environment of the building. Ways must be found that decrease staff turnover and allow students to remain in a school even if they move from a school's catchment area. Stability is a critical component of providing a secure learning environment.

The prolonged absence of any of the four components of a secure learning environment leads to an erosion of the learning climate. Providing a secure learning environment is also conditioned on the school, or external institutions, fulfilling the social safety net conditions.

Social Safety Net

Public schools are part of the social safety net. They must deal with problems that are not, or cannot be, addressed by other social intervenors—family, church, or social agencies. When students suffer from hunger, poverty, chemical or physical abuse, gang violence, or other social dysfunctions, their learning is interrupted. If a school does not deal with these social problems, their effects can dominate the school community, affecting all students (Ravich 1983). Students in central-city schools are disproportionately affected by these social dysfunctions. In addition, there is a close relationship between the two preconditions, as shown in the figure. If the social safety net functions are not fulfilled, it will be difficult for a school to provide a secure learning environment.

Urban communities are not alone in having difficulty in fulfilling the preconditions for learning. These problems are present in all communities in varying degrees and probably dominate the operating environment of public schools in other marginal communities. However, the magnitude and the isolation of poor minority students in inner-city communities means that solutions are often frustrated by the size of these problems. In addition, the large number of students affected has long-term implications for the nation as a whole. If the preconditions for learning are absent, the goals discussed next, especially academic goals, can only be achieved by a few extraordinary individuals.

Goals

Inductive reasoning was used to formulate the list of goals for public education: Academic, Social/Cultural and Economic. First, a series of hypotheses was formed as to what public school systems are expected to accomplish from observations of current practice, readings of educational history, and the application of economic theory to education policy. These hypothesized functions were then qualitatively tested to determine if they held over time, paying special attention to prominent educational reform reports written from 1887 to 1987 (Rock and Hill 1990). At the end of this process it became apparent that the seven aspects of education fit into three goals, all of which rest on the two fundamental preconditions.

Academic Goal

The academic goal is what many consider to be the primary purpose of schooling and it is the focus of the excellence debate. There are, however, three distinct stages of learning that should be recognized: the attainment of basic skills, life-long learning, and intrinsic learning. Each is a precondition to the previous level. More advanced forms of learning will not be reached if basic skills are not attained. This is shown in Figure 17.1 by the cumulative nature of the academic aspects of public education.

Basic Skills. The function of basic skills is achieved when the learner acquires the skills of reading, writing, and basic mathematics (Ch. 7). Educators do not agree as to the grade level at which these skills are achieved. Some suggest that acquisition of basic skills ends at grade three; others suggest that basic skills are acquired at the end of elementary education. The acquisition of basic skills is defined here as the point at which a person is functionally literate (they are able to follow brief written instructions, can select phrases to describe pictures, and can add, subtract, multiply and divide)—this is the threshold of literacy.

Life-Long Learning. The function of life-long learning refers to the ability to learn new skills as they relate to maintaining, or improving, one's place in the workforce. A person is capable of life-long learning if he or she can use basic skills to acquire more complex work-related skills and knowledge. Learning associated with this function is economically motivated in that acquired skills and knowledge are for occupational advancement.

Intrinsic Learning. Intrinsic learning is the idealized goal of most educators, occurring when a person is learning for personal fulfillment rather than monetary gain. The knowledge acquired for intrinsic learning is for personal, rather than occupational, growth. The knowledge acquired in intrinsic learning is not necessarily valued on the labor market and is primarily sought for the pleasure of the learner.

Social/Cultural Goal

There are are two components to the social and cultural goal: assimilation and participatory democracy. Assimilation is one of the main arguments for a school system that is not segregated by class, race, or income, what is known in the education literature as the common school. In societies that are either experiencing extensive immigration or composed of several distinct ethnic or cultural groups, publicly supported schools are often expected to transmit a shared national culture or identity. Assimilation is the foundation for the higher-order form of this goal—participatory democracy.

Assimilation. In the contemporary United States, the assimilation function includes integrating minority group members into the dominant culture and cultivating respect for cultural diversity while developing a common national identity. It is extremely difficult to assimilate minority and low-income students into the dominant culture due to spatial and economic polarization. Assimilation of African-American students, in particular, is problematic because, unlike Western European immigrants, they have been excluded from the "melting pot." Ogbu (1987) and Washington (Ch. 13) suggest that castelike social structures, as opposed to classlike structures, inhibit assimilation.

The assimilation function includes instilling in the student societal norms and basic social skills, promoting a common national identity, while recognizing and respecting cultural diversity. Most educators stress the role of public schooling in promoting good citizenship, or participating in an active democracy. This differs from assimilation in that it requires participation in, rather than observation of, democratic processes.

Participatory Democracy. The most sophisticated non-pedagogical function of public schooling is the encouragement of active citizenship: training students to become participants in national and local governments. This function requires that schools perpetuate democracy by teaching students to exercise their constitutional rights and responsibilities. The function of participatory democracy is a synonym for active citizenship. There is a close connection between this aspect and intrinsic learning because being an active participant in a democracy usually assumes that one is able to process and act upon abstract knowledge and concepts.

Economic Goal

Historically there has always been a close connection between public support for education and economic development. In fact, demands by employers for better-skilled workers and governors' reactions to the restructuring of the American economy appear to be the stimuli for the excellence in education movement and the large increase in educational funding by state governments during the 1980s. There are two sequential aspects to the economic goal: employability and economic development. These stages have been present over time, but the level of learning required to fulfill each aspect has increased as the economy has become more capital- and knowledge-intensive.

Employability. The employability aspect of education requires that schools teach students necessary, but basic, employment skills so that they can obtain entry-level positions (Figure 17.1). In the current economy people are employable at low-skill, entry-level positions when they are able to use reading, writing, and computational skills to follow routine instructions and interact with machinery in highly controlled situations. There is a close relationship between the aspects of basic skills, assimilation and employability (Figure 17.1).

The skills of reading, ciphering and numeracy must be combined with punctuality, the ability to take and follow instructions, and independent work habits—in other words the Protestant work ethic—which are tied to the assimilation aspect of public education. The achievement of assimilation and basic skills, in turn, depends on the fundamental preconditions of education being met (Figure 17.1). A person is not fully assimilated into the dominant culture if they do not play a productive role in the economy, which means that they are at least employable. Conversely, it is difficult for a person to obtain the basic skills if they have not accepted the goal structure of the dominant culture.

Employability does not require that the student be taught the learning skills required to adapt to changing technology, that is the ability to learn over one's lifetime. Life-long learning is more closely associated with the economic development aspect of education.

Economic Development. Schools respond to the economic development aspect of public education when they aid in development of national, state, or local economies. Employers have demanded higher levels of learning over time, and the education system has always attempted to respond to those demands. The economic development function requires that prospective workers (current students) be given a combination of general learning and specific training to meet the changing demands of employers (Hill and Rock 1990).

Public education plays an important role in economic development because of the risk that educational investments made by either workers or employers will not pay off. Students are often unwilling to pay the full cost of their education for two reasons. First, teenagers are notoriously present-oriented and can act irrationally (in economic terms) by not giving adequate weight to the impact their current decisions will have on their earnings over their working lives. Second, education is a human capital investment and, as such, it should be paid for over the useful lifetime of the investment, in other words over the person's worklife. But education is not a physical asset, like a house or a lathe, and cannot be attached by a bank and resold for non-payment. The public, therefore, must either make the current payments (and be paid back through the tax system), guarantee the loan, or live with the result of individuals underinvesting in their educations.

Employers are reluctant to invest in training that is not specific to a worker's current job, sometimes called generic learning, because it is of value to other employers and they will lose their investment if the employee quits. This type of training corresponds to life-long learning in today's economy. Yet it is life-long learning that is most closely associated with economic development. In today's economy, schools successfully achieve the economic development aspect of education when students achieve basic skills and are able to learn in formal and informal settings over their productive lifetimes (Figure 17.1).

AT WHAT GRADE LEVEL ARE THE NINE ASPECTS OF EDUCATION ACHIEVED?

Due to the cumulative relationship between the nine aspects of public schooling, it is apparent that not all are attained at the same grade level. The fundamental preconditions must be present in all school buildings. The preconditions are more difficult to achieve in junior high and high school buildings than in primary school settings.

Elementary schools are the proper place for students to achieve basic skills and the assimilative aspects of public education but they must be either reinforced in secondary settings if students achieved them in elementary school, or taught once again if they were not achieved (Figure 17.2). As mentioned above, attainment of these aspects of education depends on the secure learning environment and social safety net aspects being fulfilled. This is not meant to imply that intrinsic learning is irrelevant to elementary settings. To the contrary, it is nearly impossible to separate attaining basic skills from intrinsic learning at this level. After all, America's approach to education policy rests on the premise that there are many ways to teach and learn and certain children may best attain basic skills in settings that stress what appear to be rudimentary forms of intrinsic learning, such as an approach that is rich in music or the arts. The proper place to attain basic skills and assimilation is at the elementary level and elementary schools should be held accountable for these aspects of public schooling.

The other five aspects of public education are best addressed at the secondary level (Figure 17.3). These five aspects, especially life-long learning and economic development, are the focus of the excellence debate. What is missing from that debate, however, is the recognition that learning at the secondary level has four preconditions (the two fundamental preconditions and the assimilation

FIGURE 17.2

The Relationship Between the Three Standards and
Four Aspects in Public Elementary Schooling

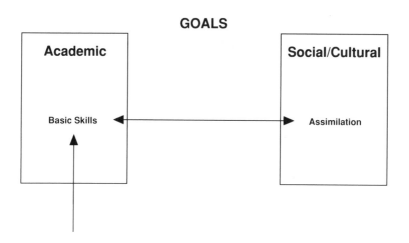

GOALS

Academic	Social/Cultural
Basic Skills	Assimilation

FUNDAMENTAL PRECONDITIONS

Secure Learning
Environment   Social Safety Net

FIGURE 17.3

The Relationship Between the Four Standards and
Nine Aspects in Public Secondary Schooling[a]

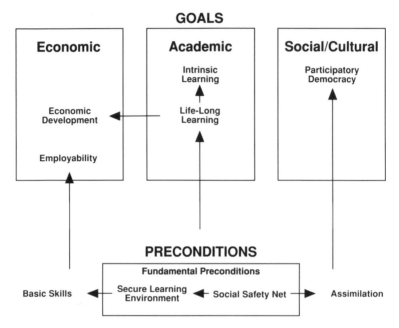

Note: [a] Secondary schools include middle schools, junior high schools, and high schools.

and basic skills aspects of education) and that these preconditions are necessary, but not sufficient, for achieving the other five aspects of education. If reforms are made in elementary schools that correspond to the path of interaction in Figure 17.2 and are not continued in secondary schools, the effort will not necessarily be wasted but the results will be seriously degraded. This model of the goal structure of public education is used to evaluate two prominent theories of educational failure.

TWO THEORIES OF SCHOOL FAILURE

Policy discussions about the perceived failure of inner-city public education have focused on the classroom, not the school. By asking what can teachers do differently and what can teachers get their students to do differently, policy makers do not threaten the existing structure of public education. Chubb and Moe (1990) indicate that this mind-set maintains the fiction that teachers are easily substituted for one another. This also implies that there is top-down control in the provision of educational services, thereby maintaining the roles of both state educational bureaucracies and local school systems' central administrations. The building principal remains an administrator under this logic and cannot become either a leader or a team-builder. This top-down controlling mind-set is a major part of the problem, and it is suggested that the opposite approach be tried: successful schools are made by implementing school-wide strategies designed to address the fundamental preconditions and the three goals of education that result in successful students. This is a bottom-up strategy for invigorating schools and it requires team work on the part of the school's administration and its teachers.

The traditional approach to educational reform imagines that policy makers—be they state legislators, state educational bureaucracies, local school boards, or central administrations of local school systems—act as if there was a direct link between policy and the classroom. The school, as an organizational whole, is assumed to be of little or no consequence. This is foolish. Chubb and Moe (1990) echo Eberts (1984) who found that many teacher union contracts attempted to maximize the autonomy of the teacher within a school, thereby limiting the role of the building administrator. This goal will interfere with meaningful reform because as an organized whole the school determines a child's learning environment.

The two theories of failure considered in this section, the theories of cultural differences and secondary discontinuity, recognize the role that factors external to the classroom play in school failure. The inability of public schools to compensate for differences in class, race, and culture are the focus of these theories, making them especially relevant to inner-city schooling. These two theoretical approaches to education lead to the conclusion that the school building is the critical focal point for reform because the teacher and his or her classroom are part of a larger social body—the school.

Cultural Difference Theory

Just as cultural compatibility is one credible explanation for school success (Coleman and Hoffer 1987), cultural incompatibility is one explanation for school failure (Vogt, et al. 1987, p. 286). The theory of cultural differences suggests that children have more difficulty learning in school when the culture in their homes is different from the culture in their schools. It is important to note that this is a theory of cultural difference; children whose home culture is different from that of school are not culturally deprived. If educators perceive that differences in culture render the student inferior, then not only will schools fail but they and the students have little hope for success.

Cultural difference theory, grounded in anthropology, is useful if one is seeking to explain why non-white, and/or non-middle-class students, "fail" (i.e., achieve below grade level). The argument for cultural difference theory postulates that "relatively narrow-range mismatches or incompatibilities between the natal culture of the children and the culture of the school at points that are critical for school success" may cause school failure (Vogt, et al., p. 276).

If differences in school and student culture adversely affect school success, then it follows that recognizing and compensating for these differences through educational practice will allow schools and students to succeed. However, specific educational practices that compensate for cultural differences between school culture and a particular home culture (Filipinos in Hawaii, for example) may not transfer to other cultural groups (African-Americans in central cities, for instance). Each set of cultural incompatibilities is hypothesized to be unique to a particular group. Therefore, it is unreasonable to expect that a universal educational strategy can correct for all cases where differences in culture result in school failure. This theory results in two important conclusions. First, there is no single best method of education. Second, a common school that does not recognize cultural differences among a multi-cultural student body is doomed; the same holds for a school with a student body that spans a wide class spectrum.

Secondary Discontinuity Theory

The cultural difference theory offers an explanation as to why non-white, non-middle class students fail in schools. It does not explain why schools are failing for some students in a particular cultural group and not for others. That is, schools are not failing for *all* poor and non-white students. Ogbu (1987) suggests that cultural difference theory does not recognize that some students from different cultures perform well in schools without modified educational strategies.

His comparative work on minority student performance in school suggests that, although important, differences in language, dialect, communication style, cognitive style and style of interaction cannot solely explain poor performance of minority students. Rather, the "nature of the history, subordination, and exploitation of the minorities, and the nature of the minorities' own instrumental and expressive responses to their treatment" is the main factor which differentiates successful from less successful minority students (Ogbu 1987, p. 317).

Discussion

These two theories of educational failure suggest that society and schools (as social institutions) contribute to the poor educational performance of minorities. The social contributions include the denial of desirable jobs, social position, and equal access to a good education to certain categories of minorities. Schools, in turn, reflect societal norms regarding minority performance by lowering educational expectations of minority students, assigning a disproportionate number of minority students to special education classes, and giving the impression that cultural differences indicate cultural deprivation, thus creating a climate of failure.

The premises of cultural difference and secondary discontinuity theories help explain why schools must address the social safety net aspect of education. These two theories suggest that when schools fail to anticipate or treat social dysfunctions, students fail. In fact, socially "inappropriate" behaviors, or dysfunctions, may become stereotypical and expected, thus cultural differences become interpreted as cultural inferiorities. Secondary discontinuity theory suggests that when minority students begin to exhibit inappropriate behaviors, they are more quickly transferred to special education classrooms than non-minority students and teachers begin to hold lower academic expectations. These minority students are then predisposed to lower achievement due to the lower expectations of the academic setting in which they are placed.

Clearly the theories of cultural difference and secondary discontinuity are related to the assimilative aspect of public education. These theories suggest that successful schools recognize the different learning styles and needs of students from various ethnic, racial, and class groups. In so doing, schools are expected to alter policies regarding educational practices and strategies in order to provide minority students with the skills required to succeed in the classroom. If schools do not attain this assimilative aspect, both theories would suggest that they did not sufficiently alter their policies. In addition, schools may actually be denigrating, rather than respecting, the different cultures of their students. The secondary discontinuity theory would further suggest that successful minority students in failing schools manage to adopt the school's culture at the expense of their own cultural heritage.

These two theories of school failure are limited, however, because they recognize only two of the nine aspects of public schooling, social safety net and assimilation. If schools do not address all nine aspects they are failing. What follows is a discussion of "successful" schools. The principles of successful schools will be examined in light of these theories of school failure and the aspects of public schooling discussed above.

SUCCESSFUL SCHOOLS

There are at least two methods of determining the characteristics of successful urban schools. One is to identify existing successful schools and compare their characteristics with both successful and failing schools. This method is used by the authors of what has become known as the effective schools literature. The second method is to transform a school that is failing, determine if the changes are successful, and document their subsequent effects. The second method was undertaken in the New Haven (Connecticut) Schools Project [NHSP]. What follows is a discussion of these two methods of identifying successful schools.

Effective Schools

Ronald Edmonds is credited with first synthesizing the similarities of effective urban elementary schools into five attributes of effective schooling (Edmonds 1979). These five attributes are: (1) strong administrative leadership, (2) high expectations for children's achievement, (3) an orderly atmosphere conducive to learning, (4) an emphasis on basic skill acquisition, and (5) frequent monitoring of pupil progress. While other researchers have modified, or added to this list, the basic attributes of effective urban elementary schools have not deviated far from Edmonds' original synthesis (*Phi Delta Kappan* 1980; Tomlinson 1980). Each of the five attributes is discussed below in relation to the nine aspects of public education (Table 17.2).

Strong administrative leadership, as defined in the effective schools literature, identifies the principal as the person responsible for providing clear goals. The current educational administration buzzword for this is "having a vision." In addition to creating this vision, the building administrator is responsible for transforming goals into a purpose to be shared by all adults and students associated with the school. This assumes that the building administrator has control over all aspects of organizing and maintaining the school.

Strong building leadership is the third component of a secure learning environment and it has been identified by Chubb and Moe (1990) as missing from most school buildings. In fact, Chubb and Moe emphasize that it is the very structure of the governance of public schooling that prevents principals from becoming leaders:

TABLE 17.2

Comparison of the Nine Aspects of Public Education with Two Theories of School Failure and Two Programs of School Reform

Aspects of Public Education	Cultural Difference	Secondary Discontinuity	Effective Schools	New Haven Schools Project
Secure learning environment	a	a	administrative leadership orderly atmosphere	school climate
Social safety net	a	recognizes	high expectations	employ parents and parent involvement
Basic skills	recognizes	a	emphasized frequent testing	academic programs
Life-long learning	a	a	a	c
Intrinsic learning	a	a	a	b
Assimilation	recognizes	recognizes	a	parent involvement and academic programs
Participatory democracy	a	a	a	b shared governance
Employability	a	a	a	attendance discipline b
Economic development	a	a	a	c

Notes: a. Overlooked.
        b. Preparation for attainment in secondary school.
        c. Premature, relevant to secondary school.

Source: Author.

It may be better to think of the public school principal as a lower-level manager than as a leader. In the public sector, the principal is a bureaucrat with supervisory responsibility for a public agency . . . Many of the important structural decisions are also taken by higher authorities . . . and many of the important personnel decisions are imposed from above as well . . . Most of the high-level rhetoric about the importance of the principal's leadership role is essentially just that. (p. 56)

Building administrators are just as Chubb and Moe describe—they are administrators and cannot become leaders until they are freed from oppressive central administrations and school district-wide policy bargaining on the part of teachers' unions.[2]

The second of Edmonds' attributes—having high expectations for children's achievement—is communicated to students and parents through policies established and implemented by teachers and administrators. These expectations may include, but are not limited to: high attendance rates, teachers making regular classroom and homework assignments, students completing those assignments, and using school hours for instructional purposes. By holding students to high standards of school-related behavior, teachers and building administrators "create a climate in which students place a higher value on achievement" (Hallinger and Murphy 1986, p. 332). The theory of secondary discontinuity rests, in part, on low expectations. By not permitting students to adopt the belief that due to their race they are less able, school personnel increase the likelihood that average student performance will improve. This is part of the social safety net aspect of education.

The third attribute of effective schools—creating an orderly atmosphere conducive to learning—is similar to establishing and maintaining high expectations for students. Both attributes directly affect the school environment and collectively place responsibility for success on students, teachers, and administrators. An atmosphere that is conducive to learning includes feeling personally safe and secure, quiet and orderly school corridors, limited vandalism, and few classroom interruptions from administrators or parents. Such an atmosphere does not suggest that classrooms be void of noise—instead they should be filled with noises that come from students sharing and working together. This is fully consistent with the definition of a secure learning environment.

The fourth attribute emphasizes the acquisition of basic skills. Students cannot learn what is not taught; therefore, if the emphasis of the curriculum is to be on basic skills then the curriculum must center on their acquisition. This attribute, more clearly than the other four, is specific to elementary education where basic skills are taught and are presumed learned. The spirit of this attribute is also related to secondary schools. Students, at any grade level, cannot pass content-oriented competency tests, perform well on standardized achievement tests, or become life-long learners if they have not acquired sound grounding in basic skills in their primary schools. The basic skills aspect of the academic goal clearly responds to this attribute.

The final attribute of effective schools is frequent monitoring of pupil progress, based on the content of what is taught in the classroom. It is necessary to monitor the success schools have in meeting their goals. This suggests that establishing a clear purpose, shared vision, or agreed on goals is but half the battle. Monitoring efforts toward attaining those goals is also essential for effective schooling. That is, frequent evaluation informs staff, parents, and students about their collective progress toward attaining the shared school vision. Two reasons for monitoring are presented in the discussion on policy recommendations.

The central hypothesis in the effective schools literature is that by altering the characteristics of a school to approximate those of effective schools, a failing school can become successful. This hypothesis, however, has yet to be proved. The effective schools approach provides an incomplete recipe for successful reform of inner-city schools because it addresses only one of the academic aspects of education, basic skills, and only parts of the two necessary foundational preconditions, the leadership component of the secure learning environment and student expectations of the social safety net.

The next section discusses the efforts of the Yale Child Study Center in transforming two failing schools into successful schools. The NHSP is one model of a comprehensive approach to inner-city elementary education. Time is spent discussing the NHSP not because it is the only approach but because of the way in which it addresses all four of the aspects of education that are relevant to elementary education and the way in which it establishes the preconditions to meet all five aspects that are relevant to secondary education.

The New Haven Schools Project

In 1968, James P. Comer and others initiated a school improvement plan in two failing New Haven, Connecticut, public elementary schools (Comer 1980, 1987). The intent of the plan was "to try to change the social system [in the school] by applying the principles of behavior[al] and social science" (Comer quoted in Brandt 1986, p. 13). The composite standardized achievement scores for the two schools were among the lowest in the city. Students in the two schools were both unmotivated and disruptive in class. Serious attendance and behavior problems existed.

The clinical (Yale Child Study Center) and educational (New Haven School District) staff who implemented the plan hoped to "establish a systematic long-term collaborative exchange between a clinical center . . . and two primary schools" (Comer 1980, p. xiv). The intervention project focused on three critical schooling components: school climate, the academic program, and staff development. In addition to modifying the critical schooling components, the project's goals included developing shared responsibility for decision making among parents and staff and developing an organizational relationship between the clinical services at the Yale Child Study Center and the educational program at the two elementary schools.

Several key groups were formed to achieve the project's goals. Most groups included school personnel, parents, and at least one person from the Child Study Center. The schools' administrative teams gave overall guidance to the project and were responsible for day-to-day school management. The schools' committees (curriculum, personnel, and evaluation) interviewed and selected staff to develop and oversee curriculum and evaluation programs. In addition to participation in these groups, some parents became part-time school employees as parent aides and participants in social and educational activities.

Through these efforts the NHSP transformed the environment of the two failing schools into successful schools. When applying the theories of school failure and the nine aspects of public schooling to the project, it becomes clear why these two schools became successful. The NHSP responded to both the cultural difference and secondary discontinuity theories of school failure. In so doing, the project directly addressed four of the nine aspects of public schooling identified: secure learning environment, social safety net, basic skills, and assimilation (Table 17.2). The program also established the preconditions required for meeting the five aspects of secondary schooling: life-long learning, intrinsic learning, employability, economic development, and participatory democracy. Achieving these aspects requires that the reforms be continued in the secondary schools that the children attend. The NHSP is a holistic approach to revamping inner-city education.

The NHSP brought parents into the decisionmaking process and hired them as part-time school employees. This action addressed three aspects of public education. First, the divergent cultures of the students' families were brought into the school, thereby improving communication between parents and school personnel. This allowed the schools to address issues of cultural differences among parents, students, and staff. When the schools systematically engaged parents of students with behavioral problems, they addressed failures identified by the theory of secondary discontinuity and improved a major component of the school's learning environment. In addition, hiring unemployed parents as part-time school workers helped to fulfill an important part of the social safety net. The participatory democracy aspect of education for the student must be fulfilled at the secondary level but involving parents in the design and execution of the program introduces this aspect of education into the family. While this does not directly address the civic component of the participatory democracy function, it does permit parents and students to feel the power of democracy.

Two of the three critical schooling components identified by the NHSP, school climate and the academic program, directly relate to three of the nine aspects of education identified. By responding to concerns of school climate, the NHSP addresses the secure learning environment function. By bringing together parents and school personnel, the NHSP created a larger school community that could address most of the non-pedagogical aspects of education by involving parents in the education of their children. For instance, students' attendance and behavior improved, addressing the aspects of assimilation and basic skills. The curriculum committee addressed the academic program component which, with appropriate planning, related to the basic skills aspect of the academic goal and established the precondition for meeting the life-long learning and intrinsic learning aspects as the child advances into secondary school.[3]

The two theories of school failure discussed here have a clear implication: there is no best way in which to educate all students. The NHSP is one successful approach to educational reform for disadvantaged students. It is an approach that is rich in resources and it changed the way in which resources were used in two elementary schools. In addition, the NHSP looked at the school as the functional unit for change—not the classroom or the school district's central administration. There must be other approaches that will be just as successful as the NHSP but have not yet been tried. Incentives must be put into place to encourage schools, which are the supply-side of the educational market, to experiment with various strategies for school improvement. It also means that incentives must be put into place that will change principals from being building administrators into leaders and to change the focus of reform from the classroom to the school as a functioning unit. The dilemma faced in the United States is in attempting to explain why the NHSP has not been widely imitated in other districts. This is just another way of stating the second question raised in the introduction to this chapter: Why has the system not reformed itself?

COMPETITION AND THE COMMON SCHOOL

Witte (1990) identifies the core of the debate over allowing greater competition in the provision of public schooling: it is essentially normative. The debate, according to Witte, is less about the desirability of competition *per se* because competition in the provision of public schooling is merely an instrumentality. Instead, the debate is about which of the seven aspects contained in the three goals of public schooling are valued and about the weight placed on each of these aspects. There is no objective right or wrong in this normative debate. There are, however, large differences about what are the desired outcomes for public schooling.

Witte discusses two of the four core values that shape this debate. First, there is a value placed on increasing average educational achievement (called "excellence" in the current education wars). This value emphasizes the connection between one aspect of the academic goal, life-long learning, and the economic development aspect of public education. Those that emphasize average achievement place a strong value on efficiency—getting the largest social return from public investments in education, while down-playing distributional consequences. The second value emphasizes the distributional, or equity, outcomes from public educational spending.

What is interesting is that both of these normative values ignore the preconditions to meeting the various aspects of education. Those that favor excellence stress the top-down imposition of exit standards for students. Those that favor equality tend to emphasize equal provision of resources (what economists would call inputs), again in a top-down manner. This value is based on the social/cultural goal of education but it is a perversion of that aspect of education. Education should be evaluated on outcomes, not inputs. Children of the disadvantaged could be hurt if a high value is placed on equality of educational inputs because supplemental funding required to meet the social safety net aspects of public education could be denied. Neither the mix of inputs nor the way in which public education is governed is necessarily questioned by those who value excellence or equality.

Excellence does not imply competition (Boyd and Kerchner 1988). In fact, the first wave of reform generated during the 1980s was anti-competitive because it was based on mandatory improvements through such devices as competency testing of students and teachers and variegated secondary school diplomas. Chubb (1988) concluded that such reforms are doomed to fail because no real incentive is offered to improve the performance of schools. Chubb goes further by concluding that reforms which are consistent with the current system of school governance (he calls this democratic control) are at odds with reforms that will improve student achievement. Chubb and Moe (1990) argue that the dichotomy between equity and efficiency in school reform is false because the current system of democratic control of education hurts both efficiency and equity and that competition (they refer to this as market control) is required.

Coleman (1990) discusses the other two values: choice versus educational egalitarianism. Coleman views choice as a valued outcome in its own right. Choice as an independent value does not relate to any of the nine aspects of public education identified in this chapter. Coleman contrasts that value with another: egalitarianism in American education. This second value is more consistent with the social/cultural goal of public education than is a strict distributional equity. Coleman states that American society places a high value on parents making choices that shape the social, moral, and intellectual development of their children. In fact, these choices embody a large part of parenting.

At the same time, Coleman states that American society places a high value on egalitarian education and that the educational system should be the foundation of a mobile social structure; that is, a structure "not fragmented by divisions imposed by segregated or exclusive upbringings" (p. x). The common school, a school open to all regardless of their class or income status, appears to be valued in its own right as the expression of the democratic ideal of egalitarianism. Is the common school a legal reality and a social myth in the modern metropolis?

Decentralized urban residential patterns, where social classes and racial groups are spatially isolated, have destroyed the possibility of existence of a common school—if it ever existed. Residential polarization, protected by the legal demarcation of city and town boundaries, means that the common school cannot exist in the modern metropolis. Schools in different districts will have unequal resources as long as educational funding is based on property taxes and they will not have similar mixes of students. The reality of residential segregation and income polarization reduces the legal reality of the common public school to a social myth.

Metropolitan area-wide school districts are required if the value of the common school and educational equity is to dominate under the current form of democratic educational control. There are two arguments against this approach to providing more equity. First, the political costs will be great because choice, which is highly valued, will be reduced significantly. Parents will resent the loss of control over an important part of their children's lives. Loss of control over their children to the state will cause resentment to increase, thereby reducing the efficacy of local government.

Orfield and Monfort (1989) noted that the only substantial gains in racial integration have been made under court-ordered metropolitan area-wide desegregation plans. They conclude, however, that political reality restricts most plans to limited reverse busing across district lines and the introduction of racially balanced magnet schools open to students from different school districts.

The second argument against metropolitan-wide school districts is that they can only bring about equity in per student funding, the provision of educational inputs and not equality in results or outputs. Under democratic control metropolitan schooling will most likely result in more unequal attainment, coupled with a degradation in average attainment.

The spatial expansion of school districts would create near monopolies that would, in all likelihood, reduce efficiency and be marked by deterioration in the attempt to meet the goal of excellence. Deterioration will occur because competition among suburban districts for the children of well-educated parents will stop and local pressure for excellence will diminish as parents feel that their ability to influence an enormous educational bureaucracy is undercut. In other words: the increased size of the district will diminish the relative effectiveness of a parent's voice, thereby weakening loyalty to the public school system, resulting in increased exit from that system (Hirschman 1970).

It is also reasonable to expect that there will be equity losses. A large democratically controlled school system will tend to produce schools that use uniform teaching methodologies based on one-way communication from the central administration to the classroom teacher. This means that the role of the school and its staff will be diminished. The problems discussed earlier in this chapter under cultural difference theory and the theory of secondary discontinuity will be exacerbated. The result will be a marked deterioration in the school's learning environment for minority group members.

Chubb and Moe (1990) present a dichotomous view of school control—there is either democratic control or market control. Weiss (1990), on the other hand, identifies five sources of control where different primary agents tend to use one mode of control, market forces being one source of control. Her point is that under the current form of governance no single form of control dominates and, therefore, no single agent dominates decision making. Weiss describes school governance as a "tapestry" of control where democratic processes are protected by a series of Jeffersonian checks and balances. Control, according to Weiss, is the "ability of one actor to limit the range of acceptable behavior of another actor, in order to achieve some policy objective" (p. 92).

Weiss makes a critical assumption in her depiction of control in public schooling—she assumes a just regime; that is, the politics of a public school system are transformational not transactional (see Ch. 9). Transformational politics in public schooling implies that schools are primarily used to enhance the life-chances of students. Transactional politics in public schooling takes place when control is used to enrich an individual or particular group. Weiss dismisses transactional politics when she states that "[i]f control granted for policy purposes is turned to personal ends, that constitutes a distortion of the control relationship" (p. 92). If the dominant use of control in the current system of governing large school systems is transformational, then the current disaggregated system of control is justified—if not, then a movement away from democratic control is warranted.

The Achilles' heel of large inner-city public school systems is the local board of education. If the board is dominated by transactional political concerns, without effective countervailing power from other interested parties, the system will fail.

School boards, in general, are weak political institutions. This is so for six reasons. First, board elections typically attract a small fraction of the electorate. Second, board members are either unpaid or poorly paid. Third, in large cities election campaigns are very expensive compared to their direct financial reward. Fourth, service on boards is demanding and time consuming due to the complexity of responding to directives from state legislatures, courts, federal bureaucrats, and the occasional parent or voter—which increases the opportunity cost of service. Fifth, membership on a school board will increase a politician's name recognition but usually to the detriment of the politician's career, this will further weaken the attractiveness of board service in large cities. Sixth, school boards have typically become deeply involved in the administration of the public school systems by voting on, or commenting on, individual contracts and personnel assignments within the system. The further a school board gets from policy, and the more deeply it is involved in administration, the more tempting transactional politics becomes and, typically, the more venial are the outcomes of the board's actions.

The combination of the expense of running for a large city's school board and low voter turnout increases the power of those with a direct economic interest in the outcome of board elections. The expense of campaigning means that contributions from groups, such as teachers and trade unions and vendors, are important. Low voter turnout implies that organized groups of voters, usually employees of the system along with their friends and families, can play a large role in the election. These conditions, coupled with the potential influence board members have on incomes and contracts, are a recipe for transactional politics.

While the above statements can typify all public school systems, large systems are more susceptible due to their size. In effect, there are scale economies at work in the politics of schooling. Political investments, hopefully just in the form of campaign contributions, are concentrated on a few individuals running for office and those individuals influence a very large amount of contracts. This makes the cost of organizing and financing campaigns worthwhile. At the same time the sheer size of the school system promotes what Olson (1982) calls "rational ignorance" on the part of many voters and parents. If voters, or parents, believe that the influence of their vote, or active use of their political voice, will not change the outcome of educational practices in their community, not spending the time and effort to become fully informed about the actions of the board is rational. This is especially true if the board is infrequently covered by the media, as is often the case. The larger the system, the more rational is ignorance on the part of the voter. Voters will only participate if the information is cheap to obtain, and that occurs when school politics become dominated by easy-to-understand issues, such as racial issues and total budget amounts and property taxes. Unfortunately, under democratic governance the voter is the only check on the board.

To simplify matters a brief examination follows of who benefits under the current system of governance of large urban school districts and who would benefit under a market system.

Under the current system the dominant beneficiaries are those who have a vested interest in school board politics and those who can protect their incomes and power through school boards. There are three groups of primary beneficiaries: politicians and their contributors, administrators, and other school board employees. Board members benefit because they can have extensive influence over the disposition of contracts and the purchase of services for the system, such as insurance, fuel, and building materials. It is expected that their contributors also derive economic benefits from the current system. In many large urban systems construction trade union members and non-teaching personnel, such as janitors, gather extremely large benefits from the system due to their contributions to the campaign funds of board members. As institutions, the teachers' union benefits from the existence of large school systems because the union's power is based on acting as a countervailing source of power to a large bureaucracy. If the bureaucracy is weakened, the union's purpose is also weakened. It is therefore in the union's best interest to minimize the role of the school building as the organizing unit and concentrate on the school system as a whole. The existence of a large school system lowers the union's average organizing and bargaining costs and maximizes the union's sphere of influence. Ineffective teachers also benefit from this system because their positions are protected through their contracts.

The only way of finding congruence between the normative values of efficiency, equity, parental control over their children, and egalitarian education—in other words a system that stresses transformational politics and fulfills all nine aspects of education—is to change the nature of control over the educational system. A new system of governance would be one that increases the roles of parents as consumers on the demand side of the education market and innovative teachers as providers on the supply side, yet retains legitimate aspects of democratic control. A purely market-based system would increase the power of these two groups but would denigrate the social/cultural aspects of public education. It would also tend to downplay the role of the taxpayer who is, after all, paying the bills. In addition, a pure market-based system of education would not change the allocation of resources to ensure that the foundational preconditions of education are met for the children of the poor.

The work of the NHSP argues for freeing up the supply side of the educational market as well and for making the focus of school reform the school building, not the classroom. Changes in the classroom have a better chance of occurring if they flow from changes in the educational approach in the building.

How Do We Get There?

How can the supply and demand sides of the educational market be freed up and, at the same time, retain democratic control over the educational system? What can be done to foster cooperation among students, families, and school personnel to improve the educational performance of children of color and of all students who attend inner-city public schools? Surprisingly, cooperation will most likely be encouraged by the injection of limited competition in the provision of education services. Limited competition will help empower parents, changing some who Darling-Hammond et al. (1985) call inactive choosers of education to active choosers. The act of choice forces parents to become more directly involved in the educational performance of their children and, less directly, in the success of the school.

Yet, unfettered competition is not desirable either. The problem with unbridled competition is that parents may choose schools based not on the efficiency of the school but on the class and income composition of the student body. If choice is made on the basis of the socioeconomic composition of the classroom, polarization will be reinforced. Darling-Hammond's work on the Minnesota experiment in educational choice and an earlier test in Alum Rock, California (Bridge 1977) indicate that unlimited choice, often called voucher plans, encourages segregation by class and race. A market-based system of educational reform must offer incentives to overcome polarization as a way of meeting the social/cultural and fundamental preconditions of education.

Spicer and Hill (1990) recommend limited choice. They state that the benefits of competition can be realized if choice is allowed, but restricted to an identified geographic area that is racially and economically balanced. This form of limited choice will promote school selection on the basis of the performance of the school and less on the socioeconomic composition of the student body. If such restrictions are not imposed, the primary beneficiaries of choice plans will be the children of the middle class, and racial and economic minorities will remain isolated.

There are six critical elements to the Spicer-Hill proposal.

First, students will be provided with vouchers to pay for their education; those vouchers would not be supplemented with private funds.

Second, the supply side of the market must be freed by allowing teams of teachers to form their own schools. If the schools do not succeed they should close and the school's employees should not have the contractual rights to move into a successful school to preserve their paychecks. Moreover, the school system should not shuttle students into the failed school.

Third, there should be frequent testing and performance monitoring of each school. There are two objectives for this testing. The first is to test the school as a means of providing parents with information about schools in a geographic area. This would be accomplished by testing a random sample of students in the school and reporting results by school and grade level. The importance of random selection, by the testing authority, is that it downplays the role of standardized testing in the curriculum. The second type of test would be performance testing of each child based on what is being taught in the classroom. The purpose of this test is diagnostic, to help aid the student's learning.

Fourth, the schools and the pool of potential students must be geographically restricted so that information about each school is easily obtained and selection is made on performance and not the socioeconomic characteristics of the student body. It may be necessary for these catchment areas to cross municipal boundaries to achieve balance. This cross-over is necessary in responding to Orfield's observations that diversified districts are a requirement to effective school desegregation.

Fifth, counselors should be readily available by a regional education office to inform parents and students of their choices. The theme, purpose, and educational philosophy of each school would be explained, as well as objective and subjective indicators of the performance of the school. This would be similar to the program offered by the Cambridge, Massachusetts, school system (Alves and Willie 1990; Chubb and Moe 1990; Elmore 1990).

Sixth, all children have a right to attend a school and will continue to under this plan but they will not have a right to attend a specific school. A child may be denied entrance or readmittance to a school for disciplinary or academic reasons. If there are large pools of unattached students (which reportedly does not occur in Cambridge), the education of pools of students could be put out to bid by the relevant public educational authority (the term school board is intentionally not used because it is hoped that they disappear).

Two points can be viewed as extensions of the Spicer-Hill proposal. The state could provide supplemental vouchers for difficult-to-educate, or difficult-to-place, children. Learning disabled, non-English speaking, pregnant, and chemical-dependent children are examples of groups that are more expensive to educate. (Students that have the objective characteristics of being "at-risk" are frequent targets of supplemental spending and this recommendation builds on that precedent.)

A public authority, such as a state school board, county or municipal government can offer bonuses as incentives for schools meeting socially motivated inclusionary goals. Such bonuses could provide a strong incentive for schools to be more balanced racially and socially. If the educational catchment areas do not cross municipal boundaries, the state must facilitate cross-boundary enrollment for the purpose of achieving racial and class balance. The incentives will be greater if the educational providers could profit for actively recruiting underrepresented students into their student body. This means attracting whites into predominantly black schools and blacks into predominantly white schools.

A competitive system will also allow for social safety net functions to be incorporated into the school building and integrated into the curriculum. If a system of restricted competition is put into place, states could allow schools to bid for social service funds. In fact, social service providers could be part of the educational staff as was the case with the NHSP. This would explicitly recognize the social safety net function of urban public schools. Again this does not mean that this will be the case in every school. It depends on the educational philosophy and marketing strategy that the school adopts.

A program of limited choice would allow for democratic and market control of public schools and increase the relative power of the three most important groups of stakeholders in the educational system—students, their parents, and teachers. In addition, the Spicer-Hill proposal would allow teams of teachers to develop educational programs that will satisfy all nine of the critical aspects of public education. This will not necessarily be a less costly plan for public education when compared to the current system. It will be more efficient and will be a major factor in healing the racial divide in U.S. metropolitan areas.

This chapter has not provided a recipe for educating African-American children, or poor children or children of inner-city residents. It provides a recommendation for educating children in a metropolis based on the premise that there is no one best way to educate all children. This recommendation does, however, address the educational problems faced by children of color and poor children in two important respects: (1) it recognizes the critical role of the foundational preconditions and social safety net aspects of public education; and (2) it identifies the impediment transactional politics puts in the way of democratic control of public education. This is a policy recommendation in which all children will benefit but children of color and children of the poor should benefit the most. Limited choice on the demand side of the educational market, coupled with a competitive group of suppliers, will make educators responsive to the needs of the child; currently it appears that the child is responsive to the needs of either the bureaucracy or to the contributors to political campaigns.

NOTES

1.   Historically there have been ten aspects of education that are important to policy makers. The tenth, labor absorption, was dropped from this chapter because it is not relevant in today's economy. During times of labor surplus, schools were used to remove young people who were potential workers from the labor market, thus preventing them from competing with adults for scarce jobs. In fact, compulsory school legislation was passed during times of extreme labor surplus. Hill and Rock (1990) and Rock and Hill (1990) discuss this aspect of public education.

2.   District-wide bargaining on wages and benefits on the part of teachers unions is congruent with the notion of educational reform. Bargaining over approaches to teaching, hiring, and other policy issues is an impediment to reform.

3.   If reforms are not continued into secondary schools, there will be back-sliding in the progress students have made. This would be similar to the results observed in Head Start programs. Evaluations of Head Start indicate that real gains are made among disadvantaged children but these gains are subject to the "fade-out" phenomenon—where the gains made by children in compensatory preschool education programs deteriorate after the second year of schooling (Nariello, et al. 1990; Reynolds 1990).

REFERENCES

Alves, M. and C. Willie. 1990. Choice, decentralization and desegregation: the Boston 'controlled choice' plan. In *Choice and control in American education*, Vol. 2, *The practice*, W. Clune and J. Witte, eds. New York: Falmer.

Boyd, W. and C. Kerchner. 1988. Introduction and overview: education and the politics of excellence and choice. In *The politics of excellence and choice in education*, W. Boyd and C. Kerchner, eds. New York: Falmer.

Brandt, R. 1986. A conversation with James Comer. *Educational Leadership* 43(5):13–17.

Bridge, G. 1977. Citizen choice in public services: voucher systems. In *Alternatives for delivering public services*, E.S. Savas, ed. Boulder, CO: Westview.

Chicago Panel on Public School Policy and Finance. 1990. *Public school databook, school year 1988–89*. Chicago.

Chubb, J. 1988. Why the current wave of school reform will fail. *The Public Interest* 90 (Winter):28–49.

Chubb, J. and T. Moe. 1990. *Politics, markets and America's schools*. Washington, DC: The Brookings Institution.

Coleman, J. 1990. Choice, community and future schools. In *Choice and control in american education*, Vol. 1, *The theory*, W. Clune and J. Witte, eds. New York: Falmer.

Coleman, J. and T. Hoffer. 1987. *Public and private high schools*. New York: Basic Books.

Comer, J.P. 1987. New Haven's school-community connection. *Educational Leadership* 44(6):13–16.

Comer, J.P. 1980. *School power: implications of an intervention project*. New York: The Free Press.

Council of Great City Schools. 1987. *Challenges to urban education: results in the making*. Washington, DC.

Darling-Hammond, L, et al. 1985. *Tuition tax deductions and parent choice*. Santa Monica, CA: Rand (R-3294-NIE).

Eberts, R. 1984. Union effects on teacher productivity. *Industrial and Labor Relations Review* 37:346–58.

Edmonds, R. 1979. Effective schools for the urban poor. *Educational Leadership* 37:15–27.

Elmore, R. 1990. Choice as an instrument of public policy: evidence from education and health care. In *Choice and control in American education*, Vol. 1, *The theory*, W. Clune and J. Witte, eds. New York: Falmer.

Hallinger, P. and J. Murphy. 1986. The social context of effective schools. *American Journal of Education* 94(4): 328–55.

Hill, E. and H. Rock. 1990. Education as an economic development resource. *Government and Policy (Environment and Planning C)* 8(1):53–68.

Hirschman, A. 1970. *Exit, voice and loyalty*. Cambridge, MA: Harvard University Press.

Jaynes, G. and R. Williams, eds. 1989. The schooling of black americans. *A common destiny: blacks and american society*. Washington, DC: National Academy Press.

Nariello, G., E. McDill and A. Pallis. 1990. *Schooling disadvantaged children: racing against catastrophe.* New York: Teachers College Press.

National Commission on Excellence in Education. 1983. *A nation at risk: the imperative for educational reform.* Washington, DC.

Ogbu, J. 1987. Variability in minority performance: a problem in search of an explanation. *Anthropology and Education Quarterly* 18(4):312–34.

Olson, M. 1982. *The rise and decline of nations.* New Haven: Yale University Press.

Orfield, G. and F. Monfort. 1989. *Status of school desegregation 1968–1986.* Alexandria, VA.: National School Boards Association.

Phi Delta Kappan. 1980. Why do some urban schools succeed? Bloomington, IN.

Ravich, D. 1983. *The troubled crusade.* New York: Basic Books.

Reynolds, A. 1990. Sources of fading effects of pre-kindergarten experience. Annual Meeting of the American Educational Research Association, Boston, April 16–20.

Rock, H. and E. Hill. 1990. The functions of public schooling: a historical perspective. Cleveland, OH: College of Urban Affairs, Cleveland State University.

Spicer, M. and E. Hill. 1990. Evaluating parental choice in public education: beyond the monopoly model. *American Journal of Education* 98(2):97–113.

Tomlinson, T. 1980. The troubled years: an interpretive analysis of public schooling since 1950. *Phi Delta Kappan* 62:373–76.

Vogt, L., C. Jordan and R. Tharp. 1987. Explaining school failure, producing school success: two cases. *Anthropology and Education Quarterly* 18(4):276–86.

Weiss, J. 1990. Control in school organizations: theoretical perspectives. In *Choice and control in american education*, Vol. 1, W. Clune and J. Witte, eds. New York: Falmer.

Witte, J. 1990. Introduction. In *Choice and control in american education*, Vol. 1, W. Clune and J. Witte, eds. New York: Falmer.

18 Race and the American City: Living the American Dilemma

LAWRENCE F. KELLER

Few topics raise as many research problems or elicit such deep emotions as race and the city.[1] *The American Dilemma,* Gunnar Myrdal's memorable comment on race relations in the United States in the 1930s and 1940s, has indelibly marked the American city and stubbornly refused to leave the American agenda.[2] Unfortunately, neither the city nor race relations have been coupled with concerns over governance, even though any lasting resolution of the dilemma requires sensible urban policies at both the state and national levels, and the ability of local government to create and sustain long-term courses of action. An effective urban policy, that is, a consistent set of goals and procedures for dealing with urban areas, can only be developed within an effective system of local governance.

Governance is the establishment of direction for a political system. Governance includes the ability to set long-term goals for a political community and to pursue these goals consistently. Goals should be related to both declared values, what the community determines to be important, and to the long-term viability of the community itself. Finally, the public sector, under a system of governance, should be characterized by institutions, that is, organizations representing and inculcating community values, such as neighborhood public schools and libraries did historically (Selznick 1984).

In essence, governance is the creation of a legitimate communal agenda and the institutional means by which to implement that agenda. The theory and nature of governance is more fully developed in Chapter 9. This chapter centers on the evolution of urban politics and the consequences for race relations. The consequences represent in great measure the failure to create governing systems that provide governance.[3]

In fact, rather than being institutionally a system of governance, many if not most local governments are embedded in an "ecology of transactional games." The games revolve around "political deals," with the political actors engaging in a web of political exchanges. Historically, the actors practiced the adage of "you rub my back, I'll rub yours." Selected politicians, and their business and other allies, have been personally enriched while the quality of life was reduced for many citizens.

Reformers consistently criticized these transactional systems on ethical and moral grounds; however, in good times the system could seem to work as various ethnic groups were integrated economically into "middle class" American urban society.[4] Integration only occurred during prosperous times because transactional politics needed a growing pie to share with newcomers. Problems arose when the pie did not grow. The system could not function well in those circumstances. Politicians often fell out over the distribution of the dwindling "spoils." Most importantly, the system had no governance capacity, the ability to create a long-term agenda for increasing the quality of life for the average citizen.

In contrast to the steady, long-term, public-oriented policy direction pursued through governance, many American metropolitan regions are spatially and racially fragmented. The fragmentation promotes self-interested politicians who seek particularistic (serving one or only a few interests) and often personally enriching ends. The danger to the modern city is the manipulation, both covertly or overtly, of the racial issue for narrow political ends. Politicians appeal to the racial and sexist prejudices of sects and ethnic groups. The appeal can establish a firm local electoral base for such politicians, especially when city councils are elected from wards or districts, because of the spatial separation of races at the neighborhood level.

Sadly, the politics of race can be, and increasingly are, played ably by politicians of all races, certainly a chilling prospect in the contemporary American central city. The politics of race are a deadly variation on transactional politics with issues phrased in and decided on in terms of race. Casting all contemporary problems in racial terms fortifies the polarization of people and power that is spatially present in the metropolitan areas. Such a system can only craft policies that tend to exclude rather than include. Thus, the policies only provide benefits to those individuals and groups with power, leaving those without power outside the system. As a result, those with the most pressing social and economic problems in the city (e.g., the underclass of the central city) are least likely to be invited to have their problems considered. The underlying problems of the city that create and sustain the underclass are not dealt with at all.

Light can be shed on why this dismal prospect came to be by examining the evolution of race relations, local politics and the city. Each will be addressed, assessing the outcomes of their confluence in the city. The examination illuminates some interesting twists to the "conventional wisdom" about the current political scene. A "clear-headed" examination is needed if America is to implement governance and politically resolve the moral issues of race.[5]

NATURE OF THE RACIAL ISSUE: POLICIES IN SEARCH OF MORALITY

Race is at root a moral issue. Economic issues such as the distribution of wealth are indeed intertwined with political issues of race. The economic issues are correlated with race because large numbers of African-Americans are poor, reflecting in large part a history of racism; but the economic issues in part transcend race. In essence, economics goes more to defining the solution rather than defining the problem. Increasingly, members of all races have been placed at economic risk since the early 1970s. As noted in Chapter 10 on black mayors, the economic decline is largely beyond the control of the fragmented local politics. Attempting to treat problems of race as an economic issue may raise demands for equal economic treatment from other groups and even individuals harmed by recent economic trends. As a result, the issues of race may be submerged if not ignored. Race is a moral issue, which if not treated as such an issue, confounds public policy generally and urban economic policies specifically.[6]

Race is a moral issue because it involves all Americans. Americans must recognize their racist past and eliminate its legacies in the contemporary society. This is not a call to empower a group politically along the lines of transactional politics. In contrast, it requires a long-term dedication to eradicating the ills of those deliberately shouldered aside in American society.

Political mobilization of African-Americans will not achieve the goal. Political mobilization was quite helpful in demonstrating the patently moral obscenity of regimes such as Bull Connor's in Birmingham. Mobilization is less useful in maintaining long-term policies to eradicate racial inequalities. In fact, political mobilization along racial lines may raise perceptions among all races that rewards are being politically driven in a transactional system. What is needed for the long term is a community effort to "level the playing field" that was racially tilted historically. Sufficient political awareness must be maintained to ensure that those occupying high positions are dedicated to the long-term task. This requires coalitions that cross racial and economic divisions. Unfortunately, development of the modern city complicates the creation and maintenance of that kind of a coalition in local politics.

THE AMERICAN CITY: ROMANCE WITHOUT LOVE

Similar to their feelings and actions about the farm, Americans often extol the virtues of central cities but prefer to live elsewhere. The ambivalence complicates governance of the metropolis and forestalls creation of a national urban policy. As a result few people like the contemporary city in all respects, fewer understand and even fewer care to think about it. (See Downs 1990, for a most insightful analysis of America's twisted urban vision.) History, as former Supreme Court Justice Holmes noted in describing the law, is indeed more illuminating than tomes of logic. Contemporary policy analysis and the general American tendency to deal with the "here and now" often distort the politics by overlooking the social context and its history.

The phrase "classical" American city may be an oxymoron if not a contradiction in terms. Large American cities arose during the American industrial revolution in the late 1800s and early 1900s. These cities were concentrated in the Northeast and Midwest regions. In some cases, industrialization transformed existing commercial cities such as New York and Boston. In other cases, relatively new cities, such as Cleveland and Milwaukee, were created. The result was a cluster of very dense, large cities dominating their region, or in the words of early researchers of the city, "creating hinterlands dependent on the city."[7] The origins and the form of central cities can be traced to these industrial cities of the Northeast and Midwest. They are "classics" as it were of American urban development.[8]

Contemporary technologies structured the early industrial city. Thus, the need of the steam railroad for gentle grades and the task of transporting thousands of workers to their places of employment without the automobile mandated diverse high-density cities. Industrial plants clustered in areas with gentle or no grades, such as rivers and lake fronts. Getting thousands of employees in and out of the plants demanded short distances from residences to plants. Jacobs' later prescription for diversity at the neighborhood level (1961) was remarkably similar to the resulting urban spatial pattern that mixed firms, offices, commercial enterprises and residences. For most purposes the city was a walking city, with extended journeys made on trolleys within and inter-urbans or railroads outside the city (Warner 1987 [1968]).

Immigrants from overseas and surrounding countryside were socialized into the employment mainstream of industrial America, usually through an ethnic community's ties to city government (through political patronage) and to industry (with the use of the foreman system in the early private sector) (Bodnar, et al. 1981).[9] Politically adept miscreants and even criminals were tolerated if not venerated, such as the infamous Boss Tweed of New York City (Mandelbaum 1990). The machines fitted transactional politics to the ethnic social organization of industrial cities.

The decentralized nature of the highly politicized administration within the political machine fit with the social reality of the ethnic neighborhood. In essence, each ethnic group had a share of public jobs through the neighborhood representative of the machine. The nexus of place and power in America was spatially rooted in the ethnic city with its distinctive neighborhoods.[10] Urban immigrants were enriched by the growing national industrial economy (though certainly not to the extent the early entrepreneurs were) and politically aligned (not integrated) through the transactional political machine.

Economically, the American city was indeed the *Private City* (Warner 1987). Immigrants from the hinterlands and from overseas were attracted to the city because of the promised personal economic gains. To a great extent, the main function of city government was to build the infrastructure for corporations which permitted, in turn, citizens to pursue their personal enrichment. As Toffler (1970) noted, schools became important training experiences for corporate workers, inculcating timeliness, obedience and perseverance—all characteristics of docile workers in authoritarian settings. (Also, see Bowles and Gintis 1976.)

Blacks were recruited in large numbers into the American city during the First World War (Kusmer 1976).[11] Racism severed the ethnic connection between community and employment for blacks (Bodnar, et al. 1981). Blacks were not accepted as a legitimate ethnic group. Consequently, as Bodnar notes, they were forced to seek opportunities as individuals in a city organized on the basis of ethnic groups.[12]

Public employment was also narrowly prescribed for blacks. They did not obtain the extensive organizational franchises enjoyed by other groups, such as the Irish and Italians. They were not an important element of the pre-World War II political machines because of the general racism. White ethnic groups often controlled city departments, such as the police or sanitation (Callow 1976). In contrast, poor white groups were deliberately pitted against blacks in many of the industrial cities within both the public and private sectors (Chafets 1990). Blacks, or at least some black politicians, did obtain some power within the political machine. However, the black community remained socially segregated and possessed few public rights in the general community.[13]

Both the private and public sectors underwent significant changes. Sadly, none provided help to black Americans. In fact, the changes complicated attempts to improve race relations generally and the plight of blacks specifically until the 1960s and later.

Early industrialization quickly concentrated production in large corporations. Management of these agglomerations remained centered on the foremen who hired, fired and directed production. However, these arrangements were highly inefficient in utilizing the new technology and controlling the large labor force. Taylor created a "scientific management" theory that centralized authority in a planning department (see Montgomery 1982 for discussion). The department utilized scientific knowledge to maximize efficiency in organizing the plants, depriving foremen of most of their authority.[14]

Scientific management severed the connections between the ethnic community and the factory just as large numbers of blacks arrived in the industrial city. Clearly, the large numbers did not diminish racism in the city. However, the large numbers did increase the community presence significantly, which may have created greater employment opportunities for blacks, as a group, had not the foremen system been terminated.

The rise of a more technologically complex economy also required professional credentials for jobs in the private sector. These requirements have increased the most in the newer industries that have replaced traditional industrial firms in the American city. One result has been to reduce job opportunities for blacks and other poorer groups.

The pattern of neighborhood/ethnic alignment with public employment also underwent two dramatic changes in the first two decades of the twentieth century. Neither change altered the plight of black Americans.

First, in some cities a political reform movement gained control of the political system. The reformers implemented the council-manager form of city government. (See Ch. 9, for details on that system.) The system was only temporary in some cities, such as Cleveland, which adopted the council-manager form of government in 1924 but abandoned it within ten years. In other cities such as Cincinnati, the system still continues. In any event, the outcome was to transform the politics of some cities in the early parts of the century and to change many of those cities in which the reformers could not change the form of government.

In reform cities, and over time even in many non-reformed cities, jobs in the public sector were allocated on the basis of merit and ability. Merit and ability were universally thought to be indicated by professional credentials, such as college degrees. The need for professional credentials often denied blacks and other poorer groups access to public employment. Though some cities such as Chicago continued to allocate public sector jobs through the patronage of an ethnic-based political machine, most cities regardless of form of government increased the professionalization of public agencies. The reform cities had a more appropriate structure for governance, but the poorer groups were excluded from meaningful participation.

Secondly, Americans began to migrate from the central city to the surrounding countryside. The movement began in some cities with the advent of more effective transportation systems such as the electric streetcar (Warner 1962). Large numbers exited from the central cities after the Second World War. The movement, one of the largest urban migrations in history, was fueled by generally favorable economic conditions and national government housing, highway and tax programs. These programs helped provide new housing for a rapidly growing white middle class. The outcome was a complicated metropolitan pattern, with proliferating governmental structures whose boundaries seldom matched anyone's perceptions of community. For many suburbanites, the "city" was a good portion of the metropolitan area. However, political structures did not match the boundaries of the expanded "city" available to the suburban middle class.

The movement to the suburbs coincided with the movement of Americans to the South and West. The only central cities whose populations increased after World War II were confined, with few exceptions, to the so-called "Sunbelt" cities. The exceptions were either idiosyncratic economic developments such as the case of Boston, or the creation of metropolitan governments which expanded the area of the central city, such as Indianapolis.[15] Several rather undesirable outcomes of these processes set the stage for current politics and issues of race in the classical cities of the United States. Not only were metropolitan areas in the Northeast and Midwest spatially segregated in terms of power, class and race, so were sections of the country. Increasingly, the more recent professional members of the middle class moved west and/or south, leaving the suburbs less capable of attacking the problems of class and race that increasingly demand a metropolitan solution.

In all parts of the country, suburbanization polarized people and fragmented public authority. Place in urban America had both racial and power connotations. The setting was not favorable for dealing with the issue of race.

RACE AND THE CITY: SEGREGATION ON A GRAND SCALE

Ironically, race relations are one part of American life that has witnessed considerable change during the twentieth century and yet has not satisfied either the majority or minority. As increasing numbers of blacks enter the middle class and the mainstream of American economic life, many remain in an underclass (see Ch. 13). Paradoxically, integration appears to have increased both tolerance and racism. American individualism can facilitate close relations among individual members of races while still maintaining group prejudices. Race does indeed remain an "American dilemma."

The lack of viable traditions around race relations handicaps efforts to deal with racism. Blacks were the one group who did not choose to come to the United States. The singular status of blacks was reflected in the preferred solution to the race problem during the first 100 years of independence. The solution was to liberate the slaves and return them to Africa. Slavery was indeed perceived as incompatible with liberty. However, integration was not an alternative. The movement to repatriate African-Americans was organizationally spearheaded by the American Colonial Society.[16] Lincoln illustrated the American ambivalence over race with his concern that slavery not be established in the emerging states of the West and that the American union be preserved. Aid to African-Americans was secondary to the preservation of the union. The "Jeffersonian" settlement of the West, that is, free men achieving independence by owning land, excluded African-Americans whether slave or free.

After the Civil War the concern for slavery ended and with it most of the concern for black Americans (see Ch. 13). While many Northern cities boomed with industrial development, the South remained a third-world society marked by repressive politics and stagnant economies.[17] The blacks' only release was to migrate to the north. The migration was relatively steady after the Civil War but became a torrent during and between the two world wars. The South seldom regretted the exit of blacks and Northern cities seldom welcomed their entrance.

Until the end of the Second World War, most northern cities maintained if not enhanced racial segregation. In contrast to the open practice of the American South, the segregation of the North was informal. But both were often deadly earnest in their racial barriers.[18] However, the 1960s marked the turning point in race relations as the children of the Affluent Society acted on the premise that equality and justice were not clandestinely footnoted parts of the American dream but were indeed meant to apply to all.

Ironically, just as many whites began fighting for more equality among the races, and a president elected from Texas quoted Martin Luther King, Jr. in Congress, some blacks erupted in riots in major American cities.[19] As in the case with blacks following the Civil War, presidential assassination played a major role in American politics.[20] One hundred years after the liberation of the slaves, the nation remained committed to solving the problems of race relations, but was more divided than ever though not only across racial lines. Economic and sociological class problems complicated race relations, deadlocking progress. Worse, political leaders failed to emerge who could attack the moral as well as the political and economic dimensions of the problem or who were interested in reforming local government for the task.

RACE AND THE MODERN CITY: INTEGRATION FOR THE FEW, POVERTY FOR THE MANY

By the end of the 1970s, more blacks than ever moved into the mainstream of American economic life. Indeed, some of the highest-paid performers in both sports and entertainment were black and an increasing number of political offices even in jurisdictions with a plurality of non-black voters were filled by blacks. Affirmative action might not have achieved all of its goals, but it did elevate blacks into higher levels of American organizations, both public and private. However, as in the case of the "glass ceiling" that Kanter noted with women in organizations, many blacks perceived that progress was stalled when the top posts were considered.[21]

More telling was that complete integration did not occur. Roles in movies and plays were not cast without regard to race. Nor was dating across racial lines generally accepted. Often, individual blacks who entered integrated institutions were treated well in general but bereft of a meaningful social life. Attempts to engage in meaningful social interaction could incur a strong reaction and was often either not attempted or sustained. Integration became an economic more than a social reality.

While upward mobile blacks found integration to have some rather ill-defined upper limits, many blacks never entered the game. They were mired in an unrelenting poverty similar to what their predecessors faced in the post-Civil War South. The reality was psychologically more difficult to face because the mass media presented an image of general affluence. Sociologically, black communities within industrial cities became more chaotic as the upwardly mobile blacks who had earlier been forced to live in segregated areas now had a greater range of choices (see Wilson 1987). The migration weakened many community institutions.

Racially, the metropolitan areas of the classical cities became fragmented. A black underclass was trapped in the central city while the surrounding suburbs became more integrated. However, the integration was limited, both spatially and economically. Even if members of both races lived in a city, they tended to concentrate by race rather than be evenly distributed throughout the city. In the central city, the underclass included members of both races though they were spatially separated to a large degree.

Spatial separation by income and race reflected some basic attitudes. The white middle class believed that segregation was wrong and racial discrimination inappropriate. However, they disagreed with affirmative action and most programs for integration. In essence, most Americans could readily identify the racial policies and practices they opposed, but were hesitant about, if not resistant to, notions of complete integration.[22]

Recent economic changes have increased the difficulty of integration. Many in the white middle class are slowly entering the lower classes with a large segment of the lower classes joining the underclass (Bluestone and Harrison 1982 and 1988). Tragically, many of the whites in the underclass share many of the racial feelings of lower classes in the post-Civil War South. Combined with the ambivalence over integration generally and affirmative action specifically, the result was a vote for more conservative racial public policies at the national level. At the local level, the fight was over a shrinking pie, often leading to increased transactional politics based on the protection of shares in a shrinking pie.

Concurrent with the change in economic fortunes, urban politics began to emphasize pursuit of special interests and group politics. For many cities, this was a continuation of "politics as usual." For others, it was a return to pre-reform politics. For example, several cities have attempted to abandon the council-manager form of city government because some managers refused to endorse commercial projects that had political backing by important interests, but whose long-term economic viability was questionable. In essence, the developments were often important for the local business community and selected political leaders. Political evolution undercut professional government and promised to polarize urban politics in an era of increasing scarcity. The tragic evolution was promoted by both academic theories as well as the self-interest of local politicians.

POLITICS AND THE CITY: INTERESTS AND DRIFT

The capacity to govern, so vital for the long-term well-being of a polity, is an ignored feature in academic theory on the public sector. It is most neglected at the local level. Instead the concern remains focused on representing interests and groups in the central cities. Thus urban politics are perceived as a contest of interests and groups with little regard for policy coherence, the longer term and even the health of the general community. All feeds transactional politics.

Fewer academics focused on the suburbs, especially the smaller cities. Presumably, the various groups and interests were to be represented. The actual outcomes of "who gets what when" were more assumed than researched. Seldom was a serious concern expressed for issues beyond the immediate legal city. The metropolitan area, the functional city, was largely forgotten. The impression of urban politics created by these lines of inquiry in political science, public administration and economics was one dominated by critically important elections because they determined representation.

Others pursued studies of public policies from a managerial perspective, appraising policies on the basis of cost effectiveness. Many of these studies used national datasets and at best indirectly measured the local political setting. The prescriptions often called for more national policies or increased funding for selected programs.

Another group from traditional public management, or a generic management school, emphasized more efficient management. Borrowing extensively from the private sector, management researchers believed that management could be improved in spite of transactional politics. It was assumed that service delivery was improved by more effective policies and efficient management regardless of the local political configuration or the spatial dispersion of race, class and power in the metropolitan area.

Governing was seldom perceived as a distinct integrative endeavor. In other words, most academics dismissed notions of transformational politics, seeing calls for morality as political rhetoric based on middle-class rule. Discrete activities—representing interests and groups, creating more effective national policies and implementing more efficient local management—were typically termed government. These activities are often divorced from an understanding of the evolution of the American city and race relations. They were almost certainly removed from everyday life and incapable of comprehending the governmental decisionmaking apparatus in that life.

The unfolding of the city, race relations and political studies indicated separate if not diverging tracks. As a result the contemporary American city is poorly equipped to grapple with the continuing American dilemma over race or the emerging economic class structure. All promise to make future progress more difficult and attempts at change more contentious.

CITY, RACE AND POLITICS: CLASS, PLACE AND POLARIZATION

The divergence has several outcomes. Politically, leadership is limited by the dominance of transactional politics. In fact, many of the most capable leaders of all races either refuse to or are excluded from entering local politics. In terms of race, segregation of the underclass and the continuation of upper limits of integration are promoted. In terms of governance, few have strategic visions and few institutions, either formal or informal, exist for implementing the visions. The city is faced with mounting social and structural problems with few weapons for the battle.

In many cases, political coalitions have formed around politicians who could mobilize crucial business interests.[23] Bolstered by the Reagan initiatives around public/private partnerships, the coalition of politicians and large developers has dramatically if not successfully transformed downtown development (Elkin 1987; Frieden and Sagalyn 1989). However, other sectors of the cities are often poorly dealt with if considered at all.

As the problems of the city increase, elections are dominated by candidates who call for innovative programs loosely connected with past initiatives. Typically, the candidates also denigrate professional management, calling public servants "bureaucrats." The constant changes in policies and management focus on short-term, often symbolic, problems. Problems such as racism which require long-term policies are ignored.

Concurrently, party influence continues to wane. Candidates for public office, especially highly visible executive offices, use city posts as personal stepping stones to higher public offices. In pursuit of visibility and electoral ambition, some elected officeholders eagerly sacrifice the service delivery capacity.

They embrace if not create alliances with interests who can finance their future ambitions (and style of living) and who need their approval for particular projects.

In essence, the local political process is dominated by transactional politics, a system of exchange for future favors (Burns 1978). This system fits well with representation by group and race which legitimate the participation of interests in public decisionmaking that centers on particularistic goals. Public policies revolve around "projects" rather than the quality of community life.

Many of the same outcomes occur in suburban cities, even those with growing economies. Small groups often control the elective political offices. In fact, many suburbs operate personal versions of small-scale political machines, typically centered on an elected chief executive. Others continue in the reform tradition with relatively strong city managers but with little ability to interface with the larger urban community or to even effectively cope with problems of class and race spilling over from the larger central cities.

If Americans do not refocus the divergent paths of race, governance and the city, urban America may experience rapid decay. Increasingly, most urban "citizens" lack a sense of community, a coherent social and political reality. Instead, they perceive a hodge-podge of polities and policies with little overall sense of a long-term direction in the public interest. The metropolitan area is marked by "complex drift," an enervating form of "the ecology of games" so well described by Long (1962). In an ecology of games, services and products are provided through a variety of self-regulating systems. Thus, newspapers pursue what they consider news in specific ways and financial institutions invest according to common processes. Without formal coordination among the diverse activities, purposes are accomplished and the larger community enriched. In complex drift, the status quo of the larger community is "locked in" by the fragmentation of community and the pursuit of self-interest.[24] Thus, public and private sectors continue along traditional lines, drifting in spite of the mounting problems. The drift makes it difficult to cope with, much less surmount, the social and racial problems that determine the quality of life in the local community.

BUILDING THE FUTURE METROPOLIS: VISIONS AND TRANSFORMATIONS

American cities can mobilize considerable resources, human and monetary, that can be focused on ameliorating if not solving the American dilemma. The changes will require that different leaders be recruited into the political system who seek a public interest rather than a political career. Being non-career officials, they need professional administrators as partners in governance. Appropriately trained professional chief executives such as city managers can best support the "amateur" politics that are necessary for transformational leadership.

As Bill Hansell, executive director of the International City Management Association, astutely recognized, transformational politics are the foundation of reform government. Professional government generally and reform government specifically, will only work if they are supported actively by a core public leadership practicing transformational politics (Hansell 1988). The new leaders must be part of a coalition that meaningfully involves talent from all races. Furthermore, an effective coalition will span the fragmented jurisdictions of the modern city.

The spanning can align public authority with perceptions of community as well as encompass sufficient resources for the city to tackle the persistent problems of race. At present, the migration of resources out of the central city deprives that public authority directly confronting problems of race and class of sufficient resources. Only a metropolitan coalition can bring sufficient resources to bear without engendering political conflict among the fragmented governments.

Exclusion of blacks and other poorer groups from employment, especially in higher positions, in both the public and private sector does not just reflect the lack of professional credentials. The lack of, and difficulty in obtaining, professional credentials reflects more than the lack of economic opportunities. To a large extent, the exclusion is a result of an inability to deal with an organizational society.

Sociologically, middle class can be defined as skill in, and comfort with, utilizing institutions for mutual benefit; that is, a middle-class person has a sense of personal esteem and sufficient knowledge about complex institutions to be able to access programs offered by the institutions in ways that also benefit the organization. For example, a good student not only gains an education but improves the operation of the school. Lower class people often lack such skills, sometimes feeling intimidated by institutions and often reacting in a fashion that may benefit neither themselves nor the institutions. Thus, economic policies may not increase life-chances unless they are used to address the lack of ability to utilize institutions.[25] Since governance depends on institutions, inability to utilize institutions inhibits improving the community as well as hindering individual advancement. The creation of self-esteem in the underclass requires educational systems that focus on the "whole" individual. Teachers need to be rewarded for promoting personal growth as well as achieving high levels of test scores.

Finally, with transformational systems of governance staffed by a multiracial coalition of dedicated public officials concerned with the city, professional chief executives who work closely with these public officials and an educational system that promotes personal development as well as acquisition of knowledge, the American city could attack the dilemma of race. The system can pursue "visions" of community through governance and finally bring justice to the troubled centers of American life.[26] All Americans must have "a dream" about justice and equity and the institutional means for bringing those dreams to life.

NOTES

1. Legally, the city is a municipal corporation. Each city is a separate legal entity with its own governing system. However, for most Americans the functional city, that is, the urban reality in which they work and play, is the metropolitan region. Taxes are a pertinent reminder of this fact; the average American pays taxes to 11 separate governments, 9 of which are local to a specific metropolitan region.

Metropolitan regions are composed of a variety of governments not just municipal corporations. The purposes and authority of each vary from state to state, sometimes quite dramatically. For example, the county is the basic unit of local government in Maryland, with school district boundaries coinciding with county boundaries. In Ohio, counties are very traditional administrative subdivisions of the state and thus relatively unimportant local governments. The difference is evident in the governing structure. Maryland counties have councils and chief executives, with some chief executives elected, others appointed. Ohio counties are run by three county commissioners, a very traditional structure that also includes a plethora of independent elected offices such as the county recorder, sheriff, etc. Thus, the term "city" has several possible and quite distinct variations in modern urban America.

In this chapter, city refers to the "functional city," the metropolitan area, unless otherwise noted.

2. In keeping with the American tradition of blaming the victim, the subtitle of Myrdal's work is "The Negro Problem and American Democracy." However, the thrust of his work is not in that tradition.

3. A governing system exercises public authority over a specified area or territory. Governance is the ability to use public authority to craft and implement a long-term agenda dealing with the problems besetting the governing system. Governing may not provide governance though governance cannot be performed without a governing system.

4. Middle class is one of those phrases with a variety of definitions reflecting rhetoric more than analysis. Later, the term will be applied in a sociological sense to interactions between individuals and institutions. Here it refers to families achieving a sufficient income for purchasing parts of the American dream, especially a house and an automobile. More importantly, the heads of the families adopted middle-class mores. The adoption was a double-edge sword; it propelled large numbers of their children into the professional world, starting in the 1950s. Ironically, the propensity to obtain a college education for their children undercut the racist and sexist society that many had desired. The 1950s and 1960s were marked by generational conflict, usually between the children who wanted a more just society, and their parents who had mistakenly assumed education would leave the injustices of American society intact.

5. The public discourse and much of social science is bedeviled by the multitude of definitions of key terms. Politics like power is a key term with many definitions. The refusal to define explicitly such terms easily confuses analysis and in the public discourse, that is, discussions about public affairs, implicit definitions create the appearance of consensus when in reality there may be several conflicting views.

Politics is most relevantly defined according to David Easton's formulation in the mid-1960s (1965). Easton contemplated the function of political systems. He determined they "allocate values," that is, determine what is and what is not important for a society. Unfortunately, American political science focused on describing the process and ignored the values. Thus, governance was scorned and local government was pictured as a pluralist process that should register the desires of all groups and interests according to their political clout regardless of the consequences on moral issues such as race or even the long-term economic health of the community. This view legitimated a transactional perspective on local government, especially the governing of large industrial cities. It is small wonder that more and more of the public is affronted by current policies and have become apathetic.

6. As Harrison and Gorham forcefully note (1990), African-Americans have been hit harder than other groups by the economic changes since the early 1970s. Race is a double whammy for individuals caught in the economic restructuring. Their data demonstrates that the economic problems of African-Americans were best dealt with during periods of economic growth, especially in basic industries.

This can be interpreted as a result of African-Americans concentrated in the classical industrial cities with their "transactional politics." Thus, African-Americans only received increments of growth after the other groups had their share. In times with no growth, they often received no increase. Thus, in Reagan's America with its contracting base of industrial capital in the central cities, African-Americans will probably lose part of their share even if they become more of a presence in the transactional political systems that characterize the central cities. The wealth continues to migrate out of the central city, either out of the country altogether or to the suburbs which are most likely to engage in a transformational political system, that is, governed by professionals who attempt to plan for a longer term and are less concerned with dividing the pie along ethnic lines.

This political dichotomy between suburbs and central cities may explain why affirmative action works best in transformational settings where middle-class blacks advance based on their credentials. It has had less impact in the systems practicing transactional politics.

7. The densities were quite remarkable. For example, Cleveland had a population of 950,000 by 1950 in an area of 79 square miles. Some cities retain high densities, such as Boston and San Francisco.

8. Classic is a descriptive title, noting where most urban institutions, formal and informal, originated. The term does not imply that these institutions are superior or even necessarily desirable.

Some of the structures of the city date to earlier times, even the Colonial era. However, it is noteworthy that city planning began at this time and the form of the central city as we know it dates from this time. For example, streets were rationally numbered, which in some cities such as Denver required renaming streets in a four-county area. (See Scott 1969.)

The urban growth after World War II has followed a different path. Thus, cities founded after WW II, or which grew large then, have a much different pattern of development as well as a different political culture. Even public images are quite different. The second and third largest cities, Los Angeles and Chicago, illustrate the difference along several dimensions, from geographic area to politics.

9. Patronage is the distribution of public jobs through politicians. Elected officeholders determine who will be bureaucrats. The early industrial plant organized tasks under the foreman system. A foreman headed "work gangs" who did a specific set of tasks, such as moving completed steel plates to the shipping section of a plant. The foreman not only supervised the actual conduct of the work but hired and fired. Legally, they were independent contractors and thus helped the company to elude any law regulating employee conditions. Sociologically, the foremen tended to hire from their ethnic community, connecting the early plants to the community.

Frederick Taylor's prescriptions for scientific management centralized work groups under managers. The centralization circumscribed much of the discretion of the early foremen. See David Montgomery, *The Fall of the House of Labor*, for the influence of Taylor's system on industrial plants.

10. Even though the melting pot may not be completely descriptive of early American industrial cities, the groups were intermingled. Jane Addams, in writing about Hull House, the first settlement house in the industrial city, noted the surrounding neighborhoods were a "labyrinth" of nationalities and creeds. In citing her work, Philpott (1991, p. 67) stated, "Despite their inclination to cluster in colonies, members of the various ethnic groups were 'more or less intermingled' in the housing, the workshops, and the public accommodations of the district. The average block had residents of eight ethnicities. No block, nor even one side of a block, was ethnically homogeneous." The most segregated group in all industrial cities, and the only group for whom segregation was justified on racial theory lines, was the black Americans, demonstrating why their claims are morally different from any other group.

11. Blacks had existed in cities from the earliest times. Crispus Attucks is one of the better known. Contrary to conventional views, some of the most prominent citizens in turn-of-the-century Cleveland were blacks (Kusmer 1976). In many trades and occupations, black providers had a predominantly white clientele.

12. Ironically, now African-Americans appear to be seeking a clearer group identity just as many professional Americans, especially those who are first-generation college educated, seek to leave such roots behind.

13. Thus, political and economic leaders of the black community became powerless, dependent upon leaders from other groups. Because of their dependence they could not exercise independent power. The later civil rights revolution of the 1960s came from the black (and white) churches and colleges, not from the black political and economic leaders.

14. Frederick Taylor's conception of science is greatly different from current definition. He referred to what some have called "technology" not science. It is important to note that fact but its explanation is beyond this topic.

15. Columbus, Ohio, is one of the few cities in the Northeast and Midwest that has been able to annex extensively and increase its population over the past two decades. In fact, Columbus is now the largest city in Ohio and is still pursuing an aggressive annexation policy.

16. The history of the American Colonial Society is quite a story. During most of his public life, for example, Henry Clay was president (Peterson 1987). The society founded Liberia with its capital named after an American who helped found the society, James Monroe. The existence of the society and its concern with slavery illustrates the American guilt over slavery and ambivalence about the presence of blacks.

Emancipation raised both political and economic problems. Slaves were economic assets whose emancipation required compensation to their owners. Ironically, after the slave trade was constitutionally closed and the cotton gin made possible the plantation system throughout the South, the breeding of slaves became quite profitable. Prior to the cotton gin, the only cotton that could be processed was grown in the coastal areas. Only the political requirements of the Civil War made emancipation feasible.

17. Repression was aimed at most southerners of all races. However, race was used as an issue to inhibit the formation of a broad coalition among the poor. Martin Luther King, Jr., was one of the few southern leaders who could appeal to both races. It was not surprising that his assassination was part of a conspiracy of a few business leaders.

18. Howard Fast is one of many authors who autobiographically capture the grim side of the ethnic, neighborhood city, especially for blacks. He relates how he was physically beaten by both Irish and Italians because of his Jewish background (even though his family did not practice Judaism). He attempted to join the "white gang" in its annual Halloween battle with the "black gang" in order to gain some degree of acceptance in his neighborhood. He was turned away, which he considered lucky, because in that particular battle, a black youth was captured by the white gang and lynched, partially due, Fast believes, to the press coverage of such events in the South.

Fast notes that most of the battles were tolerated by the police because they did not like blacks who were almost always outnumbered and thus beaten by the whites. However, in this case, the police arrested five members of the white gang who were sentenced to reform school (Fast 1990).

Russell Baker recounts growing up in Baltimore and seeing the blacks celebrate the victory of Joe Louis by becoming visible in the neighborhoods. They left their dwellings in the alleys and paraded through the streets. He notes that after the celebration they returned to their invisibility (Baker 1982). Ralph Ellison captured this element of invisibility in his moving book, *The Invisible Man* (Ellison 1952). Perhaps the most moving account of life at this time in a southern city is Richard Wright's *Black Boy* (1945).

The American dilemma is indeed a deep wound in the American psyche.

19. The choice of descriptor for the turbulence in the black ghettos does reveal the political interpretations of the researcher. In many ways the turbulence was indeed rebellion. The academic writing of the times carried on a fascinating debate over the nature of the turbulence.

20. Presidents who had the ability to control some of the more radical forces while yet pushing for progress, Lincoln and Kennedy, were replaced by vice presidents (coincidentally both of whom were named Johnson) who lacked such skills. Both vice

presidents inherited the office via assassination and because of inept political actions imperiled both their own political careers as well as the direction of race relations.

Neither Lincoln, as noted above, nor Kennedy were particularly motivated initially by concern with improving race relations. However, both had the political followings and skills to cope with such problems. Two other assassinations, those of Martin Luther Kind, Jr. and Robert Kennedy, removed potential leaders who could mobilize political support for dealing with race relations. The result was to set back programs such as affirmative action. The setbacks were unfortunate because they had a much greater change of promoting economic progress of blacks in the industrial economy of the 1960s than in the service economy of the 1980s and 1990s.

21.   Evidence of the emotions such perceptions cause abound around the use of the term "qualified." For many blacks it is not focused on the nature of the position or the abilities of the black candidates, but is a code word for end running affirmative action.

Ironically, the professionalization of American life has increased the ambivalence. Professionals, especially first-generation ones who worked hard to achieve their positions, are indeed supporters of most affirmative action concepts generally but are primarily concerned with the effectiveness of their organization. Thus, calls for qualification ring strongly especially as affirmative action has seldom been coupled with training programs designed to deal with issues of long-term job performance.

22.   Conceptually, opposition to segregation and racial discrimination is a different dimension than support for integration. This is analogous to Herzberg's discovery about motivation. He found that conditions that led to dissatisfaction by their absence, for example, did not lead to satisfaction if present. They reduced dissatisfaction (1966).

Similarly, reduction in segregation and discrimination is not equated by many with integration. Thus, the anomaly of many voters supporting liberal policies ending discrimination but opposing integrated housing and affirmative action policies.

23.   Perhaps one indicator of black progress in local politics is that many of the politicians leading the business/political coalition are black. The "progress" is certainly a double-edged sword, seldom helping the underclass or appealing to the black middle class.

24.   Entropy, the tendency of physical systems to approach a state of equi-finality (all outcomes are equally likely and thus have no organization), is a fitting analogy. Without the inputting of energy in public affairs by those with a transformation ethic and a strategic vision, local systems will continue to fragment into fiefdoms of self-interest.

25.   In the 1960s the Great Society was able to solve the predominant form of poverty at that time. The modal category of poor was the aged. Many of them had skills of interacting with institutions and thus with money were able to obtain the necessary services to improve their lives. In contrast, many of the current poor are part of an underclass, many if not most of whom lack such institutional skills. An infusion of money may not have the same effects with the underclass that it had with the aged in a previous generation.

Similarly, women as a group are better able to utilize affirmative action than are black males. Many women have self-esteem and organizational knowledge; additionally, power in a complex organization is in many ways accumulated and exercised in what many feminist theorists call feminine. Power in an organizational setting gets the results best by enlisting cooperation rather than forcing action. Females often could only get power through such indirect methods in a male-dominated society. Thus, the elimination of sexism may be easier than dealing with many aspects of racism.

26. Many organizational theorists recognize the moral basis of leadership. They build on a tradition started with Chester Barnard. Barnard (1938) astutely notes, based on his experience as an executive in the private sector, that pecuniary motives were not sufficient for an effective organization. Thus, he outlines the "functions of the executive" to include instilling moral purpose into organizational life.

Contemporary theorists such as Peters have updated Barnard to note the importance of a leader creating a vision that enlists the support of members of the organization and imbues their work with importance beyond the immediate task (Peters and Waterman 1982; see also Tichy and Devanna 1986; Kotter 1988).

Similarly, leadership in the local public sector must develop visions about the future community that enlist the support of the public and give meaning to participating in public affairs. Race relations can only be improved by leaders who develop such visions, or in the immortal words of the greatest leader on the "American dilemma," Martin Luther King, Jr., who have "a dream."

REFERENCES

Baker, R. 1982. *Growing up*. New York: St. Martin's Press.
Barnard, C. 1938. *Functions of the executive*. Cambridge, MA: Harvard University Press.
Bluestone, B. and B. Harrison. 1982. *The deindustrialization of America*. New York: Basic Books.
————. 1988. *The great u-turn: corporate restructuring and the polarizing of America*. New York: Basic Books.
Bodnar, J., et al. 1981. *Lives of their own: Blacks, italians and poles in Pittsburgh 1900–1960*. Urbana, IL: University of Illinois Press.
Bowles, S., and H. Gintis. 1976. *Schooling in capitalist America: educational reform and the contradictions of economic life*. New York: Basic Books.
Burns, J. 1978. *Leadership*. New York: Harper and Row.
Callow, A., ed. 1976. *The city bosses in America: an interpretative reader*. New York: Oxford University Press.
Chafets, Z. 1990. *Devil's night and other true tales of Detroit*. New York: Random House.
Downs, A. 1990. *The need for a new vision for the development of large U.S. metropolitan areas*. New York: Salomon Brothers.
Easton, D. 1965. *A framework for political analysis*. New York: Prentice-Hall.
Elkin, S. 1987. *City and regime in the american republic*. Chicago: University of Chicago Press.
Ellison, R. 1952. *The invisible man*. New York: Random House.
Fast, H. 1990. *Being red: a memoir*. Boston: Houghton Mifflin Company.
Frieden, B.J. and L.B. Sagalyn. 1989. *Downtown, inc.: how America rebuilds cities*. Cambridge, MA: MIT Press.

Hansell, W. 1988. The missing ingredient: a credible civic infrastructure. *Public Management* 70:4–5.

Harrison, B. and L. Gorham. 1990. Family incomes, individual earnings, and the growth of the african-american middle class. Washington, DC: Economic Policy Institute.

Herzberg, F. 1966. *Work and the nature of man*. Cleveland: World Publishing Company.

Jacobs, J. 1961. *The death and life of great american cities*. New York: Random House.

Kanter, R. 1979. *Men and women in the corporation*. New York: Basic Books.

Kotter, J. 1988. *The leadership factor*. New York: Free Press.

Kusmer, K. 1976. *The making of a ghetto: black Cleveland 1870–1930*. Urbana, IL: University of Illinois.

Long, N. 1962. *The polity*. Chicago: Rand McNally.

Madelbaum, S. 1990. *Boss Tweed's New York*. Chicago: I.R. Dee, Inc. (reprint of 1965 edition published by John Wiley, Inc).

Miller, Z. 1981. *Boss Cox's Cincinnati: urban politics in the progressive era*. Westport, CT: Greenwood Press (reprint of the 1968 Oxford University Press edition).

Montgomery, D. 1982. *The fall of the house of labor: the workplace, the state, and american labor activism, 1865–1925*. New York: Cambridge University Press.

Myrdal, G. 1944. *The american dilemma: the negro problem and modern democracy*. New York: Harper Brothers.

Palen, J. 1987. *The urban world* (third ed.). New York: McGraw-Hill.

Peters, T.J. and R.H. Waterman. 1982. *In search of excellence*. New York: Harper & Row Publishers.

Peterson, M. 1987. *The great triumvirate: Webster, Clay and Calhoun*. New York: Oxford University Press.

Philpott, T.L. 1991. *The slum and the ghetto: immigrants, blacks, and reformers in Chicago, 1880–1930*. Belmont, CA: Wadsworth Publishing Company.

Scott, M. 1969. *City planning since 1890: a history commemorating the fiftieth anniversary of the American Institute of Planners*. Berkeley, CA: University of California Press.

Selznick, P. 1984. *Leadership in administration: a sociological interpretation*. Berkeley, CA: University of California Press (originally published by Harper Books in 1959).

Tichy, N.M. and M.A. Devanna. 1986. *The transformational leader*. New York: John Wiley.

Toffler, A. 1970. *Future shock*. New York: Random House.

Warner, S. 1962. *Streetcar suburbs*. Cambridge, MA: Harvard University Press.

———. 1987. *The private city: Philadelphia in three periods of its growth*. Philadelphia: University of Pennsylvania Press (reprint of the original 1968 edition).

Wilson, W.J. 1987. *The truly disadvantaged*. Chicago: University of Chicago Press.

Wright, R. 1945. *Black boy: a record of childhood and youth*. New York: Harper and Brothers.

19 Beyond Black and White: Multicultural Understanding and the Sharing of Power

TERRI LYNN CORNWELL and SYLVESTER MURRAY

Nearly a half century ago, Gunnar Myrdal proclaimed in *The American Dilemma* that "the subordinate position of Negroes is the most glaring conflict in the American conscience and the greatest unsolved task for American democracy" (Myrdal 1962 [1944]). Readers of this book may conclude that this task remains unsolved, and that, with countries around the world looking toward American democracy as a model, that unsolved task presents a glaring flaw that must be repaired. The 1988 Report of the Commission on Minority Participation in Education and American Life stated this conclusion even more strongly:

> The credibility of democracy as a vehicle for advancing the hopes and dreams of millions of people in less-developed nations depends on our performance (*One-Third of a Nation* 1988).

The discussion and remedies presented in this book and in the literature on cultural and racial diversity, however, indicate that a growing number of Americans do recognize the importance of full equality and participation for all citizens. This chapter reinforces this goal, recognizes the progress that has been made, however slow and difficult it has been—and continues to be—and offers strategies that help build multi-cultural understanding leading to the empowerment of minorities.

Considering that American society embraced racial *inequity* long before the signing of the Declaration of Independence, the progress in race relations during the twentieth century might be considered encouraging. Increasing discourse on racial issues, particularly during the civil rights struggles of the

356

1960s, firm presidential commitments during the 1960s and 1970s, crucial Supreme Court decisions, and widely discussed academic research have helped pave the way for positive change (Shaw, et al. 1987). The Commission on Minority Participation in Education and American Life highlighted these facts in its report:

- During the 1960s the median income of white families rose by 34 percent after inflation; black family median income rose 48 percent. During the 1970s income growth slowed for all groups but "black median family income tracked closely with that of whites. (p. 7)
- Between 1977 and 1987, average scores for black students on the verbal section of the SAT tests increased by 21 points and scores on the math section increased by 20 points; scores for whites rose 1 point on the verbal test and stayed the same on the math test.
- During the 1970s only 60 percent of blacks between the ages of 18 and 24 had graduated from high school. By 1975, the figure was 65 percent; by 1985, it was 76 percent. For Hispanics, the graduation rate in 1975 was 56 percent; in 1985, it was 63 percent.

Although recent figures indicate a leveling off of educational attainment of minorities, particularly blacks, and increased difficulties in retaining minorities in higher education, it is important to highlight the fact that progress is indeed possible and has been made.

Setbacks—and evidence indicates that some ground has been lost—can be attributed to factors other than changes in attitudes about race relations. The successes of the last 25 years were achieved in a climate of economic growth with low inflation; the political atmosphere favored minority advancement; public and private sector programs targeted at the disadvantaged were adequately funded and well administered; and minority groups had developed a strengthened determination to push for change (*One-Third of a Nation* 1988). Current setbacks should be seen in the light of a weakened economy, shifts in the nature and location of jobs; a changing political consensus, both nationally and within various local constituencies; and the cutback or elimination of many programs that were targeted for minorities.

Despite changes in the economy, lost ground in government support, and the urban nexus of place, power, and polarization, individual attitudes toward race relations in the population as a whole have improved, however slightly, over the last three decades. Comparison of results of 1978 and 1990 Roper polls show that, at the neighborhood level, whites and blacks have grown more tolerant: The 1978 Roper poll of 2,000 people across the country, indicated that 28 percent of whites said they preferred "no blacks" living in their neighborhoods; in 1990 that figure decreased to 21 percent. In 1978, 8 percent of blacks said that they preferred "no whites," while in 1990, the figure was 3 percent. Similarly, the 1990 annual poll of college freshmen by the American Council on Education (Survey 1991) shows an increase in the percentage of students who said it was "essential" or "very important" to "help promote racial understanding" (up to 38 percent from 27 percent in 1986).

To some readers, these figures may seem as if little progress has been made, or, when viewed in the light of highly publicized incidences of racial violence, as if American society is slipping backward. But inch-by-inch progress cannot be dismissed lightly, and greater awareness of these violent incidents may be attributed to society's heightened sensitivity to any racial discord. This chapter is not intended to focus debate on these issues, but to provide reasons why American society must build on successes to move beyond merely modifying the attitudes of individuals toward changing institutions in a multicultural society. Incremental steps, however small, are the foundation of this process, which works toward building confidence in the majority that sharing of power with minorities can be non-threatening. As the process continues, economic and social polarization will become less extreme and inequities based on race, cultural background, and sex will begin to disappear.

The following section describes American society's shift in the direction of multiculturalism as a background for the remainder of the chapter which discusses the process of empowerment, first by changing the individual and then by changing the institution.

THE MULTI-CULTURAL SOCIETY

Although black and white race relations remain a major concern, and the African-American[1] population continues to face more serious problems in employment, health care, and education, the demographics of society are changing so rapidly—with other subgroups facing similar problems—that a shift from a "black and white view" of these issues to a "multicultural view" will become a necessity. In many cases, lessons learned in the black vs. white struggle can be transferred to the multi-cultural arena.

By the year 2000, people of color will be more than 30 percent of the population; Hispanics and African-Americans will each be 13 percent of the population. In a growing number of specific geographic areas the percentages are greater: in California, for example, the white population will be 55 percent; Hispanics, 28 percent; blacks, 7 percent, and Asians, 10 percent (Takaki 1987).

The school-aged population will also change radically by the year 2000. In 1985, 20 percent of the school-aged population was defined as minority; by 2000, 33 percent will be minorities; and by 2020, 39 percent.[2] In cities, the figures are even higher: in 25 of the country's largest cities, half of the public school students in 1989 came from minority groups (Green 1989).

This demographic data obviously predicts changes in the workforce: the white male share of the workforce by the year 2000 will drop to 39 percent (from 49 percent in 1976); the percentage of African-Americans will increase to 11 percent (from 9 percent in 1976), Hispanics to 10 percent (from 6 percent); and Asians, American Indians, Alaskan natives, and Pacific Islanders, as a group, to 4 percent (from less than 2 percent) (Solomon 1990).[3]

These workforce figures, of course, do not provide a picture of the distribution of minorities in individual organizations, where percentages are much lower at the higher levels of the power structure. For example, Table 19.1 shows the percentages of minorities in municipal administration and appointive public service positions in 1987. An appropriate goal for the year 2000 would be to increase the percentages of upper managers comparable to the percentages of

TABLE 19.1
Number of Minorities in Municipal Administration

Minorities in the U.S. Population, 1987	
Black	12%
Hispanic	7%
American Indian	< 1%
City Managers (total: 4,744)	
Black	1.1%
Hispanic	1.6%
American Indian	.2%
Assistant City Managers (total: 1,272)	
Black	3.7%
Hispanic	2.6%
American Indian	.4%
Police Chiefs (total: 6,443)	
Black	1.5%
Hispanic	1.6%
American Indian	.4%

Source: Albert K. Karnig and Paula D. McClain, *Urban Minority Administrators: Politics, Policy, and Style* (New York: Greenwood Press, 1988), p. 6.

minorities in the population. Strategies discussed later in this chapter related to the public sector have also been used effectively in the private sector.

The two important factors outlined above—the movement toward a multi-cultural workforce and the fact that minorities do not currently share management power appropriate to their numbers—are critical to this discussion. But two other facts make the situation even more critical: the entire workforce is shrinking (the baby-bust generation moving into the workforce is smaller than the baby-boom generation), and international competition is increasing. The combination of all of these factors will make the task of recruiting quality job applicants more difficult and compound the stress on institutions already struggling with the changing racial and cultural segments of the workforce. For these reasons, business, educational, and particularly governmental institutions (see discussion in next section) must prepare to go beyond merely tolerating diversity to valuing diversity.[4] Only by understanding and acting on this fact will American society be able to maintain and increase the productivity of its workforce for the twenty-first century.

CHANGING THE INDIVIDUAL

Before institutions can be modified, however, changes must occur in individual attitudes toward differences in race and culture. Throughout the history of America, society has "trained" individuals to behave in certain ways toward people of different races. Over the decades, this training has had a powerful effect on the attitudes and behaviors of whites toward African-Americans, American Indians, and Hispanics, particularly certain Hispanic subpopulations (e.g., Puerto Ricans and Mexicans), as well as the attitudes and behaviors of these minority groups toward whites.

John F. Coffey (1987) has provided a complete discussion of the evolution of what he calls "race training" and American democracy. From the Colonial period, when the white colonists developed and perpetuated public feelings of racial superiority over the American Indians, through the growth of slavery and its inherent racism, to the 1954 *Brown* v. *Board of Education* decision, individuals have been "trained" by society and its institutions to deal with issues of race in very specific ways. During the country's infancy, most Americans "chose to ignore the implications for a democratic society of exclusion and subordination based on race" (Coffey 1987, p. 115). With the emancipation of blacks following the Civil War, the federal government began to change the course of race training, and by the time of the Civil Rights Act of 1964 training to eliminate racism began in earnest.

Despite the progress in race relations during the twentieth century, the Kerner Commission in 1968 reported the existence of "two separate societies"—a statement that caused concerned religious and lay groups to join the federal government in race training and begin to intensify their programs which expanded during the late 1960s and early 1970s. By 1972, the Nixon administration began to court the Hispanic vote, and Hispanic concerns entered race training curricula. During the 1980s, with race training programs becoming more common at the state and local levels, the federal government has been able to concentrate on issues related to age, the handicapped, and sexual harassment.

As the content of race training programs evolved, so did the labels applied to these programs. During the 1970s and 1980s, labels like "human relations," "cross-cultural training," and "group relations" became common. The emphasis of such programs then shifted to issues other than race; individuals were learning "better interpersonal communication skills" or "a better understanding of other cultures." The goal of helping whites accept people of color was not stated, because "resistance to integration of African-Americans, other minority groups, and white women into the mainstream of American life had been so massive that a back door approach to integration had to be developed" (Coffey 1987, p. 122).

Race training was not enhanced in the 1980s by the policies of the Reagan administration, which often supported resistance to affirmative action programs. Furthermore, with the increasing competition in the job market and the tightening economic situation, incidences of racial tension began to increase. But, with the expanded awareness of the increasing diversity of the population following the 1990 census, race training has become training for "cultural diversity": "For many managers, the 1990s will usher in the 'decade of cultural diversity'" (Mandell and Kohler-Gray 1990).

Although all sectors—public, private, nonprofit—will eventually face a culturally diverse workforce, the public sector may be forced to deal with changes sooner and to a greater extent than the private sector. Recent trends indicate that many highly qualified young people do not consider government employment as their first choice. In a 1988 survey of 865 new members of 4 major collegiate academic honor societies (Phi Beta Kappa, for liberal arts students; Beta Gamma Sigma, for business administration; Sigma Xi, for the sciences and engineering; and Pi Alpha Alpha, for public administration) 86 percent did not think that a government job would allow them to use their abilities to the fullest and half stated that most public sector jobs were routine and monotonous (*Report and Recommendations of the National Commission on the Public Service* 1989, p. 179). With most top graduates looking to the private sector as a first career choice, competition for skilled, competent public managers will be particularly difficult as the workforce shrinks; consequently, concentrating on the recruitment, retention, and promotion of culturally diverse minorities in the public sector is essential for increased productivity.[5]

A number of successful strategies that have been used in the public sector to create and enhance a culturally diverse workforce are outlined in the following sections, and many elements of these strategies are transferrable to the private sector. Successful programs in both the public and private sectors move through an incremental process which begins by educating all individuals in the organization about cultural diversity. This "diversity training step" is followed by helping managers to understand how differences based on race, gender, age, nationality, and values influence workplace behavior and how these differences can be managed for more effective group performance. The third step moves the process to the institutional level, where substantial changes can be made to create and enhance diversity at all levels, and power can be comfortably shared by all segments of the workforce.

FROM INDIVIDUAL TO INSTITUTIONAL CHANGE

Educating or sensitizing individuals to diversity is merely the first step in a process that seeks to change the *behavior* of individuals, and changing attitudes and behavior must occur before effecting institutional change. Because the focus of this book is "black and white," this section discusses the movement from individual to institutional change by using race as the focal point.[6]

Changing attitudes and behavior—where *individual* racism is evident—is the first step in eliminating *institutional* racism, and progress in eliminating individual racism can be measured by tracking changes in *attitudes* and *behaviors*. Changes in individual attitudes can be measured by public opinion polls, while progress in eliminating the individual racism inherent in harmful behaviors can be measured by observation. But changes in individual attitudes and behaviors are not sufficient to counter policies and procedures that have been built into institutions over decades.

Built-in institutional racism is so powerful that it does not require conscious racist acts to sustain it: "Institutional racism exists when the norms of an institution are predicated on assumptions of racial equality that are not met in society. The application of the institution's policies and procedures produce racist consequences" (Rodriguez 1987, p. 184).

A commonly acknowledged example of institutional racism is the admissions policies of institutions of higher education until the late 1960s. Colleges required so-called "objective" criteria for admissions: grade point average, class rank, performance on standardized tests, etc. This policy was seemingly "color-blind," but, because of past educational discrimination, applicants of color were at a disadvantage when competing with whites for college entrance. Solutions have included use of multiple criteria for admissions purposes including special talents or abilities, community service, leadership record, essays, and interviews. Many institutions of higher education have also created summer and weekend programs, remedial courses, and tutoring services to help minorities bridge the gap between high school and college. These and other programs targeted to assist minorities help modify past inequities created by institutional racism.

Evidence of institutional racism, unlike individual racism which can be measured by opinion polls or observation of specific acts, is more difficult to ascertain. Rodriguez (1987), however, describes three ways to determine if institutional racism exists: (1) cultural values or norms (evidenced by language and value frameworks that are considered "right" or "good" by one group as opposed to another); (2) institutional procedures (evidenced by mechanisms that give one group privileges over another); and (3) effects or outcomes (evidenced by unequal distribution in economics, politics, and social status). The plain language effect of these institutional policies and procedures is:

> People of color and women are disproportionately located in lower-level positions, positions characterized by lower salary scales, little decision-making power, limited opportunities for advancement, less autonomy, and less access to information. (Chesler and Delgado 1987, p. 186)

Institutional change is possible and necessary to reverse the above inequities. A number of government agencies in Oregon, for example, have developed successful strategies to increase the representation of women in management, and these can be applied to increasing the representation of minorities, as well. A 1986 study sponsored by the Oregon Chapter of the American Society for Public Administration of seven local, state, and federal government agencies outlined several common strategies which help to combat institutional sexism. Furthermore, these strategies were found to be no different from those observed in the private sector (Bremer and Howe 1986):

- Management must have a strong commitment to the belief that women can and should participate in the management of the agency.
- Opportunities for women to be promoted from within should be improved.
- Recruiting must be improved.
- The most qualified candidate should be hired regardless of gender (if women are not among the most qualified, recruitment techniques must be strengthened and training enhanced).
- Job training and career development programs should be improved.
- Values of excellence and equal opportunity should be promoted across the organization.

During the 1980s the city of Cincinnati embarked on a plan to increase the number of minorities in managerial positions in city government. Strong commitment and leadership began at the top of the organizational structure with the hiring of an African-American city manager. Facing the years of the Reagan administration, when federal revenues were decreasing, the city was forced to reduce its existing workforce, but was still able to institute its plan to increase the number of minorities in upper-level positions. Key strategies, in addition to commitment from the top, included promotions from within, active recruiting, and the support and assistance from an all-white external business advisory committee composed of community leaders—individuals who help shape community attitudes and behaviors.

Shapiro (1987) provides a parallel example from the federal government in which a two-year organizational development program was instituted in 1970 in the Health Services Mental Health Administration [HSMHA], then an agency of the Department of Health, Education, and Welfare, to develop racial and cultural awareness and recommend organizational change. The agency's 3,000 employees, including management and staff, participated in 47 residential, indepth race training seminars and workshops. Various recommendations were implemented and the agency noted increases in the status of minority employees following the program. In 1973, HSMHA was reorganized and eliminated, but the comprehensive equal opportunity program remains a model

> in thoroughness of the intervention, the commitment of the top management, the extensiveness of the training program, the effectiveness of the organizational re-structuring, and the genuineness of the management monitoring of progress subsequent to introduction of policy statements . . . . (Shapiro 1987, p. 113)

Similarly, Rodriguez (1987) profiles institutional changes at a major hospital in Dade County, Florida. The 1980 program involved: (1) assessment of hospital practices, (2) a diagnostic phase which suggested recommendations to reduce barriers and increase sensitivity, and (3) a post-assessment and withdrawal phase. The assessment stage included a review of affirmative action reports and minutes of policy-making meetings; development and administration of discrimination and employee satisfaction questionnaires; interviews; field observations; and collection of baseline personnel data. The diagnostic phase resulted in the decision to focus on distribution of power and rewards across ethnic and racial groups. Recommendations included implementation of training and career development programs, clarification of career paths, and creation of a mentoring program.

Several examples of institutional change at colleges and universities have been profiled by Green in *Minorities on Campus: A Handbook for Enhancing Diversity* (1989). "There are no perfect models, but there are success stories," notes Green (p. 159), and she profiles the University of Massachusetts at Boston, Miami-Dade Community College, and Mount St. Mary's College. These three schools have made significant institution-wide changes and their efforts have three common elements: leadership from the top, sustained support for students, and a commitment to institutional change and diversity as part of the campus ethos (Green 1989).

The examples cited above all contain the four elements described by Chesler and Delgado (1987) as necessary for organizational change:

- Formulation of clear and specific policies
- Involvement of legitimate and credible leaders at the top
- Supportive organizational infrastructure
- Support for new behaviors from front-line actors

Furthermore, the common thread in all four elements is the important role of communication in easing the process of re-distribution of power: policies must be formulated with use of clear, consistent, and sensitive language; policy-makers must be able to communicate to all employees (and students in academic institutions) that institutional leaders are committed to change and can make it happen; a comprehensive communications infrastructure must be in place; and the communication of front-line actors (telephone operators, front-desk clerks, police, etc.) with the public must indicate that the organization itself is committed to change.

DEALING WITH CHANGE: USING COMMUNICATION TO EASE THE SHARING OF POWER

As society moves toward greater mixing of races and cultures, and individuals and institutions begin to redistribute and share power, effective communication becomes essential. In addition, as the multicultural demographic changes force the beginning of the end of a white-male-dominated society and power begins to shift, conflict is inevitable; consequently, techniques for dealing with conflict—special forms of communication—should also be put into place.

As noted above, lessons learned during the struggle between African-Americans and whites can be helpful, as both the public and private sectors move toward accepting the reality of diversity in the workplace. Again, an example from the city of Cincinnati is instructive. In the early 1980s, Cincinnati's workforce was 30 percent black. For years, many black employees were angry because they felt that each year they were pressured to donate to the United Way, which they perceived as a white organization that did not value blacks. Managers noted that work production decreased during United Way solicitation periods. Finally, in 1983, city management made the commitment to include the United Negro College Fund as part of the city-wide solicitation.

Because managers communicated to employees that the organization recognized their concerns and actually changed a specific policy, the traditional decrease in productivity of black employees was avoided, and two charities benefited from the funds that were raised.

Although organizations operate better when both managers and employees share the same culture and values, when they do not, organizations can still remain effective if co-workers are aware of and respectful of the others' differences. The above example illustrates this concept of clear communication of awareness and respect. Once this concept has been established, it should translate into a better understanding of capabilities and expectations, which, in turn, will lead to more efficient and effective attainment of organizational goals.

Steps beyond awareness involve specific organizational changes, which also depend on effective communication. An example following the awareness-building stage in Cincinnati, mentioned above, was the establishment of a Police/Community Relations Board. This board was created in place of a Police Review Board which, in many cities, often perpetuated racial conflict by being a product of the majority-white police department, by receiving most of its support from white citizens, and by not being a consistent and effective communications vehicle for citizens due to the lack of staff. The Police/Community Relations Board, on the other hand, was separate from the police department (but had the required participation of the chief of police), had an African-American staff director, and held regular meetings throughout the city, not merely at city hall. Results of the creation of this board were noted in a number of areas:

- Negative criticism ("we make complaints and nobody does anything") decreased.
- The board provided a regular opportunity for the chief of police to talk with citizen groups.
- Formation of the board provided the impetus for broader organizational change resulting in creation of the Division of Municipal Investigations, which ultimately served as a second official source to officially investigate police brutality complaints and shootings.

All of these improvements indicate enchanced communication, particularly between the community and the city government; members of the community no longer feel powerless when dealing with neighborhood police matters.

Although enhanced communication has been shown to be a key ingredient leading to comfortable sharing of power in city management, conflicts are still inevitable. As individuals and institutions move from the dominance/control model toward the empowerment/partnership model, the power shift—usually from white males to females and minorities—creates both individual and institutional tension. Green suggests the following, when implementing comprehensive institutional change:

> As you move forward, it is highly likely that conflict will emerge as a by-product of the change process. It is important to have a mechanism in place to address these conflicts, provide forums for resolution, and to prevent the escalation of conflict (Green 1989, p. 8).

A specialized communication skill that has been successful in dealing with conflict, particularly in schools, is mediation (McCarthy 1990). Comprehensive use of this technique—in which disputing parties negotiate in the presence of a trained mediator—has been used since 1983 in a magnet school in Cleveland, Ohio. The approach has been so successful—the school has the lowest suspension rate in the district and the fewest suspensions for physical violence—that mediation is now a recognized alternative in handling disciplinary problems in all the schools of the 72,000-pupil district.

Founders of the mediation program at Cleveland's Martin Luther King Law and Public Service Magnet High School [MLK-LPS] were trained by the Community Youth Mediation Program, an organization that mediates neighborhood and school problems involving youth on the near West side of Cleveland. The MLK-LPS mediation program trains students to serve as peer mediators to handle troublesome situations before they become worse. The successful results of this program are particularly impressive for two reasons: (1) the school population is racially diverse (under federal desegregation mandates, the school must maintain a maximum 75:25 ratio of black students to non-black students) and (2) students do not have to pass tests to enroll in MLK-LPS, they merely select entrance; consequently, the school is more representative of the general district population than are most magnets.

The MLK-LPS mediation program illustrates that conflict, whether racially motivated or for some other reason, can be minimized, even in the most difficult urban school districts, as was noted in an article in the *Washington Post*:

> At Martin Luther King High School, which is in the Hough area of Cleveland (where some of the nation's harshest racial clashes occurred in the late 1960s), almost 1 out of 10 students is involved in the mediation program. King is the school that local politicians praise when they want to say there is hope for inner-city public education (McCarthy 1990).

The success of mediation as a conflict-reducing technique in schools brings this book to a fitting close—with the locus of the discussion once again in the educational system. Rothenberg, in *Racism and Sexism*, stresses that substantial change cannot occur without reinforcement by the educational system (Rothenberg 1988, p. 396). Individual attitude changes taught to America's children, who at the same time are given techniques for handling conflict, will be in a much stronger position to help in the process of institutional change—where diversity is valued and the sharing of power is not seen as a threat, but as an organizational strength.[7]

CONCLUSION

This chapter began by discussing progress in correcting the racial inequities built into American society since its beginning. By the late twentieth century, data indicates that, despite gradual gains, African-Americans are still behind their white counterparts in educational attainment, income levels, and health status. But, in order to continue the progress, however slight, focus must remain on programs that have made a difference. Furthermore, these programs must be broadened to deal with the growing multicultural aspect of American society, which will have nearly one-third of its population people of color by the year 2000. The need for such programs will be even more critical in schools, where greater than one-third of the students will be minorities within a decade.

The strategy set forth in this chapter has two major steps:

- Change the individual.
- Change the institution.

For this process to be successful, institutional leaders must use effective communication techniques to ease the empowerment process. They must also recognize that conflict will naturally occur and mechanisms to deal with conflict must be in place.

Figure 19.1 summarizes the major steps that have been described in this chapter and that have been shown to be successful in comprehensive institutional change to redistribute power in various organizations in the public and private sectors alike. Leadership, management, and front-line actors must all begin with awareness building by participating in diversity training programs. This step, focusing on individual change, must continue, while steps to begin institutional change are implemented. Following the gathering of base data, organizations must then examine their affirmative action policies, recruitment plans, and internal promotion, job training and career development programs in light of both women and people of color.

Top administrators must continue to lead and monitor the implementation of major programmatic changes throughout the organization. Managers, work-

FIGURE 19.1

Major Steps in Comprehensive Institutional Change

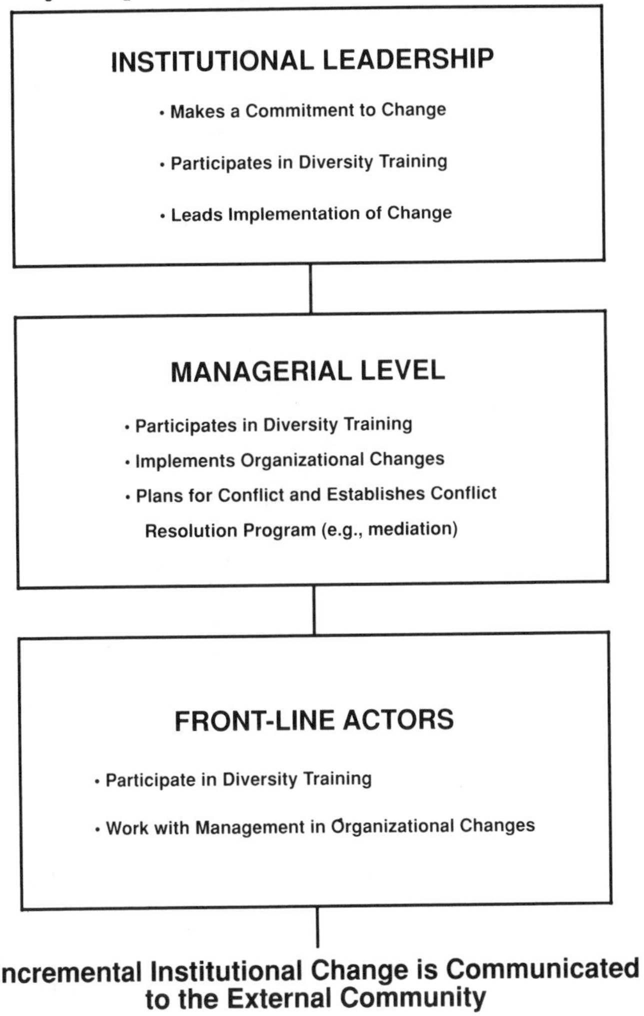

INSTITUTIONAL LEADERSHIP

- Makes a Commitment to Change

- Participates in Diversity Training

- Leads Implementation of Change

MANAGERIAL LEVEL

- Participates in Diversity Training
- Implements Organizational Changes
- Plans for Conflict and Establishes Conflict
  Resolution Program (e.g., mediation)

FRONT-LINE ACTORS

- Participate in Diversity Training

- Work with Management in Organizational Changes

**Incremental Institutional Change is Communicated
to the External Community**

ing with all front-line actors, must further refine the programs and evaluate them in light of quantitative changes at all levels of the organization. Throughout the process—of both individual change and institutional change—strong and varied communication vehicles are essential. Top leaders' commitment to change must be communicated clearly and consistently to all internal and external audiences via speeches, newsletters, and other publications, and conflict—which must be understood as natural and non-threatening—must be handled by effective dispute resolution techniques.

Of all institutions in society, schools, colleges, and universities are most appropriately positioned to lead this process. Able to reach individuals at an early stage in their development, educational institutions are an essential foundation for major societal change, and as the multicultural twenty-first century looms on the horizon, the empowerment of women and people of color should be at the top of the agenda.

NOTES

1. Hanchard (1990) has provided a discussion of the chain of terms: "colored," "Negro," "black," "Afro-American," "African-American." He notes that the debate over the last term should be broadened to extend to an understanding of the term "American" itself: "African as prefix to American as it is colloquially understood seems to suggest that the real meaning to black identity lies in the American, and this may be closer to the mark than the proponents of hyphenation would care to admit" (p. 38).

2. *One-Third of a Nation* uses figures for African-American, Hispanic, and American Indians, since they constitute 90 percent of the minority population (p. 3).

3. Another major change in the workforce is the growing percentage of women. A complete discussion of the effects of this change is beyond the scope of this chapter.

4. Green (1989) stresses the difference between the terms "diversity" and "pluralism" by noting that the former means the mere presence of different racial and cultural groups, while the latter connotes a "dynamic atmosphere of collaboration" (p. xvi).

5. Unfortunately, many educational institutions offering public administration programs have been slow to provide such courses. In a 1990 survey of the 10 Ohio universities offering degrees in public administration, none offered a specific course intended to prepare students to identify and solve workforce problems arising from diversity (Murray 1990). Furthermore, none of the programs' core courses that teach students personnel management skills had an identifiable content on managing diversity. These courses primarily taught only the rules and regulations of equal employment opportunity and affirmative action.

6. References to "racism" can be replaced, in most cases, with "sexism," "ageism," etc., and strategies eliminating "institutional racism" can also be effective in eliminating other institutional "isms."

7. The educational system can help weaken *polarization* of *place* in choice of both home and work: a Columbia University Teachers College study of black students who were randomly selected to attend integrated schools in the suburbs of Hartford found that, as adults, these individuals were much more likely than their segregated peers to move into an integrated neighborhood and to work in jobs often traditionally held by whites (Wells, *New York Times* 1991).

REFERENCES

Bremer, K. and D.A. Howe. 1988. Strategies used to advance women's careers in the public service: examples from Oregon. *Public Administration Review* (November/December).

Chesler, M. and H. Delgado. 1987. Race relations training and organizational change. In *Strategies for improving race relations: the anglo-american experience*, J.S. Shaw, P.G. Nordlie and R.M. Shapiro, eds. Manchester: Manchester University Press.

Coffey, J.F. 1987. Race training in the U.S.: an overview. In *Strategies for improving race relations: the anglo-american experience*, J.S. Shaw, P.G. Nordlie and R.M. Shapiro, eds. Manchester, UK: Manchester University Press.

Green, M.F., ed. 1989. *Minorities on campus: a handbook for enhancing diversity*. Washington, DC: American Council on Education.

Hanchard, M. 1990. Identity, meaning, and the african american, *Social Text Journal* 8(2).

Mandell, B. and S. Kohler-Gray. 1990. Managing development that values diversity. *Personnel* (March).

McCarthy, C. 1990. The mediator is the message. *Washington Post*, September 2.

Murray, S. 1990. A survey of the curricula in managing diversity provided to public management students in selected Ohio universities. Maxine Levin College of Urban Affairs, Cleveland State University.

Myrdal, G. 1962. *An american dilemma: the negro problem and modern democracy*. Twentieth Anniversary Edition. New York: Harper & Row (originally published 1944).

National Advisory Commission on Civil Disorders (Kerner Commission). 1968. Report of the national advisory commission on civil disorders. New York: Bantam Books.

One-third of a nation: report of the commission on minority participation in education and american life. 1988. Washington, DC: American Council on Education and Education Commission of the States.

Report and recommendations of the national commission on the public service. Committee on Post Office and Civil Service, U.S. House of Representatives, May 2, 1989, p. 179.

Rodriquez, A.M. 1987. Institutional racism in the organizational setting: an action-research approach. In *Strategies for improving race relations: the anglo-american experience*, J.S. Shaw, P.G. Nordlie and R.M. Shapiro, eds. Manchester: Manchester University Press.

Roper, B. W. 1990. Racial tensions are down. *New York Times*, July 26.

Rothenberg, P. S. 1988. *Racism and sexism*. New York: St. Martins Press.

Shapiro, R.M. The implementation of an equal opportunity programme within an organization. 1987. In *Strategies for improving race relations: the anglo-american experience*, J.S. Shaw, P.G. Nordlie and R.M. Shapiro, eds. Manchester: Manchester: Manchester University Press.

Shaw, J.W., P.G. Nordlie and R.M. Shapiro, eds. 1987. *Strategies for improving race relations: the anglo-american experience.* Manchester: Manchester University Press.

Solomon, J. 1990. As cultural diversity of workers grows, experts urge appreciation of differences. *Wall Street Journal*, September 12.

Survey of college freshmen finds a shift in priorities. 1991. *New York Times,* January 29.

Takaki, R., ed. 1987. *From different shores: perspectives on race and ethnicity in America.* New York: Oxford University Press.

Wells, A.S. 1991. Asking what schools have done, or can do, to help desegregation. *New York Times*, January 16.

Suggested Further Readings

Chapter 1

Douglas Massey and Mitchell Eggers. 1990. The Ecology of Inequality: Minorities and the Concentration of Poverty, 1970–1980. *The American Journal of Sociology* (March) 95:5 1153–88.

> Massey and Eggers carefully examine the causes of spatial concentration and poverty using census data from 1970 and 1980. This paper is a thoughtful and complete examination of Wilson's underclass hypothesis.

Gunnar Myrdal. 1944. *The American Dilemma: The Negro Problem and Modern Democracy.* New York: Harper and Row.

> Unfortunately, this classic two-volume work is out of print; the most recent edition was published by Pantheon Books in 1975. Myrdal's work sets forth a clear model of cumulative causation and documents the racial divide in American society at the end of the Second World War. The book is referred to more often than it is read, yet it remains a standard against which other works on race relations in the United States are still measured.

National Advisory Commission on Civil Disorders (The Kerner Commission Report). 1968. *Report of the National Advisory Commission on Civil Disorders.* New York: Bantam Books.

> The Kerner Commission documents the causes of the urban riots of 1968. The commission documented the close connection between racial and spatial polarization with poverty and political polarization in metropolitan America. The work is comprehensive and is the second classic work in this area.

William J. Wilson. 1987. *The Truly Disadvantaged: The Inner City, the Underclass, and Public Policy.* Chicago: The University of Chicago Press.

> Wilson's book reopened the liberal perspective on urban poverty. His work builds on the intellectual roots of Myrdal and the Kerner Commission. The book stands out for two reasons. First, Wilson offers a fresh and frank reassessment of the fallout from the Moynihan Report on the Negro family. Second, Wilson argues that the historical burdens of racism and the decline of manufacturing employment in northern inner cities resulted in a deprived permanent "underclass."

Chapter 2

Gunnar Myrdal. 1944. *The American Dilemma: The Negro Problem and Modern Democracy.* New York: Harper and Row.

> See Chapter 1.

National Advisory Commission on Civil Disorders (The Kerner Commission Report). 1968. *Report of the National Advisory Commission on Civil Disorders.* New York: Bantam Books.

> See Chapter 1.

Chapter 3

Henry J. Aaron. 1978. *Politics and the Professors: The Great Society in Perspective.* Washington, DC: The Brookings Institution.

> This book conveys a sense of the motivational underpinnings of the War on Poverty and how the broader, multifaceted concept of poverty was eclipsed by the Orshansky income base definition as the War on Poverty got underway.

M. Harrington. 1962. *The Other America.* New York: MacMillan Books.

> *The Other America* provides a good sense of how poverty was thought of before the War on Poverty and the similarity between the pre-War-on-Poverty concept of poverty and the current concept of the underclass.

Christopher Jencks and Paul Peterson, eds. 1991. *The Urban Underclass.* Washington, D.C.: The Brookings Institution.

> See article by Jencks for alternative definitions of the underclass and alternative estimates of its size and growth. The article by Peterson is an excellent discussion of the relationship of the underclass to poverty.

William J. Wilson. 1987. *The Truly Disadvantaged.* Chicago: University of Chicago Press.

> In Chapter 1 of this book, Wilson, undoubtedly the most thoughtful scholar of the underclass, provides an excellent discussion of the social, economic, and political context that gave rise to the underclass today.

Chapter 4

John Bound and Richard Freeman. 1990. *What Went Wrong? The Erosion of the Relative Earnings and Employment of Young Black Men in the 1980s.* Cambridge, MA: National Bureau of Economic Research.

> Confirms the sharply worsening wages of black men since the late 1970s, and offers a number of complementary explanations that reflect the growing social class heterogeneity within the black community.

Gerald Jaynes and Robin Williams, eds. 1989. *A Common Destiny: Blacks and American Society.* Washington, D.C.: National Academy Press.

Wornie Reed, ed. 1990. *Critiques of 'A Common Destiny.'* Boston, MA: William Monroe Trotter Institute, University of Massachusetts at Boston.

A collection of papers commissioned by a national network of mostly black scholars to critique the National Academy of Sciences report.

Margaret Simms and Julianne Malveaux. 1987. *Slipping Through the Cracks: The Status of Black Women.* New Brunswick, NJ: Transaction Books.

Documents the growing income and occupational gap between white women and women of color. Poses this division as a challenge to the feminist movement.

Chapter 5

Thomas Boston. 1988. *Race, Class and Conservatism.* Boston, MA: Unwin Hyman.

This book is a critique of conservative views on race and class. It has been written largely in response to works by Thomas Sowell, Walter Williams, George Gilder, and William J. Wilson. The basic thrust of the book is that racial discrimination is the basic explanation for the disadvantaged position of blacks in American society.

Robert Cherry. 1989. *Discrimination: Its Economic Impact on Blacks, Women and Jews.* Lexington, MA: Lexington Books.

This book begins by presenting the theoretical foundations for three contrasting views on discrimination: conservative, liberal and radical. Next it looks at data on racial discrimination in terms of income, employment opportunities and the impact of welfare programs from each of the three perspectives. The remainder of the book deals with sex discrimination and discrimination against Jews.

Bradley Schiller. 1989. *The Economics of Poverty and Discrimination* (fifth edition). Englewood Cliffs, NJ: Prentice-Hall.

This book provides a comprehensive review of the literature on all topics dealing with the economics of poverty and discrimination. It discusses competing explanations for poverty and discrimination and presents a wide array of data gathered primarily from the Current Population Survey. It also has a number of chapters that deal with public policy aimed at eliminating poverty and discrimination.

Chapter 6

Phillip Clay. 1989. Choosing Urban Futures: The Transformation of American Cities. *Stanford Law and Policy Review* 1(Fall):28–43.

Joint Center for Housing Studies. 1990. *The State of the Nation's Housing 1990.* Cambridge, MA: Harvard University.

Chapter 7

Gerald D. Jaynes and Robin M. Williams, Jr., eds. 1989. *A Common Destiny: Blacks and American Society.* Washington, DC: National Academy Press. Chapter 7, "The Schooling of Black Americans."

>An inclusive discussion of the progress African-Americans have made in education since the 1940s from primary education to higher education. The chapter also discusses the slowdown in progress since 1980.

Chapter 8

Gerald D. Jaynes and Robin M. Williams, Jr., eds. 1989. *A Common Destiny: Blacks and American Society.* Washington, DC: National Academy Press. Chapter 8, "Black Americans' Health."

>A comprehensive statistical overview of the state of health of African-Americans and the differential rates of illness, disability and death that persists between black and white Americans. The chapter spends considerable time analyzing the conditions that sustain these differentials, paying particular attention to socioeconomic and environmental causes.

Alphonso Pinkney. 1987. *The Myth of Black Progress.* New York: Cambridge.

>As the title suggests, this book tackles controversial issues such as affirmative action and socioeconomic status in a challenge to the increasingly popular notion that the struggle for political and social equality for African-Americans has been won. The author is especially concerned with the thesis that race is increasingly insignificant in the life chances of African-Americans, and he marshals an array of evidence to demonstrate the continuing significance of race in the fight for parity for all Americans in all spheres of life. This argument is central to the thesis of this chapter.

David P. Willis, ed. 1989. *Health Policies and Black Americans.* New Brunswick, NJ: Transaction Publishers.

>This superbly edited volume is perhaps the most comprehensive collection, at one time, of health information on African-Americans. The articles cover all the major health topics, among them mortality, health policies, health insurance, quality of life, and health statistics. It was a primary source book for Chapter 8.

Chapter 9

Charles R. Adrian and Ernest S. Griffith. 1983. *A History of American City Government: The Formation of Traditions, 1775–1870.* Washington, DC: University Press of America. Reprint of Praeger edition (1976).

>One of the few comprehensive and insightful histories of cities and their governing. Not only are the books excellent history, they are also quite readable. They demonstrate the dramatic changes that have occurred in local government and the amazing resilience of some of the traditions.

Charles R. Adrian and Charles Press. 1977. *Governing Urban America* (fifth edition). New York: McGraw-Hill.

One of the best textbooks on local government. Local government is sketched historically and related to public policies which are in turn related to the quality of life. These connections, especially the last, are all too infrequent in most academic literature.

Charles R. Adrian and Michael R. Fine. 1991. *State and Local Politics.* Chicago: Lyceum Books.

Ernest S. Griffith. 1938. *The Colonial Period.* Washington, DC: University Press of America. (The series is published for the National Municipal League.)

_____. 1974. *The Conspicuous Failure, 1870–1900.* New York: Praeger.

_____. 1983. *The Progressive Years and their Aftermath, 1900–1920.* Washington, DC: University Press of America.

Chapter 10

Rufus P. Browning, Dale Rogers Marshall and David Tabb, eds. 1990. *Racial Politics in American Cities.* New York: Longman.

An anthology covering political activities of blacks and Latinos in major American cities. The focus of the analysis is mayoral politics. A major question addressed in this anthology is how blacks and Hispanics achieve political power in urban America. The focal point of analysis is bi-racial coalitions. Cities covered include among others, Atlanta, Boston, Denver, and Miami.

Georgia A. Persons, ed. 1991. *Dilemmas of Black Politics: Issues of Leadership and Strategy.* New York: Harper-Collins.

An anthology covering the evolution of black electoral politics from the insurgency, reform-oriented style of early black mayors to the current trend toward deracialization of black politics. Chapters cover a range of mayoral contests, two state gubernatorial contests, a U.S. Senate race and a U.S. House race in which black candidates pursued a deracialized campaign strategy. Other chapters focus on changing perspectives on black leadership and the enduring dilemma of ideology in black politics.

Chapter 11

Douglas Massey. 1990. American Apartheid: Segregation and the Making of the Underclass. *American Journal of Sociology* 96: 329–57.

Massey adds to the above debate by concentrating on the spatial dimensions of poverty. He argues that racial segregation is crucial to explaining the emergence of the underclass.

Charles Murray. 1984. *Losing Ground: American Social Policy, 1950–1980.* New York: Basic Books.

> An influential, controversial book articulating the "conservative" view on the growth of poverty in African-American communities. Murray argues that federal anti-poverty programs altered the economic incentives faced by poor people, thereby encouraging out-of-wedlock childbearing and discouraging marriage and participation in the low-wage employment sector.

William J. Wilson. 1987. *The Truly Disadvantaged.* Chicago: University of Chicago Press.

> The "liberal" counterpoint to the issue. Wilson argues that structural changes in the type and location of jobs have disproportionately penalized black workers. Furthermore, expanding residential options for middle-class African-Americans have led to an out-migration of stable, respectable "role models" from the ghetto.

Two other recent compendia of articles about the causes of underclass reflect alternative disciplinary and ideological perspectives: *The Annals of the American Academy of Political and Social Sciences* 501 (January 1989) and *The Journal of Economic Perspectives* 4 (Fall 1990).

Chapter 12

K. Auletta. 1982. *The Underclass.* New York: Random House.

> This book is a good treatise on the role of personal pathology as a cause of the underclass, although Auletta is mindful of the importance of social causes.

William J. Wilson. 1987. *The Truly Disadvantaged: Inner City Underclass and Public Policy.* Chicago: University of Chicago Press.

> Wilson's book is a good treatise on the role of social structure and the emergence of the underclass and is a good counterpoint to Auletta. In the last three chapters, Wilson discusses positive responses to the problems of the underclass.

D. Ellwood. 1988. *Poor Support Poverty: Poverty in the American Family.* New York: Basic.

> This book is a very thoughtful examination of the relationship of the welfare establishment to the elevation of poverty and social distress. An understanding of the arguments of this book is an essential first step to considering policy solutions for the underclass.

Chapter 13

The Annals of the American Academy of Political and Social Sciences 501 (January 1989).

> See Chapter 11.

Sethard Fisher. 1982. *From Margin to Mainstream: The Social Progress of Black Americans.* New York: Praeger.

This volume traces the history of race relations in America from 1619 to 1980, just prior to the changes wrought by Ronald Reagan in affirmative action, the Great Society, etc. Fisher sees race relations as moving from caste to class. Due to its publication in 1982, he missed Reagan's impact on race relations. The volume is recommended as a good historical account of race relations in America and the changes those relations have gone through.

John U. Ogbu. 1978. *Minority Education and Caste: The American System in Cross-Cultural Perspective.* New York: Academic Press.

This volume gives a good exposition of the applicability of "caste" to America. It uses caste to explain the then-current state of minority education in America.

Chapter 14

See Chapter 6.

Chapter 15

Juliet Saltman. 1990. *A Fragile Movement: The Struggle for Neighborhood Stabilization.* Westport, CT: Greenwood Press, Inc.

The author analyzes organized neighborhood integration maintenance efforts in fifteen communities across the country since 1956. Successful efforts indicate the crucial role played by forces external to the community and by institutional processes.

John Goering, ed. 1986. *Housing Desegregation and Federal Policy.* Chapel Hill: University of North Carolina Press.

A carefully edited, comprehensive volume that assembles current work from economics, sociology, political science, geography and law. Evidence and analysis are presented on housing discrimination and segregation, racial attitudes and desegregation-oriented federal and local policies. The merits of alternative strategies are debated.

Chapter 16

John Goering, ed. 1986. *Housing Desegregation and Federal Policy.* Chapel Hill: University of North Carolina Press.

See Chapter 15.

Jamshid A. Momeni, ed. 1986. *Race, Ethnicity, and Minority Housing in the United States.* Westport, CT: Greenwood Press, Inc.

This book makes a compelling case that persistent discrimination, rather than minority poverty, explains the inadequate housing conditions that minority group members disproportionately face. This volume focuses on conditions that account for the unequal status of blacks and other minority groups (Hispanics, Asians, and American Indians) in housing quality and quantity when compared to their white counterparts. Collectively, the authors provide empirical evidence documenting the relationship between segregated and inadequate housing which affects minority groups in a number of settings—urban, suburban, and rural. This book expands on a point raised in the chapter; that is, the relevance of discrimination for explaining housing patterns.

Chapter 17

Anthology and Education Quarterly. 1987. 18(4).

The theme of this issue is explaining the school performance of minority students. It includes articles concerning school failures and case studies related to the education of minority children. Two of the theories of school failure described in this chapter are explained in this issue.

Janet Weiss. 1990. Control in School Organizations: Theoretical Perspectives. In *Choice and Control in American Education,* Vol. 1, W. Clune and J. Witte, eds. New York: Falmer.

Weiss disaggregates control into five types: professional norms and styles of work, political processes and institutions, administrative direction and control, market forces and pressures, and the articulation of values and ideas. She suggests that each of these types of control must be "reckoned with" as educators seek the method(s) through which educational outcomes can improve.

Heidi Marie Rock and Edward W. Hill. 1990. *The Functions of Public Schooling: A Historical Perspective.* Cleveland, OH: College of Urban Affairs, Cleveland State University.

Although the authors hesitate to recommend their own work, the only comprehensive discussion of the development of the aspects, standards, and goals of schooling can be found in this work. The evolution of the goals through the twentieth century along with contemporary definitions of each goal is discussed.

Chapter 18

J. Bodnar. 1985. *The Transplanted: The Immigrants in Urban America.* Bloomington, IN: University of Indiana Press.

_____. 1982. *Workers World: Kinship, Community and Protest in an Industrial Society 1900–1940.* Baltimore: Johns Hopkins University Press.

Realistic and empirical examinations of life in the early industrial cities from the workers' perspectives. Captures not only the "numbers," but the human side of American urban and industrial development.

Z. Miller. 1987. *The Urbanization of Modern America: A Brief History.* New York: Harcourt Brace and Jovanovich.

> Excellent and succinct overview of American urban development that encompasses political and social events. Highly readable without sacrificing detail.

W. Riordon. 1963. *Plunkitt of Tammany Hall: A Series of Very Plain Talks on Very Practical Politics, delivered by ex-Senator George Washington Plunkitt, the Tammany Philosopher, from his rostrum—the New York County Court House Bootblack Stand.* New York: Dutton.

> The classic story of how the political machine operated. Concepts such as "honest graft" depict how machine members ruled the American city.

Chapter 19

Paula S. Rothenberg. 1988. *Racism and Sexism: An Integrated Study.* New York: St. Martin's Press.

> This publication is a text-reader that integrates the study of racism and the study of sexism by providing interdisciplinary chapters covering the concerns of blacks and women, as well as those of Hispanics, Asians, and Native Americans. Topics covered include: definitions of racism and sexism; statistics related to race, gender, and class in the United States; an overview of the legal history of issues related to race and sex; and a discussion of stereotypes, language, and social control of minorities and women.

Sammie Lynn Scandlyn, ed. 1967. *101 Winning Ways to Better Municipal Public Relations.* Washington, DC: National League of Cities.

> This book gives case studies and ideas used by cities across the country to bring their citizens together in an informed manner. Although the book is over twenty years old, the case studies and ideas still have merit today.

Donald A. Schon. 1983. *The Reflective Practitioner.* New York, NY: Basic Books.

> This book suggests that the best administrators, including public administrators, add a reflective quality to their decision making that cannot be explained scientifically but that works well to motivate people.

John W. Shaw, Peter G. Nordlie, and Richard M. Shapiro, eds. 1987. *Strategies for Improving Race Relations: The Anglo-American Experience.* Manchester, UK: Manchester University Press.

> Shaw, et al., state that their book was prompted by the question, "what have we learned so far?" In response to that question, authors of various chapters provide an overview of the history of racism, equal employment opportunity, and affirmative action and detailed case studies in which organizations have been successful in combating "institutional racism." Common strategies and models for organizational change are also discussed.

Eddie N. Williams. 1975. Politics and the Black Economic Condition. Washington, DC: Joint Center for Political Studies.

This speech was given to a group that included city planners, housing officials, and architects. It explains how the physical and human parts of a city must be in harmony.

About the Authors

John P. Blair is Professor of Economics at Wright State University. He has written numerous books and articles in the fields of urban development and public policy. His latest book is *Urban and Regional Economics* (Irwin 1991). Blair received his Ph.D. from West Virginia University in 1974. In addition to his teaching and research, he is a member of the Montgomery County Planning Commission.

Mittie Olion Chandler is Associate Professor in the Department of Urban Studies of the Maxine Goodman Levin College of Urban Affairs, Cleveland State University. She received her Master of Urban Planning and Ph.D. in Political Science (public administration) from Wayne State University. Dr. Chandler has done community development and public housing consulting in Detroit, Michigan and Cleveland, Ohio. Her book *Urban Homesteading: Programs and Policies* was published by Greenwood Press in 1988.

Phillip L. Clay is a distinguished scholar of the American city. An honors undergraduate of the University of North Carolina at Chapel Hill, he holds a Ph.D. in City Planning from Massachusetts Institute of Technology (MIT) where he now teaches courses on housing, urban demographics and community development. From 1980 to 1984, he served as Assistant Director of the MIT-Harvard Joint Center for Urban Studies. Dr. Clay is the author of *Neighborhood Renewal* (1979) and co-author with Robert Hollister of *Neighborhood Planning and Politics* (1983). In addition, he has written numerous articles, reports and monographs, has lectured widely and made presentations to professional and community groups, has served on a variety of national and local committees, task forces and other policy groups, and has presented congressional testimony on issues of national housing policy. Professor Clay served as a federal court expert in a major and successful fair housing case and provides consulting services to foundations, local governments and community groups on program design, evaluation and analysis.

Terri Lynn Cornwell most recently served as Director of the Ohio Commission on the Public Service, a state-wide project assessing state and local government in Ohio and headquartered at Cleveland State University's Levin College of Urban Affairs. Dr. Cornwell, who currently resides in Virginia and serves as a consultant to nonprofit and government organizations, was also a Visiting Assistant Pro-

383

fessor of Communication at Cleveland State University. Prior to her work in Ohio, she served as legislative director for the Congressional Arts Caucus in Washington, D.C. She received an M.A. in music from West Chester College in Pennsylvania, and an M.A. in theatre and a Ph.D. in public communication from the University of Maryland.

Rudy H. Fichtenbaum is Professor of Economics at Wright State University. He teaches a course on the economics of poverty and discrimination and has written a number of articles on poverty, discrimination, and income distribution. He earned his Ph.D. from the University of Missouri at Columbia in 1980.

George C. Galster is Professor of Economics and Chairperson of the Urban Studies Program at The College of Wooster. In 1974, Galster received his Ph.D. in Economics from MIT. His principal research areas are racial segregation, neighborhood satisfaction, and preservation. Dr. Galster's recent publications include *Homeowners and Neighborhood Reinvestment* (Duke University Press 1987) and *The Maze of Urban Housing Markets* with Jerome Rothenberg, Richard Butler, and John Pitkin (University of Chicago Press 1991).

Lucy Gorham is a professional staff member for the Joint Economic Committee of the U.S. Congress. She is a doctoral candidate in the Department of Urban Studies and Planning at MIT, from which she also holds a master degree.

Bennett Harrison is Professor of Political Economy in the School of Urban and Public Affairs, Carnegie Mellon University. He received his Ph.D. in Economics from the University of Pennsylvania in 1970, and is the author, co-author, or editor of seven books and more than fifty scholarly papers. His most recent book, *The Great U-Turn* (Basic Books 1988), co-authored with Barry Bluestone, is a study of the growing polarization of income and wages in the United States. Prof. Harrison teaches political economy, economic development, labor economics, and the economics of discrimination.

Edward W. Hill is Associate Professor of Urban Planning and Public Administration at Cleveland State University's Maxine Goodman Levin College of Urban Affairs. Hill received his Ph.D. in Urban and Regional Planning and Economics from MIT in 1981. Dr. Hill is an associate editor of *Economic Development Quarterly* and a co-editor of *Financing Economic Development* (Sage 1990). He has written on public policy and education reform, regional labor markets, and the regional impact of the savings and loan crisis.

Lawrence F. Keller is Associate Professor of Urban Studies and Public Management in the Maxine Goodman Levin College of Urban Affairs at Cleveland State University where he is also the Senior Research Associate of the Public Management Program in the Levin College's Urban Center. Keller received his Ph.D. in Public Administration from The American University and holds a J.D. with a specialization in administrative law from the Law School of Vanderbilt University. Dr. Keller has published in a variety of public administration and political science journals on such topics as the policy roles of city managers, the nature of interorganizational policy networks, action research as a method of implementing public policy research, and the nature of public administration academic programs. His major focus in research is the interface of management, politics, and law in the American public sector and the implications for governance of American society.

Norman Krumholz is a professional city planning practitioner turned uneasy academic. He was Assistant Planning Director for the city of Pittsburgh (1965-69), Planning Director for the city of Cleveland (1969-79), Director of the Cleveland Center for Neighborhood Development (1979-87), and has been Professor of Urban Planning at Cleveland State University since 1985. His research has been sponsored by the Cleveland, Gund and Ford Foundations and his most recently published works include *Making Equity Planning Work: Leadership in the Public Sector* (1990), with John Forester, and chapters in *Unequal Partnerships* (1989) and the *Handbook of Housing and the Built Environment in the U.S.* (1989). He is a past President of the American Planning Association.

Sylvester Murray is Director of the Public Management Program at Cleveland State University's Maxine Goodman Levin College of Urban Affairs and Associate Professor in the Levin College's Department of Urban Studies. Murray's specialty is urban administration and management. He is former city manager of San Diego, California; Cincinnati, Ohio; and Ann Arbor, Michigan; and manager of government consulting at Coopers & Lybrand in Columbus. He holds a Master in Governmental Administration degree from the University of Pennsylvania and a Master of Arts in Economics from Eastern Michigan University.

Akwasi Osei is Assistant Professor of Black Studies and Political Science at The College of Wooster. Educated at Oberlin College, Ohio University, and Howard University, Dr. Osei's research interests are African politics, African-American political economy, and the continuing marginalization of the African continent in the international system. He is a contributor to *The Oxford Companion to Politics of the World* (Oxford University Press, forthcoming). He is currently completing a manuscript entitled "Politics and Change in a Postcolonial State," and an essay entitled "Bridge Across the Atlantic: The Political Economy of the African World." Dr. Osei previously taught at Oberlin College where he was the Director of the African Heritage House.

Georgia A. Persons is Associate Professor of Political Science in the School of Public Policy at Georgia Institute of Technology. She has published many articles on black electoral politics and recently edited *Dilemmas of Black Politics: Issues of Leadership and Strategy* (Harper Collins 1991). She also does research in the area of public policy/regulatory policy.

Erol Ricketts holds a Ph.D. in sociology and demography from the University of Chicago. He is Visiting Scholar of the Russell-Sage Foundation in New York. He recently received the American Evaluation Association's Marcia Guttentag Award for his research on the underclass. Dr. Ricketts has written on diverse subjects such as the underclass, AIDS, immigration, and education reform. His professional experiences include being the associate director of the Equal Opportunity Division of the Rockefeller Foundation, a visiting scholarship at the Urban Institute in Washington, D.C., service on the graduate faculty of the City University of New York, and health administration in New York City.

Heidi Marie Rock is a doctoral candidate in the Administration and Institutional Policy Program at the University of Chicago's Department of Education. She is currently employed as a coordinator of evaluation by Chicago's Public Schools. Before working for Chicago's Public Schools, she supervised student teachers for three years at the University of Chicago. Ms. Rock also taught at the secondary level for five years in Cleveland's public school system.

Charles Washington is Assistant Professor of Urban Studies and Public Administration in the Maxine Goodman Levin College of Urban Affairs at Cleveland State University. He received his Ph.D. in Political Science from Indiana University in 1988. Dr. Washington has taught at Jackson State University in Jackson, Mississippi, and Indiana University-Purdue University in Indianapolis. Dr. Washington spent a year studying housing problems in Zambia Central Africa and he was the Contract Compliance Manager for the city of Indianapolis before joining Levin College. His research interests include human resource management, affirmative action, urban problems, and comparative urban issues. He has published in the areas of affirmative action, human resource management, and the urban underclass.